# Revivals! Diverse Traditions

## 1920–1945

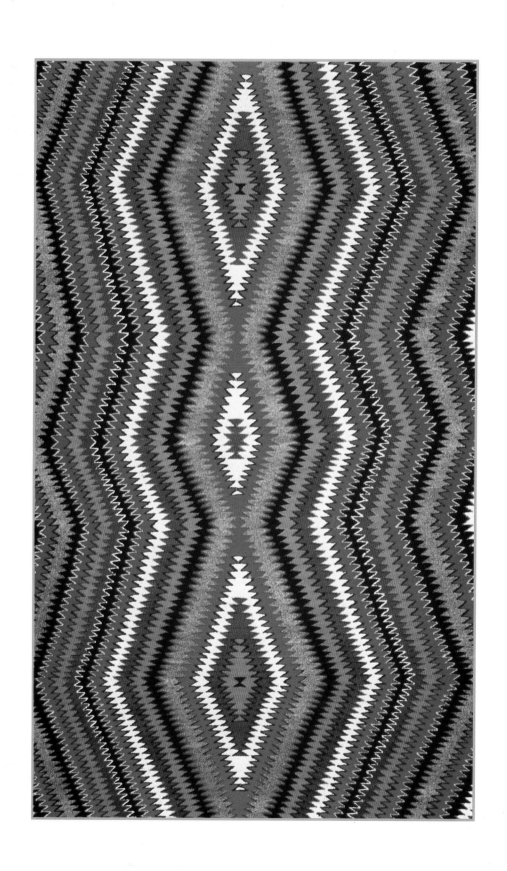

# Revivals! Diverse Traditions
## 1920–1945

The
History
of
Twentieth-Century
American Craft

Janet Kardon, Editor

with essays by

Ralph T. Coe
Harvey Green
Janet Kardon
Jane Kessler
April Kingsley
Francis V. O'Connor
Winifred Owens-Hart
William B. Rhoads
Dale Rosengarten
Annie Santiago de Curet
Gail Tremblay
John Michael Vlach
William Wroth
Hildreth J. York

Harry N. Abrams, Inc., Publishers, in association with the American Craft Museum

This book is published on the occasion of the exhibition
"Revivals! Diverse Traditions 1920–1945"
American Craft Museum, New York
October 20, 1994–February 26, 1995

The History of Twentieth-Century American Craft: A Centenary Project
Janet Kardon, Project Founder and Director
Robert Hornsby and Betsy Jablow, Project Coordinators
April Kingsley, Publications Coordinator, Assistant Editor

For Harry N. Abrams, Inc.:
Project Manager: Ruth Peltason

For American Craft Museum:
Editor: Gerald Zeigerman

Captions for pages 1–6:
Page 1: Navajo (Four Corners). *"Eye-dazzler" Rug.* 1945.
Wool, dyes, 78 x 49″. Collection School of American
Research, Santa Fe, New Mexico

Page 2: Kate Clayton ("Granny") Donaldson. *Cow Blanket.* c. 1930.
Vegetable-dyed wool, cotton, 48 x 36″. Collection
Southern Highland Handicraft Guild. Folk Art Center,
Asheville, North Carolina

Page 5: Philip Simmons. *Window Grill.* c. 1940. Wrought iron,
39 x 27″. Collection Philip Simmons

Page 6: WPA Glass Factory, Vineland, New Jersey. *Amethyst
Vase.* c. 1940–42. Glass, 16 x 4¾ x 4¾″. Collection
Newark Museum, New Jersey. Gift of the WPA Art Project, 1943

"The History of Twentieth-Century American Craft: A Centenary Project" is a decadelong program of symposia, exhibitions, and catalogues organized by the American Craft Museum to write the history of twentieth-century American craft by the year 2000. "The Ideal Home: 1900–1920" was the first in the series of planned exhibitions; "Revivals! Diverse Traditions 1920–1945" is the second.

We are appreciative of generous support that has been provided by The National Endowment for the Arts, a federal agency, and the Rockefeller Foundation. Additional support has come from the Norman and Rosita Winston Foundation, Inc.

Library of Congress Cataloging-in-Publication Data

Revivals! diverse traditions : the history of twentieth-century
American craft, 1920–1945 / Janet Kardon, editor ; with essays by
Ralph T. Coe . . . [et al.].
p.   cm.
Catalog of an exhibition held at the American Craft Museum, New
York, N.Y.
Includes bibliographical references (p.   ) and index.
ISBN 0–8109–1955–9 / ISBN 0–8109–2601–6 (Mus. pbk.)
1. Decorative arts—United States—History—20th century—
Exhibitions.   2. Handicraft—United States—History—20th century—
Exhibitions.   3. Ethnic art—United States—History—20th century—
Exhibitions.   4. Regionalism in art—United States—Exhibitions.
I. Kardon, Janet.   II. Coe, Ralph T.   III. American Craft Museum
(New York, N.Y.)
NK808.R48   1994
745′.0973′0747471—dc20       94–11076

Printed and bound in Japan

"The History of Twentieth-Century American Craft: A Centenary Project,"
including
"Revivals! Diverse Traditions,"
is made possible by a major grant
from the Lila Wallace-Reader's Digest Fund.
The American Craft Museum expresses its profound gratitude
for this award.

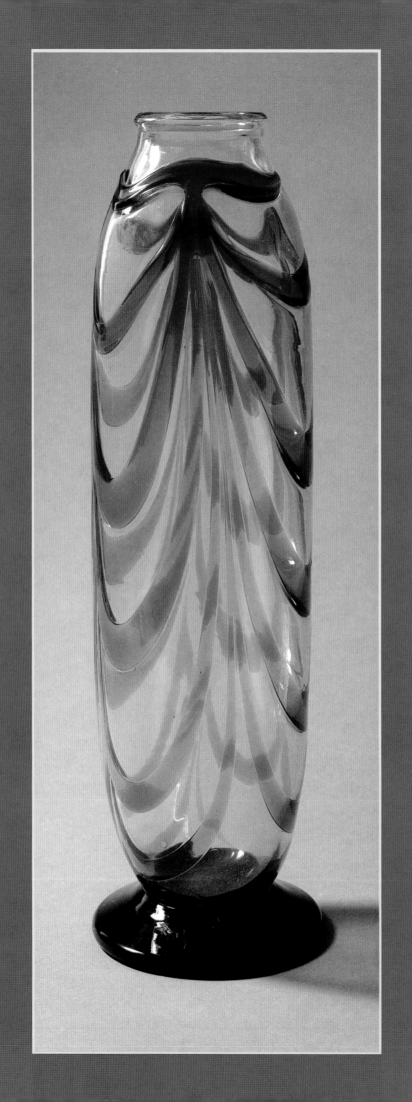

# CONTENTS

Oneidacraft
*Bombé Secretary with Bust of Lord Howe.* c. 1926
W. and J. Sloane
Wood, 98 x 46 x 25"
Collection New York State Historical Association

Domingo Tejeda
*Trastero*, c. 1937

Attributed to Benjamin Wade Owen
*Four-Handled Dragon Vase*. c. 1940s
Jugtown Pottery
Red stoneware, Chinese blue glaze, 14 x 5 x 5"
Collection Milton Bloch and Mary Karen Vellines

Henry Letcher
*Sgraffito Vase.* c. 1930s
Ceramic, 6¾ x 3½ x 3½"

Mary Saltonstall Parker
*Sampler.* 1920
Cotton embroidery on linen, 20 x 27"
Collection Peabody Essex Museum, Salem, Massachusetts

Juan Sanchez
*Retablo, Santa Librado*. c. 1930s
Gesso and water-soluble paint on wood, $9 \times 7\frac{1}{2}''$
Gift of Historical Society of New Mexico to Museum of New Mexico, Museum of International Folk Art, Santa Fe

# Contributors

Ralph T. Coe is an independent art historian who was formerly curator and director at the Nelson Gallery of Art, in Kansas City, Missouri. Among the many exhibitions of contemporary and ethnic art he has organized are "Sacred Circles: Two Thousand Years of North American Indian Art," at the Hayward Gallery, London, and "Lost and Found Traditions: Native American Art: 1965–1985," an American Federation of Arts traveling exhibition.

Harvey Green, professor of history at Northeastern University, has lectured widely in the United States and Canada. He has written many articles and reviews on American history and material culture, as well as three books: *Light on the Home: Women in Victorian America; Fit for America: Health, Fitness, Sport, and American Society, 1830–1940;* and *The Uncertainty of Everyday Life, 1915–1945.* He is at work on a study of the intersections of popular literature and material culture in the United States between 1850 and 1910.

Janet Kardon, director of the American Craft Museum and founder and director of the Centenary Project, is the editor of *Revivals! Diverse Traditions, 1920–1945.* Former director of the Institute of Contemporary Art at the University of Pennsylvania, in Philadelphia, she has curated more than forty exhibitions in her career and written and edited nearly as many catalogues. In 1980, she served as United States commissioner for the Venice Biennale and, since 1975, has been a consultant/panelist for the National Endowment for the Arts.

Jane Kessler is an independent curator and a principal partner in Curator's Forum, a curatorial consulting firm in Charlotte, North Carolina. A former curator of contemporary art at the Mint Museum, in Charlotte, she has organized numerous exhibitions of contemporary art, including works in craft media, and has written reviews, articles, and catalogue essays for national and regional publications, museums, and university galleries.

April Kingsley is curator and Centenary Project publications coordinator at the American Craft Museum. Formerly an independent art critic, curator, and historian, she has written for such major publications as *Artforum, Art International, Arts, The Village Voice,* and *Newsweek.* She is the author of *The Turning Point: The Abstract Expressionists and the Transformation of American Art* (New York: Simon and Schuster, 1992).

Francis V. O'Connor, an independent historian of American art, has written extensively on New Deal cultural programs. He is currently writing a history of the mural in America from early Native American times to the present.

Winifred Owens-Hart is a ceramist, teacher, and researcher in the history of ceramics. As professor of art at Howard University, she coordinates the art department's ceramics, sculpture, and foundation programs. She has been the recipient of the Lifetime Achievement Award in the Craft Arts, the Smithsonian Institution's Renwick Fellowship and Faculty Research Fellowship, and many other awards and grants.

William B. Rhoads, professor of art history at the State University of New York, New Paltz, has published *The Colonial Revival* as well as several articles on the Colonial revival in American architecture. His essay "The Colonial Revival and the Arts and Crafts Movement" will appear in *The Substance of Style,* to be published by W. W. Norton for the Winterthur Museum.

Dale Rosengarten, guest curator of the McKissick Museum's Lowcountry Basket Project, is the author of the exhibition catalogue *Row upon Row: Sea Grass Baskets of the South Carolina Lowcountry.* A doctoral candidate at Harvard University in the history of American civilization, she works as a research historian for various museums.

Annie Santiago de Curet is director of the Museum of Anthropology, History, and Art, University of Puerto Rico, in Rio Piedras. She has been a consultant in collections management and cultural activities to various museums, including the Smithsonian Institution. She is the author of "Recent Findings on the Art of Needlework in Puerto Rico."

Gail Tremblay is a member of the faculty at The Evergreen State College. A poet and fiber artist, she has written several articles on Native American art and photography. Her essay on the work of Navajo photographer Hulleah Tsinhuahjinnie is included in *Partial Recall,* edited by Lucy Lippard. She has also curated exhibitions of work by Native Americans for the Center of Contemporary Art and Sacred Circles Gallery at Daybreak Star Indian Art Center in Seattle.

John Michael Vlach, a professor of American civilization and anthropology at George Washington University, is currently chair of the American Studies Program and director of the Folklife Program. He has served as guest curator or consultant to several museums, including the Cleveland Museum of Art, the Institute for Texan Cultures, the Smithsonian Institution, the California Craft and Folk Art Museum, and the McKissick Museum. Among his books are *The Afro-American Tradition in Decorative Arts; Plain Painters: Making Sense of American Folk Art;* and *By the Work of Their Hands: Studies in Afro-American Folklife.*

William Wroth is one of the foremost authorities on early Hispanic arts. As curator of the Taylor Museum of the Colorado Springs Fine Arts Center from 1974 to 1983, he was responsible for "Hispanic Crafts of the Southwest," as well as its catalogue; he was also the project director and curator of the museum's "Images of Penance, Images of Mercy." Wroth served as codirector and guest curator for the Hispanic Heritage Wing of the Museum of International Folk Art, Santa Fe, New Mexico.

Hildreth J. York taught art history and directed the Museum Studies Program at Rutgers University before retiring from teaching in 1993. She has written *New Deal Art: New Jersey,* as well as articles on ancient and more recent art, and has been curator of several exhibitions.

# Researchers

Tara Leigh Tappert is writing a biography of Cecilia Beaux and organizing an exhibition of her paintings for the National Portrait Gallery. She has a degree in library science and a Ph.D. in American civilization from George Washington University.

Peggy Ann Brown is an independent scholar and editor with a Ph.D. in American civilization from George Washington University.

# Lenders to the Exhibition

Albuquerque Little Theater, Albuquerque

Mr. and Mrs. Thomas C. Babbitt, Litchfield, Connecticut

Berea College Appalachian Museum, Berea, Kentucky

Berkeley College, Yale University, New Haven

Milton Bloch and Mary Karen Vellines, Clinton, New York

Ruth Clement Bond, Washington, D.C.

Lester P. Breininger, Jr., Robesonia, Pennsylvania

Leroy E. Browne, Sr., Saint Helena Island, South Carolina

Robert S. Brunk, Asheville, North Carolina

John C. Campbell Folk School, Brasstown, North Carolina

Robert Cargo Folk Art Gallery, Tuscaloosa, Alabama

The Charleston Museum, South Carolina

The Children's Museum, Boston

A. M. Chisholm Museum, Duluth, Minnesota

Churchill Weavers, Berea, Kentucky

Cleveland Public Library, Ohio

Lizzetta LeFalle-Collins and Willie R. Collins, Oakland, California

Colorado Springs Fine Arts Center, Colorado

Teresa Rodón de Comas, Torrimar Guaynabo, Puerto Rico

Lane Coulter, Santa Fe

The Denver Art Museum, Colorado

Rosalina Brau Echeandia, San Juan, Puerto Rico

Economos Works of Art, Santa Fe

Edisto Island Historic Preservation Society, South Carolina

Harriet Clarkson Gaillard, Camden, South Carolina

Gordon William Gray, Princeton, New Jersey

Phoebe Hearst Museum of Anthropology, University of California, Berkeley

High Museum of Art, Atlanta

Sherman Holbert, Onamia, Minnesota

Howard University Gallery of Art, Washington, D.C.

M. Jeannette Lee, Mt. Pleasant, South Carolina

Eli Leon, Oakland, California

Susan Morgan Leveille, Dillsboro, North Carolina

Jan Brooks Loyd, Newell, North Carolina

Helen Bright Lyles, Washington, D.C.

The Metropolitan Museum of Art, New York

Mint Museum of Art, Charlotte, North Carolina

Ralph Siler Morgan II, Webster, North Carolina

Museum of American Glass, Wheaton Village, New Jersey

Museum of Fine Arts, Boston

Museum of Indian Arts and Culture, Museum of New Mexico, Santa Fe

Museum of International Folk Art, Museum of New Mexico, Santa Fe

National Park Service/Roosevelt-Vanderbilt National Historic Sites, Hyde Park, New York

The Newark Museum, New Jersey

New York State Historical Association, Cooperstown, New York

Nordic Heritage Museum, Seattle

Rude Osolnik, Berea, Kentucky

Mrs. Y. A. Paloheimo, Santa Fe

Peabody Essex Museum, Salem, Massachusetts

Qualla Arts and Crafts, Cherokee, North Carolina

Alberta Lachicotte Quattlebaum, Pawleys Island, South Carolina

E. Ronald and Shirley Rifenberg, Hurley, New York

Rochester Museum & Science Center, Rochester, New York

Franklin D. Roosevelt Library, Hyde Park, New York

Roswell Museum and Art Center, Roswell, New Mexico

Mrs. Jervey D. Royall, Mt. Pleasant, South Carolina

Jeanne S. Rymer, Wilmington, Delaware

Sagamore Hill National Historic Site, Oyster Bay, New York

Sandwich Historical Society, New Hampshire

School of American Research, Santa Fe

Science Museum of Minnesota, St. Paul

Philip Simmons, Charleston, South Carolina

South Carolina State Museum, Columbia

Southern Highland Handicraft Guild, Asheville, North Carolina

Sterling Memorial Library, Yale University, New Haven

Mrs. Frances R. Stroup, Spruce Pine, North Carolina

Tantaquidgeon Museum, Uncasville, Connecticut

Mrs. W. M. Thomas, Columbus, Georgia

Mr. and Mrs. Gary S. Thompson, Jr., Greenville, South Carolina

Timberline Lodge, Government Camp, Oregon

Vivian Torrence, Munich, Germany

University of Kentucky Libraries, Lexington, Kentucky

Michael Walsh, Park Ridge, Illinois

Mable M. Westbrook, Lenoir City, Tennessee

Mrs. Rosemary Keyser Wood, Ambler, Pennsylvania

Arval Woody, Spruce Pine, North Carolina

Yale University Art Gallery, New Haven

Yosemite Museum National Park Service, California

# Acknowledgments

"The History of Twentieth-Century American Craft: A Centenary Project" is the American Craft Museum's decadelong pioneering effort to organize a major exhibition series and compile a multivolume history. At its culmination, near the turn of this century, the museum will have produced the first historical overview of the American craft movement. *Revivals! Diverse Traditions, 1920–1945* is the second catalogue in this ambitious exhibition series.

"The History of Twentieth-Century American Craft: A Centenary Project," including "Revivals! Diverse Traditions," is made possible by a major grant from the Lila Wallace–Reader's Digest Fund. The American Craft Museum expresses its profound gratitude for this award.

We are appreciative of additional, generous support that has been provided by The National Endowment for the Arts, a federal agency, the Peter T. Joseph Foundation, and the Norman and Rosita Winston Foundation, Inc. The exhibition and catalogue are also made possible by generous grants from the Rockefeller Foundation.

The American Craft Museum has benefited from the expertise of the many scholars who assisted with the Centenary Project; the parturition of this book is one result of their conscientious efforts. As Centenary Project founder and director, it has been a great pleasure to work with them.

Planning for the exhibition "Revivals! Diverse Traditions, 1920–1945" began five years ago. It was agreed that the period 1920 to 1945 was too complex and varied to be encompassed within a single framework. In fact, it split naturally along two parallel temporal lines. One concerned the developments occurring within our shores that had made an effort toward national self-definition: the Colonial, Hispanic, Native American, and African American revivals and survivals—and the Southern Appalachian and other regional revivals. A different aesthetic sensibility was being sparked by European Modernism, an influence outside our shores, abetted by many of its proponents who were fleeing Nazism and emigrating to this country. In 1995, these developments will be traced in the third volume and exhibition in this series, "Craft in the Machine Age: European Influence on American Modernism, 1920–1945."

The structure for "Revivals! Diverse Traditions" was outlined in a spring 1990 symposium, "1919–1945, Multicultural and Regional Sources: Craft Revivals," and was further refined in a roundtable conference and many informal discussions that I had with the participants: Ralph T. Coe, curator and expert on Native American art; Douglas DeNatale, South Carolina State folk arts coordinator, McKissick Museum, University of South Carolina; William Ferris, director, Center for the Study of Southern Culture, University of Mississippi; Rayna Green, director, American Indian Program, National Museum of American History, Smithsonian Institution; Eugene Metcalf, associate professor, interdisciplinary studies, Miami University; Barbara Perry, former curator of ceramics, Everson Museum of Art; William B. Rhoads, professor of art history, State University of New York, New Paltz; Jeffrey Stewart, assistant professor of history, George Mason University fellow, National Humanities Center; Marcia Tucker, director, New Museum of Contemporary Art; and William Wroth, editor and curator of "Hispanic Crafts of the Southwest," The Taylor Museum. The wise counsel of these informed minds, as well as our Centenary consultant, Jonathan Fairbanks, curator of American decorative arts, Museum of Fine Arts, Boston, was invaluable to us in planning "Revivals! Diverse Traditions" and conceptualizing the important role of the diverse cultural strands that nurtured the American craft movement.

I am particularly grateful to the writers of the essays in *Revivals! Diverse Traditions, 1920–1945.* Harvey Green, professor of history at Northeastern University, who has made an extensive study of the intersections between America's history and its material culture, provides an insightful overview of this troubled interwar period. Five of the essayists, serving with me as cocurators of the main sections of the exhibition, lent their invaluable expertise to the project. Ralph T. Coe organized the Native American section, which he elucidates in his essay, "Native American Craft." Jane Kessler selected the objects from the Southern Highlands and describes their significance in "From Mission to Market: Craft in the Southern Appalachians." William B. Rhoads located important examples of the Colonial revival in the states along the eastern seaboard, and he outlines their social and political value as well as their aesthetic merits in "Colonial Revival in American Craft: Nationalism and the Opposition to Multicultural and Regional Traditions." John Michael Vlach is our curator of African American objects. His essay, "'Keeping On Keeping On': African American Craft during the Era of Revivals," elucidates the survival of certain traditions. William Wroth discusses the Hispanic revival material he selected in "The Hispanic Craft Revival in New Mexico." This publication is enhanced by the expertise of these scholars in the regional, national, ethnic, and cultural segments of our culture.

Other essayists provided a contextual background for the objects created during this period, viewed them from alternative perspectives, or focused on a single area of craft production. Winifred Owens-Hart traces the history of ceramic production in America to its African sources in her essay, "Ceramics: From Africa to America." Dale Rosengarten, who specializes in the study of the sea grass baskets of the South Carolina coastal plains, elaborates on them in "The Lowcountry Basket in 'Changeful Times.'" Gail Tremblay, a poet and fiber artist, brought her perspective as a Native American craftsperson to bear on the developments of the period in "Cultural Survival and Innovation: Native American Aesthetics." Hildreth J. York has given an overview of the federal government's support for craft during the Depression in "New Deal Craft Programs and Their Social Implications." Francis V. O'Connor, an authority on the WPA, focused on one of its many programs in his discussion of Timberline Lodge, Mt. Hood, Oregon. Curator April Kingsley, our valued coordinator of the museum's Centenary publications and assistant editor of this catalogue, worked with Annie Santiago de Curet, the director of the Museum of Anthropology, History, and Art at the University of Puerto Rico, to discuss the revival of lacemaking in Puerto Rico between the world wars, and with Ruth Clement Bond on a short account of the Black Power quilts Bond designed in the 1930s while working on the Tennessee Valley Authority project. These last three commentaries indicate the widespread and richly various craft revivals and survivals in the years between 1920 and 1945.

The extensive resource section was entrusted to the capable hands of Tara Leigh Tappert and Peggy Ann Brown, who performed their difficult task with admirable precision. Lisa Hartjens and Anita Dickhurth, our picture researchers, were amazingly resourceful at fulfilling challenging assignments. Gerald Zeigerman once again served as our tireless, conscientious editor, enabling us to maintain the same high quality of scholarship and editorial consistency established in Centenary I. It has also been a great pleasure to collaborate again with the publishing house of Harry N. Abrams, Inc., and its representatives—in particular, Paul Gottlieb, president, publisher, and editor-in-chief; Ruth Peltason, senior editor; and Carol Robson, designer.

The entire staff of the American Craft Museum has been exemplary. Robert Hornsby, former Centenary Project coordinator, and Betsy Jablow, Centenary Project coordinator, have overseen all aspects of this complex project with much organizational skill and diligence. They have been assisted by Tracey Bashkoff and Marsha Beitchman. The latter's ability to execute the myriad details of the project was of inestimable help. April Kingsley's work on this time period and her publication experience have proved highly beneficial in her role as coordinator of Centenary publications. As assistant editor, her commitment to excellence has significantly strengthened this book.

Many other members of the American Craft Museum staff have made vital contributions to the project, but I want to particularly mention Kate Carmel, senior curator; Robert Perlstein, corporate and special events manager; Lillian Piro, deputy director for internal affairs; Elizabeth Reiss, coordinator of education; Doris Stowens, registrar; Scott VanderHamm, collections manager; Carol Wood, exhibitions coordinator; Olga Lydia Valle, curatorial assistant; and Naomi Vine, deputy director for external affairs. We have had the inestimable benefit of the assistance of interns Dan Derenthal, Julie Williams, and Julie Winieski.

Special thanks go to Irene Gordon for her concerned work with Ralph T. Coe on his essay and to Michael Godfrey for assisting Jane Kessler with hers. Cinda Baldwin, Tritobia Benjamin, Charlotte Brown, Claudine Brown, Elenita Chickering, Rossie Colter, Lane Coulter, Eileen Johnson, Leslie King-Hammond, Billie Rae Hussy, Jack Lindsey, Judy McWillie, Sally Peterson, Ken Trapp, Merikay Waldvogel, and Georgia Weir have all been of invaluable assistance in identifying hard-to-find objects for the exhibition. We also want to thank Pedro Reina at the Puerto Rican Foundation for the Humanities for his kind assistance. Lastly, we are grateful to Marie Carmen Artera, Josh Brown, Judith Brundin, Annie Santiago de Curet, Marilyn Johnson, and John Moore for their thoughtful assistance in planning the exhibition installation.

The board of governors of the American Craft Museum, led with admirable vision by Jerome Chazen, chairman, has steadfastly and enthusiastically supported this project. Museums across the country have been remarkably generous in extending loans from their collections, and private lenders have kindly parted with beloved objects to make this exhibition possible. We are immensely grateful to them all.

Ultimately, our appreciation must go to the many artists, who, very often, worked in total obscurity for practically nonexistent remuneration—literally performing labors of love for their art. This exhibition and catalogue acknowledge the men and women who kept esteemed craft traditions alive. They created splendid objects. We are also grateful to those who generated interest in them and preserved their history.

JANET KARDON
DIRECTOR
AMERICAN CRAFT MUSEUM

# Within Our Shores: Diverse Craft Revivals and Survivals

by Janet Kardon

"The History of Twentieth-Century American Craft: A Centenary Project" was initiated when I became director of the American Craft Museum, in response to my perception that the vital contribution of the craft movement to our culture lacked a comprehensive overview. To confirm this need for a written history and to begin assembling the expertise required to gather the information, the first of several planning symposia was presented in 1990.[1] It was apparent that the leading figures, the issues, and the aesthetic development of craft in this century often have remained in discrete and unrelated clusters of information, separated by divisions of medium, region, or ethnicity, awaiting basic research, analysis, and compilation. The American Craft Museum has assumed the monumental, decade-long challenge of preparing the first historical survey of the craft movement in the United States.

As a conceptual framework for this project, the twentieth century has been divided into sequential time periods. For each period, a symposium is convened of specialists in each of the craft, and related, disciplines, in an attempt to identify the most significant issues and artists. Many of the scholars who will contribute catalogue essays or act as curators for the exhibitions emerge the following day from a roundtable discussion with the speakers, museum curators, and invited guests. Then, a major exhibition, documented by a comprehensive publication, is organized to reflect the history of each sequential time span. By the turn of this century, the American Craft Museum plans to have presented eight exhibitions and publications. Exhibitions are ephemeral, existing within a prescribed quotient of time, but the volumes that accompany each one will comprise the enduring history.

More than one hundred scholars and artists from across the country are now participating in the Centenary Project; they represent the disciplines of craft, the decorative arts, architecture, art history, material culture, and political and social history. Their response has been overwhelmingly positive, thus affirming a genuine critical need. "The Ideal Home: 1900–1920," the first exhibition in the series, was presented in October 1993. As founder of the Centenary Project, it is my great pleasure to introduce the second volume of this history, *Revivals! Diverse Traditions, 1920–1945*, which accompanies the second exhibition in this enormous enterprise. *Revivals! Diverse Traditions* focuses on the contribution of indigenous communities, including foreign cultures that maintained an ethnic or racial identity in our society. During the period, ongoing craft activity cohabited with revivals of African American, Appalachian, Hispanic, and Native American crafts, while the Colonial revival remained a strong presence.

The planning for this exhibition and publication began with a symposium, "Multicultural and Regional Sources: Craft Revivals," held at the American Craft Museum on May 17, 1991. Participating with me were the following experts, listed with the titles of their papers: Ralph T. Coe, "Art of the Native American"; Douglas DeNatale, "The Southeastern Craft Revival and the Reinterpretation of Regional Culture"; William Ferris, "Memory and Sense of Place in African American Crafts"; Rayna Green, "The Beaded Adidas and the Mickey Mouse Kachina: Old Thoughts, New Forms in Indian Art"; Eugene Metcalf, "Folk Art, Fine Art, and Craft: Aesthetic Definitions and the Search for a Modern American Identity"; Barbara Perry, "Rediscovering America: The Effects of Multicultural and Regional Contributions on Mainstream Craft"; William B. Rhoads, "The Colonial Revival: Nationalism and Regionalism in American Craft"; Jeffrey Stewart, "Issues of the African American Artist between the Wars"; Marcia Tucker, "'Who's On First?' Issues of Cultural Equity in Today's Museums"; and William Wroth, "The Hispanic Craft Revival in New Mexico in the 1920s and 1930s." The following day, the proceedings of the roundtable conference, which included our speakers and curatorial staff, clearly indicated that scant literature or research was available for several of the sections to be included in the exhibition. Overviews of craft produced within each individual culture, or of craft itself between the years 1920 and 1945, simply do not exist. Compared to the first exhibition, "The Ideal Home: 1900–1920," where much information had already been gathered on the Arts and Crafts movement, the years between the two world wars have been undervalued, even neglected. They require far more basic and original research.

Our task is daunting for many other reasons. The period itself is heterogeneous. In the political arena, the dual forces of isolationism and internationalism struggled in opposition. An index of the period's dichotomies would juxtapose dire poverty and conspicuous affluence; the city and the dream of retaining an agrarian economy; the Great Depression and the New Deal; Communism and Fascism; the rise of unions and Jim Crow; the destitution of the Native American's actual reservation life and Hollywood's portrayal of cowboys and Indians; the natural disaster that caused the Dust Bowl agricultural crisis and the ill-considered laws of Prohibition that encouraged the speakeasy; the deprivations of mountaineers and their romantic portrayal in certain novels and photographs.[2]

The artistic climate reflected this bifurcated political and social environment. American painting vacillated between regionalist realism and Cubist-influenced abstraction. Because the range of craft in these years was so diverse, we have chosen to devote two distinct exhibitions and publications to this twenty-five-year period, enabling us to develop parallel, if vastly divergent, points of view. This book, *Revivals! Diverse Traditions*, explores aesthetic activity that occurred simultaneously in different regions and communities within various ethnic and racial groups, which are defined by national borders as well as an adherence to history and tradition. The third Centenary exhibition, "Craft in the Machine Age: European Influence on American Modernism—1920–1945," to be presented in 1995, and its accompanying book, will focus upon newly invented forms, concerning itself with the influx of European Modernism, the rebellion against past doctrines and traditions, and the formation of a new artistic and expressive vocabulary in craft media.

In the first publication of the Centenary Project, an attempt was made to define craft. Those definitions are pertinent to our period: Craft objects originate in function, and function often emerges from spiritual or ritual imperatives; they evidence the makers' respect, even reverence, for materials, process, and techniques; and they have been created by trained professionals or individuals who are carrying on traditions transmitted from their elders. The artist is aware of the historical continuum of craft, either within the ethnic or national community or from the larger mainstream, and is often committed to extending and expanding that continuum in inventive ways. We still cling to the ideal that a single artist designs, executes, and signs the work, while allowing that, in some cases, the artist carefully supervises production in a small workshop.

In the first two decades of this century (covered in *The Ideal Home*), the incursion of industry into the making of the craft object was an important issue. In the time period of the present volume, the definition of craft is, instead, commonly obscured by a blurred distinction between craft and folk art. Lincoln

*Boston Sunday Post,* February 14, 1937. These pictures ran side by side in the newspaper, and were intended to highlight the differences between the lives of the rich and poor.

Kirstein, in 1930, attempted to clarify the situation in an early definition of folk art: "By folk art we mean art, which, springing from the common people, is in essence unacademic, unrelated to established schools, and, generally speaking, anonymous."[3] Two years later, Holger Cahill expanded the definition. He described folk art as "the expression of the common people, made by them and intended for their use and enjoyment. It is not the expression of professional artists made for a small cultured class, and it has little to do with the fashionable art of its period. It does not come out of an academic tradition passed on by schools but out of craft tradition, plus the personal quality of the rare craftsman who is an artist."[4]

From these definitions, we can perceive differences between craft and folk art. Rarely are folk artists formally trained, and most remain anonymous. Modestly, they make objects for others like themselves and probably do not consider themselves artists in origin, intent, or execution. Craft, even with its democratic aspirations, is not quite as humble. Separating folk art from craft art is particularly problematic in the quarter century under discussion; there are many objects in the exhibition that might be defined as folk art. Since we are seeking to identify the sources of the craft movement, though, it is appropriate to also examine what may be described as folk art, because its presence influenced the historical development of craft.

An undertaking as enormous as the Centenary Project necessarily requires the efforts of many experts. Nowhere is this more evident than when we survey the rich cultural diversity of the interwar period. Acknowledging the complexity of interpreting this material, we have engaged writers from within and from without the communities to assist in the preparation of this book and exhibition. It is the aim of the entire Centenary Project to bring the contributions of artists working in craft media into the larger cultural mainstream, but the particular focus of this second Centenary exhibition and catalogue is to enter the contributions of our indigenous cultures, as well as our unique, non-European, immigrant population, into the mainstream of craft in America. Many important social issues have emerged, so we have taken this opportunity to examine work that has too long been excluded from the official discourse of contemporary American culture.

Multicultural segments of our society were inspired to revive and preserve craft traditions that were endangered by industrialization and cultural homogenization. Concurrently, Colonial revival partisans venerated and preserved an Anglo-Saxon past—an attempt to figuratively whiteout foreigners and people of color. These historical repetitions blanketed the country, smothering the contribution of Hispanic Americans, Native Americans, and African Americans, as well as others who were emerging from various, often isolated, regions. While most scholars concentrated upon the Colonial revival style—even as popular culture absorbed and reflected its forms—significant components of our culture languished in the shadows of neglect or misinterpretation.

It is our thesis that an important counterculture to the powerful and popular Colonial revival was in existence. In this period, several cultures, races, communities, and religious groups were mining their own histories and reviving their own traditions, as well as creating new forms. Avoiding subsumation by the nationalistic melting pot, some peoples of ethnic, racial, and religious diversity chose to withdraw into their own enclaves.

A significant amount of ethnographic data was recorded on the objects at the time they were created, yet the artistic mainstream lacks information on these cultures. The tenets of art history, the discipline of the decorative arts, or the common definition of craft often have not been integrated with the research, which makes it difficult to align the contributions of the different cultures with related disciplines. Thus, in William Ferris's *Afro-American Folk Art and Crafts,* identification of the role of craft is the task of the discerning reader. In Janet Catherine Berlo's book *The Early Years of Native American Art History*, the objects are all considered part of art history; she does not make a distinction between craft and sculpture.[5] Most texts focus on the marketplace and anecdotal commentary, offering minimal descriptions of artists or their objects. Compounding these scholarly disjunctions and lacunae, government funding, when apportioned, particularly in the 1930s, was often accompanied by strict guidelines that frequently interfered with traditions. The results were predictably ragged—the survival of some aspects of our common culture and the disappearance or alteration of others.

Our challenge was to assemble these many separate but concurrent chapters, each written from its own point of view and utilizing its own descriptive vocabulary, each driven by different spiritual forces, its own collective memory, and with its own political agenda. It is complicated further because many of these individual histories are now in the process of intense revision. Even a review of the terminology employed indicates flux; the African American community, for example, has also been referred to as colored, Negro, black, and Afro-American—interchangeable terms in use during the past half-century denoting a shared identity.

Is our melting pot a myth? Although slavery was legally abolished in 1863, the fiery zeal of the Ku Klux Klan burned as brightly in the 1920s as the crosses it torched, and, later, when Japanese Americans were placed in internment camps, virtual imprisonment denigrated a segment of our population for the duration of World War II. Today, our effort to address the past collides with the loss of recorded history, a result of the earlier, silenced voices of nonwhite cultures. Powerful propaganda emitting from proponents of the melting pot often overwhelmed attempts to preserve traditions. This dialectic between traditional enclaves and assimilation is as powerful in this period as was the economic struggle between industry and the hand in the first two decades of the century.

Recent experience and studies indicate that, however well intentioned, traveling through multicultural territory can prove controversial in unexpected ways. As Steven D. Lavine and Ivan Karp write in *Exhibiting Cultures: The Poetics and Politics of Museum Display*, "Only when as a society we have achieved sufficient opportunity for art and artifacts of 'other' cultures to be seen can we expect this kind of controversy to become less heated. Now an exhibition often bears the burden of being representative of an entire group or region."[6] In the same publication, Svetlana Alpers notes that "in the exhibiting of the material culture of other peoples, in particular what used to be called 'primitive' art, it is the museum effect—the tendency to isolate something from its world, to offer it up for attentive looking and thus to transform it into art like our own—that has been the subject of heated debate."[7]

Since scholarship is often in the formative stages and not properly coordinated, the available information is disparate and uneven. With the exception of Colonial revival material, we must often rely upon clusters of memory systems rather than actual texts. Our challenge is further compounded by the necessity to separate, identify, and record the contributions of artists from discrete cultures working under the particular rubric of craft media. In *Revivals! Diverse Traditions*, we hope to identify the problems noted by the seminal revisionist studies and lay the groundwork for future investigations, while identifying putative differences, similarities, and crosscurrents. It would be premature for this exhibition to attempt to show development in each of the separate cultures, if, in fact, this were even a legitimate approach; we can only represent some of the most prominent artists and include a thoughtful selection, by the most qualified experts we can identify, of the most significant objects produced within the period.

The selection of objects for the first exhibition, "The Ideal Home," followed traditional craft divisions—clay, fiber, glass, metal, and wood—forming five subcategories. "Revivals! Diverse Traditions" is organized differently; our curators are experts in five major, but aesthetically very different, regional, racial, or cultural spheres. The African American section was curated by John Michael Vlach; the Appalachian by Jane Kessler; the Colonial revival by William B. Rhoads; the Hispanic American by William Wroth; and the Native American by Ralph T. Coe. In addition to selecting the objects, each curator has written an essay for this publication.[8] Several shorter texts that discuss particular projects or craft disciplines are also part of this volume.

Harvey Green has provided a political, economic, and social overview of these twenty-five years in his essay, "Culture and Crisis: Americans and the Craft Revival." The legacy of a world war and the economic disaster of the Great Depression had significant impact on artistic expression, particularly craft, since it was viewed, perhaps not incorrectly, as a social vehicle and an economic tool. Green examines the role of racism as it affected the diverse cultures under discussion, as well as differences between our urban and rural populations. Henry Ford's Greenfield Village and John D. Rockefeller's Williamsburg were built to attract those Americans who could afford to travel. These sites offered an opportunity to inculcate the public with the tenets of Colonial revivalism, undoubtedly the strongest aesthetic presence of the period.

William B. Rhoads's essay, "Colonial Revival in American Craft: Nationalism and the Opposition to Multicultural and Regional Traditions," provides the background for the emergence of the colonial form as the national style. Its wide acceptance minimized the cultural contributions of Native Americans, Hispanics, and African Americans, even as it served as a banner of Americanization to the immigrants who struggled to enter our shores. Rhoads's revisionist overview examines the pros and cons of reviving regional craft centers through machine production, whether or not it was combined with handwork. The opening of the American Wing of the Metropolitan Museum of Art, in 1924, was a major impetus to the revival of colonial-style objects. Colonial revival remains a powerful conservative presence.

Hildreth J. York surveys the impact of the multifaceted Works Progress Administration (WPA) and other New Deal federal programs that affected the development of craft as well as society itself. Certain institutions thrived under federal patronage. Francis V. O'Connor discusses Timberline Lodge, in Mt. Hood, Oregon, a 1936–37 WPA recreational project that involved a large community of carpenters, stonecutters, leather toolers, woodcarvers, cabinetmakers, metalworkers, weavers, writers, painters, and architects. Skills were taught, and they created irregular, rudely carved beams and interior details with indigenous pine, stone, and cedar. Newel posts represented birds or animals of the Mt. Hood region. Fabrics for curtains were simple and forthright: Handweavers used Oregon flax and wool as warp and woof on simple looms. Colors echoed those of earth, sky, water, and wood; motifs were borrowed from the patterning of local flora and fauna.

Of the histories of indigenous peoples in the process of revision, none is more burdened with spiritual imperatives and political controversy than that of Native Americans. In an attempt to reflect the current terminology, in most cases we chose Native American over American Indian, even though it and many previously shunned terms are currently acceptable.

The cover of Rosemont's catalogue of hooked rugs and coverlets suggested that they were still made by Virginia women in the old colonial way, at home by the hearth and the spinning wheel.

Julian and Maria Martinez, San Ildefonso Pueblo, c. 1935. Photograph by T. Harmon Parkhurst

Early in the century, under the influence of the market, a few Native American craft artists, encouraged to break with tradition, began to sign their works. Several European Surrealist painters, as well as Americans such as John Sloan and Georgia O'Keefe, were intrigued by objects from the Southwest. As a result, when Native American artifacts were collected and exhibited in New York City, they became a subject of considerable study. But the acceptance of Native American objects into the larger collection and exhibition context of art museums became legitimate only with René d'Harnoncourt's 1941 exhibition at the Museum of Modern Art, "Indian Art of the United States." At the time, d'Harnoncourt was general manager of the Department of the Interior's Indian Arts and Crafts Board. Referred to as "the aesthetic appropriation of Indian art," d'Harnoncourt's presentation of non-European material as art remains a model,[9] although it was controversial at the time. His commitment to merchandising and marketing, even within a museum context—which may have fueled the controversy—is paralleled by the efforts of certain contemporaneous Hispanic, Appalachian, and African American advocates, as well as by Eleanor Roosevelt's Val-Kill.

Attitudes and terminology have changed since d'Harnoncourt's exhibition. Native Americans have removed many artifacts—spiritual objects, in particular—from public display. Scholars have steadily revised the history, acknowledging that the Native American was trained, perhaps by inherited tribal knowledge, to make spiritual objects as beautiful as possible. It is the task of the American Craft Museum to ensure sufficient national tribal representation in just one section of a single exhibition. Ralph T. Coe carefully selected Native American objects from more than twenty tribes. He stresses Navajo and Pueblo crafts, for that is where the emphasis was during the period, but he also examines work produced in other regions of our country, work that was overlooked then and later. He considers the influence of railroad patronage, tourism, the Indian Arts and Craft Board, and the WPA. We are pleased to include the voice of a Native American fiber artist in this volume: Gail Tremblay focuses on the individuals who innovatively transformed traditional models, and discusses the social, cultural, and economic forces that influenced aesthetic developments.

William Wroth's essay, "The Hispanic Craft Revival in New Mexico," outlines the historical context of Hispanic crafts in New Mexico and the early revivals between 1890 and 1920 that legitimized Hispanic crafts. He discusses the work in the 1920s of Mary Austin and Frank Applegate, who rediscovered Hispanic craft artists and established the Spanish Colonial Arts Society. In addition, Wroth

Tinsmith Francisco Delgado in his shop on
Canyon Road, Santa Fe, New Mexico,
c. 1935. Photograph by T. Harmon Parkhurst

examines the promotion and marketing of Hispanic revival crafts, as well as the
effects of government support in the 1930s. Marketeering interventions benefited this segment of the population and outweighed the ill effects sometimes experienced in other revivals.

Hispanic aesthetics, routed from Spain to Mexico or directly to this country,
reflected European tradition, but Native American expression that often intertwined with Hispanic culture can also be perceived. Without the establishment of
certain public programs to encourage the revival of Hispanic traditions, they
might have become completely acculturated. The native market was an extreme-

Blacksmith Philip Simmons at his forge

ly important lifeline for Hispanic craft, for it enabled the producers of craft objects to earn a living.

The Harlem Renaissance, a cultural movement in New York City that spanned the 1920s, concentrated on painting and sculpture. Music by members of the African American community received critical notice even before the visual arts, and little attention of any sort was given to craft activities. Our awareness and knowledge of baskets, quilts, musical instruments, canes, and vessels is a result of the more recent scholarship of Robert Farris Thompson and William Ferris, among others. John Michael Vlach, author of the African American section, notes that despite the neglect of scholars who preferred to focus on music and painting during the Harlem Renaissance, craft traditions survived in basketry, ironwork, and quilting. Self-generated despite the paucity of government support, they thrived. Elsewhere, Dale Rosengarten discusses the developments in lowcountry basketry and Winifred Owens-Hart covers African American ceramics.

Owens-Hart has discovered that African Americans were making pottery in Jugtown, previously thought of as an enclave of traditional white potters, and that black women were gathering in each others' homes during the 1920s to paint china and to fire it in their personal-size Revelation kilns. African American ceramists were also utilizing Mayan motifs on teapots, inventing dazzling new glazes, and shaping ashtrays and bowls that would have looked perfectly at home in a modern, streamlined setting. Other surprises have been the modernistic quilts that black women made on the TVA Wheeler Dam project and the presence of black chipcarvers in a craft specialty previously thought to be the exclusive province of northern Europeans who emigrated to America.

Despite the great diversity within this particular framework, one African American paradigm underlines the urgency to apply a separate set of aesthetics in interpreting each of these cultures. Symmetry ruled the making of the Colonial revival quilt, but the unique irregularity, offbeat multistrip, and staggered composition of African American quilts reflect the impetus of different social and psychological forces. This irregularity and broken patterning has been attributed to a defense against immediate clarity and an impulse for self-protection, which dates back to the encoding of information about the Underground Railroad in the quilts.

Aunt Lou Kitchen, c. 1927–29.
Photograph by Doris Ulmann

Regional craft revivals, as in Appalachia, pose a different set of problems. Here, the traditions of artists working in craft media often were inundated by waves of good intentions, and unique expressive qualities became subsumed by the exigencies of a marketplace that was seduced by the Colonial revival. Early in the century, countless settlements were founded in the mountains of Kentucky, Tennessee, Georgia, and North Carolina. The work of what has been called Soldiers of Light and Love, linked to a conservative concept of social change, projected grossly misleading images of rural and mountain communities. Their manipulation of culture reflects a clash of ideological differences. Teachers in the settlement schools were determined to remake their students in their own images, just as instruction in craft was intended to reconfigure objects for the marketplace. Settlement schools in Manhattan and other urban areas codified expression according to an economic and moral imperative: Neutral, homogeneous products were encouraged.

Jane Kessler, curator of the section on craft revivals in Appalachia, delineates the effect of such outside forces on the distinct character of the Southern Highlands region and its vernacular pottery and other crafts. In her essay, "From Mission to Market: Craft in the Southern Appalachians," she describes settlement schools and other social-reform movements of the period, and discusses the tradition and community-based Highlands craft activity at Penland School, Berea College, and Allanstand Cottage Industries.

From 1920 to 1945, the legacy of cultural and material heritages from other continents was not yet gentrified, nor is it today, fortunately. As the outside world co-opted and often attempted to homogenize the unique spiritual and expressive styles of each of these communities, their very identity was being diluted, if not threatened with extinction. Often, this was exactly what was required for entry into the larger cultural mainstream.

We have attempted to provide a contextualized and aesthetic backdrop for craft as it emerged from multipartite communities during a complex and divergent period of our history. "Revivals! Diverse Traditions" clearly differs from most exhibitions in that there was not the customary attempt to select objects with visual or thematic consistency; the leitmotiv of this exhibition is diversity. Several of our writers refer to the cross-fertilization that has produced hybrid artifacts generated from multicultural, multinational, and diverse spiritual origins. We expect that the richness of the objects will evince the strength of these previously unaccounted visual resources.

The disparity between egalitarian and elitist elements in our society has been made apparent. We have also considered craft's social, economic, recreational, and therapeutic virtues as they compete with aesthetic imperatives. The residual effects of the WPA and the Index of American Design on craft activity now can be better observed. A concerted effort must be made to mine the records of both endeavors to further ascertain their influence on the American craft movement. Our expectation is that additional research could focus on shared crosscurrents. But, at present, the objects offer a metaphorical, iconographical, symbolic, historic, and formal feast for scholar, student, artist, and, indeed, every visually literate viewer.

JANET KARDON
DIRECTOR
AMERICAN CRAFT MUSEUM

The Great Depression and World War II were the defining events of the quarter century that began in 1920. The physical suffering and psychological damage wrought by the economic collapse left what historian Caroline Bird chillingly called an "invisible scar" on Americans.[1] The war brought death, left visible marks and deformities, and took an emotional toll on survivors of the battlefield and on the relatives, friends, and lovers of many who perished or disappeared. As important as the Depression and the war were, however, it would be a mistake to see the 1920s as less important, as an era of respite and relative ease between World War I and the Crash of 1929. The complicated position of the crafts in the United States during the Depression and World War II originated in the 1920s—and earlier.

For historians, part of the problem of the revival and survival of craft lies in the tangled roots of private and governmental support of the various experiments and socioeconomic efforts to preserve and broaden production and marketing bases of the crafts. Some advocates of the therapeutic, aesthetic, and economic worth of craft activities and their continuance arrived at their position from a concern about the continuing attraction of cities for the rural young. Others, building upon the ideas and ideals of the Arts and Crafts movement of the late nineteenth and early twentieth centuries, envisioned a resurgent crafts revival as a way to ameliorate the ill effects of industrial mass production and the accompanying alienation of the worker. Still others envisioned craft as an alternative—perhaps an antidote—to Marxist working-class radicalism. More than a few were convinced that reinvigorating a particular segment of the population's crafts would aid in a nativist racial-purity crusade that included more obviously controversial positions—eugenics and racial intolerance. Some social reformers perceived craft training as tools of uplift for the poor, and educational reformers who followed John Dewey's theories easily integrated craft into their learning-by-doing ideology. New Dealers hoped support of all sorts of indigenous craftspeople might offer a new economic answer to unemployment and poverty. Business-

Black clouds of dust, Texas panhandle, March 1936. Photograph by Arthur Rothstein

Two boys playing marbles in Washington, D.C., November 1942. Photograph by Gordon Parks

Polish religious order marching in procession at Easter High Mass, Corpus Christi Church, Buffalo, New York, April 1943. Photograph by Marjorie Collins

people saw a product they could buy cheaply and sell dearly if they could find a market, and some of those making the goods envisioned profit, especially if they were to sell directly to consumers. A few saw crafts and the people who produced them as windows to the past, or as specimens and curiosities to be nurtured and preserved.

"Discovering," supporting, and marketing the crafts in the United States have roots that return to the nineteenth century. The most analyzed contributor to these activities is the Arts and Crafts movement, an ideological descendant of the efforts of English reformer William Morris. The title of the movement is significant; art was a critical component, and many of its leaders were formally trained academic artists. Naive or traditional works of art or craft occupied an important place in their work and teaching, but more as inspiration than as model.

Some of the larger Arts and Crafts organizations—Gustav Stickley's Craftsman Workshops and Elbert Hubbard's Roycroft colony, among them—were big businesses as well as ideological statements. Others—Fellowship Farms, New Clairvaux, Elverhoj, and Byrdcliffe—were descendants not only of Morris's little pockets of craftsmen and -women in England but also of the nineteenth-century American utopian experiments, such as the Zoar, Amana, and Shaker communities. Some linked crafts with agriculture and self-sufficiency; others were closer to the socialism of nineteenth-century reformer Charles Fourier.

Enmeshed in the English and communitarian roots of the Arts and Crafts movement were less noble elements of American intellectual history—nativism and racial nationalism.[2] Ralph Radcliffe Whitehead, who founded Byrdcliffe, near Woodstock, New York, in 1903, defended his autocratic leadership with references to the incompatibility of Socialism with the family and Anglo-Saxon life.

Interest in racial purity lay, in part, behind the beginnings of amateur and academic enthusiasm for collecting Americana of all sorts—artifacts, songs, language—in the late nineteenth century. Native Americans were especially important targets in this effort, once the United States Army had relocated nearly all of the tribes to reservations. Defeated and confined, they became a safe "other," to be studied and even ennobled, especially by urban easterners. Photographers Edward Curtis and Adam Clark Vroman, among others, documented the Native American peoples, especially those of the Southwest and Pacific Northwest, and collectors, anthropologists, and museum curators accumulated vast quantities of ordinary and precious ritual materials for private and public display. The looting—and "legal" purchasing—went on despite the Antiquities Act that Congress passed in 1906, which forbid the excavation and removal of materials without official sanction, thus limiting the access of native peoples to examples of their own material cultural heritage.[3]

Native American culture exercised an important influence on the Arts and Crafts movement. Gustav Stickley's magazine *The Craftsman* regularly carried articles on the basketry, music, myths, and architecture of the native peoples.[4] Some of the Rookwood Pottery Company's most famous decorated art pottery depicted idealized images of tribal chiefs, and generic Native Americans graced advertisements for "healthy" or "pure" products.[5] By the 1920s and throughout the following quarter century, Native American craftspeople continued to produce and sell a broad spectrum of objects, including rugs and other textiles, pottery, and jewelry and other metalwork.

At the same time that interest in Native American crafts began to grow, collectors such as Henry Chapman Mercer were showing concern with the disappearance of white "pioneer" settlers and their culture. Mercer accumulated large and small tools, vehicles, firearms, household supplies, furnishings, and whatever else he could find. As he was doing so, anthropologists and folklorists came upon what they were convinced were living relics of our colonial past—the mountaineers of the Southern Appalachians. Here, thought many analysts, were the early Americans that civilization had forgotten, or missed, because of their geographic isolation and their allegedly cantankerous—and violent—everyday lives.[6] Some enthusiasts of the culture of the Appalachian peoples, such as Virginia composer John Powell, brought an intense hostility to African Americans and nearly all peoples not of Anglo-Saxon or northern European roots to bear on their collection and interpretation of music and material culture.[7]

Powell's racism and search for racial purity should be no surprise—nor should the nativism, or, at best, nationalism, of other collectors, marketers, and makers of American goods. The Russian Revolution, in 1917, and the strikes that occurred throughout the United States in 1919 augmented already potent anti-immigrant and antileft bias. Attorney General A. Mitchell Palmer, his presidential aspirations in evidence, helped foment the hysteria: "Out of the sly and crafty eyes of many of them leap cupidity, cruelty, insanity, and crime; from their lopsided faces, sloping brows, and misshapen features may be recognized unmistakenly criminal types."[8] On January 2, 1920, Palmer supervised a nationwide raid and roundup of suspected radicals. Agents hauled off more than four thousand suspects. In the next six weeks, two thousand more were arrested. Not all immigrants were suspect, however. Many of the most respected furnituremakers, metalsmiths, and glassblowers were from southern and eastern Europe. Presumably, they were uninterested in radical politics, unionization, or other Red or Wobbly (as the Industrial Workers of the World were called) ideas.

The Palmer raids, and the nativist hostility from which they grew, found support in the resurgent Ku Klux Klan, although not all nativists supported the Klan's racist violence. *The Birth of a Nation*, in 1915, D. W. Griffith's cinematic tour de force, was an adaptation of Thomas Dixon's viciously racist novel of 1905, *The Clansman*. Both the film and book were used as tools for the Klan's recruitment efforts, not only in the South but all over the Midwest, Far West, and the Northeast during the 1920s.[9]

The fear and antagonism created by job competition outside the South after World War I was a major part of the Klan's success in recruiting new members. African Americans had not been welcomed into the armed forces during the war. Kept from the battlefield, they were assigned the most degrading jobs on base and

Submarginal farm of Mollie Day, Bedford
County, Pennsylvania, December 1937.
Photograph by Arthur Rothstein

were placed in segregated living conditions. Not only was enlistment an unat-
tractive option, the demand for war-related matériel and the decline in the white
male workforce, because of enlistments, opened job opportunities that were better paying than anything African Americans had even hoped to find in the South,
where tenant farming and sharecropping or menial industrial or commercial jobs
were the norm. After the war, however, production levels dropped, white ser-
vicemen returned, and violent racism reemerged. The impact of this racial intolerance was at once obvious—in the riots and the increase in lynchings in the 1920s
and 1930s—and subtle: African American crafts were seldom the focus of those
determined to rescue or revive the culture of the "folk."

African Americans, for the most part, were left out of the various attempts
to preserve or make use of the crafts—in part because of racism, in part because
the ideologies associated with the crafts were rooted in a critique of modern
industrial civilization that seemed inappropriate to the African American experience. They had not suffered from the ill effects of mass production and industrial labor, the argument ran, because, traditionally, they were unable to get jobs or
buy the goods produced. And once such jobs opened up for them, as they had in
northern cities during World War I, they enthusiastically grabbed them, jettison-
ing their rural southern heritage of impoverished agriculture and racism. Many
critics thought they abandoned their folk roots as well. Even some sympathetic
academic analysts of African American culture assumed that the slave experience
was so wrenching and wretched that no vestige of African culture remained to be
"saved." Yet, objects such as coiled-grass and other baskets, quilts, and pottery
indicate not only that African elements of material culture survived the American
experience but that urban industrial work did not preclude traditional craft
activity.

For white Americans, industrial civilization was a riddle: It delivered material abundance to an ever-widening circle of consumers because of the wonders of
engineering and efficiency, but the realities of factory and office work also brought
dehumanization and alienation. In 1922, four important books appeared, each in
its own way drawing attention to the problem of modern industrial civilization.
Harold Stearns's *Civilization in the United States*, a collection of thirty essays,
noted that social life in the United States was characterized by an "emotional and
aesthetic starvation," caused, in large part, by the country's lack of "traditions."

Haying hands eating dinner at the C-D Ranch, Big Hole Valley, Montana, c. 1938. Photograph by Russell Lee

Stearns challenged the assertion of the Ku Klux Klan and other nativists that American civilization was necessarily and desirably Anglo-Saxon, and he complained about the gap he perceived between what Americans preached and what they practiced.[10]

Walter Lippmann, in *Public Opinion*, also criticized Americans for this trait, voicing his frustration at the difference between the idea and the reality of material progress.[11] Lothrop Stoddard's *The Revolt against Civilization* warned against the lure of the primitive, stressing eugenics (selective breeding and sterilization among humans) as an antidote to the social problems he saw around him.[12] In *Social Change with Respect to Culture and Original Nature*, William Ogburn equated the highest levels of civilization with the ability to adapt to rapid technological change. Those who maintained habits and customs of eras of lesser technological development well after the material and technological bases of society had changed suffered from "cultural lag." Ogburn maintained that this continued reliance on anachronistic practices led to tension and waste.[13]

The American Country Life Association, founded, in 1919, by a coalition of reformers, aimed to combat the problems of isolation and poverty that Ogburn and earlier "rural sociologists," such as Robert Dugdale and Frank Blackmar, had identified and to fight the demographic pressures disrupting rural life. The *Proceedings* of the group's 1929 annual meeting warned that "if the inequalities which now exist shall continue, we shall not much longer be able to keep the normal boys and girls on the farm. . . . If the flight to the city . . . shall go on as rapidly as it has in the last few years, the next generation will witness a farm population largely composed of the physically and mentally unfit."[14] This set of fears informed the efforts of the analysts who saw the southern mountaineers as historical specimens as well as those who sought to preserve their crafts and culture. Implicit in much of this analysis and programmatic action, however, was the sense of otherness and inferiority of the "backward" peoples discovered by the urbanites, business adventurers, and reformers.

Sociological investigation of urban and village life also increased in the early twentieth century.[15] By the 1920s, the idea that *community* was endangered by modern civilization provoked studies and surveys of village, city, and farm life. The most famous was that of Robert and Helen Lynd, who conducted extensive fieldwork in Muncie, Indiana. In *Middletown*, published in 1929, they exposed a

Mrs. Watkins in her smokehouse, Coffee County, Alabama, April 1939. Photograph by Marion Post Wolcott

The Lemuel Smith family saying grace, Caroll County, Georgia, April 1941. Photograph by Jack Delano

deeply held conviction that one's place in the world was a result of individual effort and that failure in the socioeconomic world was one's own fault.

*Middletown* confirmed what the popular press and popular magazines had been asserting throughout the decade: Self-help and personal responsibility were the keys to success. Advertising, which was becoming a more organized and bureaucratized profession and a critical part of the profitability of many businesses, found the vulnerable spot in the middle-class American's psyche: Success no longer seemed based on such easily quantifiable characteristics as piecework productivity but on such intangibles as "fitting in" and "likability."[16]

Self-improvement was one answer to the problem of survival and prosperity, and its leisure-time analogue, do-it-yourself projects and amateur crafts, was another. The Arts and Crafts movement had stimulated a spate of guides for would-be china painters, needleworkers, metalsmiths, potters, woodworkers, and the like. Still popular in the 1920s, these and more practically oriented do-it-yourself books and guides were offered to the amateur who wanted both to economize and gain some measure of relief from the stresses of the office. In this sense, crafts may not have been arts, as in the Arts and Crafts movement's sense, but they shared some of the same alleged therapeutic benefits.

The insecurity of the white-collar world of work was an adjunct to what many blue-collar workers had known for decades. The economic expansion of the decade included a modest increase in real wages for the working class as a unit, but the reality of day-to-day work for industrial, agricultural, and extractive workers was one of sporadic and unpredictable labor. The timber and mining industries continued their massive expansion in the upland South and intermountain West, but logging was seasonal, and mines often shut down if there was a lull in demand.[17] The same situation applied to factory work. Few laborers could count on regular employment for a full year, and workers often reported for work in the morning only to find the plant closed when demand slowed. Farmers enjoyed a brief period of high prices after World War I ended, but by the mid-1920s, prices collapsed and their Depression had begun.

Thus, vacations—one of the ways by which the middle class was supposed to reinvigorate itself—were unavailable to the working class, which got more time off than it wanted. The middle class and the wealthy, however, increasingly took to the rails and the roads in the 1920s, which brought them to parts of the country they had not seen before and, to some extent, in contact with the crafts of peoples of whom they had been only dimly aware, if at all. For Native American and Hispanic craftspeople in the American Southwest, sales of craft to this new breed of traveler became an important source of income.

Travel by auto, at best, could be an adventure and, at worst, a harrowing experience, given that roadways between cities and towns were often dirt or gravel and only occasionally signed and numbered. By the mid-1930s, federally sponsored public works projects led to the improvement of many major routes, and for the 35 to 40 percent of the workforce that escaped unemployment or underemployment during the Depression, new vacation destinations beckoned. In the mid-1920s, automobile magnate Henry Ford and oil baron John D. Rockefeller, Jr., launched ambitious historical re-creation projects that were to become major tourist destinations. Ford, who was displeased with the history of the United States he found in textbooks, began a nationwide effort to accumulate representative artifacts of American everyday life in order to refocus the attention of Americans on the country's great inventors and products. Greenfield Village was born of Ford's rural background and personal commitment to science and technology. In addition to vacuuming up all sorts of artifacts, he moved the houses and work areas of representative American greats to Dearborn, Michigan—in particular, Thomas Edison's Menlo Park, New Jersey, laboratory and the Wright brothers' bicycle shop.

Colonial Williamsburg was a different sort of project. The Rockefellers wished to restore an existing town as a way of teaching vacationing Americans about the values of democracy, individual effort, and personal responsibility. After considering New Castle, Delaware, they settled on Williamsburg; the colonial capital of Virginia, it had been the site of activities of such state luminaries as Thomas Jefferson, Patrick Henry, and George Washington. As the opening date neared, in 1935, the Williamsburg project received massive press attention. It was an immediate success with the public and with all sorts of magazines and newspapers. Decorating magazines like *House Beautiful* and *House and Garden* ran

Miner's shack, Scott's Run, West Virginia, c. 1938. Photograph by Walker Evans

Backyards, Mexican section, San Diego, California, June 1941. Photograph by Russell Lee

numerous illustrated stories of the restored town, reinvigorating Americans' fascination with the forms, crafts, tools, designs, and household objects of the colonial American past.[18]

Ford and the Rockefellers were building upon more than a half-century of American enthusiasm for the colonial. Beginning with scattered preservation efforts in the middle of the nineteenth century and accelerating after the Philadelphia Centennial International Exposition, in 1876, the Colonial revival expanded throughout the American marketplace by the 1890s. It included new buildings modeled after colonial (especially neoclassical) architecture, historic preservation and renovation of original structures, a burgeoning antiques market, the mass production of replicas and adaptations of antique furnishings, and all sorts of community celebrations and commemorations.[19]

It was both an inclusive and exclusive movement—a celebration of American nationalism and a potential way for immigrants to assimilate, as well as a means by which white Anglo-Saxon Protestants could distinguish themselves from those "others." The revival also focused the attention of some Americans on the craftsmen and -women of the early years of settlement and of the Republic. The objects of veneration of the collectors, dealers, and curators were primarily metropolitan-based, high-style furnituremakers, who were seen as in perfect harmony with their times. There was, therefore, an ironic element in the growing enthusiasm for the crafts of the rural Appalachian people that caught on in the 1920s. These "folk" were originals, and their talents and products were a continuation of the crafts that Colonial revivalists valued; unlike their forebears, though, the people themselves were seen as underprivileged, backward, and quaint.

The founders of Williamsburg, Greenfield Village, and the many other restored village projects initiated in the era consciously strove to create a special vision of the past. Workshops were re-created to prevent the disappearance of the crafts of the cabinetmaker, metalsmith, printer, housewright, weaver, and other preindustrial workers. These were "villages" with neither troublesome unions nor sit-down strikes, like those that occurred with increasing frequency after 1935, and, apparently, no unemployment and no depressions.

The Colonial revival emerged as one of the major strains of design and decorative inspiration in the material culture of twentieth-century United States, competing with the enthusiasm for machine-age streamlining and the design implications of new materials, such as aluminum, Bakelite, and plastics. But Modernist design also exerted a substantial force on the crafts, as exemplified by the work of the students and faculty of the Cranbrook Academy of Art, which was founded in 1927. Most of their work was Modernist in approach—traditional motifs appeared most frequently in textiles and ceramics, and only occasionally in metalwork and furniture—yet, like the Colonial revival, Cranbrook, in Bloomfield Hills, Michigan, also represented an old idea: the small, dedicated community of like-minded, or, at least, like-talented, individuals committed to the preservation and continuance of the crafts in an industrial society. As such, Cranbrook, like many of the utopian communities of the midnineteenth century and the Arts and Crafts communities of the turn of the century, came into being as a counterpoint to industrial production and its social consequences.[20]

The Colonial revival—as well as Modernism—gathered strength from its nationalist associations and, by the 1930s, as a source of intellectual and cultural reassurance during an economic cataclysm. In its intensity and duration, the Depression was not like previous economic downturns. The unemployment rate shot up, from 3.1 percent in 1929 to 24 percent in 1932. In 1932, 64 percent of all construction workers in New York City were out of work; between 1928 and 1933, new building starts in the United States dropped 90 percent. The lumber industry collapsed. Fifty percent of all home mortgages throughout the country were in default by 1933. Bank failures mounted at a frightening rate: 659 in 1929; 1,352 in 1930; 2,294 in 1931; 1,456 in 1932.[21]

Individuals out of work responded characteristically in a culture that, for generations, had linked economic success to personal initiative and hard work. Governmental and privately sponsored studies of the unemployed found that they commonly blamed themselves rather than any larger, impersonal forces; shame and a sense of personal failure were everywhere.[22] Popular entertainment reinforced the sense of personal responsibility and offered formulaic answers to the Depression's problems. On the radio, outsiders such as "The Lone Ranger" and "Superman" appealed to a populace that was dubious about the capability of established governmental or other institutions to solve what were unprecedented problems.

The quest for solutions to the crises of the Depression dovetailed with the ongoing strength of the Colonial revival, a discomfiture or disillusionment with industrial machine production, and a continuing interest in the crafts. A search for, and reaffirmation of, the organic and folk roots of American culture emerged as the Depression wore on. Holger Cahill organized a pathbreaking exhibition of American folk art at New Jersey's Newark Museum in 1930 and, after its spectacular success, a similar exhibition of American folk sculpture at the same institution the following year. As head of the Works Progress Administration (WPA) Federal Art Project, Cahill sponsored numerous projects and exhibitions of craftworks, and helped organize the systematic recording of important artifacts of American arts and design in the Index of American Design. The WPA sponsored more than three thousand craft projects, the Farm Security Administration supported experiments in handcraft production, and nearly every state initiated and organized craft fairs.

Eleanor Roosevelt was an enthusiastic sponsor of the crafts. With three other women, she organized Val-Kill Industries, in 1927. Val-Kill resembled earlier Arts and Crafts colonies, in that each craftsman worked on a piece from beginning to end, rather than in an assembly-line or other division-of-labor system. The furnituremakers were to copy colonial-era pieces, thus directly linking their work and the ideology of Val-Kill to the Colonial revival. Later additions to the Val-Kill Industries, notably metalworking and weaving, were less dependent upon colonial materials for inspiration. Workers at the Val-Kill Forge (1934–38) produced goods modeled after or copied from European and American sources. The Val-Kill Looms (1929–37) and the Val-Kill Weavers (1934–49) produced homespun textile goods much like those found in the Southern Highlands in the 1930s.

For consumers without the skills, finances, or desire to make the goods, the crafts movement and crafts revival of the quarter century beginning in 1920 was an option that could reaffirm some sense of commitment to American national identity. While the crafts movement at times objectified the very craftsmen and -women that proponents and merchants thought they were helping, it also provided a sense of dignity and, perhaps, the wherewithal that these individuals had not been able to garner before. In the end, the unevenly distributed prosperity of the 1920s, the economic crisis of the 1930s, and the enormity of World War II united some Americans and divided others by class, ethnicity, race, and ideology. The work and the products of craftspeople were emblems of individual and group political identity and the aspiration of the makers and the consumers. Both were altered by the exchange.

Colonial Revival
in American Craft:
Nationalism and the
Opposition to Multicultural
and Regional Traditions
by William B. Rhoads

The revival of early American craft between 1920 and 1945 was part of the larger movement, since the 1870s, to bring back colonial design. To its advocates—mostly white Anglo-Saxon Protestants—it represented America's own national style.[1] By 1920, the Colonial revival had become deeply entrenched in architecture and design; probably the most popular of the revival styles,[2] it has remained so to the present day. For the confirmed Colonial revivalist, the seventeenth- and eighteenth-century styles of the eastern seaboard were suitable for use anywhere in America, and the contributions of Native Americans, Hispanics, and African Americans to the fabric of American culture were, at best, marginal. Those who felt threatened by the influx of millions of immigrants sometimes turned to the Colonial revival as an emblem of their ancestral piety or as a tool to educate, to

## OLD DESIGNS MADE NEW

No Article of Furniture Links us with the Past as the Windsor chair. There is hardly a city or country home which would not look the better for any one of the chairs shown on this page made after models dear to us through association with New England history. They make the most acceptable of Christmas gifts.

OAK ROCKERS at **$10.50** or mahogany at **$14.00** or the Shakespeare chair made in mahogany only, shown below, at **$15.00** is just the thing for comfort beside an open fire on Christmas morning.

For DINING ROOM, sitting room or porch the chair shown above made in oak **$10.00** and mahogany **$14.00**, or the Prince of Wales chair shown below made of mahogany only at **$10.50** would be a good companion to furniture of almost any type.

THE BEAUTIFUL GATE-LEG TABLE shown above, 40 in. in diameter, in oak **$28.00**, in nut-brown mahogany **$32.00**, is useful in almost any room of the house. This same design, oval 40x54, of oak **$31.00**, or of mahogany **$36.00**, would make a delightful breakfast or dining table.

THE SLENDER AND GRACEFUL ANN HATHAWAY CHAIR shown at the left made of mahogany only, at **$18.00**, would solve the difficult matter of gift for any man of the family or for use in library or dining room.

**GUSTAV STICKLEY
THE CRAFTSMAN**
6 E. 39TH ST., NEW YORK

Gustav Stickley produced Windsor chairs at the end of his career. He claimed he had always admired them.

Wallace and Mariet Nutting posed for a pentype silhouette by Ernest and John Donnelly. They are shown in modern dress, seated on Windsor chairs, writing Christmas cards on a Pilgrim Century tavern table.

Americanize newcomers assumed to be ignorant of America's heritage.[3]

Colonial craftsmanship—widely interpreted as continuing into the early nineteenth century, until the triumph of the machine and Victorian styles—appealed to many American supporters of the turn-of-the-century Arts and Crafts movement, especially in the Northeast, because colonial craft was simple in design and sturdily made by hand. Colonial pieces could serve as appropriate models for American workers in the arts and crafts seeking native sources, just as English vernacular examples of the seventeenth and eighteenth centuries served William Morris and his English followers. Thus, Gustav Stickley based his Craftsman furniture, in part, on colonial precedent, and he praised the strength and durability of old colonial furniture and simply treated reproductions while objecting to the machine reproduction of colonial ornament.[4]

In 1917, soon after the demise of Stickley's enterprise, Wallace Nutting began to reproduce colonial furniture with a combination of machine and handwork. Nutting, as historian John Crosby Freeman has shown, was both a late disciple of the Arts and Crafts movement and "the leading popularizer of the Colonial revival during . . . the 1920s," through both his photographs of colonial scenes and his colonial-inspired furniture, made in Saugus, Ashland, and Framingham, Massachusetts.[5]

Nationalism and ancestor worship were at the root of Nutting's rationale for his revival: "There is enshrined in the forms of furniture used by our ancestors a spirit absent from the exotic shapes that come from Italy and France. We love the earliest American forms because they embody the strength and beauty in the character of the leaders of American settlement."[6] This regard for ancestral furniture was heightened, Nutting acknowledged, by the upheaval of the Great War. Tracing his New England ancestry to the seventeenth century, he found his forebears' virtues embodied in their surviving oak furniture, which he then reproduced. Seventeenth-century court cupboards, in Nutting's words, were "the noblest pieces that have come down to us." Only a little less noble, presumably, were the Connecticut sunflower chest and paneled oak chest with their sturdy foursquare lines and surfaces enlivened with applied turnings. Native oak was superior, he thought, to imported mahogany. For one influenced by the Arts and Crafts movement, eighteenth-century mahogany furniture seemed, at least until about 1927, overrefined and aristocratic.[7] His Queen Anne daybed, in walnut, began to test the limits of his taste for simplicity and restraint.

Nutting was a photographer, writer, and expert on colonial furniture but not a craftsman, so he hired "fine American mechanics," both native- and foreign-born—a veritable League of Nations, he said. Nutting had given up the ministry, yet he did not forsake his calling to mold human character. For his workers, he composed Ten Shop Commandments, "to make men while making furniture."[8] By 1936, he observed, loftily, that his foreign-born workers were as efficient and faithful as the native-born.[9]

In the Arts and Crafts spirit, Nutting claimed "to encourage individuality" in his turners, chair- and cabinetmakers—"men who love their work" and therefore would adhere to his tenth commandment: "Let nothing leave your hands till you are proud of the work." But individuality did not mean the freedom to invent, as Nutting demanded that his workers accurately copy colonial designs. Where Stickley and others freely interpreted their sources, Nutting capitalized on his reputation as an expert on American antiques—especially through his book *Furniture of the Pilgrim Century*—and publicized the fidelity of his reproductions. He was proud of the lineage of his furniture, while those who tried to be inventive with colonial design only created "mongrel mixed shapes."[10]

Nevertheless, it is clear that Nutting's own designs strayed from historical accuracy; Patricia Kane has noted a "tendency to exaggerate and re-create forms in more monumental scale."[11] A Nutting rival, Jacob Margolis (brother of Nathan Margolis, the Hartford furnituremaker), reproduced early American furniture in New York, and assured the noted antiques collector Francis P. Garvan that "my furniture would be made mostly by hand—mortising, carving, and finishing." Margolis's experience as a repairer of and dealer in antiques served to enhance the accuracy of such reproductions as the three-part mahogany dining table commissioned by Garvan for the Yale University Art Gallery in 1929, but, as David Barquist points out, Margolis's eighteenth-century-style mirror, also for Garvan and Yale, was "influenced by the early twentieth-century taste for simplified forms."[12]

Danersk furniture was first produced by "mountaineers . . . old-time chair makers" in shops in the North Carolina mountains for the New York–headquartered Erskine-Danforth Corporation, but, in 1915, most manufacturing was transferred to a factory in Stamford, Connecticut.[13] In the early 1920s, Danersk's sources were remarkably broad; the design of one painted cabinet came from Esfahān. Soon, however, the company's advertisements—directed, presumably, by president Ralph Erskine—took on an aggressively nationalistic tone, not uncommon in postwar America. In 1923, Erskine wrote a denunciation of German and French Modernism (apparently that of Art Nouveau) as well as antique "foreign elaborations," although the simpler sorts of old English and French furniture were admired and even copied by Danersk.[14]

A 1926 Danersk ad proclaimed that "the spirit of freedom" was symbolized in American furniture, whether based on George Washington's desk or a Salem desk with McIntire eagle. "These ancient symbols are dear to all true Ameri-

Assisted by Wallace Nutting, Berea College students made and sold Welsh dressers and other Colonial revival designs. From *Antiques* magazine

cans. . . . We count it our duty to make them live again in convenient forms for the homes of our generation." Furthermore, Danersk proposed that the "character and integrity" of the Founding Fathers "will be fostered in our children if we surround them in their homes today with furniture that breathes the spirit of the best American traditions." Students at Yale University might benefit from the colonial joint stools that were among the eclectic furniture by Danersk in the Linonia & Brothers Room of Sterling Memorial Library, opened in 1931. From such pieces, Danersk supposed "students are constantly absorbing vital lessons of good taste and the appreciation of honest craftsmanship."[15]

Danersk blended a not-very-strict Colonial revivalism, lingering ideas from the Arts and Crafts movement, and modern technology. Externally, a six-legged

Danersk heralded the authenticity of its reproduction of George Washington's writing table. The fluting of the legs, for example, was executed by hand. From *Antiques* magazine

highboy was "faithfully copied," but the interior could be transformed to house radio equipment.[16] Modern design was rejected: "Art is evolution, not revolution. . . . Art never casts aside the tangible beauty . . . from past ages to express itself in grotesque, awkward forms whose sole distinction seems to be that they are different." While objecting to cheap copies and quantity production, Danersk did embrace modern machinery, in combination with handcrafted details (for example, fluting of the legs of Washington's desk).[17]

Danersk's designs and ad copy oozed Americanism, but, like other manufacturers, its workers were fairly recent arrivals on American soil. The company avoided employing immigrants from southern and eastern Europe; it was proud that the three hundred craftsmen of the "Danersk Colony" were Scotch and English, "many of them . . . the sons and grandsons of Scotch and English cabinetmakers." James Rogers, for instance, came from Duncan Phyfe's hometown in Scotland, and was said to have equaled Phyfe's mastery of inlay work.[18]

The opening of the American Wing of the Metropolitan Museum of Art, in 1924, further stimulated an already widespread taste for American antiques as well as reproductions and adaptations. Lewis Mumford worried that the American Wing's popularity would lead to bad copying, "harnessing machine-productions to a sickly desire to counterfeit the past,"[19] but Ralph Erskine urged that "manufacturers and artisans" look to the American Wing and similar collections as "sources for inspiration."[20] That was precisely the intention of the wing's curator, R. T. H. Halsey. He took special delight in observing how manufacturers

R. T. H. Halsey supervised the reproduction of a grand eighteenth-century desk with George Washington associations for the New York State Historical Association's re-creation of the John Hancock House, in Ticonderoga. The desk, with other reproductions of American Wing antiques, dominated the drawing room, which was furnished by W. and J. Sloane.

increasingly drew upon the Met's collections for ideas, while "'Jazz' in art, with its utter disregard of basic principles," seemed in decline. Halsey argued for the acceptance of the colonial furniture of the American Wing as being distinctly American and expressive of the "traditions and principles for which our fathers struggled and died." He thought the "foundations" of the American Republic were threatened by "the influx of foreign ideas"; therefore, "study of the American Wing" would be "invaluable in the Americanization of many of our people" ignorant of so much American history.[21]

But Halsey was not content merely to encourage craftsmen and manufacturers. In 1925, he was president of Oneidacraft, makers of "authentic" but moderately priced early American furniture, in Oneida, New York. Oneidacraft announced that Halsey and William Sloane Coffin, vice-president, were "well known antiquarian experts" who chose the models for the reproductions that were sold exclusively through W. and J. Sloane, of New York City. Sloane's more expensive line of furniture, built by the Company of Master Craftsmen in a Georgian-cupolaed factory, in Flushing, New York, included a magnificent desk and bookcase (or tall secretary desk), whose base combined, unusually, bombé outward curving lines and a block front. A bust of General Jeffrey Amherst (victor over the French at Ticonderoga) was inserted within the broken pediment. The original of this desk (without the Amherst bust), belonging to the American Wing and probably made during the Revolutionary War, was said to have been used by Washington in the Craigie Mansion, in Cambridge. Halsey arranged for a copy of the desk, and copies of several other pieces of furniture in the American Wing, to be placed in the John Hancock House, reconstructed by the New York State Historical Association, in Ticonderoga, in 1926. Halsey was credited with ensuring that the craftsmen had an intimate knowledge of the antique sources: They "had the original pieces, not photographs or drawings, to work from. . . . They could handle and study them indefinitely and under Mr. Halsey's stimulating comment."[22]

The proprietors of the Val-Kill Shop, established in 1927, in Hyde Park, New York, were among those who turned to the American Wing for models of colonial craft. Val-Kill was a small shop producing Colonial revival, partially handmade furniture and other crafts under the sponsorship of Eleanor Roosevelt.

Eleanor Roosevelt posed with one of the Val-Kill craftsmen in 1927. Ribbon-back chairs, of the sort later made at Arthurdale, West Virginia, are to the right.

Promotional brochures assured customers of the legitimacy of the designs, some of which derived from pieces in the American Wing. Eleanor Roosevelt and Nancy Cook, the shop's manager and chief designer, consulted colonial experts, such as the museum's Charles Cornelius. Nutting's *Furniture of the Pilgrim Century* and the Nutting Collection, at the Wadsworth Atheneum, in Hartford, also served as sources,[23] and three Val-Kill designs were inspired by objects in Thomas Jefferson's Monticello. His Federal-style music rack became a magazine rack, in maple.

Although Val-Kill did produce high-style, eighteenth-century designs, it is better remembered for simpler pieces produced under Nutting's influence: bedside tables, in maple; slat-back, rush-seat chairs; and comparably restrained pewter pitchers and porringers. These were, in fact, the sorts of pieces Eleanor Roosevelt and her associates, Nancy Cook and Marion Dickerman, preferred for furnishing Val-Kill cottage and that Franklin Delano Roosevelt later wanted to use in the Little White House, at Warm Springs, Georgia. It was appropriate that these democrats who admired Jefferson and decried plutocratic excess should adopt Jeffersonian and unpretentious colonial models.[24]

"Val-Kill" is a Dutch word meaning valley stream, and some of the shop's publicity pictured the Dutch colonial Val-Kill cottage located near the stream, or val-kill. (The furniture shop was a few yards from the cottage.) But Val-Kill furniture drew upon English colonial forms and was not publicized as Dutch or reflecting regional, Hudson Valley precedent, even though Eleanor Roosevelt told an interviewer in 1929 that "we hope to make Val-Kill the center for a revival of all the old industries which were once carried on in its very hills"—weaving, rug-hooking, and metalwork.[25]

Val-Kill was intended to serve the people of Hyde Park as a source of employment. Local boys were trained—primarily in the tedious job of finishing—by Cook and her expert craftsmen, who were not from the region but, ironically (although not unusually for the period), foreign-born. Key figures were Frank Landolfa, from Italy (maker of the Jefferson-inspired magazine rack), and Otto Berge. Berge, trained as a woodworker in his native Norway and then as a restorer of American antiques in New York City, was critical of the failure of Val-Kill designs to follow historical precedent exactly.[26] But Nancy Cook was no Wallace Nutting. Eleanor Roosevelt insisted that the Val-Kill craftsman "express his own thought and make such changes as he personally desire."[27] In fact, Berge did not want freedom to invent but freedom to be a strict copyist, and this he was denied.

Val-Kill had its admirers. Decorator Nancy McClelland considered it a "serious effort to further the love of our national styles," but it was not a commercial success. Onetime New Deal economist Rexford Tugwell thought it merely "one of the futile attempts to re-create a handicraft so many well-meaning amateurs are apt to think practical."[28] Eleanor Roosevelt made another unprofitable effort, aided by Cook, in 1933, to establish colonial and hill-country crafts at the federally sponsored subsistence homestead project in Arthurdale, West Virginia, for unemployed miners "who have rediscovered the fine arts of their pioneer forefathers." Some of the furniture made at Arthurdale (under various names, including Mountaineer Craftsmen's Cooperative Association) came from local sources—notably, the Godlove chair, based on a "two-hundred-year-old family method of joining kiln-dried rungs and slats to green uprights, making an inseparable joint." The technique was given to the cooperative by a mountaineer, but some products were not indigenous; a ribbon-back chair resembled one made at Val-Kill.[29]

Under President Roosevelt, the Works Progress Administration (WPA) supported the revival of colonial crafts, as well as traditional mountain crafts, as part of its greater crafts program: The Illinois Craft Project included a shop at Petersburg that specialized in reproducing early American furniture; the Connecticut Craft Project designed hand-printed fabrics with a Colonial revival pattern; and the New Jersey Arts and Crafts Project backed the revival of handblown glass.[30] Furthermore, the WPA's Index of American Design, which was composed of detailed illustrations of old American objects, was envisioned by Holger Cahill, the index's director, as a "steadying influence and a source of refreshment" for the craftsperson and designer.[31]

In addition to the New Deal and large manufacturers like Danersk, the Colonial revival was backed by those with a local focus who favored old-fashioned individualism. In 1926, in a New Hampshire village, J. Randolph Coolidge, a retired Boston architect, and his wife founded Sandwich Home Industries. Mrs. Coolidge, especially, encouraged the making of hooked and braided rugs and the revival of spinning, weaving, and knitting. A hooked rug by Julia Moulton represented the oldest house in the community. Later, the masculine crafts of ironworking and furnituremaking produced items that were added to the stock at the organization's colonial-style shop, in Sandwich.[32]

Other New England craftspersons worked individually or in small groups. Prominent was Nathan Margolis, an immigrant whose colonial reproductions were praised by Nutting as "the best work in America."[33] After Margolis's death, in 1925, his son Harold continued the Hartford shop and maintained its reputation for high-quality reproductions with handcarving, hand-dovetailing, and hand-finishing. In 1930, Aetna Life Insurance Company commissioned reproductions of furniture in New York's City Hall, associated with George Washington and John Adams, for placement in its huge Colonial revival office building. A high-backed George Washington inaugural settee was copied both for its purported links with the Founding Father and because its stepped, fluted legs suggested an attribution to Duncan Phyfe.[34]

Arthur J. Stone and George Christian Gebelein, rival silversmiths in Massachusetts, were both associated with the turn-of-the-century Arts and Crafts movement through the Boston Society of Arts and Crafts. Stone, English-trained and Ruskin-influenced, made handwrought silver that was rooted not only in English

Val-Kill Shop. *Table.* c. 1927–37. Maple, 28½ x 19 x 14½". Collection Franklin D. Roosevelt Library, Hyde Park, New York

but also in American colonial precedent; a 1927 sugar bowl with an inverted pear shape, handwrought in Stone's shop by Herman W. Glendenning, closely resembles a mideighteenth-century Boston sugar bowl. The arms engraved on the bowl were those used by George Dudley Seymour, a notable Connecticut antiquarian and Stone's longtime patron. A tankard made in 1932 by Herbert Taylor in Stone's shop, and inscribed in memory of a Yale Revolutionary War hero, was given to the university by Seymour. In 1936, Edward Billings, of Stone's shop, adapted a 1745 bowl, made in Connecticut by Cornelius Kierstede, for a bowl to be presented to the chairman of the Connecticut Tercentenary Commission (tercentenary silver fifty-cent pieces were inset in two side panels).[35]

George Christian Gebelein, who was born in Germany, trained in Boston in the 1890s under men who used modern techniques as well as traditional ones that had been passed down from Revere and his contemporaries, or so Gebelein liked to think. Cultivating a reputation as Revere's successor, Gebelein procured old tools from the Revere family and often employed early American designs. For a 1929 coffee and tea service, he borrowed from the fluted urn body, flame finial, and engraved details of a Paul Revere sugar bowl. Often, the borrowings were at the client's request: For Francis Garvan, Gebelein made twenty replicas of the 1752 inkstand by Philip Syng, Jr., used by the signers of the Declaration of Independence and the Constitution. Gebelein disavowed most machine tools and never had more than six or seven assistants.[36] The image of the independent craftsman working with hand tools was so attractive to the modern American consumer that a large manufacturer like Gorham advertised its ware with photographs of elderly craftsmen painstakingly engraving or otherwise finishing silver.[37]

Lester Howard Vaughan was another metalsmith associated with the Boston Society of Arts and Crafts whose work was compared to Revere's. Although trained as a silversmith, Vaughan became a pewterer about 1915, and as such he competed with Reed and Barton, the company that, in 1929, claimed to be "the only survivor of early American pewter craft," retaining "absolute fidelity" to its centurylong tradition of pewtermaking. The pewter pitcher revived by Vaughan "epitomized the Colonial revival." A similar pitcher rests on a shelf of Nutting's scrolled-pewter cupboard illustrated in his *General Catalog.* Vaughan's cubic, two-drawer inkstand is of a type made in Ireland in the late eighteenth century but also included among Colonial Williamsburg's reproductions in 1937.[38]

The vogue for handwrought silver was matched by that for handwrought iron, although Samuel Yellin, the best-known artist working in iron during the period, was born and trained in Europe and inspired, primarily, by European sources. The court of his large shop in Philadelphia was enriched with French

Gothic-style gates, and his great commissions included designs suited to Gothic buildings at Yale and the palazzo-style Federal Reserve Bank in New York City. Still, Yellin's considerable collection of old ironwork included American examples, and his c. 1928 andirons for a country house near Philadelphia represent a variation and expansion upon an early American design.[39]

Between 1916 and 1921, Edward Guy reproduced colonial ironwork (a two-branched chandelier, for example) for Wallace Nutting at a forge established behind the Nutting-owned Iron Works house, in Saugus, Massachusetts, home of "the first successful iron master in America." Nutting thought Guy's ancestry—five generations of forgemen "trained in . . . Lancashire . . . famous for its cunning and beautiful wrought ironwork"—helped assure the quality of Guy's craftsmanship. (In 1922, however, Guy accused Nutting of publishing his reproductions as original colonial ironwork.)[40]

In 1919, *Touchstone,* a successor to Stickley's *Craftsman,* announced that the fashion for wrought iron, as made by colonial blacksmiths, was coming back, citing, in particular, the handwrought iron lanterns and door knockers of the W. Irving Forge, located in New York City. These were made individually, joyfully—the smith's "every blow is freighted with the love he bears his task."[41] The dull uniformity of the machine-made had been avoided, although, admittedly, Walter Irving's blacksmiths not only had the general example of antique hardware in the company's "museum" but actually worked from drawings. The taste for the look of handwrought iron and silver led some manufacturers to apply obviously imitative hammer marks on finished pieces, a practice condemned as false, "arty," by honest craftsmen.[42]

Myron S. Teller, an architect in Kingston, New York, specialized in the restoration and revival of Dutch colonial houses. Seeking historical accuracy, he amassed a collection of antique hardware and found a local blacksmith to hammer out reproductions. Proud of his early Hudson Valley Dutch ancestry, Teller employed blacksmiths of similar heritage—in particular, the brothers Abram and George Van Kleeck. Their grandfather had operated a blacksmith shop in the foothills of the Catskills, which continued to provide some of Teller's hardware; publicity for Teller capitalized on photographs of the old shop, to enhance the antique aura of his product.

Teller took pleasure in restoring family homesteads for clients of Dutch colonial lineage. In 1927, he and his partner, Harry Halverson, designed a complete rebuilding of an eighteenth-century stone house for William E. Bruyn on land in rural Ulster County that had belonged to Bruyn's ancestors in the late seventeenth and early eighteenth centuries. Newly handwrought strap hinges and latches for the main house and several new service buildings were said to be modeled by Teller upon those found in the original house and its farm buildings. Although Teller's hardware followed colonial patterns, it did not imitate specifically local Dutch ones; his travels to colonial sites led him to conclude that English, Dutch, and French settlements shared hardware designs. A thumb latch by Abram Van Kleeck for a Kingston house resembles a "roll-pointed triangle" pattern in Nutting's *General Catalog.* Thus it is less surprising that Teller's shop at Philadelphia's Sesquicentennial Exposition, in 1926, was called the Paul Revere Forge.[43]

The link between ancestry and commitment to the colonial was not always predictable. Herman Hjorth, an educator in San Juan, Puerto Rico, with no known ancestral links to Anglo-colonial America, was an expert at reproducing colonial furniture in school industrial-arts shops. Such reproductions, he believed, were valuable not only for technical and aesthetic education but as a supplement to American and English history courses. Israel Sack, trained as a cabinetmaker in Lithuania, became a noted dealer in American antiques and, through

Israel Sack, a prominent dealer in antiques, also manufactured colonial tin sconces. From *Antiques* magazine

Julia Moulton. *Hooked Rug.* c. 1930. Burlap, wool, 27½ x 43½". Collection Sandwich Historical Society, Center Sandwich, New Hampshire

this experience, "captured the true spirit of the greatness of American character as reflected in our finest furniture." He also reproduced furniture hardware and manufactured colonial tin sconces. Continuity was important to Sack, who advertised that beautiful objects served to join generations.[44]

The ancestry of the craftsperson and its impact on his or her craft was of interest to Allen Eaton, author of *Immigrant Gifts to American Life* (1932), which surveyed the distinctive contributions to American craft made by various immigrant groups. Eaton observed, in the catalogue of the Worcester Art Museum's 1943 "Exhibition of Contemporary New England Handicrafts," that "the names and patterns and objects" connected to New England craftspersons of colonial ancestry differed from those of recent immigrants as well as from those of the few Native American exhibitors. Photographs of Italian lacework by Theresa Pelligrini and Norwegian embroidery by Mrs. T. Larsson were set against the old American patterns of a Broken Star quilt by Mrs. C. B. Driver and stenciled and painted tinware by William P. Dudley.[45]

Hand-hooked rugs were in great demand in the 1920s for Colonial revival houses. Mariet Nutting, the wife of Wallace, was responsible for this aspect of the Nutting enterprise. In and around Marion, Virginia, women at home hooked rugs under the direction of Laura S. Copenhaver, from Rosemont, a house appropriately more than a century old. Although the antiquity of the hooked rug as a type was in doubt, Rosemont designs included images of colonial buildings, like Washington's birthplace. Copenhaver advertised widely—in the *Daughters of the American Revolution Magazine,* for instance.[46] To the north, six hundred New England women "associates" worked in their farmhouses for Pinkham Associates, turning out handmade braided rugs, "in keeping with the craftsmanship of Sheraton and Chippendale" and the traditions of their New England grandmothers. The company (Mr. H. T. Pinkham, president) was headquartered in Portland, Maine, but had showrooms on Madison Avenue in New York City. In an attempt to avoid mechanical uniformity, Pinkham cultivated the idea that its rugs were "the embodiment of loving thought and sentiment, for into each rug the maker has put something of her own sterling character."[47] Pinkham's rival in New England was Ralph W. Burnham, of Ipswich, Massachusetts, who employed women to hook rugs in his "rug studio."[48] The hooked-rug revival, as directed by Burnham and others, was criticized as producing merely inferior copies; the WPA's Maine guidebook complained that "the sincerity of creative craftsmanship is missing."[49]

The embroidered sampler declined in the nineteenth century, as did much handcraft, but, in 1918, George Leland Hunter called for a return to the form of embroidery that "taught so many of our fair Colonial forebears to write and spell and draw." Even as he made his plea, there was a burst of historical writing on the American sampler and other needlework, particularly by descendants of colonial needle artists, as well as a flourishing revival of colonial needlework. Some samplers were not inventive: Rosemont sold a standard sampler with spaces for date or name (up to seven letters) to be worked in as the customer ordered.[50] More original were samplers worked by individual artists, sometimes inspired by ancestral memories. Mary Saltonstall Parker, of Salem, Massachusetts, "a descendant of Colonial dames," made samplers that combined "the charming naivety of spirit of the work of her ancestors" and "old-fashioned subjects with modern-day tendencies"—the railroad and World War I home front.[51] A sampler made in 1920, near the end of her life, alludes to her illness (did she actually rest in a Nuttinglike Carver armchair?) as well as to the conclusion of World War I. Edith Kermit Roosevelt, the widow of President Theodore Roosevelt, became fascinated with her family's history. In 1925, she worked a family-record sampler, illustrative of her late-husband's career.[52]

Mary Harrod Northend, welcoming the sampler revival, noted, in 1923, that "its rejuvenation . . . is not like the old samplers, dull in color and lugubrious in sentiment, but of a gladness which links it with the spirit of modern interior decoration." Similarly, Ruth Finley attributed the contemporaneous revival of the patchwork quilt, in part, to "the modernistic trend in every branch of decoration toward brilliance of color and boldness of line."[53] The popularity of the quilt revival continued into the 1930s, perhaps further stimulated during the Depression by the opportunity it provided women for socializing and solace. Many wrote to Eleanor Roosevelt asking for a scrap of cloth to be included in a quilt, often one to be sold for a charitable cause.[54]

In southern New Jersey in the 1930s, another early American craft, handblown glass, was revived, in Clayton, by the Clevenger brothers, Tom, Reno, and Allie, elderly men whose ancestors had long been linked to glassblowing. A 1934 catalogue of Clevenger glass noted the popularity of old South Jersey glass with collectors—Caspar Wistar had established the first successful glasshouse in America in 1739, in Alloway—observing that this apparently "forgotten art" was being revived by "old craftsmen who learned their trade from their forebears in the time hallowed apprentice system." The Clevengers were "again blowing glass into the same shapes and patterns that made glass history so many years ago."[55] A 1939 catalogue of Clevenger glass, sold by the Ritter-Carlton Company on New York's Fifth Avenue, emphasized the authenticity of the handblown replicas of early American glass, notably the lily-pad pitcher in colonial blue, although Gay LeCleire Taylor has pointed out that Clevenger glass was heavier than the original and available in more vibrant colors.[56]

By 1940, the revival of handblown glass had received federal support through the New Jersey Arts and Crafts Project of the Work Projects Administration. Aging South Jersey craftsmen, who, decades earlier, had learned glassblowing, but had turned to other jobs when the glass industry was mechanized, returned to the "hand methods their colonial great-grandfathers employed." Some were descendants of Wistar's workmen, and "Wistar sand"—a high-grade silica—and Wistar formulas were used. Replicas of museum pieces and modern ware were made in Vineland for tax-supported public institutions and government agencies; none, though, was sold to the general public.[57]

Traditional pottery survived long enough in isolated localities to be taken up by sophisticated writers and collectors. Jacob Medinger was declared the last of the Pennsylvania German folk potters, although purists worried that beyond making traditional redware, "artsy folks" had induced him to flirt with foreign forms of pottery, like Spanish harvest jugs. In 1932, after learning of Medinger's death and of the commercial value assigned traditional pottery by collectors, the brothers Thomas and Isaac Stahl decided to reestablish a pottery founded, in 1847, in the Powder Valley of Lehigh County, Pennsylvania, by their father. Thomas and Isaac had worked in the pottery in the late nineteenth century; because of industrial competition, though, they abandoned their craft about 1903. In the 1930s, the Stahl pottery became a well-known attraction for its traditional Pennsylvania German, red earthenware—plates decorated in sgraffito, with poems in the Pennsylvania German dialect or Bible verses in actual German. The brothers relied primarily upon traditional tools and methods, although Isaac used an electrically driven wheel. As elderly craftsmen of another era, they themselves were attractions not only in the Powder Valley but when they gave demonstrations in Pennsylvania colleges and a Philadelphia department store. As survivors of a Germanic, non-English, early American culture, they, unlike the Dutch in the Hudson Valley, retained strong elements of their language and transported elements of their craft into the twentieth century. Germanic, but not un-American, they were drawn to patriotic themes. One plate was inscribed, "Dictators, please take notice. We Americans trust in God. In politics we are divided, but in time of war we are unided [*sic*]." How inappropriate, then, that these gentle and good Americans should find themselves adopted by Nazi propagandists as examples of Pan-Germanic culture.[58]

Potteries stemming from the Arts and Crafts movement sometimes returned to colonial forms. Mildred Davis Keyser first studied potterymaking in 1938 when attending a WPA class with her teenage daughter. Then, with advice from the Stahls, she revived Pennsylvania German-inspired redware at her Brookcroft Pottery, in Plymouth Meeting, near Philadelphia. Although not of Pennsylvania German descent, her husband, C. Naaman Keyser, was, and he stirred her interest in

Thomas (left) and Isaac Stahl stood before the kiln in Pennsylvania's Powder Valley and held examples of their 1935–42 redware. Photograph by Ernest Schaeffer

the forms of his ancestors, an interest that found expression in her pottery and in several booklets on Pennsylvania German craft she wrote and/or published. She was best known for her wedding plates, given to couples at the time of their marriage and decorated with the date and names of bride and groom. In the early 1940s, she made one to mark her own wedding in 1917.[59]

In Virginia, the James Towne Colony Pottery re-created early examples discovered in excavations at Williamsburg and Jamestown. The restoration of Colonial Williamsburg, which began in 1926, gave yet another boost to Colonial revival craft. In 1937, the first of Williamsburg's re-created shops opened: the Deane Forge, operated by the Boone Forge, of Spruce Pine, North Carolina; Ayscough's Cabinet Making Shop, operated by the Kittinger Company, of Buffalo; and the Pewter Shop, at the Sign of the Golden Ball, operated by Max Rieg, a Bauhaus-trained metal craftsman. In these shops, men in costume, "skilled Artificers, working with ancient Implements, supply many of the unusual Requirements of the Restoration, while exemplifying and explaining their Crafts to Visitors." Modern machines, however, were employed for the rough processes not evident in the final product.

Like the American Wing of the Metropolitan Museum of Art, Colonial Williamsburg also encouraged large-scale manufacturing of colonial reproductions, under the guise of "a Programme for the Promotion of Crafts." By 1937, licensed manufacturers were reproducing furniture, silver, Wedgwood ware, glass, fabrics, hardware, pewter, brass, and lighting fixtures, which were sold at the Craft House, in Williamsburg, at selected stores around the country, and through a mail-order catalogue. Authenticity was valued. Kittinger, the licensed furniture manufacturer, was obliged to employ skilled craftsmen to replicate details of "wood, construction, and finish."[60]

In theory, Colonial Williamsburg's motives were educational, not pecuniary. The reproductions were part of the overall ambition of John D. Rockefeller, Jr., that the restoration of Williamsburg should teach "the patriotism, high pur-

Poole tried to convince the public that its
pewter drew from old English and American
sources, but it was modern in its use of
simple lines.

pose, and unselfish devotion of our forefathers."[61] Most of its reproductions were
made elsewhere, yet Max Rieg, beyond training apprentices and demonstrating
eighteenth-century techniques in the re-created Pewter Shop, made quantities of
pewter for sale. One piece, a simplified version of an eighteenth-century baptismal
basin—simpler because of Rieg's method of spinning and, perhaps, as an appeal
to American taste in the 1930s—could either stand alone or be set in a Kittinger-
made mahogany basin stand.[62] For a time, Rieg displayed both his reproductions
and his Modernist designs in his Williamsburg workshop. In 1924, Lewis Mumford had proposed that spare, seventeenth-century New England furnishings
might well serve as a basis for contemporary design—the "austere qualities" of
the antiques he found comparable to Modernist German design. A few Colonial
revivalists, like Poole Pewter, tried to present the spartan simplicity of their colonial designs as modern,[63] but, in general, there was a firm barrier between the two
camps. Wallace Nutting simply declared "there is no such thing" as modern furniture. Virginia Craftsmen, Inc., makers of "authentic hand made reproductions
of antiques" (including a Pennsylvania comb-back Windsor armchair), claimed
its craftsmen "work as though the Jazz Age and the modern cult of speed had
never been heard of. As far as they are concerned, it still takes several days to go
from Harrisonburg to Washington."[64]

For most Modernists, Colonial Williamsburg and the entire Colonial revival
represented a major obstacle to the triumph of their cause. Visiting members of
the French and German avant-garde were puzzled by America's rejection of Modernist furnishings; *House and Garden* reported that the Europeans "criticize us
because we wear modern clothes and decorate our homes in the primitive style of
our colonial ancestors."[65] America was not represented in Paris at the 1925 Exposition Internationale des Arts Décoratifs et Industriels Modernes because, as
Richardson Wright explained, Georgian chairs and traditional-style pottery
would have been rejected. Europe was old and tired of old styles; America was
"so young that we are the most conservative nation on the face of the globe. We
cling to what little tradition we possess."[66]

In his 1944 book *Good-bye Mr. Chippendale,* the pro-Modernist interior
designer T. H. Robsjohn-Gibbings complained of the Colonial revival's stifling of
originality, a consequence, he determined, of Americans—women, especially—
seeking genteel status through traditional American and European furniture.[67] A
poll of the American public taken in 1945 showed Modernism lagging behind the
colonial. The public had been influenced by Emily Price Post, who snobbishly
argued in 1939 that colonial furnishings were highly suitable because so many
Americans were "of Colonial ancestry." Modern design, for Post, had one great
failing: It had no "quality of ancestry."[68]

Nancy McClelland defended the rising popularity of American colonial furniture vis-à-vis European styles by citing the roles of the American Wing of the
Metropolitan Museum of Art and Colonial Williamsburg; most important,
though, was "the revival of nationalism . . . after the world war and . . . a widespread desire to build into our surroundings the qualities that we consider purely 'American.'" The demand for such pieces was being met by "furniture
craftsmen . . . producing finely finished American furniture, carefully detailed
from historic models, and largely hand-made." For Post, McClelland, and other
Colonial revivalists, modernity and noncolonial traditional styles failed to provide
the comforting sense of rootedness and stability they required in a time of rapid
change and radical turmoil—what McClelland called "this heedless and harried
day and generation."[69]

During the New Deal era, crafts were supported by a surprising variety of federal programs. Although the size, scope, and emphasis varied from state to state, the substance of the craft programs consistently reflected the ideology of the New Deal of President Franklin Delano Roosevelt. The rationale for these programs was expressed in several statements made by FDR and other administrators that addressed the richness of our handcraft traditions and the right of our citizens to pursue lives of fulfillment. Sadly, most of the work produced by these programs, which touched the lives of several hundred thousand Americans, has disappeared.

The craft programs honored the requirement of Holger Cahill, director of the Federal Art Project (FAP), that they be socially useful. Crafts were seen as a democratization of art, a program for fruitful leisure activity, as well as an antidote to the dehumanization of the machine age. Indeed, a kind of national therapy was pursued through these programs.

The Public Works of Art Project (PWAP), a predecessor of the Works Progress Administration (WPA), provided employment for artists who qualified for its programs.[1] Exhibitions showed ceramics done by and under the direction of Edris Eckhardt, of Ohio; pottery by Maria and Julian Martinez, of New Mexico; home furnishings made in Miami; and even interior decorations made for United States battleships. One of the more unusual projects of the PWAP employed Native Americans from Santa Fe and Albuquerque to paint murals and make rugs, blankets, pottery, and jewelry for Indian service buildings.[2] Several PWAP programs continued as part of the Federal Art Project of the WPA, which operated from 1935 until 1943.

Training in craft and applied arts also occurred in the Civilian Conservation Corps (CCC), National Youth Administration (NYA), Rural Arts Program of the Agricultural Extension Service, Special Skills Division of the Resettlement Administration, and a host of recreational and educational programs. Crafts were produced under the aegis of the Department of Indian Affairs, National Forest Service, and National Park Service. Many of our National Park lodges were decorated with project-made furnishings and other handcrafted materials. Guilds in some regions of the country were supported in part by federal and state funding—for example, the Southern Highland Handicraft Guild and the New Hampshire Arts and Crafts League.[3]

The several craft programs ultimately administered by the WPA came into the federal project in 1939. Cahill's directives about the functions of and criteria for crafts were clear: The crafts entailed "the production of articles which depend for their usefulness and value upon the special qualities of design and workmanship." Mentioned as crafts were textiles, fibers, woodworking, ceramics, metalwork, leatherwork, and "miscellany." "Welfare and Production" crafts were separated from those of the WPA Arts and Crafts Program by criteria of utility versus aesthetics, while, at the same time, acknowledging their melding "at one extreme . . . with the fine arts [and at] . . . the other extreme with utilitarian production."[4]

Many attempts were made to distinguish between utilitarian and nonutilitarian crafts as well as to recognize the continuum that united them. "Old and

Hands of a WPA needleworker embroidering in black and red on gray Russian homespun linen. Como Handicraft Project, St. Paul, Minnesota

New Paths in American Design, 1720–1936" was a major WPA exhibition of art, craft, and design at the Newark Museum, in New Jersey, in 1936. Holger Cahill's introduction to the catalogue emphasized the integration of painting and sculpture with craft in the uplifting of national taste.[5] Daniel S. Defenbacher, an administrator of the Community Art Centers program, believed that the utilitarian and craft arts were necessary to the development of aesthetic sensitivity and an enriched personal and community life.[6] The degree of detail attended to by administrators of the programs was indicative of the depth and sincerity of commitment, not only to program business but to its ideology as well. Both Adrian Dornbush, director of the WPA Arts and Crafts Program, and Whitney Atchley, assistant director, reported extensively on every aspect of their field trips.[7] Dornbush typified the concern of the program for the men and women of America by responding courteously and promptly to huge numbers of letters of inquiry from the public.

The making and teaching of crafts took place in schools, museums, and community art centers across the nation.[8] A directive for a community art center in Winston-Salem, North Carolina, anticipated an exhibitions program of "furniture, pottery, textile and industrial objects of artistic and historic merit owned or produced in the State."[9] The goals and the quality of art-center programs and facilities varied; however, some survived the phasing out of federal support to become renowned national or local resources—among them, the Walker Art Center, in Minneapolis, and the Roswell Museum and Art Center, in New Mexico. In 1940, the New York World's Fair Contemporary Art Building included a WPA/FAP Community Arts Center featuring demonstrations of handcrafts along with art and performances. In Francis O'Connor's words, "Despite the project's idealist fantasy of art's social efficacy . . . the ideas which inspired the WPA/FAP . . . offered a direct challenge to the technological materialism rife at the Fair and recognized the consumer's cultural needs."[10]

The Design Laboratory offered another type of educational program: studies and training in functional design. Beginning as a New York City project to remedy the inadequate teaching of design in America, its codirectors were Gilbert Rohde and Josiah P. Marvel. The Design Laboratory wanted to function like the Bauhaus, and to train future leaders in the field as well as provide employment. The ideals and guiding principles were total design, experimentation, and the cre-

Mrs. Lizzie Chambers and Mrs. Mary Collier piecing quilts under the direction of Mrs. Octa Self. Lawrenceburg Sewing Project, Nashville, Tennessee

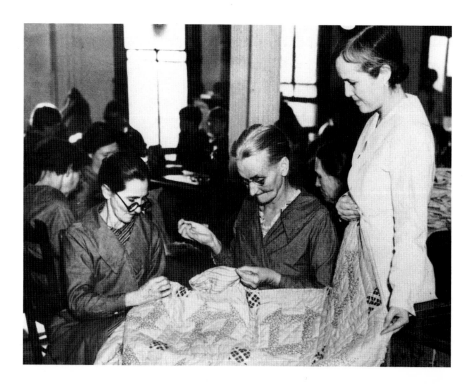

## Tours of WPA Handicraft Project Begun

GROUP tours of the Milwaukee WPA handicraft project were begun Thursday and one of the firs groups at the handicraft headquarters, 1215 N. Market st., was from the WPA household train ng center. They are watching Bart Pushee, 2145 N. 39th st., and Miss Jeanette Klatt, 1928 S. 71s t., demonstrate block printing. —Journal Staf

"Tours of WPA Handicraft Project Begun," *Milwaukee Journal*, newspaper clipping, September 6, 1940

ation of functional products. The Design Laboratory hoped to work with other agencies, such as the NYA and the CCC, in developing new talent, but a combination of debilitating WPA and labor regulations, politics, and the financial cutbacks of 1937 shortened its life. Noted textile designer Ruth Reeves and other important designers worked with the Design Laboratory. A functional-design program was also established by the Illinois Craft Project of the WPA in 1938, using students and directors of the American School of Design of Chicago, a successor to the New Bauhaus, developed by László Moholy-Nagy and other original Bauhaus teachers in Chicago. A 1940 project of this WPA program designed and produced molded-and-laminated birch furniture for the Crow Island School, in Winnetka, a modern school impressive in its educational program, architecture, and interior design. Eero Saarinen and Lawrence Perkins designed the molded chair that was produced by the Illinois Craft Project in conjunction with the Welfare Engineering Company.[11] A Division of Technical Services within the WPA worked closely with design and craft programs, offering technical and production advice. An abundance of guides and manuals for self-teaching were available to everyone.

Some areas became known for particular state or local programs; Milwaukee led the country in textile block-printing workshops. This Wisconsin program, sponsored in part by Milwaukee County and the Milwaukee State Teachers College, was developed specifically for women interested in becoming self-supporting.[12] Several examples of their work were shown at the 1939–40 World's Fair. The highest accolade for any of the programs was inclusion in the World's Fair; there, regional and local products, arts and crafts from the states, were displayed—visual paeans to the American work ethic.

New Mexico's program helped train potential artisans in furnituremaking in the traditional local Spanish Colonial style. A highly publicized representative of the New Mexico project was Patrocinio Barela, an illiterate and untrained Taos woodcarver. Originally a manual laborer on the project, his carvings were brought to the attention of administrators.[13] Barela was a prolific worker who brought deep

Patrocinio Barela and son in studio

Navajo weaver

personal and religious feeling to his work, and seems to have symbolized the potential of Everyman in a truly democratic society. The famed potters Maria and Julian Martinez, of San Ildefonso Pueblo, helped popularize and reinvigorate the ceramic traditions of Native American communities of the Southwest. They became especially well known for blackware combining highly burnished and matte surfaces. Lela and Van Gutierrez, potters of Santa Clara Pueblo, made innovations in the 1930s in polychrome pottery. These Native Americans have inspired a younger generation to carry on the Tewa pottery heritage in old and new forms.[14] The crafts project in New Mexico also attempted to revive traditions of hand-spinning, weaving, Mexican drawn-work, *colcha* embroidery, rugweaving, wrought iron, and tinwork.

Project interest in Native American culture was not limited to the Southwest. In New York State, between 1935 and 1941, Senecas of the Tonowanda Reservation were employed by the WPA/FAP to re-create the baskets, beading, blankets, and other crafts of their Iroquois heritage.[15] The FAP brought a Hopi Indian to New York City to give instruction in *kachina* dollmaking to local teachers.[16] The Indian Arts and Crafts Project of the WPA also initiated programs in Oklahoma, Montana, Washington, and other states where Native Americans were prevalent.[17]

Black Americans, for the most part, were treated as separate entities; the only "Negro" ceramics program was in Washington, D.C., at Howard University. Other art centers and galleries were established specifically in and for African American communities—that is, they were nominally segregated.[18] A touching letter from a weaver to director Adrian Dornbush, requesting information on foot-power looms, asked "if there is a place here in Birmingham that teaches colored women."[19]

Cultural handcraft traditions that were brought to America by various immigrant groups were supported in several states—for instance, Finnish and Norwegian crafts, ranging from embroidery to snowshoemaking, in Minnesota and Michigan. Sincere attempts were made to teach people the traditional arts and crafts of their parents—in some cases, already forgotten. Long-standing regional crafts, such as handweaving, basketry, and woodworking in Appalachia, received attention. Other projects attempted to reinvigorate crafts based on products of a region, such as copperworking in Arizona, or wool crafts in states where sheep were important to the local economy—Colorado, for example. Programs flourished where there was inspired local leadership. Administrators pointed to the nationally supported crafts programs in other countries, such as Sweden, as examples for the United States.

A few programs must stand for the sheer number and scope of craft activities in the various states. The ceramics program in Cleveland, Ohio, headed by Edris Eckhardt, received wide acclaim as an example of PWAP and WPA success. Eckhardt, who had been trained at the Cleveland School of Art and the Cowan Pottery, made small, finely crafted ceramic sculpture. Recruited by the PWAP, she created glazed figurines of nursery rhyme and storybook characters, as well as some larger sculptural works. The Cleveland project and Eckhardt's work were exhibited at Washington's Corcoran Gallery in 1934, among selections designated as the best of the PWAP. She continued under the WPA/FAP, working with a team that produced meticulously executed storybook figures that were extremely popular and sold well. Eckhardt's team also worked with the local WPA applied arts unit, providing sculptured ceramic plaques and decorative tiles for housing units. Her creative and administrative efforts proved so successful that her program, at one time, employed ninety people. Interested in the educational value of ceramics, Eckhardt continued to teach and to maintain her concern with the safety of art materials long after her WPA days.[20] Turning from ceramics to glass, she became known for innovative work that fused glass with gold.[21] The Akron unit of the WPA/FAP garnered attention for its printed textiles, which were placed in community rooms of housing projects—a typical project relationship of creativity, training, and social usefulness.

The unique and short-lived New Jersey Glass Project attempted to revitalize that state's hand-glassblowing industry. Southern New Jersey, with its excellent silica sands, had been a glassmaking center since pre-Revolutionary days; however, the Depression and the mechanization of the glass industry left many glass shops without work and the gaffers and their teams without employment. The WPA rented a small factory in Vineland to reemploy experienced glassmakers and train others to make traditional as well as more modern forms. Older-style glass paperweights and vessels were produced, as were the typical South Jersey amethyst and blue glass. A long and painful correspondence soon ensued between the passionately committed local WPA supervisors and the distant, seemingly heartless, central administration, in Washington. As WPA budgets began to erode, it was difficult to explain costly expenses, such as oil to keep the fires hot enough for glassmaking. The project closed, with frustrated statements from its supporters, the victim of budgets, bureaucracy, and the shifting of attention and funds by the government to the looming war.[22] New Jersey also had a WPA mosaic unit, which claimed to be unique (although impressive mosaics were certainly being made in such other states as California).[23] This unit hoped to provide employment for craftsmen and a stimulus for the large clay and tile industry of central New Jersey.[24] One of the more renowned ceramic artists of the era, Waylande Gregory, produced a major work in New Jersey, a large concrete fountain depicting the Four Horsemen of the Apocalypse—expanded by the artist to include Greed and Materialism—with extraordinary glazed ceramic figures at the rim. Gregory's work in the 1930s included decorative ceramics as well as limited editions of functional ceramics, in clays ranging from stoneware to porcelain. Gregory hoped to "pave the way for a more vital relationship between the craftsman-sculptor and industry."[25]

Timberline Lodge, on Mt. Hood, in Oregon, was a showcase for the Oregon-made crafts with which the lodge was furnished. Dedicated in 1937 by FDR, the lodge was regarded as a progressive social program to revive dormant artisanry and craft. Timberline was unusual in that it was a National Forest Service project; most lodges built under the New Deal were for the National Park Service—for instance, Paradise Lodge, on Washington State's Mt. Rainier. The interior program was directed entirely by designer Margery Hoffman Smith, the only woman at a high administrative level in the Timberline project. Fortunately, when later restoration of Timberline Lodge began, she was able to provide crucial, detailed, and accurate documentation. Timberline Lodge stands today as a grand achievement.[26]

The recordkeeping of the WPA is both overwhelming and confusing, yet reports by state supervisors rarely mention specific craftspersons. In the spirit of cooperative programs, singling out individuals was deliberately avoided. One does find references, however, to Glen Lukens, a young instructor for the WPA, who later contributed greatly to the development of ceramics in California;[27] Beatrice Wood, of Ojai, California, who, at one hundred, continues to exhibit pottery with the luster glazes for which she became famous, made pottery for the WPA;[28] and Benjamin Baldwin, the noted interior designer, who, as a young textile designer, served as a technical adviser for the WPA project in Alabama.[29]

There were clearly programs and craftspeople of high aesthetic quality, but, in general, work was traditional and conventional. Yet, there is little doubt that in paying artists and artisans to do their work, the craft programs, like the art pro-

Timberline Lodge, Mt. Hood, Oregon. Carved newel post.

Ingrid Selmer-Larsen. *The Navigator.*
1935–42. Watercolor, graphite, pen and ink
on paper, 20⅝ x 13¹¹⁄₁₆". Collection National
Gallery of Art, Washington, D.C.

grams, served as incubators for many talents during a bleak financial period.

Among the extensive records in the National Archives, two resources are particularly useful. The first is a survey by Alberta Redenbaugh, an undauntable woman who traveled the country making qualitative assessments of federally assisted craft programs.[30] Her survey was done in the hope, unfortunately not fulfilled, that the WPA Arts and Craft Program might develop production and marketing units. A complicating problem was the Fair Labor Standards Act, which invoked laws preventing the marketing of handcrafts if they were in competition with manufactured industrial products. Even though the handcraft projects were performing a useful service, as well as keeping skills alive during a terrible decade—and could not, in numbers, compete at any meaningful level—the law was vigorously upheld. It was felt that government-supported crafts should not be competing in the marketplace. Another survey, done jointly by the WPA Division of Statistics of the Women's and Professional Projects, Recreation Projects, and Education Projects for the week ending September 24, 1938, reveals that during that week, more than 28,600 persons were involved in WPA handcraft work, of whom 20,600 were women.[31] Over the course of its existence, the program employed 17,600 paid workers, and enrollees in all craft classes came to more than 612,000 people. At least three thousand ongoing handcraft projects were under the direct control of the WPA.

A project that epitomized New Deal ideology was the Index of American Design. This huge undertaking attempted to document the nation's finest indigenous, traditional, and regional arts and crafts up to and through the nineteenth century. Artists whose skills were primarily in illustration provided scrupulously detailed renderings of craft objects of traditional or historical importance. These painstaking color illustrations were considered better documentation than photographs. The idea for the Index is credited to Ruth Reeves, who became the first director.[32] C. Adolph Glassgold, at the invitation of Holger Cahill, became the director in 1937, and organized the work around several projects that were already activated in some states. To avoid duplication of particular types of objects, the decision was made to specialize. Crewelwork was to be represented by Boston examples; New York was to be a primary representative of pewter. Samples of work were sent to Washington for "searching criticism."[33] The administration dispatched concerns and information about particular and desired techniques to the several Index workshops, to encourage the best possible method of rendering an object. General instructions were spelled out at great length; size and type of paper were recommended, as well as placement of the image and materials to be used. In the service of accuracy, artists were to avoid personal expression, stylization, dramatization, or excess of any sort. It is mind-boggling to realize that twenty-two thousand plates were sent to Washington for review. The Index included depictions of crafts, such as *santos,* from New Mexico; ironwork, from Louisiana; Shaker architecture and arts and crafts; ship figureheads; coverlets; costumes; folk art—in all, an incredible variety.

Cahill and other Index administrators hoped that these visual documents would serve as useful resources for craft and industrial design in the United States, and, in fact, this was demonstrated at the 1939–40 New York World's Fair on American Designers Day, in the "American Art Today" building. Anne Frank, Ruth Reeves, Marguerita Mergentine, Gilbert Rohde, and other designers spoke and demonstrated the adaptation of historical techniques and styles to contemporary work.[34] Among the staff involved in the huge "American Art Today" exhibition and catalogue was Mildred Constantine, former Museum of Modern Art curator and writer on craft, particularly textiles.

Several attempts were made to secure funding to publish and distribute edi-

Arlene Perkins. *Appliqué Bedspread.* c. 1941. Watercolor, graphite, gouache on paperboard, 19¹³/₁₆ x 22¼". Collection National Gallery of Art, Washington, D.C.

tions of the Index to schools, libraries, and art centers throughout the country. Ultimately, complicated and nasty politics, dwindling federal financing, and the onset of World War II put an end to this hope. Wrangling continued, though, for some years over an appropriate depository for the plates. They are now in the National Gallery of Art.

The crafts projects of the New Deal, along with other federal programs, were of considerable economic importance. They provided income, self-help, and rehabilitation for the unemployed, countering the ills of the Depression as well as the more long-term effects of the industrialization and mechanization that had wiped out many artisans, workshops, and craft industries in this country. The crafts helped focus attention on traditionally marginal groups in our economy, such as Native Americans, backwoods communities, women, and the elderly. The programs exemplified and anticipated the need for fruitful leisure activities, dictated in part by changing economic and social structures, in part by a morality and work ethic that regarded idleness as a danger to social order. The programs enhanced pride in the nation's ethnic diversity and supported traditional skills. The projects and their leaders believed sincerely in the value of educating children and adults in the use of their hands. The vast number of these programs may have functioned as a benevolent and frequently paternalistic mode of social control in difficult times, yet never were so many people put in touch with creative experience. At worst, a huge number of undistinguished articles were made. At best, the programs' nonelitist art, craft, and aesthetic education provided badly needed economic assistance, work training, and pleasure, and may have even sowed the seeds of the craft renaissance of our era. Broadly speaking, this was social therapy on a far greater scale than has been previously understood.

# The WPA Federal Art Project at Timberline

by Francis V. O'Connor

The ideal of democracy inspired the various New Deal cultural programs that operated, mostly under the Works Progress Administration (WPA), between 1935 and 1942. The WPA Federal Art Project (WPA/FAP), in consequence, promoted art forms that could reach the greatest number of citizens. Thus, public forms, such as the mural and monumental sculpture, or those capable of wide dissemination, such as prints, photographs, and posters, were favored over the "closet" arts of easel painting, pedestal sculpture, and drawing. What is not often realized is that the WPA/FAP also supported the crafts—forms of creative expression open to popular usage, distribution, and appreciation—and nowhere in the country did it do so more comprehensively than at Timberline Lodge, Mt. Hood, Oregon.[1]

Mt. Hood, some sixty miles east of Portland, was so popular with skiers in the early 1920s that it needed hotel facilities to accommodate them. By mid-decade, the local U. S. Forest Service office had begun plans for a lodge at the timberline on the mountain's south slope. The early 1930s saw the private Mt. Hood Development Association established to support these federal efforts. It seized the opportunity afforded by the creation of the WPA to realize its goal, while supporting those left unemployed by the Depression. In December 1935, the WPA, the Forest Service, and the Development Association joined forces to construct the lodge. About six hundred persons, many of them skilled artisans, were employed between 1936 and 1938. Close to one million dollars was spent, with about sixty thousand dollars of WPA money going for the building's decorations and furnishings.

In style, the architecture of the lodge is the rough timber and stone construction highly favored by the East Coast rich when building their summer retreats—the famous Appalachian "camps" that rivaled in luxurious rusticity

The just-completed central lounge of the lodge, showing the variations on the blunted arch used throughout the building, the wrought-iron gates, and a variety of furniture, some with wrought-iron bases.

The guest room at the lodge, with a watercolor of maple leaves, and original furnishings, woven bedspreads, and hooked rugs.

their regal "cottages" at Newport. But, while the steep roofs of Timberline Lodge, whose two unequal wings abut a hexagonal rotunda, echo the majestic peak above, the interior reflects the spare Art Deco style of the time. Built by and for the people, it was embellished with a number of murals, oil paintings, watercolors, and mosaics. But it is the crafts—particularly the woodcarvings, metalwork, stained glass, relief carvings, textiles, and furniture designs—that set it apart.

The main entrance to the lodge provides a fine example of the skillful woodcarving to be found throughout the structure—all of which was supervised by Ray Neufer and executed by WPA/FAP artisans. The great beams that flank the door are carved down the corners to create the effect of a blunted arch—a motif repeated with variations in many parts of the lodge. Above the door is a Native American symbol of an eagle with outspread wings. The pilasters on either side have rams' heads as capitals. These introduce the visitor to a wide range of animal carvings designed by Florence M. Thomas, the most famous being the newel posts in the stairwells, each bearing the likeness of a different beast. The door itself, designed by Dean Wright and constructed of wide boards that are elegantly textured with an adze, is bound with wrought-iron strap hinges, a studded-iron border, and an elaborate knocker; in front of the pilasters are scrolled-iron foot scrapers.

The WPA's metalwork shop, under the direction of Orion Benjamin Dawson, produced an assortment of iron fixtures—from the lodge's weathervane to andirons, window grills, and a plethora of original chandelier designs. Its hand-forged ironwork is best exemplified by the two gates that separate the dining room from the main lounge. Employing Native American motifs in the borders and a row of animal heads at the handle level, the horizontal and vertical elements pass through one another at their crossings, creating a lively and intricate overall texture. The gates were designed by Dawson, Tim Turner, and Margery Hoffman (Mrs. Ferdinand) Smith.

Of all the persons responsible for the embellishment of the lodge, Smith, an interior designer and the daughter of the distinguished painter, photographer, and philanthropist Julia Hoffman, of Boston (and later, Portland), was the most influential. Appointed a director of the Oregon WPA/FAP in 1936, she was instrumental in conceiving and realizing almost all the craft projects at the lodge—most important, those related to textiles. Since the lodge was essentially a hotel, great care went into room decoration. Using a suite of botanical watercolors, created by WPA/FAP artists, to determine the color schemes of the rooms, she set about designing and supervising the weaving of drapes, bedspreads, upholstery, and hooked rugs from such unlikely materials as old Civilian Conservation Corps (CCC) uniforms and blankets, whose pedestrian khaki served as ground for a variety of colorful appliqué strategies. Ultimately, the furniture in the lodge, designed by Smith and constructed by WPA/FAP workers under the supervision of Neufer and Dawson, joined together many other crafts: woodworking and carving, an extensive variety of upholstery patterns, and, very often, wrought-iron legs and arms.

Timberline Lodge is a masterpiece of 1930s American craft design. Dedicated on September 28, 1937, by President Roosevelt, "as a monument to the skill and faithful performance of workers on the rolls of the Works Progress Administration," it still serves the people for whom it was created.

A profound shift in attitude toward Native American craft occurred in the United States between 1920 and 1945. Early in this period, the principle of assimilation, long maintained to be the natural course for America's Indian population, would meet its first tenacious resistance in the person of John Collier. The prevailing view was expressed by Ray Lyman Wilbur, Secretary of the Department of the Interior during the Hoover administration: "The red man's civilization must be replaced by the white man's. . . . The Indian must give up his role as a member of the race that holds aloof, while all other races enter into our melting pot and emerge as units of a great purpose."[1] This prescribed cleansing was forcefully countered by Collier, who, at the outset of his career as an advocate of Indian rights, cited his "*greatest* hope" at the end of a list of reforms that he proposed to achieve within twenty years: "to keep alive the Pueblo civilization with its cultural elements. . . . To make possible for these archaic communities to live on, and to modernize themselves economically . . . while yet going forward with their spiritual life."[2]

Collier had dedicated his life to social and economic reform, working in social service agencies to aid the Americanization of immigrants in New York City and California. During a five-month stay in Taos, New Mexico, in 1920–21, he became familiar with the rhythms and forms of pueblo life. This helped focus his attention on Native Americans for the next quarter century. From 1933 to 1945, he served as Commissioner of Indian Affairs.[3]

Many of the organizations that were initially formed to protect Indian land rights were also seriously concerned with the support and development of Indian crafts. Although successive administrations invited officers of these organizations to discuss the government's policies, the proposals were never put into practice. In 1927, under stress of increasing attacks, the incumbent Secretary of the Department of the Interior commissioned a report from the Institute of Government Research, directed by Lewis Meriam.[4] In addition to the recommendation of a general policy based on the recognition of positive aspects of Indian culture, the report strongly endorsed the development of Indian arts and crafts and warned against the imposition of an industrial system as a replacement for handcrafts. The report even listed the standards the government should maintain: "products that were characteristically Indian, of good materials, of good quality of execution, of good color and design, usable unless intended for display, unique or original so far as compatible with other requisites, tagged with the government's guarantee of genuineness and quality, and priced fairly."[5] Most significant for the future, the report recommended that the federal government retain for several years "at least one competent person, who with the assistance from temporary specialists could go into the matter thoroughly."[6]

It was not until five years later, under the Roosevelt administration, that the Meriam proposals and Collier's ideas were activated. A committee organized by Secretary Harold B. Ickes, in January 1934, to consider the whole problem recommended, among other proposals, that a government agency be formed for the purpose of promoting Indian arts and crafts. In late August 1935, Congress passed the act that provided for the establishment of an Indian Arts and Crafts

Wiyot. Elizabeth Hickox. *Basket Jar with Lid.* c. 1930. Redwood root and bear grass, 9¼ x 9½ x 9½". Collection Denver Art Museum, Colorado

John Collier, appointed Indian Commissioner by President Roosevelt, talks with Chief Coyote Runs and Chief Yellow Tail, of the Montana Crow tribe. This picture was taken at the Capitol, in Washington, D.C., while the Senate was deciding unanimously to recommend Collier's confirmation, April 1933.

Board in the Department of the Interior, the function of which was "to promote the economic welfare of the Indian tribes . . . through the development of Indian arts and crafts and the expansion of the market for the products of Indian art and craftsmanship."[7]

Of all the personnel decisions Collier made during his career, it is possible that none was so significant as his selection of René d'Harnoncourt, first as assistant and then, in 1937, as general manager of the Indian Arts and Crafts Board.[8] The procedures d'Harnoncourt pursued in his work with Indian arts and crafts followed the method he had developed through his transactions with Mexican Indians: to work with each tribe as a separate entity. The key to his success, he noted, "involved background research; careful consideration of the past history and present condition of each tribe; and, most important of all, close contact and cooperation with local Indian leaders and local Indian Service administrators."[9]

Although d'Harnoncourt is justly famed for the major exhibitions of Indian arts and crafts he directed—at the 1939 Golden Gate International Exposition, in San Francisco, followed by the 1941 exhibition at New York's Museum of Modern Art—the extraordinary range of his—and thus, the board's—accomplishments is revealed in a three-page list of activities covering the years 1936 to 1939. Among them are the establishment of standards of genuineness and quality for Navajo, Pueblo, and Hopi silver and turquoise projects; reviving the declining art of spinning among the Sioux Choctaw Indians of Oklahoma; developing an arts and crafts project among the Coeur d'Alene Indians at De Smet, Idaho; stopping the use of false labels; and devising marks of genuineness to distinguish all handmade Alaskan Indian and Eskimo works from imitations.[10]

The increasingly grim development of the European political situation in the 1930s introduced an unsavory xenophobic aspect into the American scene in the later years of the decade. Questions were raised in Congress as to why a foreigner—that is, d'Harnoncourt—was making public policy and was being paid with public money. Congressional antagonism to the New Deal was expressed by cutting appropriations. As the country entered the war, antagonism became increasingly vicious, with a parade of hostile testimony against the activities of the board, repeated attacks on d'Harnoncourt, and continuous reduction of funds. On January 19, 1945, Collier submitted his resignation to President Roosevelt.

# FROM ETHNOLOGY TO ART: A CHART OF CHANGE

In this consideration of the arts and crafts produced by Native Americans during the period between the two world wars, limitations of space oblige us to forgo considering the accomplishments of many tribes. The objects included in the exhibition have been selected to convey a general aesthetic context. Some are seminal works, others are representative of their class, and a few, though minor, are nonetheless of interest. All these articles were intended for display, and none abuse Indian privacy or intrude on tribal sensibilities.

Adhering to what seems to have been the primary artistic preference of the period, the majority of the objects are from the Southwest, but New England—an area omitted from the three major exhibitions of Indian art mounted during these years—is included. The material is organized by geographic region, with subcategories of individual craft media described in each region. A double standard is at work here, a middle ground reconciling both the artistic accomplishments and judgments of the period and personal preference, which is a specific of any act of curatorial selection. Thus, there is no strict reconstruction of the period's critical view of itself, which was, in truth, directed by others than Native Americans.

## THE SOUTHWEST
### Pottery

In her 1929 book on Pueblo pottery, Ruth Bunzel states, "It is important to realize at the outset the very slight extent to which modern potters utilize known resources. It is neither lack of resources nor lack of knowledge that makes modern Pueblo pottery the stereotyped product that it is."[11] Today, it is difficult to regard the rich efflorescence of southwestern pottery after World War I as "stereotyped." Actually, it is no more routine than earlier historic pottery types; early pots are simply more rare and carry the patina of time. Both Santo Domingo and Cochiti Pueblos were producing highly traditional pots—among them, bowls for ceremonial use, libation vessels, dough bowls, ollas, and storage jars, in addition to the figurines of singers, vaqueros, and mermaids long made for export.

"The art is near extinction at Santa Clara, Sia [Zia], Santa Ana, and Laguna," Bunzel continues,[12] a conclusion that would seem to contradict the earlier statement. Potterymaking was certainly not extinct at Santa Clara, not with such potters as the Tafoya family in residence. It was, actually, becoming more specialized, but, perhaps, with less good work. Zia was embarking on extended production of large, white-slipped ollas (water storage jars) decorated with painted bird and rainbow designs, which are now considered archetypes of Pueblo ceramic art. At least one major potter was left at Zuni—Tsayuitsa—who produced a masterpiece, a highly traditional storage jar with featherlight designs that attain a streamlined character all their own.

In a more recent book, we find, "After 1880, convenient and safe transportation led to the tourist trade of the modern era, with its generally decadent influence on the serviceability of the pottery."[13] It is true that a great deal of poor-grade pottery was made during this period; pottery walls may have become thinner but the shapes could be, correspondingly, more graceful. At its best, Pueblo pottery had become so beautiful, it cried out not to be used.

Displacement of function was counterbalanced by artistic diversity, as in the work of Acoma ceramist Mary Histia, who made pots with a red clay body that Bunzel notes was "practically extinct,"[14] incorporating familiar designs. She also made pots in the traditional form for presentation pieces, one of which carries the

Zia. Isabel Medina. *Water Jar.* c. 1938. Clay, paint. Collection Museum of Indian Arts and Culture/Laboratory of Anthropology, Museum of New Mexico, Santa Fe

blue eagle, the motto "We Do Our Part," and the acronym NRA, in celebration of the National Recovery Act passed in 1933.[15] While the phoenixlike eagle copies a political device, the designs that frame it are purely Native American.

Some Acoma pottery that reflects knowledge of ancient Anasazi Tularosa ware could almost be mistaken for the originals. A large, micaceous buff clay jar by Rose Cata, of San Juan Pueblo, incorporates the incised hatch designs found on ancient Potsowi incised ware, but the form is modern. There was an explicit desire at San Juan Pueblo in the early 1930s to combine the old and the new, which produced a highly creative, easily identifiable contemporary ware that is in turn strongly associated with the past.

An inventive black pottery was shared equally by San Ildefonso and nearby Santa Clara Pueblos after World War I. A fascinating convergence of the primitive and the modern—oversize plates, concave-shouldered jars, wide-bodied storage vessels, and double-spouted wedding jars—it was combined, when appropriate, with matte-black designs of an increasingly Art Deco strain (San Ildefonso) or streamlined indented designs, notably a bear paw, incised flutings, and, toward the end of our period, sgraffito ware (Santa Clara).

In 1918–19, San Ildefonso potter Maria Martinez and her husband, Julian, first fired a new type of black-on-black pottery jar, with an *Avanyu* (water serpent) circling the midbody and shoulders of each piece—an undulating, sinewy design that became a sine qua non for their famed pottery as well as a symbol of the pueblo. One of the most extraordinarily personalized uses of this new decorative technique appears on a blackware plate: an image of Maria and her husband taken from a portrait that had been painted by a friend, Santa Fe artist Henry C. Balink. Julian carved the image into clayslip in the flattest possible relief and inscribed their names. This type of personalization could only have occurred in Pueblo art when a special reciprocity was established between Anglo and Indian sensibilities. Santa Clara blackware of the late 1920s is celebrated for the evenness of firing and high level of polishing that are evident in the monumental olla by Margaret Tafoya.[16]

Nothing expresses more succinctly an awareness of vernacular Art Nouveau and early Art Deco tall ceramic vases—a staple in dry-goods stores across the country at this time—than the cylindrical Hopi version, a hand-raised ceramic vase in traditional buff-colored clay and with striking, symbolically balanced designs. Better examples, such as this one, document the natural affinity that existed between Indian ethos and the emergent manifestations of *style moderne*, encouraging a dialogue that flavored much Indian art of the 1920s and 1930s.

Were it not for its more insistent stylization, the intricate, panel-separated feather design on a Santo Domingo jar, c. 1920, could be dated to the nineteenth century, though its flaring shoulders, delicate scale, and everted rim show a latent infatuation with current market niceties. Much Zia Pueblo work has a sense of formal dignity and gravity that harks back to the past. The rainbow and bird designs of Zia and Acoma storage jars and ollas may well derive from nineteenth-century Hispanic *colcha* embroidery and Pennsylvania Dutch slipware and pottery.[17]

During the decades between the wars, the potters were open to new forces of intellect and choice, and many of those options came from outside—part of a continuing dialogue between the indigenous and the dominant cultures that reached a peak in this time of increased contact and communication.

Textiles

The dynamic of the interchange is better documented in Navajo weaving, for the practitioners of this craft were more open in their relationship with traders than

the secretive and close-knit Pueblo communities. Since the turn of the century, trading posts had exercised supervision over the design and color of Navajo rugs. These rugs had displaced the personal wearing blanket of the nineteenth century, an indication of the influence a changing market had upon the weaver. For many years, the quality of Navajo weaving declined through this commercialism, especially with the myriad loosely woven and indifferently figured, so-called pound blankets (rugs) produced for the cheaper market. In the 1930s, a small number of traders sensitive to these deficiencies, and dedicated to improving the quality of woven work, entered this milieu. One of the most prominent figures was Sallie Lippincott, who, with her husband, Bill, bought the Wide Ruins Trading Post on the Navajo Reservation in 1938.

"When my husband and I bought the post, the Navajos in that area were making very poor rugs, the kind that were sold from knocked together stands along Highway 66," Sallie Lippincott recalls. "The wool was not well cleaned or well spun. The bordered designs were the kind that originated in Oriental rugs or were crossed arrows and swastikas, and the colors were red, black, and white. Admittedly, these were the designs thought of as 'Indian.' But we had come to the reservation to work in the National Park Service at Canyon de Chelly and . . . we had seen the really beautiful rugs that the weavers there produced and were sold at Cozy's [H. L. McSparron] post. We hoped to guide the Wide Ruins weavers into the production of beautiful rugs too. We knew they were capable of such work."[18]

Incoming rugs were judged by their weight—with more wool meaning higher quality; then, spread out in the back room, their good (and occasional) bad points were discussed. The Wide Ruins Navajos (men as well as women) experimented with every possible source of dyes, "even dipping their wool into flooding arroyos when the waters ran red or brown from violent summer storms."[19] Plants again became the principal sources for colors, some of the old people remembering their ancestors' recipes. Yarns had to be well cleaned and carded. The black or brown borders that had become standard in Navajo rugs were no longer acceptable; instead, horizontally striped rugs from Chinle were hung up as models, to recall the old, striped wearing blankets.

A typical Wide Ruins rug marks an early stage in the development of the type woven for the trading posts at Chinle, Crystal, and Pine Springs (which was taken over by the Lippincotts in 1945). It has the stripes but not the refined vegetal colors, and because it features three cow heads across the middle, it can be classified as a pictorial rug. Later rugs were filled with realistically rendered scenes of Navajo life.[20]

The term *revival* has been used freely in conjunction with twentieth-century weavings and pots that recall older prototypes, but this does not adequately convey the naturalness with which discontinued techniques and designs are reclaimed. What seems arbitrary to whites is, to Native Americans, simply part of the continuous process of learning, relearning, and affirming the endless cycle of tradition. The 1945 interpretation of an "eye-dazzler" transitional blanket/rug of the 1880s and 1890s is not a copy in the ordinary sense. With its tight outlining and somber coloration, it is, rather, an elegiac meditation on the joyous colors and wildly syncopated repeat patterns of the prototype. It was probably made by someone familiar with the weavings of her mother and grandmother.

Another type of weaving, the *Yei* (Navajo religious figures) rug, derives from traditional, sacred sandpainting motifs. A typical example has a central panel, with Yei figures and symbols surrounded on three sides by a rainbow-figure border. When Yei textiles first appeared around 1900, they broke a taboo against

Navajo. *Yeibeichai Rug* (Lukachai type). c. 1930. Wool, 50 x 88". Collection School of American Research, Santa Fe, New Mexico. Gift of Mr. and Mrs. Gustave Baumann

public display of sacred imagery; tribal conservatives even feared that making such weavings could cause blindness. By the early 1920s, as tourists' curiosity about Navajo beliefs assured a ready market; these attractive textiles became repetitive in response to demand.

The climax of ceremonial Navajo weavings made in this period was a monumental series of outsize tapestries intended for formal display. Profound religious statements, they depict the sandpaintings that accompanied Navajo curing chants, during which the patient was placed upon the painting, which, afterward, was ritually destroyed. The series was executed to preserve a record of the Navajo religion under the authority of Hosteen Klah, a revered medicine man and weaver who collaborated with Bostonian Mary Cabot Wheelwright in founding the Museum of Navajo Ceremonial Art in Santa Fe in 1937 (now the Wheelwright Museum of the American Indian).[21] A very large Klah-supervised tapestry of a Nightway (*Hastseyalti*) Chant is a tour de force, probably woven in part by Klah (the areas about the legs) and in the main probably by his niece Mrs. Jim (Irene) Manuelito. The sacred order of the figures, as they appear during the process of making the sandpainting, could not be replicated in the weavings, but the image was preserved for all time.

## Basketry

California's Mono Lake Paiute made-for-sale basketry is of exceptional quality. Its basketmakers were famous and collecting was vigorous.[22] Credit for this burgeoning of basketmaking must go to the annual Yosemite Park Indian Field Days, held between 1916 and 1929, with their popular juried basket competitions. Carrie Bethel worked on her masterpiece for four years. Thirty-two inches in diameter, it is the second largest basket known to have been woven by a Native American; the colossal basket made by Lucy Telles is only an inch or two larger. The rhythmic play of disconnected motifs across the globular surface of Bethel's creation is as striking as the weaver's masterful control. Whereas the Telles basket remained in the possession of its maker and was widely exhibited, Bethel's basket was purchased immediately upon completion and disappeared from view, "never receiving the publicity or fame that Lucy Telles' giant achieved."[23]

One California-desert Chimuhuevi basket, in the traditional shape, has the sparsely placed decorative geometric accents that give this tribe's work an orientalizing appearance. A Western Apache basketry tray is large, round, and shallow, with geometric figures alternating with animals and checkered bands. Between 1880 and 1920, Apache tray baskets and ollas were *the* representative baskets collected in the Southwest. Subsequently, the quality was not maintained and decline slowly set in. The stitching became looser and wider-spaced than what is usually found in the prime efforts of the Apache tribe.

## Silverwork

Lavish use of turquoise became a hallmark of Navajo and Zuni silverwork, originally learned shortly after the midnineteenth century from Mexican silversmiths and southern Plains makers of German (nickel) silver bridles and belts. The period is characterized by greater aesthetic variety and, as more turquoise mines were opened, very elaborate settings. A Navajo girl's outfit from about 1930 conveys a vivid impression of the splendor displayed at public and religious events—a Squaw dance, a *Yeibeichai* dance, or the Gallup ceremonial festival. The Fred Harvey Company's mass-produced bracelets for the tourist trade were often embellished with generic stamped cutout thunderbirds. As tourism developed, more and more Navajo, Zuni, and Pueblo silversmiths sold work directly to traders or worked for them. Fine concha belts and other wearable objects were also made, which, after being used by native people, were often sold through the pawn system to Anglos.[24]

Zuni. *Silver Bracelet with 24 Turquoises.* Silver, turquoise, 3 x 1¼". Collection National Museum of the American Indian, Smithsonian Institution, New York

## NORTHWEST COAST

The decline of Northwest Coast traditional arts during the Depression presents perhaps the most discouraging development in the history of Native American art. Carved totem poles, house posts, and masks, potlatch ceremonial gifts, and Chilkat blankets had offered much to world culture from precontact times to the beginning of this century.

Among the Makah in the extreme northwest of Washington State, such leaders as Charley Swan (dancer and culturalist), Young Doctor (spiritual leader and carver), and Frank Smith (carver) prevented fading traditions from dying out. It was chiefly because of Makah and Quilleute basketmakers that a viable market for products was maintained. Among the Tlingit of the Alaskan panhandle and the southern coast of Washington State, however, a heavy (though not terminal) toll

The totem pole carved by John Wallace and his son Fred at the 1939 Golden Gate International Exposition, San Francisco, that was installed outside the Museum of Modern Art, New York, for the exhibition "Indian Art of the United States," January 22–April 27, 1941. (Courtesy the Museum of Modern Art, New York)

was exacted by missionization, along with other disruptive influences on native ceremonial life, and the displacement of the old clan system by secular European American materialism. Much was lost and, until recently, little replaced. Nevertheless, the northern Tlingit town of Angoon remained a ceremonial center and Sitka an educational one, and some Chilkat blankets were being made, notably by Jennie Thlunaut, as recently as the 1930s and 1940s.[25]

In 1946, when art critic and curator Katherine Kuh was sent to Alaska by the Bureau of Indian Affairs to prepare a report on totemic art, she was appalled to find that "the U.S. Forest Service, without benefit of archeological or anthropological direction, [had] instituted a program in which the local Civilian Conservation Corps undertook to rehabilitate—but, alas, more often to dismember and copy" woodcarvings in numerous areas.[26] In her report, she urged that these carvings receive immediate attention. Twenty years later, she revisited the area and found her "worst fears justified." Scarcely any of the works remained, having been either burned or left to rot. "Nor," she wrote after this second journey, "shall I soon forget the public servant who assured me that 'nothing had been thrown away but the originals.'"[27]

A major woodcarver, John Wallace, remained in the northern Haida enclave of Prince of Wales Island at the southern tip of Alaska. With the assistance of his son Fred, in approximately four months Wallace carved a thirty-foot-high totem pole at the 1939 Golden Gate International Exposition, in San Francisco. Although commissioned by the Department of the Interior, it was—except for a more elaborate coloration than the customary Haida red and black accenting—a totally traditional and remarkable feat of carving. By technical understanding of animal-crest formal relationships, and by the expression of this family legend to

Jennie Thlunaut with a Chilkat blanket she completed about 1930

which the carver had rights, the pole was in effect a paean to the origins of Haida carving art: Raven, depicted at the top, dives to the bottom of the sea, where, with the aid of various supernatural helpers, he finds totem poles at the home of Killer Whale and brings one of them back to the Haida people. Third in a line of totem pole carvers, John Wallace has been hailed as "a complete master of all the techniques and traditions of the art."[28]

# PLAINS

Hollywood movies established a stereotype of the Plains Indian: There was the good Indian, of the Tonto variety, but also many bad ones who rejected the white man's road. Southwestern Indians could remain Indian, but Plains Indians were removed from any sense of the present. In addition to the appalling poverty and degrading living conditions of reservation life for the Plains tribes, there was the problem of maintaining values in the face of pressures of assimilation. The traditional balance of life had shifted from an all-encompassing ceremonial calendar to a schedule geared to farming and ranching. At best, the Sun Dance, the central ceremony of Plains reaffirmation and renewal, was no longer staged continuously but was broken up into sections so that participants could check on their cattle and crops. At worst, it was abbreviated, or simply not held at all.

## Apparel

Despite the cultural disruptions, the arts of the Plains Indians continued to manifest themselves, often with remarkable color in beadwork and quilting. Craftspersons found an outlet for the finery associated with the powwow, a tribal get-together of great and varied social complexity, often with quasi-spiritual as well as social overtones. Increasing intertribal social contact, because of cars and trucks, encouraged the spread of design motifs and dress codes. One of these was the jingle dress, originated by the Ojibwa in either Minnesota or Canada in the 1930s, with its rows of little metal cone "jingles" that sounded like sleigh bells when the wearer danced. By using readily available tin cans, the owner was spared the expense of beadwork or home-tanned hides, which accounts for the spread of this dress style to the eastern Plains and beyond. Simpler examples made of cheap, stained muslin could still make a distinctive impression at a powwow or tribal celebration.

After 1915, the output of the Crow tribe of Montana weakened, since its classic white-bordered, beaded designs on shirts, martingales, tobacco bags, and moccasins merged with other influences—among them, Oriental rugs—much as Acoma potters may have absorbed Pennsylvania Dutch motifs. The elegance associated with traditional Crow beadwork was undiminished, however, and beaded objects, such as the purse in this exhibition, demonstrate a scintillating union of traditional Crow aesthetics and modern streamlining.

A Blackfeet beaded robe of the 1940s might be mistaken for a nineteenth-century example in the stepped-diamond patterns of its beaded roundels, called a mountain design. The width of the beaded strip, however, confers a twentieth-century sense of drama on the intended wearer.

Traditionally, Plains dolls were not intended as portraits. In 1941, Assiniboin dollmaker Juanita Tucker changed this situation with a pair of dolls that represented Two Guns White Calf and his wife, a son and daughter-in-law of the last Montana Blackfeet chief.[29] The apparel on the figures is recognizably Assiniboin, but Blackfeet in style. Tucker was strict in her interpretation; her dolls were neither playthings nor souvenirs. Since they were probably made after Two Guns White Calf died, and possibly from a photograph, they were an intentional memorial.

From the central Plains, two powwow-related, brightly dyed quill Sioux breast ornaments continue the pursuit of dramatic emphasis. The man's necklace, from about 1920, with its V-shaped, quill-wrapped rawhide strips and trade mirrors, originated among the Omaha for use in a military dance, which became the

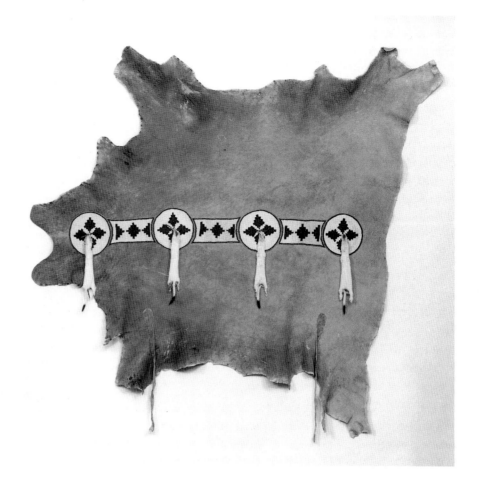

social Grass Dance as it moved westward; the woman's piece, with chevron and diamond devices, dates from about a decade later, when decorative features were more discreetly worked into the color-field.

NEAR AND EAST OF THE MISSISSIPPI
Ribbonwork

Silk ribbons, no longer fashionable in post-Revolutionary France, were unloaded on Prairie and Great Lakes Americans through traders in New France. The tradition of using patterned ribbon appliqué as decorative accents and borders on women's clothing traveled southward, and, shortly after 1850, ribbonwork was basic to the costume of the Mesquakie of Tama Settlement, Iowa. A skirt made by Susie Poweshiek in about 1930 recalls the ribbon appliqué tradition of folded overlaid patterning, remarkably unchanged a century later.

By 1900, ribbonwork had reached the northeastern Oklahoma prairies, where the Osage turned the process to remarkable use as borders embellishing large wearing blankets for women. Despite a tendency toward display during the 1920s and early 1930s (the oil-rich days of Osage oil head rights), many Osage blankets were masterpieces of the medium, and a rich but delicately sumptuous harmony was often lavished upon them, with fastidious spacing of rows of discreet geometric motifs punctuating the ribbon border.

Birchbark and Quillwork

Ottowa. Anna Odeimin. *Round Box with Floral Cover*. 1925. Birchbark, porcupine quills, 2 x 5¾ x 5¾". Collection Little Traverse Historical Society, Petoskey, Michigan

In 1938, a particularly successful Works Progress Administration (WPA) workshop program was initiated in Michigan among the Ottawa to ameliorate both the decline of interest in quillwork and the dire economic situation. By making involvement in arts and crafts a profitable economic activity, the program succeeded in generating work in which traditional styles and designs were created with excellent construction techniques, as the documented WPA quillwork boxes produced between 1940 and 1941 demonstrate.

## Beadwork

About 1850, the Great Lakes tribes—Ojibwa, Winnebago, Menominee, and Potawatomi—developed a beaded bandolier bag worn on stately occasions by tribal leaders. Originally adapted from the military shot pouch, it expanded in size until it became a decorative symbol of status and power. After 1920, production declined; old bags were still used, but new ones were rarely made. During the early 1930s, however, a group of bandolier bags emerged from the Lake Lena Ojibwa, an enclave of the Mille Lacs Band. One member of the tribe, Negannegesheg, an expert canoemaker and respected elder, was instrumental in leading an annual Lake Lena Ojibwa celebration. According to tradition, his sister, Mrs. John Benjamin, supervised the making of the customary floral, beaded, bandolier bag, one for each of the several years the celebration was held. Exactly how many of these bags were made, and their current whereabouts, except for this example, is not known.

A purely commercial ethos is expressed by an Ojibwa fully beaded vest, which probably served as a promotional item outside the Native American world. As such, this tour de force echoes the federally sponsored writers guides to the states published during these years. Here, folk art and Indian beadwork technology meet head-on. Too well executed to be a casual product, it is probably the work of one of the more accomplished beadworkers at Mille Lacs or Leech Lake; however, it is so singular in its subversion of the traditional use of beadwork as to defy attribution.

## THE EASTERN RIM: NORTH AND SOUTH

The most impressive WPA project devoted to the art of a single tribe—in this case, the Seneca Iroquois—was undertaken by the Rochester Museum & Science Center between 1935 and 1941. Under the guidance of museum director Arthur C. Parker, himself part Seneca, the Indian Art Project employed about one hundred Iroquois from both the Cattaraugus and Tonawanda Seneca reservations. They produced more than six thousand works—among them, a rich variety of beaded clothing, jeweled silver brooches, antler combs based on archaeological examples of the seventeenth century, masks, wooden utensils and dishes, clubs, paddles, and woven splint baskets. This project provided an opportunity to create types of objects rarely made in the late 1930s, such as burl bowls and ladles.

## Woodcarving

The first specialist appointed by John Collier to serve as a field representative for the Indian Arts and Crafts Board was Gladys Tantaquidgeon, a Connecticut Mohegan and a tenth-generation descendant of Chief Uncas, leader of the Mohegans. Today, in her midnineties, she manages the family museum on Mohegan Hill, near Uncasville, Connecticut. With her father, John Tantaquidgeon (Chief Matahga), and her brother Harold, they kept southern New England Indian culture alive during the interwar period, particularly the arts of splint basketmaking and woodcarving.[30]

For the first time, Tantaquidgeon objects have been allowed to leave the family museum: John Tantaquidgeon's *Wolf Stick* (Mohegan means "wolf"); Harold

A typical Osage blanket

A. Tantaquidgeon's *Crooked Knife*, with his personal sign, a dotted *X,* and his nickname, "Hat," carved into the handle; and a bowl that Harold carved with the knife. Once ubiquitous among Woodland Indians, crooked knives were used to pare splints for basketmaking and carving bowls and utensils, and for whittling canoe parts. Personal items were embellished on their handles with an endless repertoire of flora and fauna and other forms, even figureheads. They convey an intimacy in keeping with New England reticence, as does the wolf stick, which seems elegiac compared with the bold assertiveness of Great Lakes or Plains carving of similar import.

## Basketry

The most eminent New England artist of the turn of the century was Tomah Joseph, a brilliant Passamaquoddy leader whose talents as a birchbark engraver remain unsurpassed. His son, Sabattis Tomah, carried on the tradition, both in carved and birchbark items, such as a wastebasket with freely rendered anecdotal designs.

Eastern Woodland Indian art of this period is distinguished by the brown ash splint baskets made by all the maritime tribes, the Iroquois, and the Great Lakes people. Included in this exhibition is a Penobscot splint "shopper" basket with Hong Kong twine, indicative of the 1930s, together with the block on which it was made. These blocks were not merely utilitarian, they were precious heirlooms, and the old ones are still treasured in maritime Indian families.

Although there is contention as to whether splint baskets of early Swedish and other Scandinavian settlers influenced the making of Woodland Indian baskets, the river-cane basket tradition of the Southeast, practiced by the Cherokee, Choctaw, and Koasati, has a pre-Columbian origin. A woven river-cane Cherokee storage basket indicates how well this ancient art survived during the interwar period.

The period we have traversed constitutes a crossroads between the Native American past and the beginnings of the present. As outdated as its concerns may now appear, there are elements that foreshadow today's preoccupations: the ever-increasing number of Native American art exhibitions; the introduction of social reforms for minorities as an open, positive, and visible national responsibility; identification of the ongoing tensions among assimilation, acculturation, and Indianness. There was often a "father-knows-best" attitude toward the greater Native American community, which rankles in retrospect. Yet, it was John Collier who helped start the Native American, however haltingly, on the long and painful road to self-determination. In the eyes of enthusiasts, particularly in the Southwest, Native Americans had been transformed from anthropological specimens into artists.

The Native American peoples have a long tradition of making beautiful things in craft media. Although it is difficult to generalize about the aesthetic production of such a diverse group of cultures, most indigenous nations developed richly symbolic visual images that were used on clothing, pottery, wooden bowls, boxes, and spoons, on leather pouches and parfleches, on various kinds of house walls, and on a wide range of ceremonial objects. A few designs functioned only as decoration; many, though, including abstract designs, evoked complex levels of meaning, keeping tribal members mindful of important stories or histories and helping them stay in harmony with the beings in the circle of things that supports life. The making, using, and trading of beautiful objects has kept alive the cultures from which they come.

Before the Europeans arrived, Native Americans did not distinguish between craft and fine art. Over time, the European and, then, Euro-American invasions dispossessed indigenous peoples of the land and resources that allowed them to maintain their traditional economies.[1] Forced to live on reservations and to attend schools run by their conquerors, they learned to make framed paintings, something that Europeans defined as art, for the first time. Native students were urged to paint secularized pictures of indigenous life, especially of ceremonies, and even of spiritual beings. For instance, at the Santa Fe Indian School, Dorothy Dunn, the director, encouraged young Navajo students to paint pictures of *yeis* and students from the pueblos to paint pictures of *kachinas*, the respective tribes' religious figures.

Some schools did teach crafts—weaving, pottery, basketry, beadwork, and silversmithing—that were familiar to people of European ancestry. In much the same way that a market was created for Native paintings, the schools, the Bureau of Indian Affairs, and the various associations that tried to support Indians worked to develop a market for craft objects. The Indian Arts and Crafts Board was founded in 1936, the marketing of native crafts one of its main functions. But, usually, it was only among themselves that native people, in spite of the disapproval of missionaries and government agents, refined the necessary skills to make ceremonial objects, to practice traditional healing, or to practice the gift-giving required to commemorate such traditional activities as name-giving or remembering and caring for the dead.

Even during the 1930s, when the Bureau of Indian Affairs was under the direction of John Collier and Willard Walcott Beatty, there were still teachers from the older generation who believed native culture was primitive, and they worked to subvert the official policies that supported the teaching of even secularized, watered-down versions of indigenous arts and culture in the schools. Many who wished to preserve native culture had highly subjective views of what it was, and wanted to define for indigenous people what was valuable and worth preserving. Some were only interested in the things they considered marketable; others were disenchanted with the industrial culture of the United States and sought to lock native culture in an ethnographic present that was essentially nonindustrial and static. Such people, in describing Native Americans as being unfettered by the evils of civilization and existing in a more natural state, denied them their contemporary and historical reality.

Native Americans comprise more than three hundred nations in geographically diverse regions. Their experiences with outside influences are often so profoundly different that to discuss issues of survival, revival, tradition, and innovation for so many different nations is nearly impossible. On the East Coast, for example, the first trade between Native and Euro-Americans began in the early 1600s, and, by the late 1700s, the objects made for use inside the Iroquois community were different from the ones being made for trading with Euro-Americans. Over time, the materials and techniques used for each affected the other. This process of developing a separate style for trade outside the community, letting it evolve, and then incorporating it within the objects used in the native community was not written about by outsiders. As a result, most Americans have a limited view of what has been made, since they do not attend activities in the longhouse—the communal site of Iroquois ceremonies and political meetings.

By contrast, on the West Coast, the area that was to become the states of Washington and Oregon was not colonized until the early 1880s. In 1855, the United States made treaties, and the reservation period began. The treaties controlled trade between native people in the United States and the British colony of Canada, redirecting markets for both raw materials and finished goods. Soon after, natives of the Olympic Peninsula began to market baskets in Seattle. By 1920, they had developed a basketry style characterized by pictorial patterns of animals and people, done with natural and dyed bear grass, usually on cedarbark warps. This trade supplemented their traditional hunting and fishing economy, as did agricultural labor. There were also woodcarvers like Joseph Hillaire, of Lummi, who carved totem poles for his people, for the Suquamish, and for a Euro-American oil company in Bellingham. The Lummi did not have a tradition of carving large poles, although they did carve canoes and other objects; Hillaire borrowed the concept from work being done in British Columbia. The poles were highly individualistic in style and untraditional in their use of commercial paint, but, like the smaller poles carved in the area, they told traditional stories and histories. In the 1930s, Hillaire created a latter-day Lummi style of carving that is still honored by the Lummi for the way it kept indigenous culture and tradition visible in the community.

Perhaps half of the things most Americans think of today as traditional southwestern Indian crafts are hybrid forms that developed from a complex series of interactions with traders, Mexican owners of haciendas, mestizo farmers and vaqueros, and Euro-Americans. By the 1920s, some artists maintained such traditional art forms as pottery, but others worked in forms learned by their forebears while they were captives on haciendas, prior to the United States defeat of Mexico in 1845. Despite their lack of freedom, they benefited from the development of a long succession of blanket styles, rugs, and jewelry, which they used or traded with other indigenous people as well as nonnatives.

On the Plains in the 1920s and 1930s, there were contemporaries of people like the Lakota holy man Black Elk, who, having grown up before the reservations were established, had experienced the difficulties associated with the wars that lost them their territory. Although they were familiar with the imagery and skills required to make traditional objects, they lost access to many of the materials they had used to make these beautiful things. Materials like buffalo hide, pigment from areas to which people were unable to travel, and dyes from plants that western-style farming was making rare or extinct were no longer easily obtained. Cowhide replaced other types of leather, and the use of trade materials, such as beads and cloth, in the making of Plains art increased. A number of new styles developed to accommodate these materials, styles that evolved throughout the era of craft revivals.

In Alaska, the first settlers were Russians, who established missions and trading relationships. After the United States purchased the right to colonize the territory, contact became well established in southeastern Alaska. Missionaries burned totem poles, masks, and houses to destroy the imagery they associated with traditional religion. Other artifacts were shipped to distant museums or used to decorate city plazas. The land and resources were exploited by settlers, but many other native people had little contact with outsiders and continued to live traditional lives. Even in the years from 1920 to 1945, some craftspeople had easy access to the traditional materials that were by-products of an actively practiced fishing/hunting economy. There was still access to the first-growth trees (those never clear-cut by foresters) required to make totem poles, although, in the face of outside opposition, only a few carvers continued to make them. Carving on the old scale was uncommon, but basketry continued to flourish. Trade introduced cloth, beads, and mother-of-pearl buttons to many communities, and these were accompanied by innovations in style; only in the past forty years, though, has development seriously endangered the materials for making many of the traditional art forms.

Having made an overview of native craft, it is important to concentrate on the work of specific artists, such as the Hopi potter Nampeyo and the San Ildefonso potters Maria and Julian Martinez, to explore other issues. Southwestern potters had a precontact tradition of making and pit-firing pottery. By gathering and processing local materials, they eliminated the need for outside trading for art supplies. Nampeyo, who began work before the turn of the century, continued until her death, in 1932. Her daughters did important work between 1920 and 1945, as did the Martinez family. By being shown pottery from archaeological digs in their ancestors' villages, both Nampeyo and Maria Martinez were inspired to revive the older, supposedly purer, more aesthetically pleasing pottery traditions in their pueblos.

Nampeyo was born on First Mesa, in the town of Hano, sometime around 1860. Her first works were unsigned utilitarian bowls, water jars, and storage jars that were used in the village. When her husband was working on an archaeological dig run by Jesse Walter Fewkes, at Sityatki, a prehistoric Hopi village in Arizona, she became interested in the pottery being unearthed. Incorporating some of the abstract design elements of the Sityatki polychrome ware into her work, without slavishly copying them, Nampeyo made pots primarily for a nonnative market; in doing so, she managed to devise a way in which people were able to enter the cash economy without leaving First Mesa or offending a Hopi sense of balance. As an anthropologist who could verify the ties to precontact tradition, Fewkes created a timeless ethnographic present for Nampeyo's work, about which buyers of her pottery could romanticize. This pottery also fit the taste for abstraction that educated buyers were developing in the post–World War I period. Nampeyo's work influenced First Mesa pottery for the next thirtysome years.

The story of Maria Martinez begins, like Nampeyo's, with her husband working at an archaeological dig, this one at Tuyuoni, New Mexico. The excavations were led by Edgar Lee Hewett, whose team of ten researchers included Kenneth Chapman, an artist, and Jesse Nusbaum, an anthropologist. When they saw her utilitarian pottery, with its thin, even walls and perfectly round symmetrical shape, they spoke with Martinez about the pottery they were uncovering.[2] The next year, she went with her husband to the dig as a cook and studied the pottery shards being unearthed. Hewitt asked her to experiment, to try to make a pot like the ones he had found. Since she did not paint, Julian, her husband, agreed to

Nampeyo with a piece of her pottery

paint the designs. Over time, Maria found ways to make both the polychrome ware and the blackware pots they were excavating. Studying the old pots, she chose to use finer clay and volcanic ash for tempering. With the help of the researchers from the dig, she started to market her pots.[3]

Like Nampeyo, Maria had nonnative experts discussing the way in which her designs revived ancient traditions. This tale of revival may seem odd because Maria was such an innovator; she may have been inspired by old things but she very quickly invented new forms. The finish on her pots was actually shinier and more beautiful than the finish on the shards from the dig. Even though some of her early pots were influenced by the shapes of the unearthed pots that were reconstructed, in a few years she began to make totally new designs based upon European pottery. To satisfy a trader, for example, she made her first set of plates. Soon, the demand was so great, her sisters and other expert potters at the pueblo began to help make the blackware dishes. Occasionally, because nonnatives asked her to, she signed her pottery. Like Nampeyo, Maria was helping not just her family but her pueblo to enter the cash economy while remaining at San Ildefonso and maintaining the culture. Many of the early pots were large, with complex and powerful designs by her husband, who was a fine painter. Maria's family and friends made a large number of pots with Julian's popular adaptation of a Tuyuoni feather design, and, like Maria and Julian, they began to innovate and create new styles over time.

Collaboration rather than individualism has often been a characteristic of Native American craft practice. Working together, cooperating, sharing, doing things that make it possible for the people to survive as a community—these are positive values, and they did not eliminate chances for innovation, change, or the revival of old traditions. The community was a training ground in which the work made by younger, less skilled people supported the complex, more challenging work of highly skilled craftspeople.

Certain issues keep reappearing in Native American craft like a refrain. Some nonnatives who claim that work is purer, more authentically indigenous, or more beautiful because it is inspired by precontact art believe innovation and outside influence cost the loss of one's culture. Others, usually outsiders, feel that one must let go of tradition to be modern and important, to be in the vanguard. Looking at craft in the dominant culture since the turn of the century, however, one sees evidence of appropriation from every culture on earth. In a similar spirit, it was Maria Martinez's prerogative to make blackware pottery inspired by pre-Columbian work and plates inspired by European dinnerware, and to let her husband paint them with traditional designs slightly altered by the Art Deco aesthetic of the time, itself often reflective of Native American forms.

Innovative developments occurred in weaving as well as in pottery in the Southwest. Hosteen Klah used an art form learned by his ancestors from the Spanish—wool tapestry weaving—to make traditional images in ways that transformed tradition. A highly unusual man, Klah was steeped in Navajo culture. He was a *hatali*, a singer of the Nightway, Mountainway, Chiricahua Windway, and Hailway chants, and as the only Hailway singer on the reservation at that time, many anthropologists wished to work with him. Franc J. Newcomb, a self-taught ethnographer who lived on the reservation with her husband, a trader, was taken to her first sing by Klah, studied with him, and eventually wrote a book about him, *Hosteen Klah: Navajo Medicine Man and Sandpainter*.[4] Studying to be a hatali is an arduous process; there are many things to learn: songs, prayers, the use of hundreds of herbs, and the intricate sandpaintings that must be precisely reproduced for the ceremonies to bring the patient back into harmony. Ceremonies may last several days, and the men who perform them are very learned.

Among Klah's friends was Mary Cabot Wheelwright, from Boston, who, as a result of her work with him, founded the Wheelwright Museum of the American Indian, in Santa Fe.[5] It was Klah's dedication to the spiritual traditions of his own people that attracted both Wheelwright and Newcomb; and it was for Newcomb that he first did drawings of the sandpaintings. Although Klah began weaving rugs at the World's Columbian Exposition, in 1893, he did not weave his first sandpainting textile until 1919.[6] Both Newcomb and Wheelwright encouraged him in the production of these textiles.

As well as being hatali, Hosteen Klah was also *nadle*—a word that translates most closely as "transformed"—which means that although Klah may have been born a man, he grew to assume, as well, the role of a woman. He did women's work—weaving is a woman's job among the Navajos—and was a person of great gentleness. Being both hatali and nadle, he had the knowledge required to make sandpainting textiles. Klah was not the first person to weave these textiles, but he is certainly the best known.[7] Because he was so unusual, and so many people had studied Navajo chants with him, he became the subject of much scholarly writing. Between 1919 and 1937, when he died, he wove about twenty-five textiles, all

Portrait of Hosteen Klah with one of his large sandpainting textiles

from chants he had performed as a hatali.[8] He also trained his nieces, Mrs. Sam (Gladys) Manuelito and Mrs. Jim (Irene) Manuelito, to weave them, and he wove a number in collaboration with Irene.[9]

At the time Klah began weaving, people were still unsure of the effect that using this imagery on textiles might have on Klah and his family. That they suffered no ill effects, and that the rugs sold for prices ranging from seven hundred and fifty to six thousand dollars—far more than for an ordinary rug made during the period—caused skeptical people on the reservation to reevaluate the way such spiritual imagery might be used. Sandpainting images are much more stylistically proscribed than many other types of religious imagery; the form may seem exotic and its meaning mysterious and traditional to an outsider, but this secularized representation of divine beings was a real innovation in traditional Navajo practice at the turn of the century. When Klah and other Navajos started to paint and weave pictures of the gods and then sell them, they were creating a new relationship with these religious figures.

Artists outside the Santa Fe market often have received less national attention than those from the Southwest. Perhaps not quite as famous as Nampeyo, Maria and Julian Martinez, or Hosteen Klah, Annie Burke was very important to Pomo basketry. Inheriting one of the most complex and beautiful basketmaking traditions, the Pomo made many different types, but they are best known, perhaps, for what English-speaking people called their treasure baskets. Used at traditional Pomo marriage ceremonies, these baskets, which held the shell money given by the wife's family to the husband's, were adorned with feathers and shell beads and had beautiful abalone-shell ornaments hanging from them. Pomos had several styles of both coiled and twined baskets, in a number of shapes and a wide variety of sizes. After trading began with outsiders, some Pomo basketmakers even incorporated glass beads, threading them directly on finely split sedge root as they coiled. The principal materials used in Pomo basketry are willow and sedge root, both the natural white root and the dyed black root, which allow the weaver to create boldly contrasting designs. To add a third color to the designer's palette, some baskets also used redbud twigs. Split sedge root is a fine material, and on a few older Pomo coiled baskets as many as sixty stitches of sedge have appeared in one inch of coiling. This time-consuming procedure resulted in beautiful and complex designs.

Elsie Allen came from a long line of Pomo basketweavers. In her book *Pomo Basketmaking*, she conveyed the admiration she had for the work of her grandmother and mother, whom she often watched weave. Her grandmother died in 1924, but her mother, Annie Burke, wove and taught basketweaving to their young relatives during the American craft revival. Burke showed her work at fairs and demonstrated basketry to nonnatives, to instill in them a sense of the skill and genius of Pomo cultural traditions. Allen herself only wove three baskets during this period: The first was buried with her grandmother; the second with her great uncle; the last, after making the rounds of her family, was finally buried with her brother-in-law. Because of work and childrearing, Allen's principal basketmaking activity was helping her mother gather materials, a time-consuming and labor-intensive seasonal activity that made it possible for her mother to weave. When her grandmother died and all her baskets and basketry materials were buried with her, as was Pomo custom, Allen felt a deep loss; there had not been enough time to study with her or to study her baskets. Soon after, Annie Burke decided that she did not wish to be buried with her baskets; she preferred to let Allen keep them so that after her children grew up, she could study and finally be able to make baskets full time. When Burke died, in 1962, Allen buried her without the baskets, in spite of the disapproval of many of her relatives. At the time, Allen was sixty-two and had been weaving baskets steadily for a year.[10]

There were other traditionalists who made an effort to keep particular craft techniques alive. Many are known only to their reservations, and one comes across their names rarely, if at all. Ida Blackeagle, a Nez Percé woman, was the principal teacher of Rose Frank, a well-known weaver of cornhusk bags who used the powerful, nineteenth-century geometric designs one sees in museum collections and at powwows. An innovator, Blackeagle incorporated geometric images of human figures into her bags and placed them in relation to symbolic areas of abstract design. Frank's revival would not have been possible without Blackeagle's daring ideas and flawless technique using jute, twine, cornhusk, and dyed yarn.[11]

Blackeagle did not weave the traditional designs but, instead, developed her own figurative style. She was following a tradition of innovation in which natural and trade materials, ancient techniques and modern improvements are valued equally. Contrary to popular stereotypes, Native Americans have never lived in an ethnographic present; instead, they are part of the evolving contemporary culture. When they are inspired by older styles, they revive them for thoroughly contemporary reasons. They innovate within a circle of changing tradition.

## THE HISPANIC CRAFTS TRADITION

In the colonial era, 1596 to 1821, the isolation of New Mexico from the rest of the Hispanic world made it necessary for craftspeople to produce goods locally, drawing on traditions brought north from Mexico.[1] Beyond utilitarian activities, such as weaving, blacksmithing, woodworking, leatherwork, and masonry, a few more specialized crafts were practiced. Local painters and sculptors made religious images—*santos*—for the Catholic churches and homes of the colony; jewelers produced delicate items of both gold and silver; embroiderers made distinctive *colcha* embroideries; and straw-appliqué was used to decorate picture frames, boxes, crosses, and other items. The methods and materials utilized in all these crafts derived primarily from European traditions brought to Mexico from Spain, perpetuating early Spanish forms and motifs. Some crafts were also strongly influenced by the surrounding Pueblo, Navajo, and other Indian cultures.

These local crafts were vigorous expressions of the highly unified social order that existed there until the twentieth century. Hispanic life in New Mexico reflected the unity of a pre-Enlightenment Europe dominated by Catholic religious and communal values, at the same time incorporating some aspects of the equally unified world view of the Indians. Beginning in 1846, with the American occupation of New Mexico, a radically different world view was imposed upon this still coherent social order. Not only was the economic role of handcrafts vitiated by the American presence but their cultural value was disdained.

In certain crafts, however, New Mexican craftspeople of the late 1800s were expanding rather than contracting their repertoire. The craft of tinwork blossomed because of the availability of large tin cans used to bring in goods from the eastern United States. At the same time, New Mexican carpenters took up the new tools brought by the Americans, as well as newly available milled lumber to create innovative furniture and architectural woodwork, characterized by a delicate use of applied decoration and creative adaptations of popular American forms. Filigree jewelrymaking flourished and was especially popular with Anglo-American women. By the 1890s, Hispanic weavers in one area had begun to make blankets for the newly burgeoning tourist trade, although at first their work was marketed by traders as another form of Indian weaving. By the end of the decade, however, most traditional crafts had lost their economic viability.

## ANTECEDENTS OF THE REVIVAL

The attitude of disdain toward Hispanic cultural forms gradually gave way to one of appreciation and interest, at least among some sectors of the Anglo-American population. The opening of the railroad brought not only slick commercial products and their purveyors but a more cultured group of eastern Americans, who were attracted by the Indian and Hispanic cultures and the climate and landscape. With their arrival, the important role of the early Spaniards in the culture and history of New Mexico began to be recognized and promoted.

In the early 1900s, the director of the Museum of New Mexico, Edgar L.

Anonymous. *Rio Grande Blanket.* c. 19th century. Wool, synthetic dyes, 86½ x 48". Collection International Folk Art Foundation at the Museum of International Folk Art, Museum of New Mexico, Santa Fe

Hewett, and his staff recognized the values of the Hispanic architectural tradition and actively promoted the revival of indigenous forms. Two important public buildings in Santa Fe helped to spur an architectural revival: the restoration of the Governors Palace, in 1913, and the construction of the Fine Arts Museum, from 1916 to 1917. The new art museum was based on the New Mexico building at the Panama-California Exposition, in San Diego, in 1913. Designed by Ira and W. M. Rapp under the watchful eye of Hewett, it was a conscious adaptation of elements from Hispanic colonial mission churches at San Felipe, Acoma, Laguna, and other pueblos. The research for the new museum and for other revival public buildings led inevitably to an awareness and appreciation of early Hispanic New Mexican interior furnishings. In 1917, Kenneth Chapman, director of the art museum, with the assistance of Jesse Nusbaum and Sam Huddleson, designed and built the furniture for the Women's Reception Room "after old Spanish models found in out-of-the-way places in New Mexico where woodcarvers and craftsmen in the early days fashioned the furniture and embellishments of the home."[2]

Anonymous. *Straw Appliqué Box.* 19th century. Straw, wood, 5¼ x 8 x 4". Collection Spanish American Arts Society, Inc., at the Museum of International Folk Art, Museum of New Mexico, Santa Fe

## CRAFT REVIVAL EFFORTS IN THE 1920s

Mary Austin, the writer, was one of the first Anglo-American proponents of Hispanic New Mexican cultural forms. On her first visit to New Mexico, in 1918, she began researching the cultural patterns of rural Hispanic villages as part of an Americanization study for the Carnegie Foundation. This fieldwork, undertaken with the aid of Mabel Dodge and Tony Luhan and artist Gustave Baumann, made her an immediate enthusiast of both the verbal and visual arts of the rural Hispanics. In 1919, she published a seminal article on the rich tradition of Hispanic verbal arts—poetry, song, and drama—which she proclaimed to be "equal to any folk product of the Old World" and superior to much contemporary poetry of the cultured world.[3]

In 1923, Austin moved permanently to Santa Fe and allied herself with her neighbor Frank Applegate in an attempt to revive Hispanic cultural forms. A sculptor and painter who had emigrated from New Jersey in 1921, Applegate actively began collecting Hispanic santos—folk statues and paintings of popular Catholic saints—and other domestic crafts, such as furniture, ironwork, and textiles. In sharing an enthusiasm for these crafts, Austin and Applegate determined that even though the knowledge and skill to produce them still existed among the people, few pieces were still being made. In 1925, with the support of other Anglo-Americans in the Santa Fe cultural community, they founded the Society for the Revival of Spanish-Colonial Arts, renamed the Spanish Colonial Arts Society four years later.[4]

The term *Spanish colonial arts*, which soon became the common designator of these Hispanic crafts, was apparently originated by Austin: "We hung up for some time over the name, but I had already been hard pressed for a phrase by which to describe the descendants of the Spanish Colonists, other than the misleading term *Mexicans*. . . . I remember insisting to Dana Johnson [editor of the *New Mexican*] that the term was in public use, though I myself was the only person who had used it, and to my relief he took it up and began to popularize it. Spanish colonial art became a subject of interested comment in the press."[5]

Austin's shying away from *Mexicans* and her use of *Spanish colonial* introduced a bias into the study of Hispanic crafts that persists to the present day. Scholars and popular writers have emphasized the Peninsular Spanish roots of these forms while downplaying the Mexican and Indian antecedents. In fact, all Spanish colonial crafts in New Mexico came first from Mexico, where centuries of usage distinguished many of them from the more distant Peninsular prototypes,

Anonymous. *Straw Appliqué Wood Niche with Santo.* 19th century. Straw, wood, 10¼ x 6 x 4¼". Collection Museum of International Folk Art, Museum of New Mexico, Santa Fe. Bequest of Cady Wells

and Southwest Indian influences must be accounted for as well. The large majority of surviving examples are not colonial at all; they were made after 1821, the end of the colonial period.[6]

The activities of the newly founded society included the collection and preservation of early pieces and the encouragement of craftspeople through annual exhibitions and prizes at the Santa Fe Fiesta. Although the first exhibition at the 1926 fiesta elicited only fifteen entries, there was much more interest the next year, and prizes were awarded for blanketweaving, tinwork, figure carving, braided and hooked rugs, and crochet. In 1930, the establishment of the society's Spanish Arts Shop, in Santa Fe, provided a continuous outlet, giving further incentive to the revival.

The question of what was to be revived became an issue among members. A laissez-faire position, adopted by artist Andrew Dasburg and, to some extent, Frank Applegate, welcomed innovation, with the attitude that the artists' work be allowed to sink or swim on its own. Others, such as industrialist Cyrus McCormick, Jr., insisted that revival work be based directly upon earlier prototypes, dismissing any form of innovation. This attitude, to the extent that it was successful, restricted craftspeople to narrow antiquarian standards. Although McCormick complained about innovative work, two of the first artists to be encouraged by the society worked in nontraditional styles—the woodcarvers Celso Gallegos and José Dolores López. Gallegos worked in a rough but vigorous carving style, producing figures in the round and atypical relief carvings of popular saints, as well as secular images, in which the background areas were completely cut out. López, encouraged by Applegate to produce santos, carved such powerful images as *Our Lady of Light*, again in a nontraditional style, intricately decorated with chipcarved designs and left unpainted. López's descendants, now in the fourth generation, continue to carve figures in his style.[7]

Some members of the society, however, cast themselves heroically as saviors of the crafts, seemingly oblivious to the fact that, for the Hispanics, the crafts did not need to be "discovered" but were well known and, in many cases, still practiced. Thus arose a paradoxical situation in which parallel traditions existed simultaneously within a single medium. There were, for instance, three separate forms of Hispanic weaving flourishing in the 1920s. In more isolated areas, the original blanketweaving tradition had never died out. Since the 1890s, weavers in the village of Chimayo had successfully adapted the tradition to the tourist market by using commercial yarns and adding popular southwestern motifs, such as arrows, swastikas, and thunderbirds. In addition, the Spanish Colonial Arts Society had spawned a revival of carefully made copies of traditional nineteenth-century pieces owned by its members.

With well-intended, if, at times, heavy-handed idealism, Austin and others saw the craft revival as a means of protecting rural Hispanics from loss of cultural identity while affording them economic independence. Given prejudice, language problems, and lack of education, Hispanics who were unable to compete successfully for good jobs often ended up in poorly paid laboring, factory, and service positions. The few individuals who successfully entered the materialistic Anglo-American system did so at the risk of being alienated from cherished spiritual and familial values at the heart of their culture. As one elderly Hispanic village woman warned her children who were attracted to the Anglo world, "Watch out . . . you can become a slave without even knowing it. You can be white and have money but not own your soul."[8]

The craft revival offered the possibility of preserving the local community in which the spiritual values and creative powers of the people could thrive. For the Hispanic, the option of working as a creative artist was clearly superior to enter-

Woodcarver José Dolores López with his statue *Our Lady of Light,* carved for the Public Works of Art Project, c. 1934. Photograph by T. Harmon Parkhurst

ing the ranks of the urban poor and becoming dependent upon the homogenized mass culture of Anglo-America. Mary Austin, John Collier, and New Mexican sociologist George I. Sanchez, among others, looked to Mexico and to Gandhi's India, where they saw ambitious, well-funded programs for village and personal self-sufficiency based upon vigorous craft-based cottage industries.[9] They hoped that a similar model might work for both the Hispanics and the Indians of the Southwest.

## GOVERNMENT AND PRIVATE SUPPORT OF THE CRAFTS REVIVAL IN THE 1930s

After the onset of the Depression, in 1929, the University of New Mexico, followed by other state and federal agencies, began to formulate educational programs in which artisanal training was a crucial part. The most important program, and one of the earliest, was initiated by the State Department of Vocational Education (SDVE), under the leadership of Brice Sewell. A sculptor by training, Sewell came to Albuquerque in 1928 and taught in the university's San José Training School. The San José Project, as it was later called, was an innovative pilot program to improve the education of rural Hispanic children. It had been inspired by Mexico's post-Revolutionary educational program to establish rural schools in isolated areas. In both the Mexican and New Mexican programs, it was soon realized that craft training was an essential element. In 1930, the San José Project appointed Brice Sewell and Mela Sedillo as supervisors of craft vocational programs. In the first project, the residents of a Spanish-speaking barrio in Albuquerque built their own school by traditional adobe construction methods. Teaching was bilingual—a radical idea for the day—and traditional crafts were taught.[10]

While employed by the San José Project, Brice Sewell issued a statement, in 1932, on "The Problems of Vocational Education in New Mexico," in which he proposed to "create and build small new industries in the villages which may be owned and operated by local capital. Only such industries will be set up as will utilize local natural resources." In this document, he reported that the university had conducted a survey of crafts in the northern part of the state and had found that leatherwork, woodworking, weaving, adobe construction, ceramics, and glassmaking would be viable village industries, all utilizing local materials.[11]

In 1933, Sewell was appointed State Supervisor of Trade and Industrial Education, with a mandate to teach traditional crafts in rural communities throughout the state. In this way, the idealistic efforts of the Spanish Colonial Arts Society and the pilot programs of the University of New Mexico achieved fruition in a very practical plan to alleviate the difficult economic conditions of rural people. The SDVE program under Brice Sewell became the central element in the crafts revival of the 1930s. Sewell's strategy was clear: first, to establish in rural communities new vocational schools for teaching traditional Hispanic crafts; second, to develop a curriculum of the highest quality, assuring the production of authentic New Mexican work; third, to develop marketing outlets for the work produced in the schools so that strong cottage industries could replace the state-run schools.

Sewell was certainly successful in his first two goals. By 1938, there were forty vocational classes in schools throughout the state, thanks to his careful use of existing funding and his skill at utilizing the array of new federally funded programs available. He worked closely with such well-funded programs as the National Youth Administration (NYA) and the Emergency Education Program (EEP) and Federal Art Project (FAP) of the Works Progress Administration (WPA). Sewell insisted that the work be of high quality, based upon authentic New Mexican prototypes: "It has been found that for the handmade products to

Anonymous. *Chimayo Blanket*. c. 1910. Wool, synthetic dyes, 84½ x 40½". Collection International Folk Art Foundation at the Museum of International Folk Art, Museum of New Mexico, Santa Fe

Anonymous. *Colcha Sample with Double Eagle*. c. 1935. Embroidery. Collection Joy McWilliams

Native Market. *Fireplace Screen*. c. 1936–38. Iron. Collection Mrs. George Paloheimo, Sr.

Pedro Quintana. *Tin Sample for Frames*. c. 1935. Terneplate, 4 x 6½ x ½". Collection Lane Coulter

be saleable, the student must be thoroughly grounded in the knowledge of the best examples of the past, particularly the Spanish Colonial, and the finished article must be superior in beauty and durability to the machine-made product."[12]

Belying the notion that crafts had died out, Sewell was quickly able to find a considerable number of Hispanic artisans, as well as some Anglos, to serve as teachers in the vocational schools. Among them were furnituremakers Maximo Luna, Elidio Gonzales, and Abad Lucero. Textile instructors included Dolores Perrault Montoya, Stella Garcia, Carmen Espinosa, Celina Vigil, and David Salazar. Tanning and leatherwork, tinwork, ironwork, and ceramics were also part of the curriculum.

Sewell ensured quality and authenticity through careful research carried out by staff members Carmen Espinosa and William Lumpkins, among others, and published a series of mimeographed booklets containing plans that were used in the schools.[13] The SDVE *Weaving Bulletin*, for instance, included plans for building looms and many careful drawings of nineteenth-century Rio Grande blankets, as well as innovative blanket designs by Taos artist Gisella Lacher. Crisostoma Luna, wife of furnituremaker Maximo Luna, learned to weave in the Taos Vocational School under Dolores Perrault Montoya, and she produced fine handspun and natural-dyed Rio Grande revival blankets based upon the prototypes in the *Weaving Bulletin*.[14]

Sewell recognized and attempted to confront the problem of marketing the crafts produced in the vocational schools, for their economic viability was to be the deciding factor in the success or failure of the program. Along with vocational training, he instituted classes in salesmanship, retail merchandising, and related skills, which were focused particularly on the marketing of Hispanic crafts. In spite of efforts to reach a national market, the major outlets were local. Much of the success of the program came from other governmental bodies in the state. Infused with federal funds, they placed large orders for interior furnishings for new office buildings, schools, and other institutional uses. With the end of the New Deal, this artificially inflated market diminished drastically. Sales to the private sector were also quite vigorous in Santa Fe, Albuquerque, and other large communities in the region, where Hispanic furnishings were extremely popular among wealthy Anglo-Americans who wished to create a southwestern ambience in their homes.

The major value of the SDVE program was that it provided craft training to a large number of individuals and helped them get through the difficulties of the decade. With the onset of World War II, federal programs began to evaporate, as all attention was focused on the war. The SDVE quickly changed its emphasis from craft training to classes in sheet-metal work, welding, airplane engine mechanics, and other subjects vital to the war effort. War-related employment was plentiful and paid highly, again drawing the young people out of the villages and virtually eliminating the economic need for the craft programs. After the war, craft training was reinstituted by the SDVE under the leadership of Henry Gonzales, but, lacking the federal support of the 1930s, the program never regained its importance.

## THE NATIVE MARKET AND OTHER PRIVATE ENTERPRISES

With the deaths of Frank Applegate and Mary Austin, the Spanish Colonial Arts Society's Spanish Arts Shop was replaced in 1934 by a more ambitious project—the Native Market—conceived and funded by Leonora Curtin, who, with her mother, Mrs. Thomas Curtin, had been an early supporter of the society. The Native Market was intended to re-create the milieu of a traditional crafts market as once may have existed in old Santa Fe, with not only items for sale but craftspeople working in the public space. The Native Market served as the major retail outlet for the products of Brice Sewell's vocational schools, as well as for items by the market's own craftspeople and many others.

Pedro Quintana. *Filigree Necklace*. c. 1925. Silver, turquoise. Necklace length: 18"; pendant: 3 x 1¼". Collection Mrs. Pedro Quintana

Weaver Dolores Perrault Montoya, an SDVE instructor, helped to set up the Native Market. Among the craftspeople employed were tinworker Pedro Quintana; colcha embroiderers Tillie Gabaldon Stark and Deolinda Baca; weavers David Salazar, Margaret Baca, and Valentin Rivera; spinners Maria Martinez and her daughter Atocha; and furnituremaker Abad Lucero. Pedro Quintana had been trained as a filigree jeweler by his father, Alejandro Quintana. With Sewell's encouragement, he quickly mastered tinwork, producing a variety of finely wrought decorative tin items, such as mirror frames, candelabra, and niches. Tillie Gabaldon Stark adapted the traditional colcha embroidery to the making of such smaller items as pillows and curtains. In 1932, David Salazar taught weaving for the SDVE at the vocational school in Galisteo before joining the Native Market; there, he helped to revive the traditional checked material known as *jerga*.[15] By 1937, more than three hundred and fifty craftspeople were reported to be selling their work through the market, and a branch store was opened in Tucson, Arizona. Although sales were vigorous, the market remained dependent upon Leonora Curtin's generosity for its survival. In 1939, she turned over its operation to a committee of craftspeople; within six months, lacking her support, the market permanently closed.[16]

The Native Market was not the only retail outlet for Hispanic crafts in New Mexico, and, in fact, it faced stiff competition from a number of private businesses operating in Santa Fe and elsewhere. In Chimayo, where a weaving revival had begun in the 1890s, the Ortega and Trujillo families had long been successful in marketing their distinctive textiles, and they employed other local weavers to assist them. In Santa Fe, the weavers Preston and Helen McCrossen had been hired by the Spanish Colonial Arts Society in 1930 to manage the Spanish Arts Shop; in 1931, though, they quit and opened the Kraft Shop, in a neighboring room in Sena Plaza, to exhibit and sell their own weaving. By 1938, they were employing seventy-two weavers, most of them Hispanic. In 1930, Celima Padilla had started Santa Fe Weavers; in 1938, she was featuring custom-woven handspun and vegetable-dyed products. The Knox Weavers, founded in 1933 by retired Kansas City businessman E. M. Knox, had, in 1938, a new building, "with twenty-two looms and some forty weavers, all young Spanish Americans with weaving in their blood."[17] Other weaving operations in Santa Fe in 1938 included the Burro Weavers, Southwestern Arts, and R. H. Welton's Southwestern Master Craftsmen, which employed six weavers using only handspun vegetable-dyed yarns.

These shops did not limit themselves to revival pieces; they produced yardage for draperies, rugs, custom-made clothing, and neckties, and enjoyed considerable success in reaching out-of-state markets. The McCrossens, between 1935 and 1938, sold more than seventy-five thousand handwoven neckties annually in foreign as well as United States markets, while the Knox Weavers claimed to have sold one hundred sixty thousand of their handwoven neckties in 1937.[18]

Locally made furniture was available at a number of outlets, such as the Spanish Indian Trading Company, run by Eleanor Bedell, former manager of the Native Market, and, in Taos, at Harry Simms's Craft O'Taos Studios. Southwestern Master Craftsmen, in Santa Fe, offered a complete line of interior furnishings made by Hispanic artisans—draperies, tinwork, ironwork, furniture, and rugs: "The glamorous tradition of the Hacienda lives on in the highly skilled crafts of the Spanish-American . . . his creations will lend your home its most distinctive touch."[19]

Decorative tin items could be purchased from traditional tinworker Francisco Delgado and his son Eddie, and from Francisco Sandoval, another traditional Santa Fe tinworker, who had learned the trade from his father in the 1870s.[20] At least four Anglo metalworkers produced Hispanic tinwork in the 1930s: Benjamin Sweringen and Bruce Cooper, proprietors of the Spanish Chest; Majel Claflin, who also worked on the Index of American Design for the WPA Federal Art Project; and Robert Woodman, who made tin for such revival architects as John Gaw Meem.[21]

The efforts of the revivalists such as the Spanish Colonial Arts Society, the government agencies, and the Native Market were part of a much larger picture of Hispanic craft production in the 1930s. It included many traditional craftspeople, who did not need reviving as much as they needed a market, and aggressive and savvy Anglo-American artisan-entrepreneurs, who were quick to adopt Hispanic forms and employ Hispanic artisans to do the work.[22]

## THE NATIONAL YOUTH ADMINISTRATION AND THE FEDERAL ART PROJECT

Among the federal programs with which the SDVE worked in the 1930s, the heavily funded National Youth Administration (NYA) was more interested in quantity than quality, attempting to educate and employ as many young people as possible. By 1938, the NYA had thirty-five hundred young Hispanics on its rolls, all of them benefiting from some aspect of vocational education. NYA funds paid for the living expenses of the students and many of the other school expenses of the SDVE, which was responsible for providing the craft training.

In contrast to the NYA, the Federal Art Project (FAP) was a small program focused upon quality. Led by painter Russell Vernon Hunter, a former vocational-school instructor under Brice Sewell, the FAP employed not only painters and sculptors, most of them Anglo, but a select number of Hispanic artisans as well. To employ them, Hunter had to convince WPA/FAP national director Holger Cahill of the cultural importance and aesthetic value of Hispanic crafts. Cahill was uncertain until he received a visit in 1936 from Leonora Curtin, whose forceful personality and commitment to the cause of the Hispanic revival convinced him that crafts could be incorporated into New Mexico FAP projects as long as they did not overshadow the work of the painters and sculptors. Thanks to Hunter and Curtin, the New Mexico FAP was one of the most active craft program in the country.

Craftspeople were utilized mainly to decorate public buildings, in particular the local art centers and theater built under the auspices of the FAP. Many of these buildings, which had murals painted by FAP artists, were tastefully decorated in

David Salazar. *Jerga*. c. 1936–38. Wool, 356½ x 27½". Collection International Folk Art Foundation at the Museum of International Folk Art, Museum of New Mexico,

Spanish Colonial style by Hispanic artisans selected by Russell Vernon Hunter. Hunter carefully reviewed the work produced in the SDVE and NYA programs and chose those craftspeople he felt were the most accomplished. In addition, he discovered some himself, most notably the carvers Patrocinio Barela, of Taos, and Juan Sanchez, of Colmor, and the painter Pedro Cervantes, of Texico, New Mexico, who did decorative work as well as easel painting for the FAP. A self-taught artist, Patrocinio Barela carved small statues from unpainted juniper in a simple style reminiscent of primitive art. Many of his pieces, such as *The Annunciation of the Birth of Jesus*, are personal interpretations of traditional Catholic imagery. Barela and Pedro Cervantes were propelled by Hunter into exhibitions in New York City at the Museum of Modern Art and other locations, and their work received adulation in the national media for its folk and primitive qualities.

Local art centers were established by the FAP in Roswell, Melrose, Las Vegas, and Gallup. In addition, the FAP decorated and furnished Albuquerque's Little Theater; the Carrie Tingley Hospital, in Hot Springs; the dining room at the New Mexico School of Mines, in Socorro; and other buildings. In many of these projects, Hunter was personally responsible for the overall design, carefully supervising specific objects as well as the craftsmanship of their makers.

The Little Theater, which opened in 1936, was the work of noted revival architect John Gaw Meem and had a facade mural by FAP artist Dorothy N. Stewart, of Santa Fe. Its interior was decorated with tin wall sconces and niches made by master tinworker Eddie Delgado; in the niches were Patrocinio Barela's small, yet striking juniper-wood sculptures. The stage curtain was decorated in colcha embroidery by a group of Albuquerque women under the direction of Stella Garcia. Ironworker Pete Garcia contributed wrought-iron railings for the stairs and to surround the orchestra pit. Hunter added to the traditional Hispanic repertoire by designing benches and chairs upholstered with Stella Garcia's embroidered fabric. All the furniture in the theater was built under the direction of woodworker George Segura and his NYA students at the Spanish-American Normal School, in El Rito. Today, the Little Theater continues to be an important community institution, with many of the original furnishings still intact.

Some of the furniture was decorated with delicate straw-appliqué designs, a traditional Hispanic craft that Hunter was particularly interested in reviving. Straw appliqué had very nearly died out; Hunter found only one person in the state still doing it—Ernesto Roybal, of Española. He employed Roybal on the FAP and encouraged him to do very fine, traditional strawwork.[23]

The WPA/FAP-sponsored Roswell Museum, which opened in 1937 and, today, is an important regional art center, also received Spanish Colonial treatment in its architectural design and interior furnishings. Most of the interior rooms, such as the director's office, were decorated in typical Hispanic revival style, but for the Ladies' Lounge, Hunter revived New Mexican territorial period furnishings, showing the effect of American fashions on Hispanic artisans after 1850: "The decorations in the Ladies' Lounge produce an effect of a period which might be called New Mexico Federal. After the Native craftsmen began to see the household articles imported by wagon trains, their copies of eastern furniture possessed a rather heavy kind of grace."[24] In addition to furniture, the lounge contained a four-foot-high embroidered dado around its walls, in imitation of the calico trade cloth used for that purpose in the territorial period.

Tin light fixtures in the museum were made by Eddie Delgado and Margaret Parrish. Woven rugs were the work of the NYA students in the Los Lunas SDVE weaving school, supervised by the FAP. The stage curtain was colcha-embroidered by young Hispanic women in Roswell, who were paid by the NYA and supervised by the FAP, with designs based upon an old textile in the collection of

Ernesto Roybal. *Straw Appliqué Cross.* c. 1936–40. Straw, wood, 7 x 5 x ¾". Collection Joy McWilliams

Office interior, Roswell Museum. c. 1940, with furnishings made by WPA/Federal Art Project workers.

James Macmillan, of the Spanish Indian Trading Company, in Santa Fe. The furniture, which included chairs with nontraditional colcha-embroidered upholstery, was made in the museum's own basement shop under the direction of woodworker Domingo Tejada. One striking *trastero* (cabinet) was decorated with straw-appliqué designs.

Wall niches held santos made by Juan Sanchez, a gifted young carver and painter from Colmor, who was crippled. Sanchez, hired on the FAP by Hunter to copy important early examples of santos, used as his sources old pieces in museums, private collections, and churches. His *St. Peter* is a careful copy of a nineteenth-century statue by José Rafael Aragón in the church at Córdova, New Mexico. Sanchez was one of the only Hispanic artisans in the 1930s to revive the traditional arts of painted wooden statuary and panel painting.

In a sense, the work of Russell Vernon Hunter was the crowning achievement of the 1920–40 Hispanic craft revival, for it combined both aesthetic and economic motives. Craftspeople produced high-quality work to furnish public spaces, thus creating a total "Spanish Colonial" ambience and increasing public awareness of the Hispanic craft tradition at its best. At the same time, the WPA/FAP provided income for these craftspeople and helped to further their careers.

Hunter also showcased Hispanic crafts in a set of renderings of original pieces, *Portfolio of Spanish Colonial Design in New Mexico*, published in 1938. E. Boyd wrote the text and did the original renderings; a large number of FAP artists, including Juan Sanchez, Eliseo Rodriguez, Ernesto Roybal, and several other Hispanics, handpainted the plates printed from Boyd's originals. An edition of two hundred copies was issued. This project was a forerunner of the WPA/FAP's Index of American Design, in which some of the same New Mexican FAP artists did renderings of Hispanic objects.[25]

## THE SIGNIFICANCE OF THE HISPANIC CRAFTS REVIVAL

On the one hand, the revival can be seen as a colossal and expensive failure. Huge sums of money were spent on projects, with little result. The world was bent on its inevitable course toward further mechanization of human life; handcrafts no longer had a vital role to play, as their demise during World War II demonstrated. The market created was both artificial and limited: The government-generated market was artificial because it depended on massive amounts of federal funds; the private market was limited to the wealthiest sector of the Anglo-American population.

On the other hand, the revival planted a seed. A large number of Hispanic men and women learned a craft. It gave them pleasure to make things with their hands, not only to sell but also to furnish their own homes. Today, in northern New Mexico, many Hispanic homes are still graced with traditionally made furniture and weavings from the 1930s as are some public buildings, such as the Harwood Foundation Museum and Library, in Taos, and the Little Theater, in Albuquerque. This skill gave Hispanics an option for employment and proved a hedge against both economic hardship and rapid assimilation. They had the option to be artists, not merely cogs in the great American economic machine.

It is commonly believed that the revival died with World War II and that crafts did not see the light again until the second revival began in the 1970s. In fact, a strong continuity was maintained between the two revivals. Many Hispanic artisans continued to work after the war, producing work in the medium they had mastered in the 1930s. The 1950 *Directory of New Mexico Craftsmen*, an admittedly incomplete source, listed eighty-two Hispanic artisans by place of residence and medium.

In the recent revival, which was under way in the 1970s, many of the surviving craftspeople of the 1930s played an important role as teachers of a younger generation. This revival, now in its third decade, is more solidly based upon a new and still growing appreciation of Hispanic forms, and the crafts made today are vibrant expressions of tenaciously held cultural values. Although some scholars and ideologues may criticize the motivations and manipulations of the revivalists of the 1920s and 1930s, today's craftspeople do not. Many of them now make much or all of their living from their handwork. They are conscious of the debt they owe to their predecessors in the revival, an earlier generation that foresaw the potential of a crafts revival leading to economic independence within, not outside of, the cultural community.

Roswell Museum. Hand-embroidered stage curtain by female National Youth Administration needleworkers, c. 1938.

Needlework, weaving, and lacemaking have been intimately intertwined with Puerto Rican history. Diego Alvarez Chanca, a doctor and companion to Columbus on his second voyage, was impressed by how much cotton the people had spun and by how well woven the cotton blankets were. "They owe nothing to those of our country," he said of the excellence of their weaving.[1] The crafts of looming and weaving were practiced by the indigenous women, who also produced shawls, petticoats, hammocks, and other cloth and cord articles. They also made baskets and pottery with equal skill.

Even as far back as Columbus's arrival, the production of textiles by native women transcended the needs of the family and community to form part of the island's commercial production.[2] During the colonization of Puerto Rico, in the sixteenth century, Europe was experiencing a true boom in the demand for woven lace, and the colonizing women brought skills and techniques that found fertile ground in the natural abilities of women of all socioeconomic levels. The manual dexterity of both colonizers and natives proved of fundamental importance in these early times.

Devout women, both within the convents and without, made clothing for the statues in the Catholic churches, cloths for the altars, and vestments for the officials; in the convents, they made these for local use as well as for churches on the Continent. The missionary Order of Notre Dame came to the island in 1915 to establish schools, one of which, the School of Notre Dame, in Puerta de Tierra, stayed in operation until the 1970s. When Father Hof, the school's founder, discovered the beautiful needlework being made by impoverished women in the area, he decided to emphasize its study. By making contact with tourist ships, Father Hof created a market for the embroidery, openwork, and lace (*encages de mundillo*) produced in the school. An altar cloth made at the School of Notre Dame is typical of the needleworkers' virtuosity. Done in openwork on three sides, it was approximately four meters in length. At least five weavers worked on the design in special stitches that created solid and shaded areas. The cloth required terraced borders on both sides, an added difficulty that necessitated unraveling of extreme precision.

The establishment of the schools coincided with a great demand for needlework in foreign markets, and many of the designs worked out at the school and other centers during this boom period exhibited a repertoire of popular motifs: landscapes, country homes, *flamboyanes*, and figures playing instruments—calabashes, guitars, maracas, and drums. Even the roasted pig has been immortalized in a number of tablecloths and hand towels. These motifs were designed, most likely, for tourists and for export; they are not found in pieces made for use in the home, nor in any of the sampler books. Typical designs for home use tended toward repetitive floral motifs—garlands and stylized flowers—and birds. Geometric motifs are rare. Usually, both the fabric and the embroidery (or weaving) are white—apparently an aesthetic preference, since many of the sampler books are rich in color, probably in order to differentiate certain designs from others.

Bobbin-thread lace had a special place in the Puerto Rican life and economy between 1920 and 1945. After World War I, the United States began searching

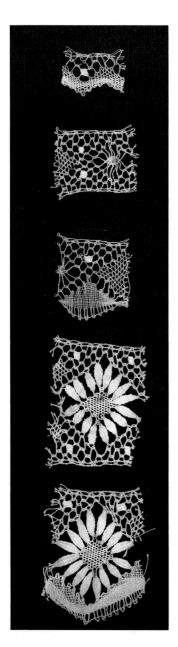

Marcelina Molinary. Five lace samples. 1925. Collection Rosalina Brau Echeandia

for places other than the Continent to find lace and lace trimmings to import. At the same time, many Puerto Rican men were going to the United States to find work, leaving their wives and children at home. In an attempt to support themselves and their families, some women, particularly on the northern shore of the island in and around the port of Aguadilla, revived—or increased the time they spent on—the making of lace. The port became a place of exchange where Marines and, later, commercial ships bought handmade lace by the yard for shipment back to the United States. The women preferred using shiny so-called Japanese thread, which was actually made in Spain and brought in to the port until the onset of World War II.

Home life often revolved around the making of lace. The demand kept girls of every social level busy. Even in affluent families, a young girl's industriousness was encouraged; in poorer situations, it was essential. Many women recently interviewed recall being shown how to make simple lace patterns at the age of six or seven. Even in the first or second grades, poorer children often found themselves spending two or three hours before school making lace; then, after school and chores, lacemaking continued into candlelight, the weaver's feet tucked inside burlap sacks to protect them from mosquitoes.

Often, women gathered in one another's homes to make lace together, enjoying the sense of community as well as the pleasure of passing on their skills to their children. The joy of creation established a rapport between generations, but it meant something more to the women. They speak of how the thread they wove into lace was a skein of cultural memories, personal feelings, and real historical events bound into a tangible object that could be enjoyed for generations. One woman spoke of the way "children's games, furtive looks, a son's sighs, hunger, and joy were caught in the links and weave of the lace, appearing as daisies, garlands, and vines."[3]

With the advent of war, Japanese thread was no longer available. In addition, the industrialization of needlework, along with a legal ban on cottage industries, forced women out of their homes and into the workforce. By 1950, only a few practiced their art, but it was enough to allow for a revival in the 1960s and 1970s when the Institute of Puerto Rican Studies began an effort to reestablish lost traditions. The craft skipped a generation and became "The Art Which Our Grandmothers Taught," as it was presented in the title of a 1980 exhibition.[4] Now, bobbin lacemaking is thriving once again.

Carmen Vasquez Gonzalez and her pupils in the Baldoristy de Castro School, San Juan, Puerto Rico, June 1925.

## "Keeping On Keeping On": African American Craft during the Era of Revivals

by John Michael Vlach

The 1930s, often remembered as the period of the Great Depression, witnessed widespread excitement over the "discovery" of local craft traditions. The handwork usually associated with the preindustrial age, which had been so widely celebrated by many members of the socially elite at the turn of the century, was now recognized as being wonderfully alive within the nation's ethnic, racial, and regional communities. Major exhibitions were staged in Buffalo, Albany, Rochester, Cleveland, Minneapolis, Omaha, and New York City to recognize and celebrate the "immigrant gifts" of craft skills brought from Europe.[1] In New Mexico, the Spanish Colonial Arts Society promoted the weaving and woodcarving of Hispanic villagers, traditions that could be traced back to the eighteenth century. The Southern Highland Handicraft Guild, founded in 1929, engaged in an active marketing program on behalf of thousands of Appalachian artisans. The federal government, affected by this wave of enthusiasm, took several initiatives; in 1935, to cite just one instance, Congress created the Indian Arts and Craft Board, making it part of the Department of the Interior.[2] With such interest in homegrown crafts, African Americans could not remain immune, and some black leaders were swept along by this renewed appreciation for the work of the hand. In 1937, A. Philip Randolph, the prominent black trade unionist and political leader, upon visiting some craft classes sponsored by the Works Progress Administration (WPA) in Harlem, suggested that such experiments might be "the cultural harbinger of a true and brilliant renaissance of the spirit of the Negro people in America."[3]

There was, however, a crucial and telling difference between the sort of WPA-sponsored activities that Randolph had witnessed and the kind of work that was being promoted on behalf of other ethnic and regional groups. The Harlem Art Workshop offered classes in drawing, painting, sculpture, maskmaking, linoleum cut-and-block printing—all of which were genres of studio art. Howard University art professor James Lesesne Wells provided the instruction, with the assistance of painter Palmer Hayden. At the Harlem YMCA, a related crafts instruction program included, in addition to painting and sculpture, opportunities to learn soapcarving, woodworking, radio and aircraft work, and chipcarving.[4] While other cultural groups reviewed their respective histories to find authentic sources of craft expression, at these WPA centers black students were introduced to either *official* academic forms of art or to popular leisure-time hobbies. The craft traditions of black Americans were simply overlooked.

A number of circumstances help explain why these programs were not grounded in black cultural history. Many black urbanites, having only recently arrived in the North, wanted to distance themselves from their southern experiences.[5] Since their craft skills were often techniques for salvage and repair—a means, basically, to run a farm with little cash—they could be dispensed with easily in a city setting. Certain traditional objects, like quilts, remained desirable, and needle skills were still regarded as useful, but the demands of wage-earning work left little time for stitching bedcovers or making dresses; it was more expedient just to buy what one needed at a store. Furthermore, if they accepted the promo-

Aaron Douglas. *Aspects of Negro Life: An Idyll of the Deep South*. 1934. Oil on canvas, 58 x 1187". Schomburg Center for Research in Black Culture, New York Public Library, New York

tional pitch that the urban North was a land of promise, as many black migrants had, then they were bound to reject the old rural South. For many blacks, the South was a region dominated by misery and injustice; understandably, they thought it best just to forget it and its adherent folkways.

The Harlem Renaissance, a cultural movement in New York City that lasted from about 1919 to 1929, provided the growing black-urban population with new goals and aspirations, but it granted no sanction for the resurgence of African American craft skills. The period saw an outpouring of African American literature, music, and art that was marked by a discernibly fresh outlook. People of color everywhere took pride in these artistic developments and were filled with a new confidence. In 1925, Howard University philosopher Alain Locke set forth a manifesto of sorts in *The New Negro*. In his book, he attempted to identify the spirit of this movement—a quality of mind present in Harlem that was "prophetic" for the future directions of all black Americans.[6] In order for the cause of the "New Negro" to be advanced, the values of the "Old Negro" would have to be discarded. For Locke, and those who followed his lead, the crafts, without a doubt a legacy of the "Old Negro," were therefore best ignored.

The African Americans who had recently left the South and its neoplantation ways of near servitude were certainly ready for this message. In 1930, more than 50 percent of all blacks in Louisiana, Mississippi, and South Carolina still worked on farms.[7] For them, and for the thousands of other northward-migrating blacks, new skills held the promise of meaningful employment, higher wages, and ownership of property, as well as the chance for social respectability. The old ways, by contrast, suggested drudgery, debt, and exploitation.

Locke, however, did not recommend the wholesale abandonment of all folk traditions; rather, he proposed that a new identity be founded in old customs. But when he called attention to African American folk art, he emphasized only music, oral literature, and dance, and he deliberately rejected any possibility that blacks might look toward craft traditions as a worthwhile cultural resource. The years of slavery, he wrote, had "severed the trunk-nerve of the Negro's primitive skill and robbed him of his great ancestral gift of manual dexterity." With respect to crafts, the African American was a "cultural zero."[8] In this way, he stilled further inquiry, for who would investigate a subject presumed not to exist?

Locke's vision of African American folk culture focused so strongly on the oral and the performing arts that three centuries of southern experience were presented as a period when black people engaged in little more than brutish labor

Anonymous. *Face Vessel*. c. 1840–80. Stoneware, kaolin, 9 x 7¼ x 7¼". Collection High Museum of Art, Atlanta, Georgia. Purchased with funds from the Decorative Arts Endowment

Anonymous. *Four-Handled Jar*. November 16, 1834. Stoneware, alkaline glaze, 18¾ x 17½ x 17½". Collection The Charleston Museum, South Carolina

and, from time to time, found solace in the gifts of song and story—an interpretation that actually was rendered by Aaron Douglas on the walls of the Schomburg Center for Research in Black Culture in 1934.[9] In *The New Negro*, Locke made only cursory reference to craft skills, observing that although the "plastic and craft arts predominate" in Africa, "there is little evidence of any direct connection of the American Negro with his ancestral arts."[10] One was left to conclude—as Locke himself would later write—that there was no worthwhile indigenous African American craft tradition upon which a "New Negro" might draw. Against this background, it is not surprising that new craft programs for the young black population of Harlem promoted the carving of animals out of bars of soap or the building of model airplanes.

The irony is inescapable: At the very moment that three centuries of African American experience in the crafts were being overlooked, other cultural groups were actively reviving or recovering their native craft traditions. Although pioneering scholarship in the 1940s on African American art began to illuminate some of the obscured history of black craftsmen in the antebellum period, only the faint outlines of this saga were sketched out.[11] Still unrecognized were the achievements of black potters at Edgefield, South Carolina, who fashioned both sturdy utilitarian ware and sculptural vessels in the shape of heads, which recalled, perhaps, ancestral forms from central Africa. One man, remembered only as Dave, now stands out clearly—not only for the witty poems he incised on the surfaces of his pots but because, in his day, he made the largest stoneware vessels known anywhere in the South.[12] Equally forgotten was that black people in the eighteenth century controlled the coastal waterways from Virginia to Georgia with their remarkable abilities in small-boat navigation and fishing and their expertise in boatbuilding. In fact, slave craftsmen are now credited with contributing to the invention of distinctive hewn-log watercraft in the Chesapeake region.[13] Slave censuses taken throughout the first half of the nineteenth century show that although blacks were trained in many trades, they proved especially proficient at woodworking, and were particularly active as carpenters, masons, and plasterers—that is, in housebuilding. Consequently, they deserve to be credited for building much of the South, both rural and urban, plain and majestic.[14]

Within their quarters, slaves on plantations not only performed the mundane tasks necessary to maintain themselves and their families but, on occasion, embellished their lives with creative acts almost too numerous to count. They carved wooden canes with all sorts of designs. They made quilts with bright and lively patterns. They fashioned musical instruments, ranging from panpipes to fiddles to banjos. They wove baskets and caned chair seats. And they made shoes and assorted items of clothing. In light of prevailing racist attitudes in America suggesting that blacks were incapable of taking care of themselves, all of these acts were charged with revisionist significance. Perhaps just as important as this history of competence was that black artisans continued to do all of these things and more after the period of slavery, and they were still doing them in the 1930s.[15] Thus, the African American craft tradition did not have to be revived; it had never died.

Even though the great migration had brought millions of blacks to the North, and eventually was to transform African Americans chiefly into an urban people, in the 1930s and 1940s more than 70 percent of the black population was still located in the South and relatively close to its historical roots. Many would have been seen, in Locke's terms, as "Old Negroes." They were a sizable group, prone to look with suspicion on new, progressive ways; they felt that it was better just to "keep on keeping on" and to put their trust in familiar, commonplace pursuits.

# BASKETRY

As the Harlem Renaissance was reaching its apogee, hundreds of black women living near Charleston, South Carolina, were vigorously making coiled-grass baskets, a craft that had been practiced continuously in their area since the late seventeenth century. During the 1930s, this tradition was changing, as more and more basketmakers were visible along the sides of the highway, on street corners, and in the central market of Charleston. Described to tourists as "basket girls"— an intriguing aspect of the area's local color—they were artisans who recognized that by making their traditional baskets, they could better support their families. But there was something else, too: In their old, familiar baskets, they saw a way to exert greater control over their personal lives.

The coiled baskets found in the coastal regions of South Carolina and Georgia had been a basic element of the technology used to raise, harvest, and process the rice upon which the local plantation economy depended. A tangible element of African-derived culture, these baskets, or, at least, the techniques used to make them, were imported right along with the African laborers brought here to work in the fields. Although planters were usually wary about letting their slaves engage in old African ways, they made an exception when they realized the great utility of these baskets. The most important types included winnowing trays—known locally as rice fanners—and carrying baskets of various sizes. Since these workbaskets were intended for outdoor use in the fields and mill yards, they were tough and durable. Fashioned with thick coils of marsh rushes about an inch in diameter, they were stitched together with strips of oak or palmetto stem. Simple in form, they had flat bottoms about two feet across and straight sides that flared out at a slight angle. About 1850, a second type of African American basket appeared in the region. Made of softer, more pliable bundles of sweetgrass and strips of palmetto leaf, they were intended for household use. Common examples included breadbaskets, cake baskets, clothes hampers, sewing baskets, hot plates, and flower baskets, which were based on popular forms or personal designs. Made with small coils about a quarter inch in diameter, in a seemingly limitless number of fancy shapes, sweetgrass baskets were called "show" baskets, because they allowed their makers to show off their fertile imaginations. Thus, for about a half-century, two modes of basketry coexisted among African Americans in the lowcountry—the plain workbaskets made primarily by men and the more expressive show baskets made by women.[16]

The Civil War brought an end to most of the rice plantations. During the last decades of the century, most American rice production shifted to other states. Consequently, the need for most of the workbaskets was eliminated. But the show baskets, whose connection was chiefly to domestic routine, were still made as needed. This women's tradition remained hidden within the home until the first decades of the twentieth century, when the basketmakers learned that white people were very curious about their craft.

In 1916, a Charleston merchant named Clarence W. Legerton established the Sea Grass Basket Company. He began to buy up large numbers of the local baskets to sell in his downtown store, as well as to customers across the country via a mail-order operation. Today, some of the older basketmakers from Mt. Pleasant, a small town just north of Charleston, can still recall the occasions when Legerton came to their various settlements and paid twelve dollars for as many baskets as would cover a whole bedsheet. Shops from other coastal Carolina towns were soon requesting baskets, too, but the basketmakers figured they could do better by working for themselves. Some began to trek to the ferry landing at the edge of the Cooper River, to hawk their baskets to the crowds waiting for the boats to

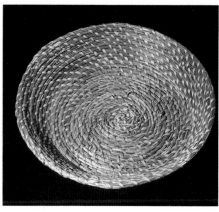

Anonymous. *Basket*. 19th century. Sweetgrass, palmetto cane, 5½ x 26½ x 26½". Collection The Charleston Museum, South Carolina

Charleston. In the early 1920s, this rutted dirt track was paved and transformed into U.S. Highway 17, the Ocean Highway, and, later, in 1929, a two-lane bridge was completed across the Cooper River, linking Charleston with Mt. Pleasant. These improvements helped bring a large and steady stream of travelers directly past the basketmakers' front doors. It was at this time that many of them took up highly visible positions along the roadside—first, with chairs and cardboard boxes and, later, in stands built with cast-off scraps of wood. There were only a few stands in the 1930s; by 1949 though, they had grown to thirty-one.[17] No exact census of artisans was taken at the time, but it was estimated that about three hundred basketmakers were actively sewing baskets in the vicinity of Mt. Pleasant. This rather sudden burst of activity may have seemed to outsiders like the revival of an old craft; for the basketmakers, it was merely the moment when they chose to display a formerly closed-door behavior to the public. The craft was not revived; it was being shown off in a new way.

Institutional attempts to revive African American coiled basketry in South Carolina during this period—most notably at the Penn Normal, Industrial, and Agricultural School, on St. Helena Island—had little success when compared to developments among the Mt. Pleasant artisans. Basketmaking classes led by experienced craftsmen were offered annually at Penn Normal from 1905 until about 1950; the appeal of those baskets faded appreciably during the 1930s, though, and 1944 found only eight girls and no boys enrolled in the basket class.[18] One might argue that the efforts of Penn Normal flagged because the school lacked the readily accessible market of the Charleston region; much more important was the absence of a community eagerly committed to preserving its ethnic heritage. At the time that a mere handful of young girls showed up to make baskets in St. Helena, hundreds of women, as well as a few men and boys, were offering baskets seemingly all over Charleston and Mt. Pleasant.

The money earned from sales during the Depression years—about seventy-five cents for the average basket—was motive enough to pursue this craft actively; more important, though, must have been the satisfaction of making interesting artifacts intimately connected to one's own history and tradition. When required to sew baskets for Clarence Legerton's commercial enterprise, basketmakers found themselves aesthetically crimped by his demands. For the most part, he wanted baskets he could ship easily in bulk loads—small baskets and shallow trays, bowllike forms without tops that were able to nest inside one another. These minimal forms, although authentic expressions of the local tradition, provided little creative challenge. They were, in fact, the type of baskets usually made by novices, and they constituted less than 15 percent of the traditional repertoire for show baskets. But when the basketmakers took charge of their own sales, they were free to create any form that came into their heads. Their roadside stands, normally stocked with baskets made by several family members, plus some made by a few neighbors, began to bristle with imaginative forms. New baskets imitated the lines of milk cans, spittoons, flower vases, thermos bottles, pitchers, and even pressing irons. Standard forms were often thoughtfully blended; a fanner basket might be given the handle from a market basket to become a new type of flower basket. Innovations of all sorts were tried out; there were experiments with changes in materials, stitching techniques, sizes, and shapes. Individualized containers known as "own style" baskets became more commonplace. In preserving their centuries-old craft, basketmakers discovered a heady liberation and a means of self-empowerment. Once these qualities were realized, they no longer accepted the meager prices offered by wholesalers. The steadily increasing number of active basketmakers is compelling evidence that they much preferred to be in business for themselves. The local enthusiasm for this craft has remained so constant that, today, it is estimated that approximately fifteen hundred African Americans are involved in basketmaking in some capacity in the Charleston-Mt. Pleasant area.[19]

## BLACKSMITHING

Blacksmithing in the Charleston area provides another example of an African American craft that became more prominent in the 1930s. Enslaved black ironworkers, as well as a few free blacks, had been active in Charleston since the late eighteenth century. By 1848, blacks had achieved almost complete parity with their white competitors; in that year, forty-four African Americans were listed as blacksmiths in the city census.[20] African American blacksmiths continued to tend to local ironwork needs in the late nineteenth century and the first decades of the twentieth; they even dominated in some branches of the trade, such as horseshoeing and wheelwrighting.[21] Although factory production and new modes of transportation eliminated the need for blacksmiths in almost every region of the country by the 1930s, in Charleston there was a resurgence in ironwork.

The survival of blacksmithing in Charleston, unlike the basketmaking of nearby Mt. Pleasant, was due to an individual rather than a collective effort and must be credited to African American ironworker Philip Simmons. Born in 1912, Simmons began his apprenticeship in this venerable craft in 1925, when he was only thirteen, and he has remained at the trade for more than sixty-five years.[22] Over the course of his career, Simmons faced many challenges, but the most critical was his shift from the general trade of blacksmithing to the more specialized field of ornamental ironwork.

Philip Simmons learned blacksmithing from Peter Simmons (who was not a blood relative), a man born into slavery in 1855. Seventy years old when Philip Simmons showed up one day at his shop, Peter's experiences provided young Philip with a bridge back to the antebellum period and a pathway into the deep history of the local black community. In fact, in 1925, Charleston still resembled a nineteenth-century, if not an antebellum, city in some essential ways. As horse-drawn wagons were still commonly used for waterfront transport, there were plenty of wagons to build and repair, wooden wheels that needed to be tired with metal rims, and horses whose iron shoes required regular replacement or adjustment. Farmers from the surrounding countryside regularly brought their plows to be fitted with new points, and since Charleston was a port city, there were requests for all sorts of "boat iron," such as keels, rudders, chains, and anchors. The blacksmith remained "king of all the trades" as other workmen came to have their metal tools either sharpened or repaired. Philip Simmons learned all aspects of blacksmithing: wainwrighting, wheelwrighting, horseshoeing, toolmaking, and angle smithing. Three decades into the twentieth century, he was fully versed in the basic skills of the previous era.

As Simmons was becoming a master of iron, though, the industrial revolution seemed, finally, to catch up to Charleston. About 1926, motorized trucks began to replace the horse-drawn drays, and local businessmen predicted a quick demise for the city's dozen-or-so blacksmith shops. The dire forecasts, however, proved premature; it turned out that the new trucks, just like the horse-drawn wagons, still required the blacksmith's attentions.

Philip Simmons assumed full control of the blacksmith shop when he was only twenty-one. It was 1933, and the decline in his business caused by many of the innovations of the modern age was accentuated further by the effects of the Depression. Before he could even consider another line of work, he was approached by architectural restorationists who were just beginning to preserve

Iron gate at No. 2 Stoll's Alley, Charleston, South Carolina. Photograph by Philip Simmons

Iron gate at No. 9 Stoll's Alley, Charleston, South Carolina. Photograph by Philip Simmons

many of Charleston's older buildings.[23] According to Simmons: "First, everyone destroy the old architectural structure of the house. [But] when they keep the value . . . they keep it then. Finally, they demand it. Then it become a compulsory that you don't tear it down—an old house—or tear down an old wrought-iron fence. . . . You see I could—we had the forge—start on the forge, and you roll these things like the old craftsmen used to do. The young people then, they didn't do it. They went the fast way. So we stop, stopped right there, and pick up all the work."[24]

Modern factory production eliminated most of the blacksmith's business, but machines could not duplicate the distinctive and telling features of hand-forged wrought-iron scrolls. Since the preservation codes mandated by the Historic Charleston Foundation required the use of original materials and construction techniques, a new, previously unanticipated demand arose for a blacksmith's skills. Simmons's comment on the beneficial impact of the local preservation movement is both terse and accurate: "That thing really helped."[25] Encouraged by his new clientele, he stayed at his anvil while other blacksmiths retired or moved on. By the 1950s, Simmons was the only blacksmith still listed in the city directory.

The key to Simmons's professional longevity was due to more than his bravery in holding on to declining trade or his cleverness in shifting between branches of the ironworking trade; it was his readily apparent talent that ensured him the opportunity to work for most of this century. Good work proved to be the best means for getting more work, and the beginning of his career as an ornamental ironworker provides a clear example. His first decorative commission, in Charleston, was for a tall walkway gate at No. 9 Stolls Alley, an enclosed residential court tucked away in the city's historic Battery District. The gate included several of the most common local motifs—S and C scrolls and spears—and the design of the gate screen was set out in the common Charleston quadrant pattern. The other home owners in Stolls Alley were so impressed that no sooner had Simmons finished this commission, then the owner of No. 2 also wanted a wrought-iron gate in his yard. In its general pattern, this gate was similar to the one at No. 9, but smaller in scale, and it contained some rarely used, reversed J curves. Then, the owner of No. 5 requested both a gate and a railing for her front steps. Her request for a gate that was similar to yet different from the others was satisfied with a design that consisted of two intersecting J's flanked by long-stemmed flowers fashioned mainly from scrolls and loops. A close look reveals, however, that the core of the design echoes the structural arrangement of the upper half of the gate at No. 9. Two things were happening in Stolls Alley: Simmons was incrementally developing an approach to design in which he would simultaneously repeat and improvise upon the local ironwork patterns, and he was forging a reputation as a trustworthy artisan. The Stolls Alley commissions served as a launching site for his new career. Each job became an advertisement for the next, not only in this out-of-the-way side street but for the rest of Charleston as well. Simmons, in fact, became so well known, he never had to advertise. Seeing his work was proof enough that he had a superior command over the Charleston tradition of ornamental ironwork.

His most important commissions and greatest honors were to come much later, but in Stolls Alley, Simmons proved to himself that he was capable of meeting the demands of decorative work, and he began to study seriously the subtleties of the ironwork in Charleston's different neighborhoods. During the 1930s, he charged himself, in effect, with maintaining historical standards for the entire city. Simmons says of his research: "I notice in doing this work you got to know the different neighborhood. Some people, you'll go there, don't know what's all

Quiltmaker at her frame, Hinesville, Georgia, 1941. Photograph by Jack Delano

about. You got to study this thing. Put a lot of time in studyin' it. Just like you get books on Charleston—study the wrought iron—I walk around here and see what the other man got."[26] Armed with this knowledge, he was ready not only to satisfy himself, and his clients, but Charleston's sense of history. The streets of this city, dressed as they are with more than two hundred of his gates, fences, window grills, and other wrought-iron embellishments, provide testimony enough to justify that Philip Simmons deserves to be known as the dean of the Charleston blacksmiths.

## QUILTING

In the 1930s, there was no pronounced revival of African American quilting. The strength of the tradition was manifested instead by the smooth reassurance of cultural continuity. Since quilted bedcovers made with layers of cloth were unknown—and, of course, not needed in tropical Africa—black Americans first must have learned of them while being held as slaves on plantations. Basic ideas about form and technique emanated from the master's "big house" to the slave quarters, and, soon, quilting was regarded as a normal household skill. When interviewed in the 1930s, John Van Hook, from Macon County, North Carolina, like former slaves throughout the South, recalled that there were "plenty of quilts . . . plenty of good warm cover in those days." Some slave quilters, like Fan-

Mattie Burnley. *Trapezoid Quilt*. c. 1935–45. Cloth, 98 x 90". Collection Eli Leon

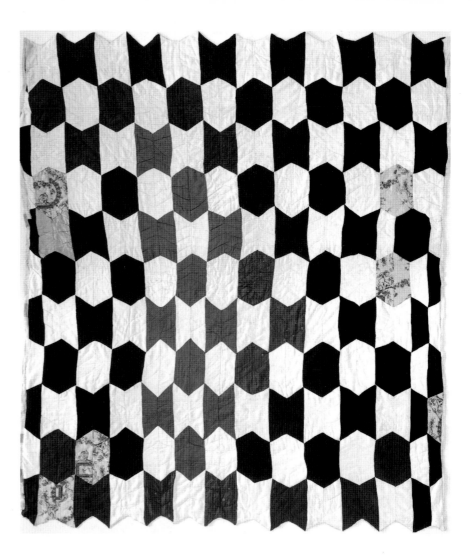

nie Moore's mother, became so proficient that "she have to piece quilts for the white folks, too."[27]

Many quilts made by African American artisans conform to the expectations of the dominant white society and, for the most part, are symmetrically balanced in design, featuring either a centrally located motif, surrounded by bordering elements, or a grid of blocks, all of which carry the same pattern. The careful planning, precision, and order seen in these textiles are hallmarks of the Anglo-American folk aesthetic. Not without appeal for some black quilters, they employed these designs even when producing bedcovers for themselves. Consequently, a number of patterns with European American origins were incorporated into African American repertoires. Commonplace motifs, such as log cabin, Dresden plate, robbing Peter to pay Paul, lone star, and nine patch, have been well known to black needleworkers since at least the early nineteenth century. The *Wild Goose Chase Quilt* made by Lucy Sims, of Galveston, Texas, about 1925, as well as the *Windmill Blades Quilt* made by Nellie Cox, of Rankin County, Mississippi, about 1935, both illustrate that these patterns were carried on well into the twentieth century. Even if they were not African American in origin, they certainly became so by creation and use. The journey of a quilt design across racial and social boundaries is finally completed when a black quilter assigns it a new name. This happened when Pecolia Warner, of Yazoo City, Mississippi, humorously referred to the ubiquitous log-cabin motif—a square composed of narrow strips of cloth concentrically arranged around a small central block—as a "pig in a pen."[28]

In addition to the quilt designs generated from repeated blocks, African American women pieced quilt tops in strip units. This technique, also known among white quilters, is more widespread among blacks. Moreover, white quilters usually regard stripping as an expedient way to make everyday quilts rather than the bedcovers that will best enable them to show off their artistic skills. In fact, they consider the format so rudimentary that novice quilters first will be shown how to run up a number of strips in order to compose a quilt top, before moving on to block formats that are regarded as more challenging.[29] By contrast, black women, at least since the 1860s (and probably earlier), have regarded the strip quilt as a favored mode. Today, it is sewn with pride by accomplished artisans in almost every black community where quilting is practiced. The strips are not merely run from one end of the quilt to the other, as might be expected; rather, they are manipulated in myriad ways to create designs that will seem off-balanced and even inept to one unfamiliar with the genre. The first-time viewer of an African American strip quilt is most likely to see it as a crazy quilt, for that is the genre of Anglo-American textile closest in feeling. The randomness of the strip quilt, however, should not be mistaken for "craziness," for the seeming chaos is just that—deliberately planned or allowed. The lack of expected order provided by a symmetrical grid is not the absence of order but the presence of another kind of order, which arises out of the circumstances of African American culture.[30]

One of the reasons for the popularity of the strip format among black quilters may be that it provides a means to slip past the rigid rules of block designs. At some level, one might experience a feeling of liberation, a quality of decided importance to a socially oppressed population. The appeal of strip patterns may also be tied to ancestral traditions recalled from Africa, where textiles are commonly woven in long narrow bands, cut into desired lengths, and sewn edge to edge to create a usable piece of cloth. The formal similarity between these African textiles and African American strip quilts is simply too close to dismiss as mere coincidence. That two distinct modes exist within the tradition of black quilting confirms the presence of what W. E. B. Du Bois described as a quintessential trait of black culture—a feature he called "two-ness." This useful and elegant term accurately describes the dual black-and-white sources of African American culture and their complex interaction.[31]

The intertwining of these two textile traditions over the span of the twentieth century has produced a hybrid style of African American quilting, marked by the fusion of an improvisational design approach with the vocabulary of Anglo-American motifs. Sometimes, the innovation will consist only of a change in scale—and a single log-cabin block, usually not larger than six inches on a side, will serve as the entire quilt top. In other instances, the rules for symmetry or clarity will be violated and a central medallion will be set slightly askew and hidden against a background of seeming clutter. The reinterpretations of standard forms are as numerous as the quilters who devise them. Although it is impossible to identify the specific time or place that this distinctive behavior originated, it was certainly a common African American practice by the 1940s. The *Double Wedding Ring Quilt* made by Anna Pennington Sampson, of Fulton, Arkansas, serves as a compelling example. It is readily apparent that Sampson was familiar with this standard pattern consisting of rows of intersecting rings, but it is equally clear she preferred not to pursue it completely. Her quilt is so dominated by large pieces of red cloth that the rings, which are thicker than one normally encounters, actually become secondary elements. In place of a ring pattern, one finds, perhaps, rows of what may be seen as large blinking or winking red eyes. It is not hard to detect the liberating effect of this quilt. Eli Leon reports that when a group of black women saw this quilt for the first time, "These five stately women, a moment before so sweet and serene, started to hoot and stomp until the house shook. The room became a stadium; the fans gone wild. It was an exhilarating experience."[32]

Such enthusiastic reactions guarantee that black improvisatory quilting will continue for some time.

Revivals, in spite of their encouraging rhetoric, are, ironically, symptoms of decline—programs of reform intended to rescue or restore a way of life that seems imperiled. Usually, a farsighted leader articulates a call to action to a small group of peers, and, together, they attempt to rouse the masses on behalf of their program. The benighted group is shown how to save itself, or, if it is too far gone, teachers and other experts are sent to help. Movements of this sort were being initiated in various places across the United States between 1920 and 1940. Nothing like this happened to African American artisans; there was no revival of their craft traditions, for, in the first half of the twentieth century, their traditions were still largely intact. During the era of craft revivals, African Americans were, for the most part, still a rural people who made daily use of woodworking, sewing, and other skills. Those with more specialized skills, like blacksmiths, chairmakers, and basketmakers, could have used some economic assistance when the Depression hit, yet no organized program designed expressly to help blacks was forthcoming.

The arts programs of the Harlem Renaissance, the most likely context for a revival of African American crafts in the 1920s, focused almost exclusively on the promotion of painting and sculpture. The same orientation was seen as well in the many WPA arts workshops that were developed for black communities and offered during the next decade.[33] Since black institutions of higher learning treated the crafts more like a system of penance than a valuable cultural legacy, they, too, were not destined to sponsor a significant crafts program.[34] But even without the advice of experts and institutional support, several black craft traditions managed to persist reasonably well. These examples of craft resurgence can be credited directly to the courage and perseverance of the artisans who remained confident of their received traditions. That confidence, when coupled with an adequate market, proved to be a feasible formula for craft continuity. The conditions for black artisans in the Charleston area, if not always the most favorable, at least turned out to be workable. In quilting, the most widespread African American craft tradition in the United States, one finds great continuity with historic precedents as well as exciting changes that constantly expanded the genre. Quilters experienced periods of upswing, but these were not really revivals, only the bursts of activity caused by artisans going into action to provide quilts when they were needed. During the era of revivals, African American crafts were able to survive on their own merits as they eluded the well-intentioned "therapy" of a craft revival recommended by outsiders.

The period between the world wars was a critical time for African American coiled-grass basketry. As agriculture declined and industrial opportunities generated by World War I lured hundreds of thousands of rural black southerners north, coiled basketry on the South Atlantic coast could have gone the way of gourd and earthenware vessels, wooden mortars and pestles, palmetto fans and thatching, oxcarts and sorghum mills. Indeed, of the two branches of lowcountry basketry, the bulrush workbasket, which was the men's branch of the tradition and once essential to rice production, almost did disappear. Sweetgrass basketmakers, on the other hand, were able to take advantage of a new market, increase their output, and expand their repertoire, allowing the women's branch of the tradition to flourish.

Both branches of coiled basketry had their champions. Progressive white educators at the Penn Normal, Industrial, and Agricultural School, on St. Helena Island, southeast of Beaufort, South Carolina, began in 1904 to promote bulrush basketmaking among black sea-island boys. Enrollment in Penn Normal's basketry department peaked before 1918, but the program remained an important part of the school's curriculum for another three decades. During these same years, in response to an increase in demand from retail merchants and tourists, sweetgrass basketmakers in the vicinity of Mt. Pleasant, across the Cooper River from Charleston, increased production of household "show" baskets, as their makers called them. Sweetgrass basketmaking took another crucial step forward in 1930 with the invention of the basket stand, and has gained further momentum since the 1960s—an indirect beneficiary of the national struggle for civil rights. Separated by some seventy-five miles, the two revivals developed independently, apparently unaware of each other. One was self-consciously conservationist—a school curriculum introduced by educators from outside the culture; the other was a spontaneous, community-based endeavor, highly adaptive and decidedly entrepreneurial.

## OLD-STYLE BASKETRY

"Native Island Basketry," as it was called in the curriculum of the Penn Normal, Industrial, and Agricultural School,[1] began as a manual-training program, reflecting ideas about the unity of art and labor that were at the root of the Arts and Crafts movement.[2] Instruction in basketry, carpentry, cobbling, harnessmaking, blacksmithing, and wheelwrighting was intended to provide hand-and-eye training[3] and to foster industry, precision, and persistence[4]—character traits critical to economic success. For administrators and teachers, coiled basketmaking had a cultural dimension as well: It connected sea islanders with their African past. "This industry," declared the school's *Annual Report* of 1910, "was brought from Africa in the early slave days" and belongs "as truly to the Negro as the Indian basket belongs to the Indian." Principal Rossa Belle Cooley wanted her school to do for African Americans what others were doing for Native American crafts.

The link with Africa was direct. Alfred Graham, Penn's first basketry instructor, had learned the craft from his African father. Graham, in turn, taught his

George Brown, instructor of native island basketry, Penn Normal, Industrial, and Agricultural School, St. Helena Island, South Carolina. Photograph by Leigh Richmond Miner

grandnephew George Brown, who ran the basket shop from 1916 until 1950. "This is the only real Negro craft inherited from African forefathers," the 1930 *Annual Report* asserted, "and is so beautiful it seems important to preserve it. These baskets were useful in the field in plantation days and have been adapted for home use." The basketmakers themselves valued baskets for their utility. To them, baskets were a "necessity for daily life," explained George Brown's son, Leroy Browne, who graduated from Penn Normal in 1934. "Every type of basket they made was a useful basket."[5]

Penn Normal's administrators offered to pay cash for baskets made at home, and sold them, along with products of the school's shop, through the mail and craft outlets in Charleston, Philadelphia, and Boston.[6] Basketmakers could use the income to pay their property taxes and hold onto their land. In some years, the school purchased more baskets than it sold, and business declined dramatically during World War I. By the early 1920s, the shop's enrollment had dropped by 50 percent. Yet, claimed the 1924 *Annual Report*, the demand for baskets "has been steadily increasing"—presumably among the northern philanthropists who supported Penn Normal and comprised the audience for the annual reports. Five Leigh Richmond Miner photographs of baskets, basketmaking, and the gathering of rush for the baskets graced the retrospective 1924 issue, and so did, for the first time, a price list for St. Helena baskets.

Penn Normal was not the only purveyor of bulrush workbaskets. In the early 1920s, one day each week, basketmakers from the islands southeast of Charleston debarked from thirty- and forty-foot picketboats at Adgers Wharf, bearing produce and oysters in jars to trade at an old, established firm called Hurkemps, and bulrush baskets for Nathan Yaschik, a new merchant in town. Twenty to thirty islanders arrived at 150 King Street. Yaschik, who had come to Charleston in 1913 and started in business pushing an ice cream cart, gave his suppliers credit slips or merchandise in exchange for baskets, and, twice a year, took his stock to sell wholesale at the Baltimore Bargain House.[7]

Basketmakers from islands farther south peddled their ware in Savannah and, later, from roadside vegetable stands.[8] Caesar Johnson, Hilton Head's best-known basketmaker, who was born in 1872, learned the craft as a small boy. Besides garden produce, he carried fish, oysters, strings of dried mullet, and bas-

Prize-basket display of a class taught by George Brown, Penn Normal, Industrial, and Agricultural School, St. Helena Island, South Carolina. Photograph by Leigh Richmond Miner

kets, too, for sale in the city. He remembered one basket customer in particular, the late Judge Gordon Saussy, who bought two of his big baskets to show his children how things used to be in "the old days gone by."[9]

At the northern end of what was once the Rice Kingdom, on Waccamaw Neck, in Georgetown County, bulrush baskets had likewise achieved the status of antiques among white people nostalgic for the old regime and souvenir hunters with money to spend. The Pawleys Island Hammock Shop, which opened in 1938, carried rush workbaskets made by Welcome Beese, who had been born into slavery on Oatland Plantation, in All Saints Parish. The shop's owner, "Doc" Lachicotte, also stocked Mt. Pleasant baskets. In the Hammock Shop's first sales brochure, he applauded the aesthetic innovations, "such as ingenious pine needle trim," of the sweetgrass forms, but he also promoted the rice fanner, or winnowing basket, for its sentimental value as a nearly lost art. He described Welcome Beese sitting in front of the shop, patiently weaving, and, no doubt, meditating upon these "changeful times."[10]

It is an irony of modern life that a traditional practice such as basketmaking tends to attract attention just as it is about to pass out of existence. Sea island baskets entered the iconography of the Harlem Renaissance through the work of a German American artist named Winold Reiss, best known today as illustrator of the movement's manifesto, *The New Negro*. In the fall of 1927, Reiss was invited by *Survey Graphic*, a social welfare journal aimed at a northern, reform-minded audience, to travel to South Carolina and draw portraits of the black sea-islanders.[11] In ten days, Reiss produced some sixteen portraits, among them romantic images in pastel of the young basketmakers.

Alfred Graham, the first basketmaking instructor at Penn Normal, Industrial, and Agricultural School; his wife, Susan, is sitting on the porch of their house, St. Helena Island, South Carolina, 1909. Photograph by Leigh Richmond Miner

Abraham Herriott pounding rice on Sandy
Island, South Carolina, c. 1930. Photograph
by Frank G. Tarbox

Other young basketmakers near Darien, Georgia, posed for Robert Winslow
Gordon, first director of the Archive of American Folk Song. Gordon photographed a basketry class supervised by one of his informants, Mary C. Mann, a
deaconess in the Episcopal Church, who ran a school that prepared young black
women for domestic service. In Gordon's photograph, she stands primly behind
her class of seven girls and one young boy as they sew baskets beneath a tree.[12]

Toward the end of the 1930s, fieldworkers for the Works Progress Administration (WPA) found a few old-timers still making baskets. On Waccamaw Neck,
Genevieve Chandler interviewed Welcome Beese.[13] Her colleague Bayard Wootten photographed Abraham Herriott on Sandy Island, pounding and winnowing
rice.[14] Wootten captured the transitional moment—when bulrush basketmaking
was in decline and sweetgrass in ascendancy—in a remarkable image that, unfortunately, was not included in her portrait of the city, *Charleston: Azaleas and Old
Bricks*.[15] Diffident yet proud, a black woman stands on a street corner holding a
cylindrical sweetgrass pocketbook over one arm and a sweetgrass sewing basket
in her hand; poised on the wall beside her is an enormous bulrush "head-tote"
basket overflowing with flowers and ferns, in its decorative reincarnation from a
workbasket.

Fieldworkers for the Savannah Unit of the Georgia Writers' Project, under the leadership of Mary Granger, set out with a definite mission in mind: to document African "survivals" along the Georgia coast. They interviewed several basketmakers, including John Haynes, near Old Fort in the northeastern section of Savannah, and Isaac Basden, of Harris Neck, a blind basketmaker, born in 1878, who made fanners and large, round baskets about twenty inches in diameter, with tightly fitting covers.[16]

Hard on the heels of Granger's troops, a young anthropologist named William Bascom, trained by Melville Herskovits at Northwestern University and fresh from a year studying Yoruba culture in Nigeria, drove to Savannah in May of 1939 to do a summer's research. In the course of his inquiries, he spent an afternoon with Isaac Basden, recording in detail how Basden learned the craft and noting his current prices—forty cents for a fanner, a dollar for a shallow basket, and a dollar fifty for a large one. On Sapelo Island, Bascom was told, fanners were still used to winnow rice, and people on the north end of St. Simon could make them as well. But the days of the rice fanner clearly were numbered. An informant in Savannah owned one that had been passed down in her family, and, Bascom tersely noted, she "doesn't want to sell it."[17] The old farm tool had become an heirloom.

Oddly enough, Bascom seems to have been unaware of the basket shop at Penn Normal; if he had known of the school's thirty-five year commitment to preserve native island basketry, surely he would have interviewed George Brown. Nor did he visit Mt. Pleasant, where a revival of the other branch of the low-country tradition had been under way for a generation.

## THE SWEETGRASS REVOLUTION

The same year, 1916, that Brown became an instructor of native island basketry at Penn Normal, basketmakers near Mt. Pleasant began what amounted to a revolution in form, function, materials, and, above all, the marketing of sweetgrass "show" baskets. The makers tended to be women, although men gathered materials and boys learned how to sew. Basket "sewers," as they call themselves (coiled basketry is sewn rather than woven), incorporated a new decorative feature—long-leaf pine needles overlaid on the sweetgrass to make bands of dark and light rows. Adapting traditional styles and inventing new ones, Mt. Pleasant sewers developed a large basketry repertoire designed to appeal to the middle-class housewife: bread trays, tablemats, flower and fruit baskets, shopping bags, hatbox baskets, missionary bags (round handbags said to be modeled on a form that Quakers used to carry their Bibles), wide-brimmed hats, clothes hampers, sewing, crochet, and knitting baskets, spittoon baskets, wall pockets, picnic baskets, thermos bottles or wine coolers, ring trays, cord baskets, cake baskets, wastepaper baskets, and wide, shallow trays still called by the old name, fanner.

The catalyst of the sweetgrass revolution was an enterprising engineer named Clarence Legerton, remembered by basketmakers today as "Mr. Lester" or "Mr. Leviston," who had come to Charleston to run his uncle's book and gift shop on King Street. About 1916, with European imports in short supply, Legerton began commissioning large quantities of Mt. Pleasant baskets, selling them wholesale through his Sea Grass Basket Company and retail from the shop.[18] Under Legerton's patronage, coiled-grass baskets became a viable cash crop in a cash-poor economy. People who had never made baskets before, or who used to make them but had stopped, were encouraged to learn from one of the "originals."[19]

The diffusion of skills radiated from the vicinity of Boone Hall Plantation, where black families still lived in brick cabins their ancestors had built in slavery.

Seagrassco Catalogue, Legerton & Co., Charleston, South Carolina. Collection Clifford Legerton

The center of sweetgrass basketmaking was Hamlin Beach, a settlement founded during Reconstruction, when property owners gave or sold small parcels of land to the Negro families who worked for them.[20] Sam Coakley, a patriarch of the Hamlin community and progenitor of many of today's sewers, took a leading role in negotiating the basket deal, relaying orders, and collecting the finished product for Legerton's inspection.[21] At first, Legerton bought between three and four thousand dollars' worth of baskets a year. In 1920, he changed the name of the company to Seagrassco and stepped up his advertising campaign. Although he purchased fewer baskets, he increased his markup to more than 90 percent and continued to turn a handsome profit.

Fifteen years after Legerton entered the picture, the sewers found a way to bypass middlemen and directly reach the market that drove past their doors every day—tourists traveling the coastal highway to Florida. By 1930, with the paving of Highway 17 and the completion of the Cooper River Bridge, basketmakers began setting out their baskets, on chairs or overturned boxes, on the side of the road. Soon, a distinctive structure evolved. It consisted of posts or saplings set upright in the ground with strips of scrap wood nailed horizontally between them, covered by a roof of burlap or tin. Nails served as pegs for hanging baskets. Behind the stands, sheds were hammered together and outfitted with stoves, beds, and chairs, to provide some comforts for the basket sellers. A few women turned their premises into "shops," where they displayed the work of several sewers.

As a stage in the marketing of baskets, the stands were a great advance. They allowed sewers to display their work with minimal overhead and, most important, to charge the retail price. "I set up a stand back when there were hardly any stands on the highway," recalled the late Irene Foreman. "Me and Hessie Huger set up a stand in 'Four-Mile.' [Settlements along Highway 17 North are named for their distance from Charleston.] Mr. Leviston paid twenty cents for a twelve-inch piece. If you sell them yourself, you can get double that, all of fifty and seventy-five cents for a basket."[22]

Basket stand near Mt. Pleasant, South Carolina, September 1938. Photograph by Bluford Muir

The stands also freed basketmakers from the constraints of commission work, which called for specific quantities of a limited number of styles. "You can make your basket the way you want and you can make them the price you want," said Evelyina Foreman, who, as a youngster, helped her mother fill orders for Legerton.[23] By 1949, thirty-one stands were counted along a two-mile stretch of road in the vicinity of Christ Church. "Gleaming" automobiles pulled in front of the makeshift structures, reported the *News and Courier*'s Jack Leland, appreciating the contrast. "Persons from the large and modern centers of this country's industrial areas" stopped to look at "an importation of the artistry of African workers."[24]

Times certainly had changed. In a few remote settlements, fanners still served their original function, but, by and large, coiled baskets had become commodities in a nonagricultural economy. The cash value of "old-style" basketry helped keep it in production, but the market for bulrush workbaskets remained, in William Bascom's words, "very very limited."[25] Isolated from the mainland and regular road traffic, sea islanders had no access to anything like the tourist trade Mt. Pleasant sewers could count on. Sweetgrass basketmakers also had other advantages. Finer and more flexible than bulrush, sweetgrass was adaptable to a wider range of forms and functions. Basketmakers could experiment with decorative elements and develop the aesthetic side of their tradition, breaking down the barriers between craft and art.

Sweetgrass basketmaking offered a group of African American women a way to earn money without bosses or middlemen, to exercise their imagination and judgment, and to work with family members in a collective enterprise.[26] Combining exceptional talents as artists and entrepreneurs, Mt. Pleasant sewers have been able to earn a small but significant income from their work. For more than seventy-five years, the sweetgrass basket has contributed materially and spiritually to the survival of the community. The basket has helped sustain a pattern of settlement in which relatives live in close proximity and skills pass naturally from mother to daughter. It has provided a way to support one's family and to affirm the faith of the grandparents "that God was never a minute late or a penny short."[27] "I know God does this," basketmaker Marie Rouse said in a recent interview. "There were fourteen of us. Time we made a basket, we could sell it and go to the store and buy some things. . . . It's a gift from the Lord."[28]

The hand production of baskets remained feasible because sewers did not expect more than a marginal income, and because there were few competing opportunities. It also survived because the basketmakers' mostly white clientele valued baskets, whether as utilitarian objects, souvenirs, or symbols, and wanted to buy them. Credit for the tradition's persistence rests chiefly with the sewers themselves and their ability to make a virtue of necessity. Twenty years ago, recognizing that the sweetgrass supply was diminishing as a consequence of coastal development, Mt. Pleasant sewers reached back into their tradition and rediscovered rush, using it in conjunction with sweetgrass to add strength and color to large sculptural forms. Today, the bulrush basket has been reborn.

# Ceramics: From Africa to America

## by Winifred Owens-Hart

The role played by African Americans in all of the crafts has been systematically misrepresented or underrepresented from the beginning, leaving a heritage vacuum for subsequent generations.[1] Recently, however, many historians, anthropologists, ethnologists, and artists have begun to take a new look at the material culture of African Americans and, in particular, at the ceramics they produced. As these artifacts are viewed with unbiased eyes, the African contribution begins to provide important keys to understanding the development of American cultural history. In documenting the story of American ceramics, art historians must wedge all of the contributions into the clay, to use a ceramics metaphor, in order to produce the true American vessel.

### FROM AFRICAN APPRENTICESHIP TO AMERICAN CAPTIVITY

The story of African American clayworkers and their ware begins in the pottery villages of Africa. The study of African ceramics has focused on the sculptural aspects of the medium—the magnificent Nigerian portrait heads in fired clay, for instance—rather than on the utilitarian forms. Very little attention has been paid to the fabrication of African pottery. It is through oral histories that we can examine the generational transfer of information via the apprenticeship system, which, historically, has produced utilitarian African ceramics.

For hundreds of years, the apprenticeship system has been the means by which information has been transferred from generation to generation. In ceramics, the art form was (and still is) usually passed within the family structure from father to son or mother to daughter, but, occasionally, children outside the family are brought to a master craftsperson who is paid a small fee to take on an apprentice.[2] This tradition is so old, it predates the diaspora of the slave trade. Of the thousands of Africans who did not perish during the Middle Passage, some undoubtedly were potters who lived to produce again on American soil.

Colonoware has been identified primarily in Virginia, South and North Carolina, and Georgia, but it is a general category of pottery made by indigenous peoples and Africans in the colonies. Leland Ferguson, the anthropologist, has defined Colonoware as "all low-fired, handbuilt pottery found on colonial sites, whether slave quarters, the 'big house,' or Indian villages."[3] Obviously, as Ferguson points out, shards and intact pottery found closest to slave quarters are more likely to have been made by African immigrants than any other examples of Colonoware. Basing his information on a Works Progress Administration (WPA) slave history of Shad Hall—whose grandmother Hester was carried to America at the end of the slave trade and who believed the pots he grew up with had been made in Africa—Ferguson concluded, "Of course, Shad Hall may have been mistaken in thinking that Hester's pots were brought from Africa. She may have made them years before he was born, on the Georgia coast. Whichever, Hester was one of the last of hundreds of thousands of African women who might have brought the skill of potting, if not whole pots, to their new American home."[4]

Traditional practices of African clayworkers extended beyond Colonoware, which tended toward the sparsest simplicity. Of the many potential carryovers,

Henry Letcher, c. 1937

114

glazed face jars[5] probably represent the last African American pottery that reflects visually unadulterated African imagery. Forced acculturation of Africans placed them as production potters in the developing ceramics cottage industry of the late nineteenth-century South. The two best-known instances occurred in Edgefield, South Carolina, and eastern Texas. Edgefield became known for its ash-glazed stoneware, and a slave named Dave became its most famous potter. Dave was "owned" by Dr. Abner Landrum,[6] a scientifically minded entrepreneur who established the stoneware pottery and published a newspaper. Landrum took the highly unusual, and risky, step of teaching Dave to read and write (something actually outlawed in many areas of the South). Dave threw some of the largest pots of the time. It has been boasted that the large pickle vessels he made were thrown with three hundred pounds of wet clay. He inscribed many of his vessels with rhymes, some alluding to his plight as a slave, such as, "Dave belongs to Mr. Miles/wher[e] the oven bakes & the pot biles."[7]

Dave the Potter. *Storage Jar (Great and Noble Jar).* May 13, 1859 (signed and dated). Stoneware, 29 x 26 x 26". Collection The Charleston Museum, South Carolina

Some of the nation's best alkaline- and salt-glazed pottery of the antebellum period was produced by African American slaves. After the Civil War, in Guadalupe, Texas, John Wilson set up a pottery in which his son-in-law and a number of slaves produced ceramic ware. The post-Emancipation Wilson ware was "characterized by salt and local slip glazes," according to Georgeanna Greer. "Ovoid in form, the storage jars had strong, well-defined cavetto rims, as well as lid ledges with the mouths quite different than those seen at the earlier pottery."[8] Wilson admitted at the time that he knew nothing about the manufacturing of ceramics when he began the business, and his master potter was apparently a slave. Many such instances occurred in which the slave was at least as knowledgeable as the proprietor. Constitutional Emancipation marked the beginning of the official entrepreneurship of African American ceramists, but, since three of John Wilson's former slaves took the name "H. Wilson and Company," their identities remained hidden.[9]

Dave the Potter. Storage jar with inscription, "Dave Belongs to Mr. Miles/wher[e] the oven bakes & the pot biles." Collection The Charleston Museum, South Carolina

## THE INVISIBLE AFRICAN AMERICAN CERAMISTS

"You are soon watching the bony, black hands knead the clay, then coax it into a stately two gallon jug," wrote Margaret Morley in *The Carolina Mountains.*"[10] Books on the history of American ceramics often include the potters of Jugtown, but they never mention the presence of any black potters. Rich Williams, however, was an African American who, like the other Jugtown potters, made his living wedging clay and turning pots in rural Carolina early in the twentieth century. He may not have been the only person of color working clay in the Carolina mountains when Margaret Morley made her study, but if there were others, they are not named by historians. Williams's marvelous stoneware jugs and storage jars are often alkaline-glazed brown with bluish tints. Morley describes him as being old in 1913, but Williams worked until the late 1920s and possibly into the 1930s. His ceramics are only now coming to light in private collections.

African Americans were invisible participators in just about every other aspect of American ceramics, including china painting, an art form long associated with women with considerable leisure time on their hands. Yet, it is far from likely that Rubie (Kesiah) Booker Lucas was the only black woman in Washington, D.C.—or the country—painting scenes and decorations on premade porcelain blanks (as they are termed) in the 1920s. In fact, it was recently discovered that she and her friends often gathered together to paint china in one another's homes, enjoying the talk as much as the activity.[11] When scholars do focus on this neglected art form, many more African American practitioners may be identified.

Rubie Lucas's gorgeous *Poppy Vase,* c. 1920, is slender at the bottom and rises

Rich Williams in the potter's shop.
Photograph by Margaret Morley

to a gentle, bulbous top. The shape of the vessel is accentuated by the large, blooming flowers she painted on the surface. How she learned to render imagery so realistically remains a mystery, although there is some indication that she may have acquired the technique of china painting at the Phyllis Wheatley YWCA, near her home, in Washington, D.C. The three-dimensionalization of the poppies is similar to that seen on Rookwood pottery. On a cocoa set, Lucas painted elaborate designs closer to the outlined floral imagery found on Pewabic ware. Like the rest of her lusterwork, a mint green and gold luster plate was fired in a kerosene-heated Revelation kiln installed in her living room. Despite the obvious love of her craft that such a risky undertaking indicates, Lucas gave up china painting to enter the workforce in the late 1920s. Her last, prizewinning pieces are dated 1925, according to her daughter, Helen Bright Lyles.[12]

Although far from color-blind, the WPA and other Depression-era government projects did give financial support to black artists as well as white. Often, like William E. Artis, they were also encouraged and supported by the Harmon Foundation, a philanthropic organization that, beginning in 1925, awarded prizes to black artists of merit and mounted exhibitions of their work that circulated throughout the United States. Artis had taken classes at the Art Students League

Rubie (Kesiah) Booker Lucas. *Cocoa Set.* c. 1925. Luster-painted ceramic. Collection Helen Bright Lyles

Sargent Johnson. *Teapot.* c. 1941. Ceramic. Collection The Oakland Museum, California. Gift of Dorothy Collins Gomez

and with Augusta Savage in her Savage School of Arts and Crafts, in Harlem, in 1932; later, he studied ceramics at Alfred University, in Alfred, New York. Better known as a sculptor, primarily of expressive busts in terra-cotta, he also made many hand-formed, glazed ceramic vessels in free-form modern styles.

Sargent Johnson, another often-exhibited artist active in the WPA and a recipient of the patronage of the Harmon Foundation, made figurative sculpture in lacquered wood or clay. In addition, he painted, enameled metal, and created sculptural ceramic abstractions. *Forever Free*, 1933, the wood sculpture that has helped sustain his reputation, was also executed in fired clay, glazed to approximate the sheen of the lacquered surface. Johnson was strongly affected by the ideas of the Harlem Renaissance; as a result, he studied African art as well as the art of his American forebears in the South. "The slogan for the Negro artist should be," he said, "'Go South, young man.'"[13] Johnson also made many trips to Mexico; that they influenced his pottery is evident in a 1941 teapot, in the collection of the Oakland Museum, with its stylized snake and animal motifs on the lid and handle.

Elmer Brown was a product of the WPA ceramics program in Cleveland, Ohio, headed by Edris Eckhardt from 1933 to 1941. For one of Eckhardt's projects, the illustration of famous American tales, Brown created *Rip Van Winkle*, a ceramic tableau depicting the game of ninepins. Brown had come to Cleveland in 1931 and studied at the East Side Settlement House (now Karamu House). He was a multifaceted artist—painting murals, acting in the Settlement House Theater Company with his friend Langston Hughes, as well as creating utilitarian ceramics.

Howard University, in Washington, D.C., was one of the few WPA locations for ceramic projects for "colored Americans,"[14] and Henry Letcher, a graduate of both Howard and Ohio State, was its ceramics instructor. A practicing ceramist, his beautiful, wheel-formed 1936 *Sgraffito Vase*, in the collection of the art gallery at Howard, has an opaque, sea-green slip glaze with sparingly applied dark blue on the abstract plant motif carved in relief around the sides. The university also has an unadorned, bluish-green glazed vase ending in a delicately thrown lip.

Not all ceramic artists benefited from or needed the support of the WPA. Isaac Hathaway, of Tuskegee Institute, in Alabama, and later, Joseph Gilliard, of Hampton Institute, in Virginia, developed two of the earliest ceramics programs in predominantly African American institutions during the 1940s. These men trained generations of ceramists practicing their art today.

Isaac Hathaway attended Alfred University to study ceramics, in 1919 and, again, in 1941. He was called the dean of Negro ceramics because of the ceramics departments he established at Tuskegee in 1937 and at Alabama Polytechnic, in Auburn, ten years later. A recognized sculptor, he designed numerous United States coins and created official portrait busts. Hathaway was active as a ceramist and teacher until the 1960s, but, unfortunately, his ceramic production has remained unavailable for study since his death.

Joseph Gilliard has retired from teaching at Howard University, where, for more than four decades, he exerted a profound influence on generations of young ceramists. Amazingly innovative in both aspects of ceramics—form and glaze—he invented a special wheel on which one could throw thirty- and forty-inch vases or storage jars. His alchemistic obsession with glazes and experimentation with radical temperatures produced some startling new effects, such as a gold-flecked glaze of unusual radiance. In the 1940s, he was casting organic forms and combining them in abstract configurations. Equally competent as a metalsmith, Gilliard combined lathe-turned metal units with ceramic forms in highly unusual ways.

Speaking in the metaphorical language of clay, one might say that African Americans, historically, have been the "grog" in the American ceramic body. Grog is hard-fired clay that has been crushed or ground into various size particles; it strengthens the clay body the way aggregate strengthens concrete, making it "stand up," as potters say. A weaker pot is produced when the grog is excluded. History's biased exclusion of an important part of the aggregate in American ceramics has weakened the national clay body. The recent practice of accurate inclusion—of "working in" or "wedging," in potter's terminology—of artists like Dave the Potter or Sargent Johnson can only strengthen the walls of our national vessel.

Ruth Clement was born into a highly accomplished family. Her father was a Methodist bishop who spoke out against racial discrimination; in 1946, her mother was the first African American to be named Mother of the Year. As an educator with a master's degree in English from Northwestern University, she has made a lifelong commitment to community service. In the early 1930s, she married J. Max Bond, Ph.D., who later became a college president, and together they raised a distinguished family of their own.[1] But in 1934, Max Bond was the top black administrator in the Tennessee Valley Authority (TVA), and, despite the couple's college credentials and background, being black meant living in segregated construction housing of the most rudimentary sort.[2]

The TVA had been established the year before to develop the water and land resources of the Tennessee River Valley. It was one of the first New Deal projects of the Roosevelt Administration and involved the construction of twenty-six major dams to prevent flooding, irrigate land, and generate electricity. Proud to be working on the TVA, the Bonds were determined to make their living quarters not only habitable but special; they tried to devise home furnishings particular to their new environment, for what Ruth now calls "TVA rooms." Max set aside time for his workers to build steps and make repairs, and they also made furniture from "trees that were cut right there on the compound." Ruth remembers that "the roughness of the branch and all was there. The chairs—one was a rocker—were made with the rough, unplaned limbs of the trees as they grew."[3] Everything in her own home, except for the bedsprings and mattresses, was created on-site. The rocker, straight chairs, tables, and bedsteads, which she helped design, were made of bent willow and pine logs.[4]

Ruth Bond soon started working with the women in their little colony, "showing them how to use the things at hand. . . . We made curtains for the windows out of flour sacks that we got from the man down at the bunkhouse, where he cooked for all the people. We made corn-shuck rugs and rag rugs. I redesigned some other things for them and made the patterns for the quilts. I did the designing on a big piece of brown paper, cut out the pattern, and picked the colors of the cloth, but it was the women themselves who did the quilting. Some of it was finer than others. A woman [Grace Reynolds Tyler] down in Chattanooga did the best work. She made the quilt that I consider *the* prize TVA quilt."[5]

The beautiful *TVA Quilt* that Grace Reynolds Tyler made from Ruth Clement Bond's pattern featured a full-length black silhouette of a man holding a lightning bolt in his upraised hands. Unfortunately, it has disappeared. But Bond designed a smaller *Black Power Quilt*, in which a black fist holding a thunderbolt fills the field below a radiant sun and the American flag.[6] We know of it from an appliqué version made by another woman on the TVA project, Rose Marie Thomas.

According to its designer, the full-figure *Black Power Quilt* represented the power that electricity was to bring into everyone's life, but very soon it became identified with the concept of Black Power itself. Bond recalled how this came about: "My husband had interns down there who came from all of the black universities in the area, like Fisk and some of the others. I think it was the first black

*9— Waiting for the Doctor. Baby Clinic.*

*Jane Emma Bond*

Ruth Clement Bond's daughter, Jane Emma Bond (standing third from left), with other TVA workers and families, waiting for the doctor at the baby clinic, established by J. Max Bond, at the TVA dam site, c. 1934. Photograph by Ruth Clement Bond

internship program they had in the South. They gave help anywhere they could to the people working on the dam—with their reading or whatever—and they worked, too, to build. I designed a quilt that I called the *TVA Quilt* because it was all about electricity. I put in the hand of this black figure a big bolt that was, to me, power, but not physical power, like knocking people down; it was about bringing the power, electric power, to the area. And these young fellows said, 'Oh! *Black Power*,' and they seized upon that. I've been told by several who were there that that's where the term *Black Power* came from. It became so popular, meaning that the blacks were coming into power; but that's not what I meant at all."

Bond's comments to Merikay Waldvogel about the abbreviated, black-fist version of the *Black Power Quilt*, however, indicate that the young men were not far off in their interpretation of its meaning: "We were pushing up through obstacles—through objections. We were coming up out of the Depression, and we were going to live a better life through *our* efforts. The opposition wasn't going to stop us."[7]

Traveling to nearby construction villages to meet with the women, Bond organized about five groups, some at the dam as well as others in the small towns near her in Alabama. "They weren't industrialized," she recalled, "but they quilted beautifully. They knew how to crochet, to knit, and to make corn-shuck and braided rugs. We dyed the sacks we got from the cook and made rugs. I was teaching them color and design, and sometimes we'd read.[8] Some of them used magazines and mail-order catalogues to paper their walls. We were trying to bring something—a little harmony or beauty—into the home that wasn't there. I was just helping extend their own interests and widen their horizons—trying to make

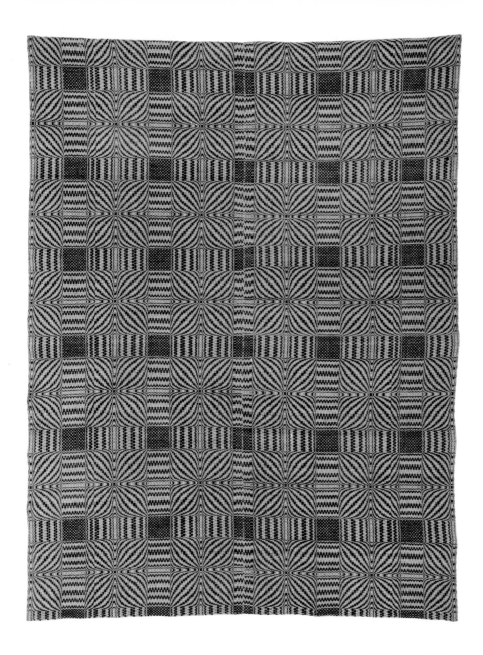

Winogene Redding. *"Blooming Leaf" Pattern Coverlet.* 1932. Wool, cotton, 85 x 60".
Collection Arrowcraft Shop, Gatlinburg, Tennessee

as the looms and materials with which to weave, she established Allanstand Cottage Industries in 1897, at a small crossroads called Allanstand. In 1908, she opened a retail shop in Asheville that operated independently until 1932, when ownership was transferred to the Southern Highland Handicraft Guild.

### Berea College

About the time Goodrich found her inspiration, William G. Frost, president of Berea College, in Kentucky, had a similar experience upon seeing the homespun bedcoverings in his students' homes.[9] He recognized the value of the coverlets as both a means to advance outside interest in the school and to use as gifts for the school's northern patrons.

Berea College was a Christian school for Appalachian youth, who worked in the Berea College Student Industries in lieu of paying full tuition. This was a practical solution aimed at helping the Appalachian people, but it also reflected the same philosophy toward the value of handwork as that of the mission schools.

Berea became an important center for the craft revival. In 1911, Frost invited a Swedish weaver, Anna Ernberg, who taught weaving in New York City, to head the school's Fireside Industries. There, she developed a new, smaller loom that was easy to transport, and brought her own sensibilities to bear on the

Penland Handicrafts. *Plate with Etched Pine Branch*. c. 1940. Copper, ½ x 12 x 12". Collection Jan Brooks Lloyd

weavers' designs. Frost, like Goodrich, encouraged both tradition and change. They were forming a new tradition—one shaped by the external influences of the marketplace rather than the internal influences of a closed community.

By 1920, there were one hundred and fifty mission schools in the mountains.[10] Some were more influential in the craft revival than others, and they soon became associated with one particular craft. In Kentucky, the Hindman Settlement School became known for basketry, and Pine Mountain Settlement School for quilts. The Berry Schools, in Georgia, became known for weaving, and Pleasant Hill Academy, in Tennessee, for woodcarving.

## THE DEVELOPMENT OF CRAFT SCHOOLS

Out of the reform movement, three craft schools grew, adapted, and survived: Arrowmont School of Arts and Crafts, in Tennessee, and Penland School of Crafts and the John C. Campbell Folk School, in North Carolina.

### Arrowmont

In Tennessee, Gatlinburg became the chosen site of the settlement school sponsored by the Pi Beta Phi sorority of Swarthmore College, Pennsylvania. At the time, it was considered the largest altruistic project of any fraternity or sorority in the United States. The organizers were influenced by the weaving and basketry at Allanstand. In 1925, the school's director hired Winogene Redding, of Massachusetts, to head the weaving industry. Redding not only embodied social-reform goals in her thinking but also heralded the beginning of the new era, wherein marketing and consumer education were paramount concerns: "We want those who buy our weaving to realize that they are not buying just an article, but that they are supplying some woman with contentment and perhaps food."[11] She recruited from within the community, and in a year's time, thirty weavers were working in their homes. Introducing her own designs and patterns, she shepherded the process and the final products in the same way that Goodrich and Ernberg had done.

Arrow Craft Shop (later, Arrowcraft) was established in 1926, on the school grounds, as a separate marketing entity. Items were made for a tourist market, and a mail-order catalogue was produced in the 1930s. By 1945, 242 women had woven for Arrowcraft. That same year, the University of Tennessee organized its first Summer Craft Workshop at the Pi Beta Phi School. Out of this workshop program grew the Arrowmont School of Arts and Crafts, which, to this day, offers workshops and exhibition opportunities for contemporary craftspeople.

Penland Weavers. *Wall Hanging.* c. 1930. Linen, wool, 57 x 32½". Collection Berea College Appalachian Museum, Kentucky

### Penland

Although the social-reform movement in the Appalachians was shaped primarily by women for women, there were men other than William Frost who played important parts. The Reverend Rufus Morgan, a native North Carolinian, returned after seminary school to establish the Appalachian Industrial School for men, women, and children, at Penland, under the auspices of the Episcopal Church.

His sister, Lucy Morgan, joined him in 1920 to teach and to help revive mountain weaving, a goal he had set for the school. Having learned to weave at Berea College, Lucy Morgan procured the looms designed by Anna Ernberg. By 1924, she had established a thriving cottage industry, marketing the items at resorts and fairs; the Episcopal Church, as well, supported the efforts through purchases. The need for a central location where weavers could share ideas and patterns, and plan marketing strategy, led to the construction, on school property, of the Weaving Cabin in 1926. Pottery and, later, metalwork were added and, in 1928, Lucy Morgan's craft industry became the Penland Weavers and Potters. A *Table Runner*, c. 1930, is woven with a summer-winter weave that makes the back pattern the reverse of the front, and features the Pine Tree, a common Penland design motif. At the time the runner was made, it sold for ten dollars.[12] The pewter and copper pieces are also typical of the Penland Weavers and Potters' designs.

Penland School of Handicrafts (later, Penland School of Crafts) grew out of the summer Weaving Institute that began in 1928 when Edward Worst, of Chicago, author of *Foot-Power Loom Weaving*, came at the invitation of Lucy Morgan to instruct the weavers. Worst later invited Swedish weaver and loom designer Margaret Bergman. During the 1930s and 1940s, other crafts found their way into the curriculum: jewelrymaking, metalwork in pewter and copper, lapidary, block printing, and even shoemaking. Lucy Morgan's extraordinary efforts, and her ability to garner support from both inside and outside the community, resulted in a craft school that, by the 1950s, attracted students and faculty from all over the world. Her belief in the spiritual and therapeutic value of craft were manifest in the leadership of Bill Brown, her handpicked successor in the 1960s. Brown, a sculptor and graduate of Cranbrook Academy of Fine Arts, married the tradition of mountain crafts to the academic world of fine arts, while adhering to the basic philosophies established during the craft revival.

### John C. Campbell Folk School

The third important revival center was the John C. Campbell Folk School, founded in 1925. Campbell was the director of the Southern Highlands Division of the Russell Sage Foundation, which supported many of the reform efforts in the

Wool processes: spinning wool and winding skeins. Photograph by Olive Dame Campbell

Southern Highlands. After Campbell's death, in 1919, his widow, Olive Dame Campbell, made a tour of successful Scandinavian folk schools that had found solutions to the problems of the disintegration of rural life. She chose to model the school, which bore her husband's name, along the lines of Danish schools, even adding such cultural accoutrements as Danish songs and dances.[13]

The school was dedicated to preserving rural life and trying to keep young people from migrating to the cities. Carving, which was first taught by Muriel Martin, became the hallmark activity of the school, but standardization rather than individual expression was emphasized. Blocks of wood were provided, and ideas, like patterns, were offered by the instructor. Some carvers, such as Jack Hall, distinguished themselves, however, through special skills or aesthetic eccentricity. The Brasstown Carvers grew out of the program and continues to work in cooperation with the school.

## ARTS AND CRAFTS IDEALS

Many of the goals of the early mission schools remained intact, but the craft revival of the 1920s and 1930s found its voice more through the ideals of the Arts and Crafts movement than Christian rhetoric. Although the movement did not manifest itself in the style of objects of the Southern Appalachians, its ideas fueled this revival. The heart of the revival was weaving, in itself a reflection of John Ruskin's ideals. He had urged women to weave and spin in order to strengthen moral values and deflect the dehumanizing effects of the industrial revolution. The influence is clear in the idealistic and high moral tone used by Frances Louisa Goodrich, Winogene Redding, Olive Dame Campbell, Lucy Morgan, Rufus Morgan, and Allen Eaton.

Eaton, of the Russell Sage Foundation, was brought to the Highlands after a chance meeting with Olive Dame Campbell. His participation in the craft revival proved long and significant, and his 1937 book *Handicrafts of the Southern Highlands* remains the only compendium of schools, craftspeople, and objects of the Southern Appalachians.

For Eaton and others, the Arts and Crafts ideal was tied to the belief that rural life and the "idealized peasant" were the healthy alternative to oppressive city life.[14] Eaton believed that the split-oak baskets, walnut rockers, coverlets, quilts, and other handmade objects were imbued with a mission. Appalachian crafts, in their simplicity of form and function and their use of natural, indigenous materials, were perfect symbols of untouched American culture, the virtues of usefulness coupled with beauty and the rejection of mass production. They established the identity of the craftsperson as independent and self-sufficient and, therefore, unquestionably free.

## FROM MISSION TO MARKET

In the late 1920s, the nature of the craft revival began to change: The focus shifted emphatically from social-reform work to cottage industries. Out of the mission schools and fireside industries grew many independent, self-supporting craft industries that had diversified to include baskets, pewter- and copperwork, brooms, dolls, toys, furniture, and quilts. Among them were the Spinning Wheel, organized by Clementine Douglas, and Biltmore Industries, established by Mrs. George Vanderbilt, in Asheville, North Carolina; the Churchill Weavers, established by Carroll and Eleanor Churchill in Berea, Kentucky; and the Tryon Toymakers, established by Eleanor Vance and Charlotte Yale, in Tryon, North Carolina.[15]

## The Southern Highland Handicraft Guild

Sparked by an address that Allen Eaton gave in 1926 at the annual conference of Southern Mountain Workers, in Knoxville, Tennessee, many of the independent craft industries formed a cooperative coalition. Representatives of eleven groups met at the Weaving Cabin, at Penland, in 1928, and, by 1930, the Southern Highland Handicraft Guild was formed.[16] Two years later, the membership consisted of twenty-five centers, including representation from the Cherokee Indians.

The promotion and marketing of craft were the dual goals. As the guild grew more powerful, it set standards and influenced products and design. It also recognized the importance of adapting the mountain crafts to the consumer: "The handwoven articles reached the city markets, lovely of quality and make, but out-of-date as to style. City women would look over the wares offered in mountain craft shops and bazaars and sigh regretfully that they were of last season's mode."[17]

At a 1935 meeting of the Southern Highland Handicraft Guild, it was announced that several experts from New York would be coming to advise on style and marketing. The two experts were Ruth Reeves, recognized at that time as the dean of textile designers, and Dorothy Carmer, who was to advise on production and sales.

The shops, the marketplace, the Southern Highland Handicraft Guild, and the tourist industry all contributed to the transformation of craft. Historically made for use in the home or for barter among neighbors, crafts became a thriving industry, responsive to the desires of outsiders. Basketmakers who, traditionally, had made split-oak or willow baskets to carry eggs or gather berries now made magazine holders as well. Weavers made placemats in addition to coverlets. Pewterwork met the needs of Depression-era consumers who could not afford silver.[18] The dulcimer became the emblem of mountain music, replacing the fiddle and the banjo, which were far more typical and preferred by Appalachian musicians. Consumers preferred the delicate sound and implied-Medieval ancestry of the dulcimer to the twang and whine of less romantic instruments.

During this period, crafts were hybrids of both past and future, often embodying conflicting attributes. They were authentic as well as affected. They were conceived within a barter system and matured within a market system. They were silent in terms of authorship, yet uniquely individual.

## FROM ANONYMITY TO CELEBRITY

With the influence of the marketplace came the concept of the individual maker. Earlier, makers eschewed individuality. The creation of baskets, furniture, and woven goods following a prescribed tradition was one means by which both the community and the family maintained their identity and continuity. Unique vision in the making of objects was coincidental and secondary.[19]

A quilt by Beulah Marshall, for example, reflects the interest in the Colonial revival apparent in many quilts of the 1920s and 1930s, and it is also an extraordinary example of individual expression. "I'm an artist with a needle," said the maker.[20] But this piece and other quilts, baskets, brooms, chairs, and iron tools were not made as a part of any organized effort, nor were they noted or singled out during this period. Many of the surviving objects from the Southern Highlands are by unknown makers.

Even at the beginning, as publicity came to the makers, individuals remained indistinguishable from the group. The objects offered were identified, for instance, only as items by the Penland Weavers, the Spinning Wheel, or the Tryon Toymakers. In the exhibition catalogue of the Southern Highland Handicraft

Shadrach Mace. *Chair*. c. 1930. Oak, 35¼ x
20 x 16". Collection Robert Brunk

Guild show, circulated by the American Federation of Arts in 1933, there is an
odd mix of attributions—some to individual makers and some to the umbrella
group under which the maker worked. The names themselves vary from credit to
credit and are difficult to recover. Often, such colloquialisms as "Granny" and
"Aunt," used as terms of respect and affection in the mountains, obscured the
actual first names.

As the revival progressed and personal expression and experimentation were
encouraged, individual craftspersons began to gain recognition. Writers and
newspaper reporters, chroniclers like Eaton and photographers like Doris
Ulmann, accentuated individual makers and gave them heroic status. Craftspeople became characters in a story, and their words part of the narrative. We know
the stories and lives of people like Shadrach Mace, the Woody brothers, Aunt
Cord (Cordelia) Ritchie, and Granny (Kate Clayton) Donaldson because of the
attention bestowed upon them by the organizers of the craft revival.

Toward the end of this era, the craftsperson gained recognition in one of two
ways—through exceptional workmanship in a traditional manner or through
innovative expression. Shadrach Mace, for instance, continued to construct chairs
in the tradition of his pre–Civil War forefathers. Function was the primary aesthetic criterion in the chairs of Mace, who said, "If you want your company to stay,
get yourself a settin' chair. If you want 'em to leave in a hurry, get yourself one of
the ladderbacks."[21]

Daniel Boone, VI, like Mace, was not making wrought iron because of any
revival movement but was part of a long line of smiths dating back to pre-
Revolutionary days. He worked primarily as a functional blacksmith until 1926,
when he was hired to work on the Williamsburg restoration. The expanding market and interest in craft created a large clientele for Boone and his student Bea
Hensley, who still makes the same fireplace sets today that he did in the 1940s.[22]

Craftsmanship also eclipsed individual expression in the chairs of the Woody
brothers; beauty derived from a strict adherence to pride in workmanship. The
Shakerlike philosophy of this family is expressed in the words of Arval Woody,
quoting his grandfather, Arthur: "He always said a man should put his best into
every chair as if it was the last one he'd ever make and would have to answer for
it the rest of his life."[23]

Others broke from tradition in surprising and delightful ways. Aunt Cord
Ritchie, who married the founder of the Hindman Settlement School, was known
for her traditional willow baskets, but she exercised an uncommon surge of individualism in her *Dream Basket*. The name itself implies a willingness to imagine
and to loose the object from its purely functional past. With her usual materials—
willow dyed with the red brown from the inner bark of the spruce tree—Aunt
Cord Ritchie created the *Dream Basket*, with three spiral handles, and said it was
"just made up."[24]

Granny Donaldson created scarves and other functional pieces at the request
of Louise Pittman, the business manager of the John C. Campbell Folk School.
Like Ritchie, Donaldson felt free to imagine. At the age of ninety, she denied any
outside connection to the Italian cow blankets that were presumed to be her inspiration: "I didn't have no pattern or nothin' to go by. Just imagined 'em." Her real
inspiration was a baby blanket left in her house by a neighbor.[25] Like Ritchie, Donaldson began to see the possibility of making something that had no specific function. She decided to make a piece the size of a baby blanket to hang on the wall.
Pittman "took a fit over it," she said, and encouraged her to make the cow blankets that subsequently were sold all over the world.[26] The spirit of the artist is in
the work of these makers. They began within the confines of an ordered tradition,
but, swept up in the vitality of the revival movement, they found their individual

voices.

People such as Ralph Morgan, who learned to make pewterware at Penland, foreshadowed the contemporary craftsperson working alone for financial return. Morgan made pewter at home for sale to individuals and wholesalers. One summer, he rented a building by the side of the road and set up shop, thereby partially supporting himself as he worked his way through medical school. Eventually, he established the Riverwood Pewter Shop, in Dillsboro, North Carolina, which is still in operation.[27]

Tom Brown, who learned carving at the Pleasant Hill Academy, in Tennessee, established himself with a narrative and figurative style that was notably similar to that of Thomas Hart Benton. Brown (whose larger sculptural pieces were never shown in the South) used his carvings to support himself while he studied sculpture at the Art Institute of Chicago; the Corcoran School of Art, in Washington, D.C.; and the Rinehart School of Sculpture, in Baltimore.[28]

Rude Osolnik and his wife, Daphne, who were both at Berea College—she as a student, he as a teacher—stood squarely at the juncture where tradition collided with change. When Rude began to apply the tenets of good design and individual expression to the age-old craft of woodturning, he helped to transform that field forever. His turned bowl from the mid-1940s is a prime example of the direction this craft was to take in the following decade. Daphne, whose bold wool blanket was similar to those made through Berea's student industries, was a producing craftsperson. Along with Rude, she became instrumental in the development of the Southern Highland Handicraft Guild.

## SOUTHERN POTTERY

The shift from utility to nonutility, from barter to marketplace, and from community to individual is particularly evident in the evolution of pottery in the region. The folk pottery of the South, although not connected to the mission schools or the reform movement in the mountains, was definitely part of the transformation that took place during the revival period.

Most of the pottery activity in the South was concentrated in North Carolina. The majority of the potters were clustered in the Catawba Valley and Piedmont areas, and they can be distinguished by the shapes and glazes of their pots. For example, alkaline glazes were characteristic of such Catawba Valley potters as the Reinhardts and Burlon Craig. Salt glazes were predominant in the work of the Craven family and, later, Ben Owen, at Jugtown.

The relationship between craft and available material is apparent in their work. North Carolina offered a wealth of varied and excellent clays, perfect for the production of stoneware and earthenware. As potter Enoch Reinhardt said, "It looked good enough to eat when you took it out."[29] The potters also found lime and wood ash for flux, and sand, flint, and iron slag for glazes. These resources dictated distinctive colors and textures, while the needs of the neighbors dictated style and function.

Charles Zug, an authority on southern pottery, describes the years from 1900 to 1940 as an era of decline and transition. Need for the pottery, and, therefore, the demand for it, was undermined by the mass production of cheap glass and metal containers, the growth of large dairies and markets, improved methods of transportation and refrigeration, and Prohibition. But the tourist trade in North Carolina, as well as the active intervention of people from outside the area, created a shift once again from a closed system of exchange to a market-driven industry. Potters began to make "fancy wares," which were decorative in nature rather than functional, and began to experiment with glazes, shapes, and technology.[30]

The Catawba Valley potters, holding closely to traditional forms and glazes, continued to produce utilitarian, alkaline pottery in at least thirteen shops throughout the 1920s and 1930s.[31] Some potters achieved a mastery of their craft, and their individual hands became easily recognized. Burlon Craig still makes pottery in the Catawba Valley, in the tradition of his earliest predecessors. He is known for the beauty of his glazes, made from wood ashes and glass ground from soda bottles and glass containers saved for him by his friends.[32] Craig made only a few face jugs—the comically ugly visages now associated with this group of potters—until the 1970s, when the tourist trade demanded increased production. Like Mace and the Woodys, he is the master of a singular tradition that makes function the preeminent concern.

The Reinhardt Brothers, Enoch and Harvey, traditional turners in the Catawba Valley, were exceptionally skilled potters. They distinguished themselves by making functional ware, such as storage jars, and also by mastering swirl technique, which combines two colors of clay turned together, as seen in their *Teapot and Cover*.[33] The Hilton Pottery; Oscar L. Bachelder, at his Omar Khayyam Pottery; and Walter B. Stephen, at his Pisgah Forest Pottery, placed great value on innovation, which makes their work unique and easily distinguishable. This group of potters, along with the Busbees, in Jugtown, was primarily responsible for transforming North Carolina pottery from the more common utilitarian ware to art ware.[34] The Hilton Pottery was notable not only for its colorful glazes and the use of deep cobalt blue on the edges of the ware but also for the liberties taken in surface decoration, such as painted scenery or the application of designs in relief.

Oscar L. Bachelder clearly represents the shift from production pottery to art pottery. Bachelder was a visionary, a self-taught philosopher who spent forty years as a journeyman potter working in twenty-eight different states. In his late fifties, he came to North Carolina and set up his own pottery with the help of his friend Robert Gudger. There, he made a line of production pottery, but always with a mind toward the creation of what he called "art goods." "I longed to shape vases in all the lovely forms that flitted through my brain."[35] And so he did, at the shop that he eventually named the Omar Khayyam Pottery. His work is distinguished by its sensitive and elegant forms and by rich surfaces, devoid of decoration. Most notable is his use of a mirror-black glaze of his own making.[36]

Stephen perfected an exquisite crystalline glaze that even Bachelder, his friend, could not imitate. He was known throughout the United States for his distinctive, if somewhat quirky, cameo ware, which he claimed had been developed by his mother at the Stephens' pottery, in Tennessee.[37] Using porcelain slips to create the designs, he employed popular iconography depicting a not-so-distant pioneer past.

The American themes in the work of Stephen and his contemporaries paralleled the search for a true American art reflected in much of the painting and sculpture of the 1930s and 1940s. For example, the wagon-train imagery—seen also in work from the Spinning Wheel weavers, in Asheville—has become trivialized over time and associated with the West; however, it is directly referential to the early settlement of the Southern Highlands and to the trade routes that subsequently ended the isolation.

Jacques Busbee [James Littlejohn] and Julianna Busbee, of Raleigh, built the Jugtown Pottery, in Moore County, in 1922, enlisting Charlie Teague and Ben Owen, two of the local potters. Aware of the wishes and demands of their market, the Busbees suggested that Owen and Teague look to Oriental cultures and traditions for their forms and glazes. As Julianna Busbee put it, "This was an injection of art into the country potter."[38] The Cole Pottery, Royal Crown Pottery, Auman Pottery, Log Cabin Pottery, and Pine State Pottery were among the many successful ones that flourished in this period, when handmade ware boasting a traditional heritage also met the stylistic demands of the day.

## THE IMPACT OF THE CRAFT REVIVAL IN THE SOUTHERN HIGHLANDS

The period between 1920 and 1945 was a time of tremendous change for crafts in the southern mountain regions. Both the objects and the craftspeople were part of a movement that had its basis in social reform, found voice and meaning in the Arts and Craft ideology, and, ultimately, was shaped by a successful marketing effort. Craft was rooted in romantic and sometimes naive idealism, and then transformed by a peculiarly savvy understanding of twentieth-century consumerism.

Critics of the reform movement revivals, such as David Whisnant, cite the naïveté of its leaders and their inability to halt the brutal encroachment of the coal and timber industries or to keep intact the colonial traditions; nor were they able to prevent children from leaving their mountain home. Despite Whisnant's assessment, they did, however, establish a series of thriving cottage industries that provided economic relief for mountain women, and, more significantly, they created a social network, keeping in place a sense of community.

Two forces operated in tandem in the Southern Appalachians between the two world wars: the preservation of tradition and the rejection of tradition. Lucy Morgan's Penland Weavers was using its newfound income to buy false teeth.[39] Meanwhile, not more than one hundred miles away, at Black Mountain College, Anni Albers was transplanting the theories of the Bauhaus and vehemently rejecting traditional weaving materials and techniques.

Nevertheless, Penland School, Arrowmont School, and the hundreds of craft organizations and individual studios that thrive today in the Southern Appalachian region arose directly out of the missionary schools—often still existing on the same grounds. The values of the early reformers have also been carried forward, even though most of the craftspeople who espouse them are unaware of their origins. Many influences have come to bear on the field of contemporary craft, but the legacy of this period continues to shape craft in the second half of the twentieth century.

# AFRICAN-AMERICAN
# TRADITIONS

*Opposite:*
Amalia Lowery Holmes
*Strip Quilt.* c. 1927
Cotton, 76½ x 69"
Collection Lizetta LeFalle-Collins and Willie R. Collins

Susan Pless
*Strip Quilt.* c. 1940s
Cloth, 86 x 81"
Collection Eli Leon

Wini Austin
*Log Cabin Quilt Top.* c. 1920–30
Cotton, 76 x 85"
Collection Robert Cargo Folk Art Gallery

Anna Mae Grace
*Pig in the Pen/Spiderweb Strip Quilt.* c. 1943
Cloth, 91 x 74″
Collection Eli Leon

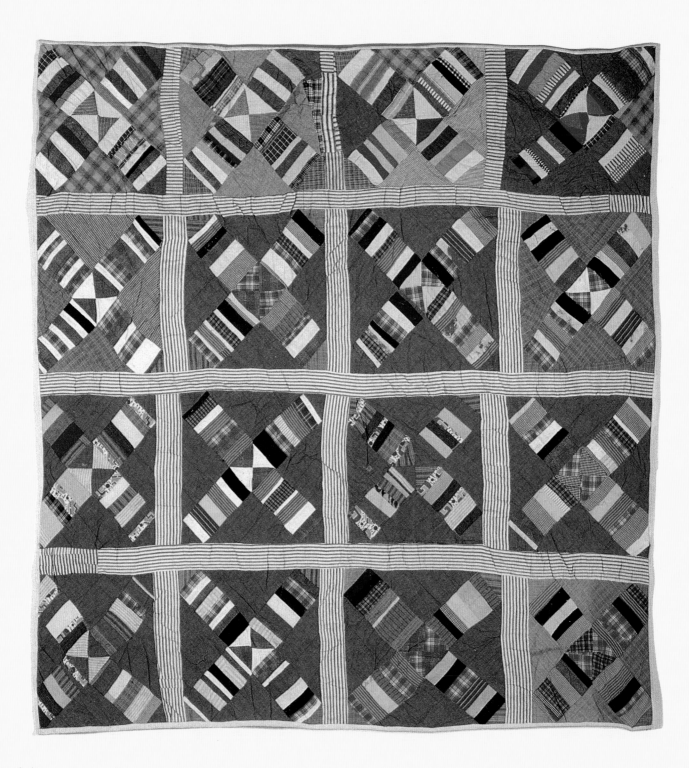

Peaches
*Spider Legs Variation Quilt.* c. 1930–40
Cotton, 77 x 72″
Collection Robert Cargo Folk Art Gallery

ennington Sampson
*Wedding Ring Quilt*. c. 1940s
7½ x 82½"
on Eli Leon

Rose Phillips Thomas
*Tennessee Valley Authority "Lazy Man"*
*Appliqué Quilt.* 1934
Designed by Ruth Clement Bond
Cotton, 85¾ x 70"
Collection Ruth Clement Bond

Rose Phillips Thomas
*Tennessee Valley Authority Appliqué*
*Quilt Design of a Black Fist.* 1934
Designed by Ruth Clement Bond
Cotton, 11¼ x 13"
Collection Rose Phillips Thomas

*Opposite:*
Rose Phillips Thomas
*Tennessee Valley Authority Appliqué*
*Quilt Design of Man with Crane.* 1934
Designed by Ruth Clement Bond
Cotton, 13⅝ x 17¼"
Collection Rose Phillips Thomas

Anonymous
*Sea Island Basket.* c. 1930s
Rush, 4¾ x 17¼ x 17¾"
Phoebe Hearst Museum of Anthropology,
University of California, Berkeley

Caesar Johnson
*Hilton Head Basket.* c. 1930
Rush, palmetto butt, 11 x 14 x 14"
Collection South Carolina State Museum

Welcome Beese
*Waccamaw River Rice Fanner Basket.* c. 1935
Rush, oak splints, 4⅝ x 20½ x 20½"
Collection Alberta Lachicotte Quattlebaum

George W. Brown
*St. Helena Island Sewing Basket with Lid.*
1940
Bulrush, palmetto, 4½ x 8 x 8"
Collection Leroy E. Browne, Sr.

Anonymous
*Cross-handled Basket.* c. 1930
Sweetgrass, pine needles, palmetto leaf,
10½ x 9 x 9″
Collection Harriet Clarkson Gaillard

Anonymous
*Cradle-shaped Field Basket.* c. 1920s
Rush, palmetto butt, 7 x 25¼ x 16¼″
Collection Edisto Island Historic Preservation
Society, South Carolina

Anonymous
*Mt. Pleasant Sewing Basket with Lid.* c. 1920
Coiled sweetgrass, palmetto butt, cloth,
Confederate bill, 3⅞ x 7½ x 7½"
Collection Edisto Island Historic Preservation
Society, South Carolina

Sorena Jefferson Linnen
*Covered Sewing Basket.* 1929
Sweetgrass, palmetto leaf, pine needles,
2½ x 3½ x 5½"
Collection M. Jeannette Lee

Maggie Mazyck
*Sewing Basket with Contents.* c. 1930
Coiled sweetgrass, palmetto leaf, 6 x 10¼ x 10¼"
Collection Mrs. Jervey D. Royall

*Below:*
Anonymous
*Covered Basket.* c. 1920s
Sweetgrass, palmetto cane, 2¾ x 5⅛ x 5⅛"
Collection The Charleston Museum, South Carolina

Ellis Wilson
*Dish*. c. 1940s
Pottery, diameter: 7⅛″
Collection Howard University
Gallery of Art, Washington, D.C.

Rubie (Kesiah) Booker Lucas
*Green Luster Plate*. October 1921
Ceramic, 1¹⁵⁄₁₆ x 8⅝ x 8⅝″
Collection Helen Bright Lyles

Rubie (Kesiah) Booker Lucas
*Poppy Vase.* c. 1920
Ceramic, 9⅞ x 3½ x 3½″
Collection Helen Bright Lyles

Henry Letcher

Henry Letcher
*Blue Vase.* 1934
Ceramic, 8¼ x 4 x 4"
Collection Howard University Gallery of Art, Washington, D.C.

Rich Williams
*Storage Jar.* c. 1930s
Stoneware, 14⅝ x 36 x 36"
Collection Mr. and Mrs. Gary S. Thompson, Jr.

Rich Williams
*Decorated Storage Jar.* c. 1930s
Stoneware, 13¼ x 33 x 33"
Collection Mr. and Mrs. Gary S. Thompson, Jr.

William E. Artis
*Bowl.* c. 1945
Ceramic, 4¾ x 7 x 7"
Collection Howard University Gallery of Art,
Washington, D.C.

*Below:*
William E. Artis
*Dish.* c. 1945
Ceramic, 11⅝ x 9⅛"
Collection Howard University Gallery of Art,
Washington, D.C.

*Opposite:*
William E. Artis
*Dish.* c. 1945
Ceramic, 8 x 5¼"
Collection Howard University Gallery of Art,
Washington, D.C.

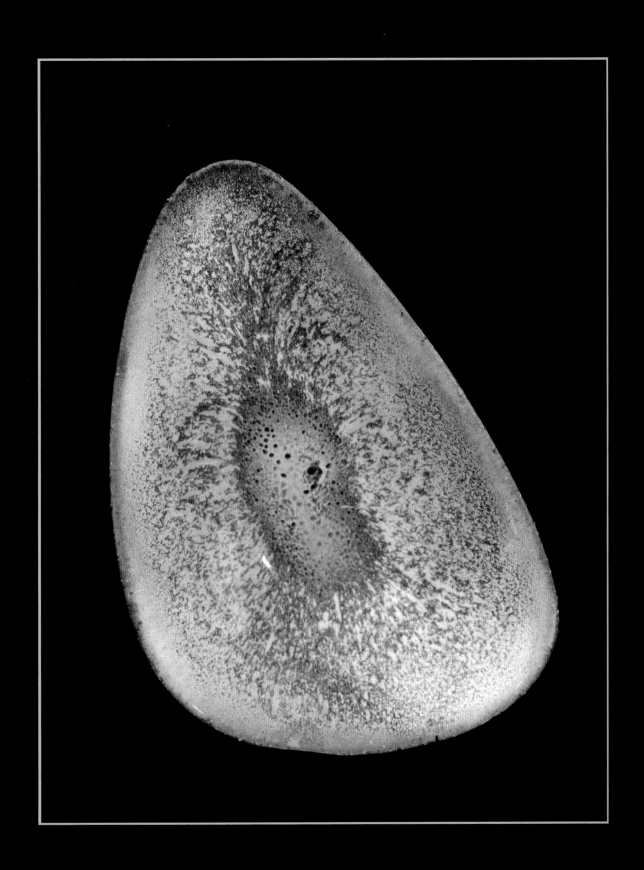

Ned Cheadham
*Table.* c. 1910–30
Painted mixed hardwood, 29½ x 22 x 22″
Private collection

Anonymous
*Gullah Cane.* c. 1939
Wood, length: 34″
Phoebe Hearst Museum of Anthropology, University
of California, Berkeley. Bascom Collection

152

## APPALACHIAN

Walter Benjamin Stephen
*Vase.* c. 1930
Porcelain, crystalline glaze, 11¼ x 6″
Collection Southern Highland Handicraft
Guild. Folk Art Center, Asheville,
North Carolina

*Opposite:*
Walter Benjamin Stephen
*Cameo Vase.* 1944
Pisgah Forest Pottery
Stoneware, cobalt-blue glaze band, 13¾ x 5½ x 5½″
Collection Mint Museum of Art, Charlotte, North Carolina.
Gift of Dr. and Mrs. Arthur Mourot

Ruffin Cole
*Jug with Wooden Stopper.* c. 1935–40
Salt-glazed stoneware, wood, 19¼ x 11″
Collection Mint Museum of Art, Charlotte,
North Carolina. Gift of Mint Museum Auxiliary
and Daisy Wade Bridges

Attributed to Benjamin Wade Owen
*Four-Handled Dragon Vase*. c. 1940s
Jugtown Pottery
Red stoneware, Chinese blue glaze, 14 x 5 x 5″
Collection Milton Bloch and Mary Karen Vellines

Benjamin Wade Owen
*Pair of Candlesticks*. c. 1922
Jugtown Pottery
Stoneware, cobalt-blue decoration, 11¼ x 5⅓″
Collection Mint Museum of Art, Charlotte, North Carolina.
Gift of Mint Museum Auxiliary and Daisy Wade Bridges

Ernest Auburn Hilton
*Vase.* c. 1935
Earthenware, glass glaze, 4 x 6 x 6″
Collection Mint Museum of Art, Charlotte,
North Carolina. Gift of Daisy Wade Bridges

Enoch William
Alexander Reinhardt
*Teapot and Cover.* c. 1935
Stoneware, 6½ x 3½ x 3½″
Collection Mint Museum of
Art, Charlotte, North Carolina.
Gift of Mint Museum Auxiliary
and Daisy Wade Bridges

161

Charles C. Cole
*Garden Urn.* c. 1940
Earthenware, 15¾ x 12⅛″
Collection Mint Museum of Art,
Charlotte, North Carolina.
Gift of Mint Museum Auxiliary
and Daisy Wade Bridges

Oscar L. Bachelder
*Pitcher.* c. 1928
Stoneware, Albany-slip glaze, 11¼ x 7¾ x 6⅓″
Collection Mint Museum of Art, Charlotte, North Carolina.
Museum Purchase

Burlon B. Craig
*Voo Doo Jug.* c. 1935–40
Stoneware, alkaline glaze, porcelain teeth, 19 x 12″
Collection Mint Museum of Art, Charlotte, North Carolina.
Gift of Mint Museum Auxiliary and Daisy Wade Bridges

Anonymous
*Egg Basket*. c. 1940–50
Oak splint, 14½ x 18 x 15½″
Collection Robert S. Brunk

Mary Prater
*Oak Splint Basket*. c. 1930–40
Oak splint, 8 x 9 x 8¼″
Collection Robert S. Brunk

Margaret Carson Revis
*Corn-shuck Dolls.* c. 1920
Corn shucks, corn silk, ink; female figure: 10½ x 3 x 2″; male figure: 12 x 3 x 3″
Collection Southern Highland Handicraft Guild. Folk Art Center, Asheville, North Carolina

Cordelia Everidge ("Aunt Cord") Ritchie
*Dream Basket*. c. 1920. Willow, 8 x 13"
Collection Southern Highland Handicraft
Guild. Folk Art Center, Asheville,
North Carolina

Rowena Bradley
*Cherokee Basket*. c. 1940–50
River cane, walnut dye, 11 x 11"
Collection Robert S. Brunk

Cherokee
*Storage Basket.* c. 1920–40
River cane, walnut, bloodroot dyes, 11 x 21 x 21″
Collection Robert S. Brunk

Kate Clayton ("Granny") Donaldson
*Mountain Cow Blanket.* c. 1930–35
Vegetable-dyed wool, cotton, 34 x 33″
Collection Berea College Appalachian Museum, Kentucky

Kate Clayton ("Granny") Donaldson
*Cow Blanket.* c. 1930
Vegetable-dyed wool, cotton, 48 x 36″
Collection Southern Highland Handicraft Guild. Folk Art Center,
Asheville, North Carolina

Anonymous
*Coverlet, Overshot Variation of Sunrise.* c. 1940
Wool and cotton, 106 x 77"
Collection Southern Highland Handicraft Guild. Folk Art Center, Asheville, North Carolina

Beulah Watkins Marshall
*Washington's Plume Quilt.* 1931–35
Cotton, 72 x 74″
Collection Mable M. Westbrook

Churchill Weavers
*Cloth 65, Kashan Stole.* 1931
Wool, 35 x 85"
Collection Churchill Weavers

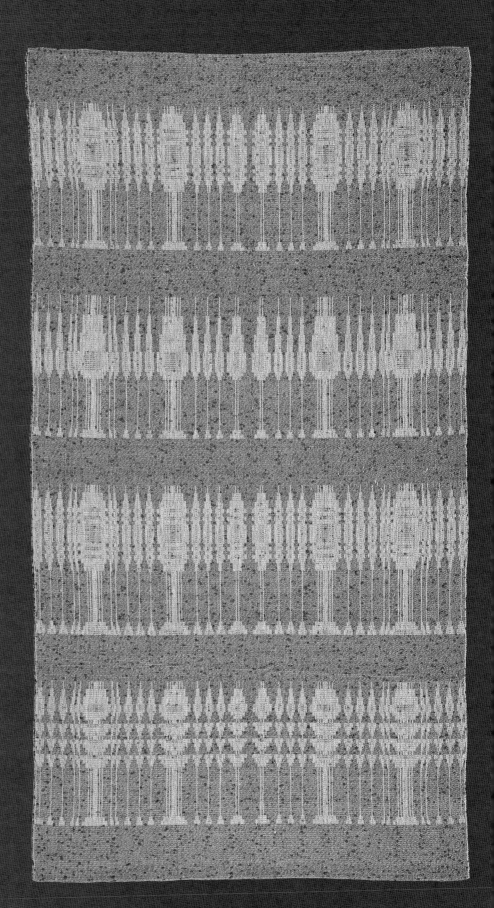

Penland Weavers
*Table Runner.* c. 1930s
Wool, cotton, summer-winter weave, Pine Tree
pattern, 31 x 60"
Collection Berea College Appalachian Museum,
Kentucky

Margaret Bergman
*"Constellation" Tablecloth.* c. 1937
Cotton, 35 x 37½"
Collection Nordic Heritage Museum, Seattle

Shadrach Mace
*Ladder-back Chair.* c. 1940–50
Walnut, 45¼ x 17½ x 14¼"
Collection Robert S. Brunk

Arval Woody
*Dining Chair.* c. 1930
Walnut, 32 x 17 x 13½"
Collection Arval Woody

Anonymous
*"Love Seat."* c. 1930s
Wood, woven corn shuck, 38 x 37½ x 17″
Collection Susan Morgan Leveille

Penland Weavers and Potters
*Pewter Plate with Etched Floral Design.* c. 1935
Pewter, 1 x 9⁷⁄₈ x 9⁷⁄₈"
Collection Jan Brooks Loyd

Ralph Siler Morgan II
*Shallow Bowl.* c. 1930
Pewter, 1¹⁄₂ x 12 x 12"
Collection Ralph Siler Morgan II

Daniel Boone, VI
*Fireplace Set.* c. mid–1940s
Iron, screen: 28 x 32″; holder: 38 x 14″;
shovel length: 30″; andirons: 20 x 13″ each
Collection Mrs. Frances R. Stroup

Tryon Toymakers
*Carved Gothic Bench.* c. 1936
Walnut, 17 x 20 x 9½″
Collection Robert S. Brunk

Tom Brown
*Cow and Calf*. c. 1940
Carved walnut, 6 x 6 x 3¼″
Collection Southern Highland Handicraft Guild.
Folk Art Center, Asheville, North Carolina

W. J. Martin
*Carved Turkey*. c. 1930
Wood, 5½ x 1½ x 4″
Collection John C. Campbell Folk School,
Brasstown, North Carolina

Park Fisher
*Dulcimer*. 1933
Cherry wood, 36¾ x 2⅛″
Collection University of Kentucky Libraries, John
Jacob Niles Collection

Rude Osolnik
*Turned Bowl*. c. 1940
Walnut, 2½ x 19 x 18″
Collection Rude Osolnik

Wallace Nutting
*Ballfoot Chest of Drawers.* c. 1917–36
Walnut, pine, brass, 42 x 39¼ x 19¼"
Collection Gordon William Gray

Wallace Nutting
*Carver Armchair*. c. 1917–36
Maple, rush, 47 x 24¼ x 18″
Collection Gordon William Gray

Oneidacraft
*Bombé Secretary with Bust
of Lord Howe.* c. 1926
W. and J. Sloane
Wood, 98 x 46 x 25″
Collection New York State
Historical Association

Wallace Nutting
*Queen Anne Daybed.* c. 1917–36
Mahogany, rush, 39¾ x 25 x 75½"
Collection Gordon William Gray

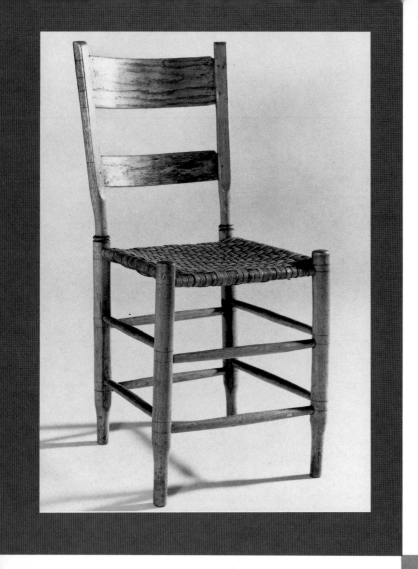

Samuel Isaac Godlove
*Godlove Chair.* c. 1937
Maple, hickory, 33 x 16 x 13″
Collection Jeanne S. Rymer

*Above right:*
Val-Kill Shop
*Ladder-back Chair.* c. 1930
Wood, 44¼ x 22 x 16½″
Collection National Park Service/Roosevelt-Vanderbilt
National Historic Sites

Mountaineer Craftsmen's
Cooperative Association
*Sewing Rocking Chair.* c. 1937
Maple, hickory, rush, 38 x 18 x 34″
Collection Jeanne S. Rymer

Virginia Craftsmen, Inc.
*Pennsylvania Windsor Chair.* c. 1930
Wood, 48 x 36 x 30"
Collection Yale University Art Gallery,
New Haven

Danersk
*Joint Stool.* c. 1930
Oak, 19 x 19 x 13"
Collection Sterling Memorial Library,
Yale University, New Haven

WPA Glass Factory, Vineland, New Jersey
*Pitcher.* c. 1940–42
Glass, 7⅝ x 6 x 6″
Collection Newark Museum, New Jersey.
Gift of the WPA Art Project, 1943

Clevenger Brothers
*Lilypad Pitcher.* 1939
Glass, 9⅝ x 6 x 6″
Collection Museum of American Glass,
Wheaton Village, New Jersey

WPA Glass Factory, Vineland, New Jersey
*Amethyst Vase.* c. 1940–42
Glass, 16 x 4¾ x 4¾"
Collection Newark Museum, New Jersey.
Gift of the WPA Art Project, 1943

Timberline
*Balcony Writing-Table Chair.* 1937
Wood, 29½ x 29¾ x 23⅛″
Collection Friends of Timberline

*Balcony Writing Table.* 1937
Wood, 40¼ x 35¼ x 29½″
Collection Friends of Timberline

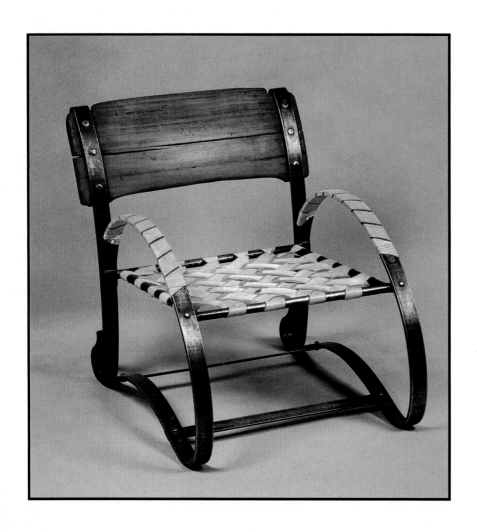

Timberline
*Lounge Chair.* 1937
Iron, rawhide, 30¾ x 25 x 32½″
Collection Friends of Timberline

Isaac Stahl
*Plate.* September 9, 1940
Clay, 1⅝ x 8⅛ x 8⅛"
Collection Lester P. Breininger, Jr.

Mildred D. Keyser
*Wedding Plate.* 1938
Red clay, 2½ x 14 x 14"
Collection Mrs. Rosemary
Keyser Wood

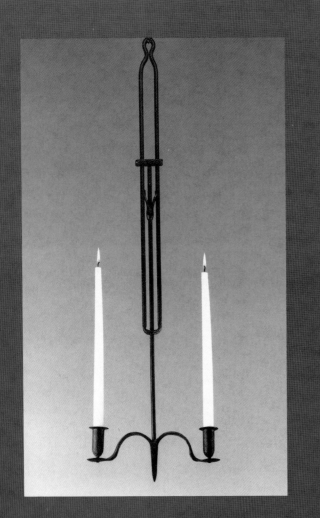

Abram Van Kleeck
*Door Knocker*. c. 1928
Wrought iron, 5 x 4⅝ x 4″
Collection E. Ronald and Shirley Rifenberg

Wallace Nutting and Edward Guy
*Chandelier*. c. 1920. Wrought iron, 46½ x 11½ x 1¼″
Collection Gordon William Gray

Abram Van Kleeck
*Thumb Latch*. c. 1928
Wrought iron, 14⅜ x 3¼ x 4″
Collection E. Ronald and Shirley Rifenberg

Samuel Yellin
*Andirons*. c. 1920s
Wrought iron and brass; each: 29 x 17 x 20″
Collection Metropolitan Museum of Art, New York.
Friends of the American Wing Fund, 1992

George C. Gebelein
*Inkstand.* c. 1930
Silver, 7⅞ x 10³⁄₁₆ x 10³⁄₁₆″
Collection Yale University Art Gallery,
New Haven. Gift of Mrs. Edwina
Mead Gagge

Val-Kill Industries
*Porringer with Decorative Handle.* c. 1930
Pewter, 1¼ x 4 x 4″
Collection Franklin D. Roosevelt Library
Gift of Mrs. Robert Abelow

Lester Howard Vaughan
*Inkstand.* c. 1930
Pewter, ceramic, 4 x 3¼ x 3¼″
Collection National Park Service/Roosevelt-Vanderbilt
Historic Sites

Lester Howard Vaughan
*Pitcher*. c. 1930. Pewter, 6¹/₁₆ x 7⅞ x 5⅛"
Collection Yale University Art Gallery,
New Haven. Marie Antoinette Slade
Fund

Herbert Taylor
*Tankard*. 1927
Silver, 7 x 8 x 8"
Collection Berkeley College,
Yale University, New Haven

Lester Howard Vaughan
*Cream or Mayonnaise Set.* c. 1927
Pewter, bowl: 7⅛ x 4¹¹/₁₆"; ladle: 4⅝ x 5⅝"
Collection Yale University Art Gallery, New Haven. Gift of Mr. and Mrs. W. Scott Braznell

Max Rieg
*Bowl.* c. 1937–50. Pewter, 2½ x 10½ x 10½"
Collection Yale University Art Gallery, New Haven. Gift of Mr. and Mrs. W. Scott Braznell (1983.27)

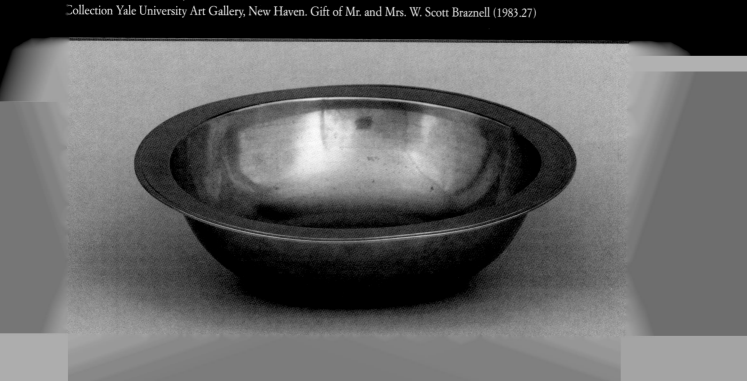

George C. Gebelein
*Coffee and Tea Service*. 1929
Silver, coffeepot: 8¼ x 9½"; teakettle: 12¼ x 9"; teapot: 8¼ x 9½"
Courtesy Museum of Fine Arts, Boston. Anonymous Gift

Herman Glendenning
*Sugar Bowl and Creamer*.
1927 and 1928
Arthur J. Stone Associates
Sterling silver, ivory, sugar
bowl: 6¹/₁₆ x 3¹/₁₆ x 4¾; creamer:
4⅛ x 2⁷/₁₆ x 2⅞"
Collection Yale University Art
Gallery, New Haven. Bequest
of Peter J. Meyer

Edward Billings
*Connecticut Tercentenary Bowl.* 1936
Arthur J. Stone Associates
Silver, 4¼ x 10½ x 10½"
Collection Mr. and Mrs. Thomas C. Babbitt

*Below:*
Arthur Stone
*Small Bowl.* c. 1920–30
Silver, 2¼ x 4 x 4"
Collection Berkeley College,
Yale University, New Haven

Edith K. Roosevelt
*Sampler*. 1925
Cloth, 20¼ x 16¾"
Sagamore Hill National Historic Site, National Park Service

Great Mother, let me once be able
To have a Garden, House, and Stable,
That I may read, and ride, and plant,
Superior to desire, or want;
And as health fails, and years increase,
Sit down, and think, and die in peace.
Matthew Prior

So she (Mercy) said within her self, If my neighbor will needs be gone, I will go a little way with her and help her.
Saint Elizabeth.

A large upper Chamber whose window opened toward the Sun-Rising: the name of the Chamber was PEACE.

Bunyan
A Shep. herd of Souls.

The Mill will never grind with the water that has passed.

Bunyan

1920

Mary Saltonstall Parker

Armistice

VICTORY

Mary Saltonstall Parker
*Sampler.* 1920
Cotton embroidery on linen, 20 x 27"
Collection Peabody Essex Museum, Salem, Massachusetts

Native Market
*Painted Chest with Stand.* c. 1930s
Pine chest: 14 x 29 x 13¾";
stand: 10½ x 35¼ x 17¼"
Collection Mrs. Y. A. Paloheimo

Native Market
*Storage Chest.* c. 1930s
Pine, 15¾ x 33⅞ x 15⅜"
Collection Mrs. Y. A. Paloheimo

Domingo Tejeda
*Trastero.* c. 1937
Wood, straw, iron, 66½ x 42 x 15"
Collection Roswell Museum and Art Center

José Dolores López. *High Chair*. 1920s
Juniper and pine, 23 x 10 x 10¼". Spanish Colonial Arts Society, Inc., Collection on loan
to Museum of New Mexico, Museum of International Folk Art, Santa Fe

Native Market
*Table.* c. 1930s
Pine, 28¾ x 35⅞ x 47⅝″
Collection Mrs. Y. A. Paloheimo

Native Market
*Chair.* c. 1930s
Pine, wool, 34 x 24 x 26″
Collection Mrs. Y. A. Paloheimo

George Segura
*Chair.* c. 1936–40
Pine, 40 x 22 x 19″
Collection Albuquerque
Little Theater

201

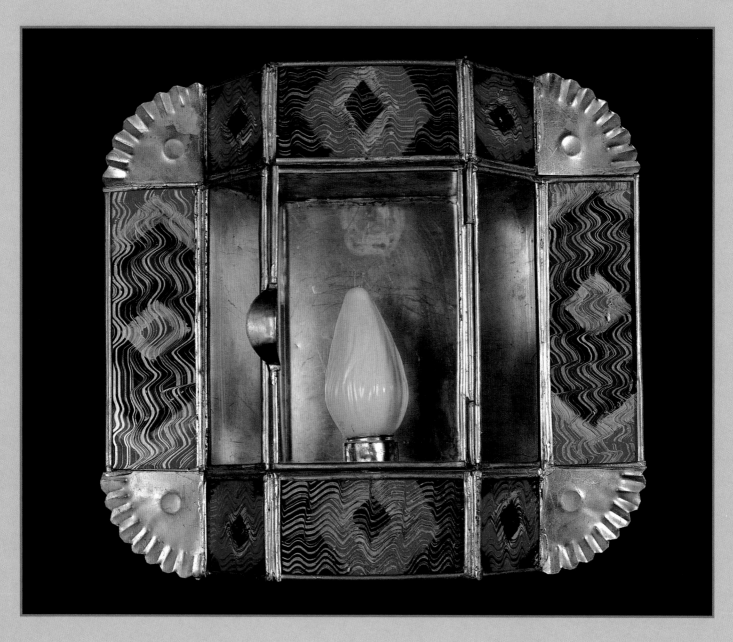

Pedro Quintana
*Tin Nicho*. c. 1935
Terneplate, reverse painted glass, 10½ x 12 x 4″
Collection Lane Coulter

Francisco Sandoval
*Lantern*. c. 1930
Tin, glass, 17 x 5 x 4½″
Collection Museum of New Mexico, Museum of
International Folk Art, Santa Fe

Native Market
*Candlesticks*. c. 1930s
Iron, 11 x 4 x 4″
Collection Mrs. Y. A. Paloheimo

Tillie Gabaldon Stark
*Colcha Pillow.* c. 1936–38
Cotton, wool, 14¼ x 18″
Collection Mrs. Y. A. Paloheimo

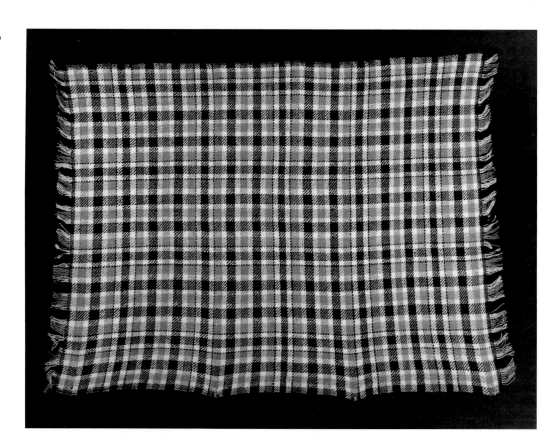

Crisostoma Luna
*Jerga Shawl.* c. 1938
Wool, 39 x 57″
Collection Lane Coulter

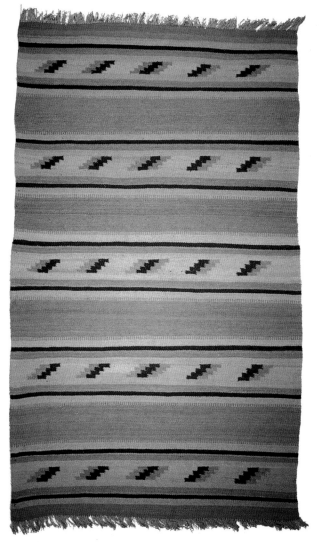

Anonymous. *Carson Colcha Embroidery*. c. 1930s.
Wool, 82 x 52″
Gift of Historical Society of New Mexico to Museum
of New Mexico, Museum of International Folk Art,
Santa Fe

Crisostoma Luna
*Rio Grande Revival Blanket*. c. 1938–39
Wool, 70 x 42″
Collection Colorado Springs Fine Arts Center

School of Notre Dame
*Baby's Receiving Blanket*. 1935
Irish linen, pulled thread edging, 42 x 42″
Collection Teresa Rodón de Comas

Anonymous
*Bobbin Lace Bedspread*.
1934
Cotton (Japanese thread),
170 x 71″
Collection Rosalina Brau
Echeandia

Anonymous
*Lace Insert*.
c. 1938–40
Cotton thread,
3 x 265″
Collection Rosalina
Brau Echeandia

Anonymous
*Girl's Blouse*. c. 1920
Battenburg lace, length: 20″
Collection Teresa Rodón de Comas

Encarnacion Ubarri
*Wedding Bedspread*. 1922
Linen, cotton (Japanese thread), 84 x 83″
Collection Rosalina Brau Echeandia

José María Apodaca
*Box.* c. 1930. Tin, glass, wallpaper, 6 x 9 x 6½″
Spanish Colonial Arts Society, Inc., Collection on loan to Museum of New Mexico, Museum of International Folk Art, Santa Fe

Celso Gallegos
*San Gorge Relief Carving.* c. 1920–30
Pine, 9 x 11½ x ¾"
Spanish Colonial Arts Society, Inc., Collection on loan to Museum of New Mexico,

Patrocinio Barela
*Anuncio del Nacimiento.* 1936–39
Juniper, 15 x 6 x 3″
Collection Colorado Springs Fine Arts Center

Celso Gallegos
*Holy Family Relief Carving.* c. 1920–30
Wood, 13¾ x 6¼ x 2¾″
Ann and Alan Vedder Collection of the Spanish Colonial Arts Society, Inc., Museum of
New Mexico, Museum of International Folk Art, Santa Fe

Federal Art Project. *Straw Appliqué Wood Niche with Santo.* c. 1930. Straw, wood, 10⅛ x 5½ x 4½"
Collection Museum of New Mexico, Museum of International Folk Art, Santa Fe

Sam Matta
*Crucifix.* c. 1930s
Carved stone, 13 x 9 x 8"
Caddy Wells Bequest to Museum of New
Mexico, Museum of International Folk Art,
Santa Fe

José Dolores López
*Straw Appliqué Cross.* c. 1920s
Straw, wood, 11½ x 5¾ x 3"
Spanish Colonial Arts Society, Inc., Collection on loan to Museum of New Mexico,
Museum of International Folk Art, Santa Fe

Juan Sanchez
*Retablo, Santa Librado.* c. 1930s
Gesso and water-soluble paint on wood, 9 x 7½"
Gift of Historical Society of New Mexico to Museum of New Mexico,
Museum of International Folk Art, Santa Fe

Susie Poweshiek
Mesquakie *Skirt*. c. 1930
Wool, ribbon appliqué, silk; length: 36″ Collection Vivian Torrence

Ojibwa. *Jingle Dress.* c. 1930s. Cotton, ribbon, metal jingles, skirt length: 30¼"; blouse length: 22"
Collection A. M. Chisholm Museum, Duluth, Minnesota

*Opposite:*
Sioux
*Man's Necklace.* c. 1920
Otter fur, leather, quills, brass tacks, ribbon,
tin cones, feathers, mirrors, 48 x 22″
Collection The Denver Art Museum

Sioux
*Woman's Breastplate.*
c. 1930
Rawhide, quills, glass and brass
beads, leather, tin cones, 39 x 11″
Collection The Denver Art
Museum

Ojibwa
*Minnesota Vest.* c. 1940
Glass beads, cotton thread, 22 x 23 x 6″
Collection James Economos

Rose Spring
Iroquois
*Beaded Skirt* (detail). 1937
Wool, silk ribbon, glass beads, 34½ x 64″
Collection Rochester Museum & Science Center, New York

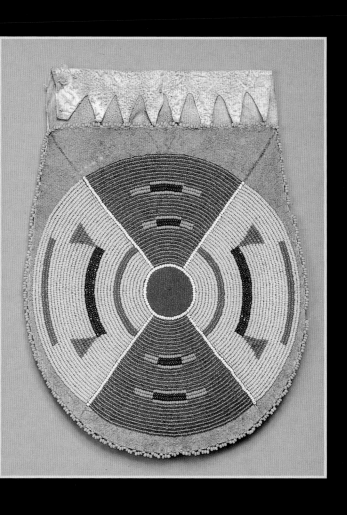

Crow
*Purse*. c. 1920–40
Leather, beads, 8 x 8"
Collection The Denver Art Museum

Ojibwa
*Bandolier Bag*. 1931
Beaded velveteen, 43 x 16"
Collection Sherman Holbert

Juanita Tucker
Assiniboin
*Commemorative Dolls (Blackfeet style): "Two Guns White Calf and His Wife."* c. 1941
Leather, beads, height: 12″ each
Collection The Science Museum of Minnesota. On loan from Northwest Area Foundation

Navajo
*Girl's Dress and Blouse with Jewelry.* c. 1930
Rayon, velveteen, silver, turquoise, dress length:
14″; blouse length: 8″
Collection Michael Walsh

Arnold Sundown
Iroquois
*Circular Silver Brooch*. 1940
Silver, diameter: 2³⁄₄″
Collection Rochester Museum & Science
Center, New York

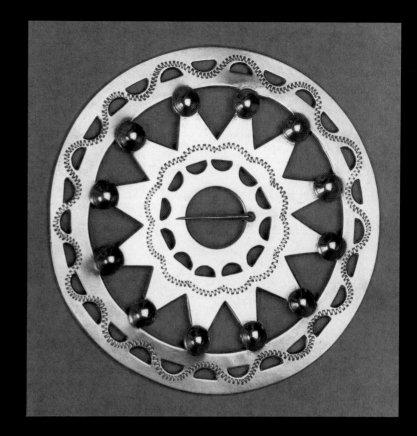

Navajo
*Concha Belt*. c. 1920s. Silver, turquoise,
leather, 3 ¹⁄₄ x 39 ¹⁄₄″. Collection Museum of
Indian Arts and Culture/Laboratory of
Anthropology, Museum of New Mexico,
Santa Fe

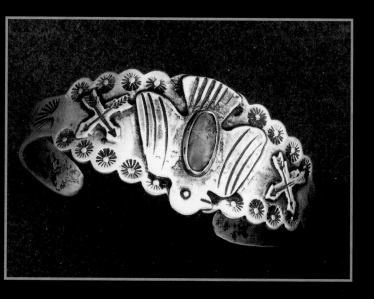

Navajo
*Bracelet.* c. 1920
Silver, ¹⁵/₁₆ x 2½"
Collection Museum of Indian Arts and Culture/Laboratory of Anthropology, Museum of New Mexico, Santa Fe

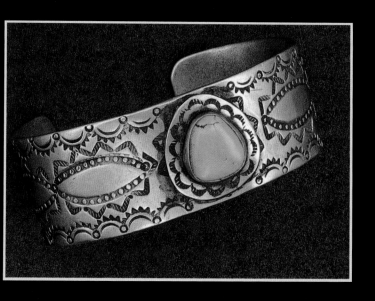

Navajo
*Revival-Style Bracelet.* c. 1930
Sheet silver, 1 x 2½"
Collection Museum of Indian Arts and Culture/Laboratory of Anthropology, Museum of New Mexico, Santa Fe

223

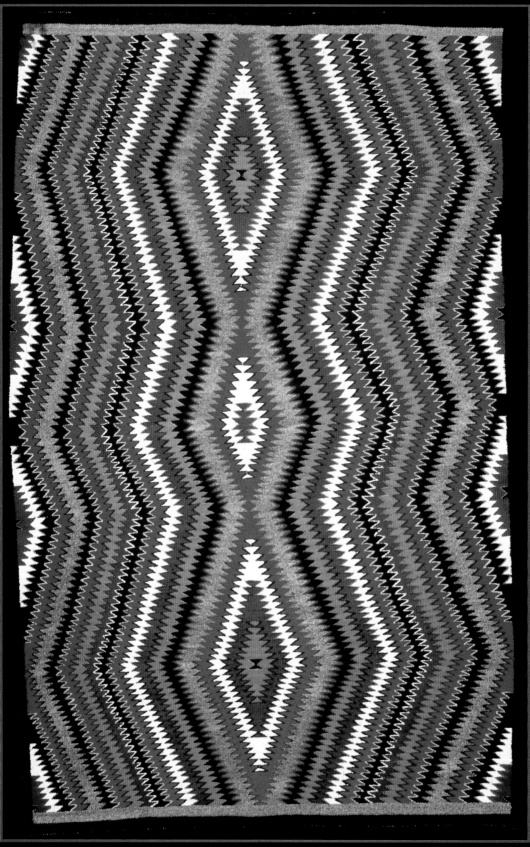

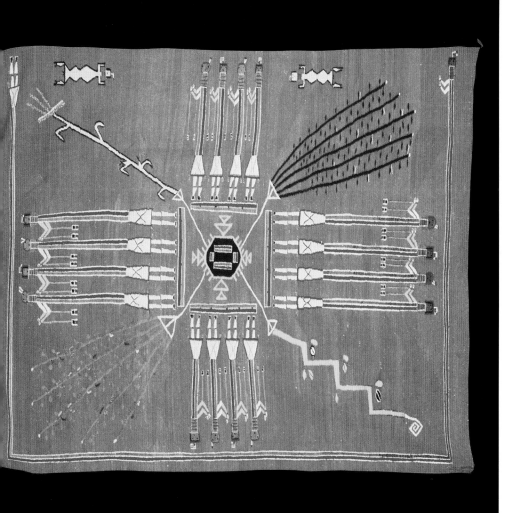

Hosteen Klah and Irene Manuelito
Navajo
*Nightway Sandpainting Tapestry.* c. 1925–30
Wool, dyes, 84 x 100″
Collection School of American Research,
Santa Fe, New Mexico. Gift of Miss Mary
Cabot Wheelwright, Alcalde, New Mexico

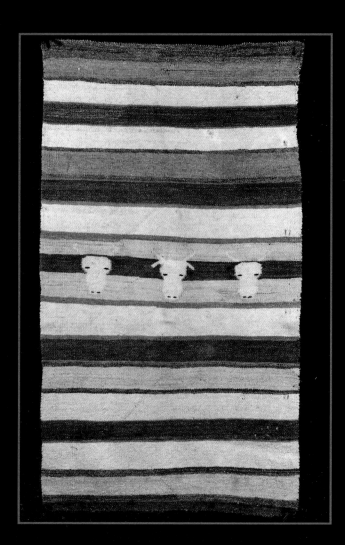

Navajo
*Wide Ruins Rug.* c. 1939
Wool, vegetable dyes, 53½ x 30½″
Collection School of American Research,
Santa Fe, New Mexico. Gift of Sallie Wagner

Penobscot
*"Shopper" Basket and Mold.* c. 1930s
Basket: ash splints, braided paper cord,
8 x 13 x 7″; mold: wood, 9½ x 14 x 5″
Collection Children's Museum, Boston

Hopi
*Large Coiled Basket* (*kachina* and terrace
designs) c. 1920. Bunched grass, 16 x 18 x 18″
Collection School of American Research, Santa
Fe, New Mexico. Given in memory of Margaret
Moses

Western Apache
*Basket.* c. 1920
Fiber, 5¾ x 21¼ x 21¼″
Collection Museum of Indian Arts and Culture,
Santa Fe, New Mexico

226

Carrie Bethel
Mono Lake Paiute
*Basket*. c. 1930s. Sedge root, redbud, bracken fern root, 21 x 32½ x 32½"
Collection Yosemite Museum, National Park Service

Lottie Stamper
Cherokee
*Wastebasket*. 1930
River cane, 16 x 13 x 9½"
Collection Qualla Arts and Crafts

Sabattis Tomah
Passamaquoddy
*Wastebasket*. c. 1920
Birchbark, sweetgrass, spruce root, 13½ x 12 x 12"
Collection Children's Museum, Boston

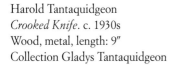

Harold Tantaquidgeon
*Crooked Knife*. c. 1930s
Wood, metal, length: 9"
Collection Gladys Tantaquidgeon

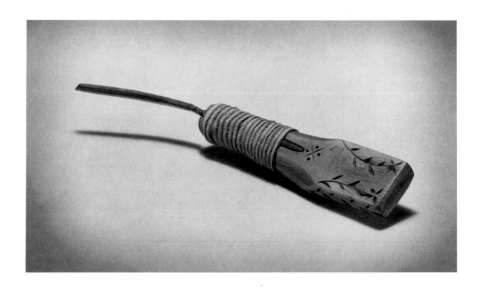

Chimuhuevi
*Jar-shaped Basket.* c. 1920
Sedge, 5 x 6 x 6"
Collection School of American Research,
Santa Fe, New Mexico. Indian Arts Fund

Matahga
*Wolf's Head Club.* c. 1930s
Wood, 18 x 3 x 2½"
Collection Gladys Tantaquidgeon

John and Harold Tantaquidgeon
*Bowl with Incised Carving.* c. 1930s
Maple, 16 x 9½ x 3½"
Collection Gladys Tantaquidgeon

Hopi
*Cylindrical Vase.* c. 1910–20
Clay, paint, 10½ x 6 x 6"
Collection Museum of Indian Arts and Culture/Laboratory of Anthropology,
Museum of New Mexico, Santa Fe

Lucy Lewis
Acoma Pueblo
*Seed Jar.* c. 1910–25
Clay, paint, 6 x 11½ x 11½″
Collection School of American Research, Santa Fe,
New Mexico. Gift of Carlos Vierra

Rose Cata
San Juan Pueblo
*Large Incised Jar.* c. 1930
Micaceous clay, 15¼ x 16½"
Collection School of American Research, Santa Fe, New Mexico. Amelia White Estate

Isabel Torebio
Zia Pueblo
*Large Storage Jar.* c. 1920–22.
Clay, paint, 17 x 21 x 21"
Collection School of American
Research, Santa Fe, New Mexico.
Gift of H. P. Mera

Santo Domingo Pueblo
*Jar* (Santa Melchor type). c. 1920–40
Clay, paint, 9¾ x 11¼ x 11¼"
Collection School of American Research,
Santa Fe, New Mexico. Gift of Sheldon
Parsons Memorial Collection

Maria and Julian Martinez
San Ildefonso Pueblo
*Portrait Plate*. c. 1920
Blackware, diameter: 12½″
Collection School of American Research, Santa Fe, New Mexico

Margaret Tafoya
Santa Clara Pueblo
*Large Olla*. c. 1928
Blackware, 23 x 21″
Collection School of American Research, Santa Fe, New Mexico

Mary Histia
Acoma Pueblo
*"National Recovery Act" Jar.* c. 1930
Ceramic, 10½ x 13 x 13"
Collection Franklin D. Roosevelt Library, Hyde Park, New York

This resource section highlights the artists, scholars, arts advocates, government and private agencies and institutions, major exhibitions, important arts and cultural publications, craft shops and production centers, and educational institutions that were important to the revival of American crafts in the period 1920 to 1945. During these years, the United States suffered its worst economic depression. To move the country toward recovery, the government developed a variety of federally assisted programs, including a number that supported arts and crafts activities. Through arts programs in this era, Americans reevaluated their own national heritage. The result was a resurging artistic interest in the revival of the colonial—both northern European and Hispanic—and a preoccupation with the survival and preservation of Native American and African American culture. The resource section of the next volume in this series will list artists, advocates, institutions, etc., important to craft influenced by European Modernism during this same period.

The artistic and cultural landscape of the period is suggested in this resource section. Short biographical entries are presented on various artists whose works exemplify the revival and survival themes. Listed as well are scholars and arts advocates who played significant roles in forwarding and championing the multifaceted elements of these themes. Federal programs and other private endeavors instituted by these scholars and advocates are enumerated. Their contributions include the pursuit of research, the collection of artifacts, the establishment of schools and museums, and the development of regional centers and cooperative guilds where crafts could be promoted and sold. The genesis of the revival and survival of myriad American crafts is suggested by the various programs and institutions established during this time period.

This resource section, a pioneering effort, provides an introductory outline that indicates the work remaining to be done. Our guidelines were to present the material in as useful a format for future scholars as possible and only to present data that we considered reliable. The material has been gathered from wide-ranging and often ephemeral sources, and, when possible, complete information is given. The biographical entries list the full and most common name, the birth and death dates and locations, and the person's craft, occupation, or position. For the institutional entries, where names often change, the current name is listed last, and the founder is named, when known. In addition, dates of operation are provided. This information ranges from institutions that are still active—indicated by the word "present"—to those entries where a founding date is available but, at present, there is no certainty of the closing date. These entries are listed with a dash. Cross-references for artists whose contributions are best understood in the context of another artist's career or in the framework of a particular enterprise or institution are listed in the index. *See also* references are provided between the artist entries, the scholar and advocate entries, the cottage industry entries developed by the various schools, and the school, organization, and literary entries to which they are also connected.

## BACHELDER, OSCAR LOUIS
Born 1852, Wisconsin; died 1935.
Ceramist

Bachelder worked for forty years as a potter in twenty-eight states. His interest was first stimulated by a visit to the Philadelphia Centennial International Exposition, in 1876. In 1914, he established a pottery shop with Robert F. Gudger in Buncombe County, North Carolina. After Gudger left the business, Bachelder named his company Omar Khayyam Pottery. He was one of the first potters to make art ware.

*See also Omar Khayyam Pottery:* CRAFT SHOPS AND PRODUCTION CENTERS—CERAMICS

## BALINK, HENRY C.
Born 1882, Amsterdam, The Netherlands; died 1963, Santa Fe, New Mexico.
Painter

In 1917, Balink moved to New Mexico, living first in Taos then relocating to Santa Fe in 1923. He painted Pueblo Indians, including a portrait of San Ildefonso potters Maria and Julian Martinez. In 1927, he received a commission from the Marland Museum, in Ponca City, Oklahoma, to paint portraits of Oklahoma Indian chiefs. Balink's handcarved picture frames reflected the Indian and southwestern themes of his paintings.

## BARELA, PATROCINIO
Born 1908, Bisbee, Arizona; died 1969, Taos, New Mexico.
Woodcarver

Barela moved to Taos as a child and began carving in 1931. First employed as a manual laborer for the New Mexico WPA, Barela became recognized as a skilled, self-taught woodcarver and was employed by the arts and crafts project. He produced numerous carvings and was best known for making *santos* and other simple religious figures out of juniper. Not a traditional *santero* (a maker of santos), Barela's work was closer in feeling to the primitive art of Africa and Oceania and the stone figures of Easter Island.

## BAUMANN, GUSTAVE
Born June 27, 1881, Magdeburg, Germany; died 1971, Santa Fe, New Mexico.
Painter, printmaker

Baumann was active in the Spanish Colonial Arts Society, serving on the committee for permanent collections. He painted Indian figures and local landscapes and designed woodcuts based on Indian pictographs found in northern New Mexico.

*See also Society for the Revival of Spanish-Colonial Arts:* GUILDS AND SOCIETIES

## BERGE, OTTO
Born 1894, Norway; no death date available.
Woodworker

Berge learned woodworking from his father, a wheelwright and coachmaker. He came to the United States in 1913 and held different woodworking positions. In 1920, Berge began working for a New York City antiques shop, learning how to restore furniture and make furniture to order. He was employed by Val-Kill Industries from 1927 to 1936. After the shop closed, co-owners Eleanor Roosevelt, Nancy Cook, and Marion Dickerman gave him machinery, and he opened a shop behind his home.

*See also Val-Kill Industries:* CRAFT SHOPS AND PRODUCTION CENTERS—GENERAL

## BERGMAN, MARGARET OLOFSSON
Born June 22, 1872, near Rörösjön, in Jamtland, Sweden; died 1948, near Breidablik, a Scandinavian settlement north of Poulsbo, Washington.
Weaver

Margaret's mother taught her to weave when she was seven, and by the time she was a teenager, she was producing textiles for her mother's customers and winning regional awards. Emigrating to the United States in 1901 to marry John Bergman, she set aside weaving for family needs, returning to her craft in 1914 and doing custom work from 1918 to 1930. Her reputation evolved from an ability to visualize complex, multishaft weaves, to create original patterns based on structures such as summer and winter weave and damask, and to then translate them to the loom. In the 1930s, she conducted weaving schools in Tacoma and Annapolis, Washington, taught seminars throughout the Pacific Northwest and parts of British Columbia, and participated in various summer programs, such as the Penland School of Handicrafts. To meet her students' demand for weaving equipment, she designed, patented, and produced the Bergman Suitcase loom and Bergman Floor loom, two folding frame looms that collapsed when fully warped. Margaret helped found weaving guilds in Tacoma, Seattle, and Kitsap County, Washington. During World War II, she developed a new weaving structure called the "Margaret Bergman technique."

## BETHEL, CARRIE
Born July 4, 1898, Lee Vining, California; died February 24, 1974, Lee Vining.
Basketmaker

A Momo Lake Paiute, Bethel learned to weave baskets as a child. In 1910, she successfully completed her first creation, a three-rod basket made with a split-willow background and an unusual red-bud and bracken fern root design of ducks and flowers copied from a crochet book. By the 1920s, Bethel was an accomplished basketweaver and a prominent competitor in the Yosemite and June Lake Indian Field Days. In the 1930s, she began producing distinct miniature beaded baskets that were neatly executed in a variety of complex patterns with small, multicolored beads. Bethel enjoyed a special artist-patron relationship with James Schwabacher, who purchased most of her larger baskets. In 1939, she gave demonstrations at the Federal Building Indian Exhibition at the Golden Gate International Exposition, held on Treasure Island, near San Francisco. Her baskets were sold at the trading post there.

*See also Golden Gate International Exposition—Federal Building Indian Exhibition:* EXHIBITIONS

## BOND, RUTH CLEMENT
Born Louisville, Kentucky; no dates available.
Interior and textile designer, quiltmaker

In 1934, Ruth Clement Bond moved to the Wheeler Dam construction village along the Tennessee River in northern Alabama, where her husband, J. Max Bond, was the top black administrator for the Tennessee Valley Authority. College educated, with a master's degree in English, she began working with the women living in the area, making window curtains from flour sacks, corn-shuck rugs dyed with local herbs, and quilts, both from popular patterns of the day and from designs developed by Bond.

## BROWN, MARY LOU ("MOTHER BROWN")
Born 1891, Lee County, Texas; died 1979, Riverside, California.
Quiltmaker

Brown grew up around Giddings and Austin, Texas, but moved to Dallas, where she spent most of her life. While in college, her daughter, Elfreda Ford, befriended Helen Nathaniel, a girl whose parents had died when she was young. When Helen had her first child, Brown stayed with her, and the two women formed a lifelong bond. Sometime in the 1940s, Brown made a strip quilt for Helen that earned the nickname "the loud quilt." Continuously used by Helen's family, it was kept on the sofa to be used as a cover while watching television.

## BROWN, TOM
No dates available.
Woodcarver, sculptor

Brown learned woodcarving at Pleasant Hill Academy, in Tennessee, where he also taught. He sold his sculpture to finance his education at the Art Institute of Chicago; the Corcoran School of Art, in Washington, D.C.; and the Rinehart School of Sculpture, in Baltimore.

## BURNLEY, MATTIE
Born c. 1897, Tyler, Texas; died 1990, near Madera, California.
Quiltmaker

Burnley learned quilting from her grandmother. Married at fourteen, she did fieldwork and housekeeping while raising six children. In Dallas, in the late 1930s or early 1940s, she and her cousin Cora Neal made strip quilts in an unusual trapezoid pattern that Neal had copied from a quilt found in a Goodwill store.

## CATA, ROSE
fl. 1930s, San Juan Pueblo, New Mexico.
Ceramist

Cata is known for creating a large micaceous clay jar with a hatched design on the upper body, which reflects the artistic direction in the 1930s of the San Juan Pueblo potters. Combining the old and the new to produce a highly creative original, the hatching on Cata's jar suggests traditional Potsowi incised ware found in contemporary archaeological excavations, but the jar form itself is modern.

## CERVANTES, PEDRO
Born Wilcox, Arizona, 1915.
Painter

Employed by the Works Progress Administration's Federal Art Project (FAP), he received national exposure when his painting was displayed at the 1936 Museum of Modern Art FAP exhibition. European service during World War II provided the opportunity for Cervantes to study the great masters. Returning to New Mexico, he studied at the Hill and Canyon School and opened a commercial-art business in Clovis.

## CLAFLIN, MAJEL
Born Michigan; no dates available.
Tinsmith

Claflin studied at the Art Institute of Chicago and served an apprenticeship with a Chicago tinsmith. To gain an understanding of old designs, she studied early tinwork and visited native Spanish Americans. Claflin reproduced old patterns and created new designs. She also made renderings for the WPA Federal Art Project's Index of American Design.

*See also Federal Art Project (FAP)— Index of American Design:* GOVERNMENT AND PRIVATE AGENCIES AND INSTITUTIONS

## COLE FAMILY
fl. 1780s–present, Catawba Valley, Randolph County, North Carolina.
Ceramists

For two centuries, or nine generations, the Cole family has produced pottery in the eastern Piedmont of North Carolina. The Coles trace their ancestry back to Great Britain, where potters of the same name are recorded in both Staffordshire and Wales. Shortly after the Civil War, Evan Cole (1834–1895), a member of the fifth generation, established one of the largest shops in North Carolina, producing stoneware bottles stamped "Cole & Co." Evan's sons, including Ruffin Cole

(1859–1931), represent the last generation to make traditional utilitarian forms. Ruffin worked as a turner in a shop set up by his brother Franklin. In the twentieth century, family members, including Ruffin's son Charles Cole (1887–1967), took an active role in the renewal of the pottery industry. Today the family runs four shops: Seagrove Pottery, Seagrove, North Carolina; J. B. Cole Pottery, Montgomery, North Carolina; and two different Cole family potteries in Sanford, North Carolina.

## CRAIG, BURLON B.
Born April 21, 1914, near Henry, Lincoln County, North Carolina.
Ceramist

Burlon Craig is the single remaining link between the potteries of today and a heritage of folk pottery that extends back two centuries in the North Carolina Catawba Valley. As a boy growing up during the Depression, Craig exchanged wood gathering for the opportunity to learn pottery from his neighbor Jim Lynn. Following World War II, he opened his own operation in Vale, North Carolina, using the old shops and kiln built by the Reinhardts during the late 1930s. Digging his clay by hand from the bottomland on the south fork of the Catawba River, Craig turned a variety of traditional forms on his treadle wheel and created stoneware and pottery distinguished by its glass and wood-ash alkaline glazes. His pieces were fired in a long groundhog kiln. Craig focused his production on utilitarian items, such as pitchers, crocks, and flower pots, until 1976, when he was encouraged to expand his repertoire. At that time, he began making anthropomorphic forms—snake urns, ring jugs, and face jars—which became popular with collectors. Craig stamped his pieces "B B Craig, Vale, N.C."

## DAVE THE POTTER
Born 1780; died 1863.
Ceramist

Abner Landrum established a pottery in the Edgefield district of South Carolina between 1810 and 1820. He owned a slave named Dave whom he taught to read and write. After being employed as a typesetter on Landrum's newspaper, *The South Carolina Republican,* Dave was given over to Landrum's son-in-law, Lewis Miles, to work in his pottery, Miles Mill. Dave made the largest stoneware vessels known anywhere in the South, and was the only slave to sign and date his work. His pottery is wide-shouldered and features couplets and witty poetry.

## DELGADO, EDDIE
Born 1883; died 1966.
Tinsmith

A tinsmith for more than forty years, Delgado followed in the footsteps of his father, Francisco. Together, they produced light fixtures for the Albuquerque Little Theater. In 1928, Delgado became the proprietor of Delgado's Curio Shop, in Santa Fe.

## DELGADO, FRANCISCO
Born 1858; died 1936.
Tinsmith

A stenographer and bookkeeper for various federal and state agencies, Delgado made decorative tin items on a part-time basis. After he retired in 1929, he opened Colonial Tin Antiques, in Santa Fe, New Mexico. With his son Eddie, he made tin wall sconces and niches for the Albuquerque Little Theater.

*See also Works Progress Administration—Albuquerque Little Theater:* GOVERNMENT AND PRIVATE AGENCIES AND INSTITUTIONS

## DONALDSON, KATE CLAYTON ("GRANNY")
fl. 1920s–60s, Brasstown, North Carolina.
Seamstress, quiltmaker

"When I was a little thing," Granny Donaldson remembered, "I learned to weave and spin and card. But crocheting was what I liked best, and that's what I settled down to doing with a purpose." In the 1920s, she began making scarves and other items for Louise Pittman, business manager of the John C. Campbell Folk School. She was soon inspired to make blankets that combined crocheted and appliquéd human figures, animals, flowers, trees, and other designs displayed on backgrounds of homespun or linen. These twenty-four-inch decorative squares were stylistically similar to Italian Po Valley blankets, in which symbolic figures proclaimed the spirit of life and decked the backs of cows on certain festive occasions. Known as the "Cow Blanket Woman," Donaldson's renditions were first purchased by Pittman and were ultimately sold worldwide.

*See also John C. Campbell Folk School:* SCHOOLS

## DOUGLAS, AARON
Born 1898, Topeka, Kansas; died February 2, 1979, Nashville, Tennessee.
Muralist, illustrator

Douglas combined Modernism and Africanism in his murals, which included work at Fisk University, in Nashville, Tennessee, and the Sherman Hotel, in Chicago. Among his best-known works is *Aspects of Negro Life;* created under Public Works of Art Project (PWAP) sponsorship for the New York Public Library, this four-paneled mural traces the roots of African Americans from the African jungle to their place in the American city. Douglas also contributed illustrations to *Crisis*, W. E. B. DuBois's magazine, and to *The New Negro*, Alain LeRoy Locke's volume on the cultural contributions of African Americans. In 1939, he founded the art department at Fisk University, which he chaired until his retirement, in 1966.

*See also Locke, Alain LeRoy,* The New Negro: BOOKS AND PERIODICALS

## ECKHARDT, EDRIS
Born 1907, Cleveland, Ohio.
Ceramist

A graduate of the Cleveland School of Art, Eckhardt was a student of R. Guy Cowan, of Cowan Pottery, which promoted ceramic sculpture. In 1933, she worked for the Public Works of Art Project, producing popular nursery-rhyme figures for use in public library programs for children. From 1935 to 1941, Eckhardt directed the Cleveland Department of Ceramic Sculpture for the WPA Federal Art Project. The group produced large-scale sculpture for public housing projects, as well as three-dimensional pictures of American life. In 1953, Eckhardt successfully experimented with fusing gold and glass, an Egyptian technique that had been employed two thousand years earlier.

## FISHER, PARK
Brasstown, North Carolina; no dates available.
Musical-instrument maker

Fisher taught local boys to make wooden boxes and other simple objects. As a teacher at the John C. Campbell Folk School, he helped make a large dulcimer.

*See also John C. Campbell Folk School:* SCHOOLS

## GALLEGOS, CELSO
Born 1864; died 1943.
Woodcarver

A resident of Agua Fria, New Mexico, Gallegos carved *santos* and other religious pieces from 1910 until his death. His santos were carved from pine; he did not add the gesso and paint finishes characteristic of the work of other *santeros*. Gallegos's neighbors, who considered him a religious man, often asked him to read prayers for them. His pious nature contributed to his popularity as a santero, as community members considered work to have greater merit if the creator lived an exemplary life. Encouraged by the Spanish Colonial Arts Society, Gallegos also made nontraditional pieces, including canes and finger rings.

*See also Society for the Revival of Spanish-Colonial Arts:* GUILDS AND SOCIETIES

## GEBELEIN, GEORGE CHRISTIAN
Born November 6, 1878, Wivestenselbitz, Oberfranken, Bavaria; died January 25, 1945, Wellesley Hills, Massachusetts.
Metalsmith

After training and working as a silversmith for Goodnow and Jenks, in Boston (1893–97), Tiffany and Company (1898–1903), and the Handicraft Shop, in Boston (1903–9), Gebelein opened his own shop, Gebelein Silversmiths, in 1909. It is still in operation in Boston today. Influenced by the skill and craftsmanship of colonial New England, he became known for domestic and ecclesiastical gold and sterling silver works, which he designed and fashioned by hand. Turning down offers to mass-produce his designs, he preferred to create individual pieces, using tools that had once been owned by Paul Revere. Gebelein presented informal lectures and demonstrations at his studio and became an expert on early American silverware, which he also collected.

## GLENDENNING, HERMAN
Born 1906; no death date available.
Silversmith

Glendenning worked for Arthur J. Stone Associates, producing handwrought silver. While he remained basically faithful to colonial design and method, he also adapted Colonial revival models. After Stone sold his shop in 1937, Glendenning worked for George Erickson, until 1971. He then established his own shop in Gardner, Massachusetts.

*See also Arthur J. Stone Associates:* CRAFT SHOPS AND PRODUCTION CENTERS—METALS

## GONZALES, ELIDIO
Born Cimarron, New Mexico.
Furnituremaker

Gonzales specializes in making hand-carved Spanish Colonial furniture, a skill he learned at the Taos Vocational School, where he later became an instructor. Under the WPA, he made furniture for the Gallup, New Mexico, Courthouse and taught for the National Youth Administration (NYA). His furniture is sold through his New Mexico shop, El Artesano de Taos.

## GRACE, ANNA MAE
Born 1914, Evergreen, Alabama.
Quiltmaker

Grace's daughter, Bennie Bell, remembers sleeping under her mother's *Pig in the Pen/Spiderweb Strip Quilt* in the early forties, when she was a child. About 1950, the Grace family moved from Alabama to Pensacola, Florida.

## GREGORY, WAYLANDE DeSANTIS
Born June 13, 1905, Baxter Springs, Kansas; died August 18, 1971, Warren, New Jersey.
Ceramist, sculptor

While studying art, Gregory worked as a printer, sign painter, and toy designer. As a 1931 fellow at the Cranbrook Foundation, in Bloomfield Hills, Michigan, he experimented with glazes produced by mixing clay with minerals and oxides. Gregory also investigated how to produce massive ceramic sculpture with the necessary supports. Among his best-known works are the *Fountain of the Atoms*, a sixty-foot fountain with representations of earth, air, fire, and water, which welcomed visitors to the 1939–40 New York World's Fair, and the *Four Horsemen of the Apocalypse*, a concrete fountain in New Jersey.

## GUDGELL, HENRY
Born 1826, Kentucky; died 1895.
Woodcarver

Although only one known cane demonstrates Gudgell's skill, this piece is generally judged to be the finest African American carved walking stick. Gudgell made the cane for John Bryan in 1867. It is divided into two sections: The upper section features geometric designs; the lower section includes such naturalistic figures as a lizard, tortoise, and man. Born a slave, Gudgell also worked as a blacksmith, wheelwright, coppersmith, and silversmith.

## GUTIERREZ, LELA
Santa Clara Pueblo, New Mexico; no dates available.

## GUTIERREZ, VAN
Santa Clara Pueblo, New Mexico; no dates available.
Ceramists

In the 1930s, the Gutierrezes experimented with polychrome pottery. They used local colored earth for paint, working with it until they produced the gray, brown, rose, and pink colors that characterized their work. Before 1956, their work reflected styles typically seen at the Santa Clara Pueblo; after that, they developed their own motifs, including anthropomorphic designs outlined in black and filled in with green, blue, white, light red, or brick red.

## GUY, EDWARD
No dates available.
Metalsmith

From 1916 to 1921, Guy worked as Wallace Nutting's ironmaster at the Saugus Iron Works. A descendant of five generations of forgemen trained in the Lancaster, England, region, Guy was proud of his ability to produce pieces in the English style. The Saugus catalogue listed fireplace furniture, candlestands, chandeliers, and door knockers, among other pieces. Guy produced items for the company's inventory and filled special orders. In 1922, he contacted bookstores and libraries to protest that several iron pieces identified as colonial works in Nutting's *Furniture of the Pilgrim Century* were actually reproductions he had made in 1918 while employed at Saugus. Nutting never responded to the charges.

*See also Nutting, Wallace,* Furniture of the Pilgrim Century (of American Origin): 1620–1720: BOOKS AND PERIODICALS

## HATHAWAY, ISAAC SCOTT
Born April 4, 1874, Lexington, Kentucky; died 1967.
Sculptor, teacher

Hathaway was educated at Chandler College, Lexington, Kentucky; Pittsburg College, Pittsburg, Kansas; and the New England Conservatory of Music. He developed the ceramics program at Tuskegee Institute in the 1940s and became head of the ceramics department at Alabama State Teachers College, in Montgomery. Hathaway was known for his portrait busts, the most famous of which are those of Frederick Douglass, Paul Laurence Dunbar, and Booker T. Washington.

## HAYDEN, PALMER
Born 1893, Wide Water, Virginia; died February 18, 1973, New York, New York.
Painter

Hayden worked for the Public Works of Art Project, painting the marine subjects that became his specialty. In 1926, he won a gold medal in the Harmon Foundation competition. He assisted James Lesesne Wells at the Harlem Art Workshop from 1933 to 1935.

*See also Harlem Art Workshop:* SCHOOLS

## HICKOX, ELIZABETH CONRAD
Born 1873; died 1947.
Basketmaker

A Native American basketweaver in northwestern California, Hickox produced most of her work between 1890 and 1930. Although raised as a weaver in the Katuk tradition (a nation living in the inland mountains), she was half-German and half-Wiyot (a nation that lived along the coast in and around Humboldt Bay). Native American baskets of northwestern California were produced from natural fibers that included hazel, willow, and woodwardia fern, which were considered gifts from ancient spirit beings. By using these sacred fibers as the raw material, baskets became important cultural symbols that were actively included in traditional ceremonies. Hickox developed an individual style through the innovative use of color and dramatic figure-ground relationships. Her specialties included ceremonial capped and lidded trinket baskets, many of which were sold through Grace Nicholson, the preeminent dealer in Native American baskets, in Pasadena, California.

## HILTON, CLARA MAUDE COBB
Born August 11, 1885, Catawba County, North Carolina; died July 10, 1969, Marion, North Carolina.
Ceramist, dollmaker

Soon after her marriage, in 1903, to Ernest A. Hilton, Maude went to work at the Hilton-Ritchie family pottery, making utilitarian jars, milk crocks, and flower pots. When aluminum and glass containers reduced the demand for stoneware, the company began making art ware. Maude advocated the change and contributed to the company's new efforts with skillful underglazes and by painting flower designs, nature scenes, and bands of color on tea sets, flower pots, and vases. Her favorite design was the dogwood blossom; in addition to painting, she fashioned blooms out of light clay, affixing them to darker, natural clay vases before they were dried and fired. In the 1930s, when she and her husband were managing their own pottery, Maude began to experiment with the making of clay animals and dolls. When her husband became ill and was forced to leave the pottery business in 1946, Maude's interest in ceramic doll-making accelerated. She used molds to form the dolls' clay heads, arms, and legs, and then completed their features with paint in lifelike colors and shiny black for the hair and shoes. Maude stuffed the dolls' soft bodies with cotton, and designed and sewed their clothes. The dolls sold well, and after she died, her daughters continued the tradition.

## HILTON, ERNEST AUBURN
Born 1878; died 1948.
Ceramist

Hilton learned how to make traditional alkaline-glazed utilitarian stoneware from his family, which operated several potteries in the Catawba County, North Carolina, area. At nine, he began working with his father at the Hilton Pottery, near Newton, North Carolina. In 1899, he joined the Oak Grove Pottery and, a few years later, the family-owned Hilton-Ritchie Pottery. In 1918, Ernest and his brothers Shuford Daniel (1875–1947) and Claude Watson (1880–1946) opened the Hilton Pottery at Propst Crossroads, North Carolina. With the support of pottery collector Mrs. M. G. Canfield, of Woodstock, Vermont, Ernest consulted a chemist who suggested the different oxides that produced unusual colors. Ernest's wife, Maude, encouraged the company's transition from utilitarian pottery to art ware. In 1927, they founded E. A. Hilton Pottery Company, in Oyama; seven years later, they moved the business to Pleasant Garden, where it remained in operation until 1953.

*See also Hilton Pottery:* CRAFT SHOPS AND PRODUCTION CENTERS—CERAMICS

## HISTIA, MARY
Born 1881; died 1973.
Ceramist

Histia was considered one of the Acoma tribe's great potters. Through the auspices of the Indian Arts and Crafts Board, and the efforts of Indian Affairs Commissioner John Collier, her work was distributed to United States embassies and government offices throughout the 1930s and 1940s. At the time, it featured realistic bird motifs, and one of her best-known pieces was a tall-necked jar emblazoned with a phoenix-like eagle in honor of the National Recovery Administration. Prior to the pottery revival inspired by whites in the 1920s, Histia's work was more traditional, but she later adopted revival styles. Her descendants carry on the pottery tradition.

*See also John Collier:* SCHOLARS AND ADVOCATES' BIOGRAPHIES

*Indian Arts and Crafts Board:* GOVERNMENT AND PRIVATE AGENCIES AND INSTITUTIONS

## HOLMES, AMALIA LOWERY
fl. 1920s–30s, Placquemine, Louisiana.
Quiltmaker

Holmes was an active strip quilter in the Placquemine area.

## HUDDLESTON, SAM
Born 1874, near Dallas, Texas; no death date available.
Furnituremaker

For nearly twenty years, beginning in 1893, Huddleston worked for the Indian Service, teaching industrial arts at Indian schools in Oklahoma, Arizona, Nevada, and New Mexico. In 1912, he joined the staff of the Museum of New Mexico, in Santa Fe. One of his assignments was to help stabilize Indian ruins at Gran Quivira, Jemez, and Chaco Canyon. In 1916, Huddleston helped design and build furniture for the Santa Fe Fine Arts Museum.

## JOHANNESEN, KARL
Born 1890, Brooklyn, New York; no death date available.

## JOHANNESEN, ROY
No dates available.
Furnituremakers

Born in the United States, the brothers were taken to Norway by their mother after the death of their father, where they learned cabinetmaking. Returning to this country, they were employed at Val-Kill Furniture Shop to make reproduction furniture that was the industry's specialty.

*See also Val-Kill Industries—Val-Kill Furniture Shop:* CRAFT SHOPS AND PRODUCTION CENTERS—GENERAL

## KLAH, HOSTEEN
Born 1867, Bear Springs, New Mexico; died February 27, 1937, Gallup, New Mexico.
Weaver, medicine man

Klah was considered one of the greatest Navajo medicine men of his time, who knew more than one thousand sacred and ancient chants. Said to be a hermaphrodite, he was a weaver, a profession not usually held by Navajo men. With the encouragement of Mary Cabot Wheelwright and Franc Newcomb, he began incorporating sacred sandpainting symbols into his weavings. Klah only wove sandpainting rugs for the chants that he was qualified to sing, including Nightway, Shootingway, and Mountainway. He constructed a special loom to weave these large tapestries, using wool from brown sheep to resemble the sand background. With Wheelwright, he helped establish the Museum of Navajo Ceremonial Art, in Santa Fe, New Mexico, now the Wheelwright Museum of the American Indian.

*See also Gladys and Irene Manuelito:* ARTISTS' BIOGRAPHIES

## LAEMMLE, DAVID
No dates available.
Painter

Laemmle was among the artists who demonstrated their craft at Santa Fe's Native Market in the early 1930s. He decorated furniture and painted glass panels for tinworks, collaborating with tinsmith Pedro Quintana, among others. His reverse glass paintings are reminiscent of pieces produced by the Rio Arriba Painted Workshop in the late nineteenth century, although his use of orange, black, blue, and white places him with his contemporaries.

*See also Native Market:* CRAFT SHOPS AND PRODUCTION CENTERS—GENERAL

## LANDOLFA, FRANK
Born Italy; no dates available.
Furnituremaker

Landolfa learned cabinetmaking at his family's furniture factory in Italy. He emigrated to New York City to set up a shop that was to be linked with the family's business. When this venture proved unsuccessful, he taught evening vocational courses. In 1927, Landolfa was recommended to Eleanor Roosevelt for his furnituremaking skills. As the first Val-Kill Industries employee, he helped Nancy Cook purchase equipment and set up the shop; he also recruited other Italian immigrants to work at Val-Kill. In the early 1930s, Landolfa left Val-Kill, but he continued to make and restore furniture. Thirty years later, he was hired by the White House to restore furniture during President John F. Kennedy's administration.

*See also Val-Kill Industries:* CRAFT SHOPS AND PRODUCTION CENTERS—GENERAL

## LÓPEZ, JOSÉ DOLORES
Born 1868, Córdova, New Mexico; died 1937, Córdova.
Woodcarver, furnituremaker

During the revival of Spanish Colonial arts and crafts in the 1920s, López was one of the first to renew the art of carving religious images. Encouraged by the Spanish Colonial Arts Society, López turned a hobby into a profession, initiating a style of carving unpainted wood figures with stylized features and carefully incised decorative patterning that has come to be known as the "Córdova style." Although he originally concentrated on animal forms, he later carved *santos* and other religious figures. Many of Córdova's woodcarvers are related to him.

*See also Society for the Revival of Spanish-Colonial Arts:* GUILDS AND SOCIETIES

## LUKENS, GLEN
Born 1887, Cowgill, Missouri; died December 10, 1967.
Ceramist, teacher

An important ceramist, Lukens moved to California and served as a professor of ceramics at the University of Southern

California from 1936 to 1966. His teaching style reflected an interest in developing the creative potential of his students—an attribute he had employed earlier when helping to rehabilitate soldiers wounded in World War I. In 1945, he traveled to Haiti, at the invitation of the government, to help develop ceramics as a home industry. In his own pieces, Lukens combined oxides and desert stones to produce distinctively colored earthenware.

## LUNA, CRISOSTOMA
fl. 1930s, Taos, New Mexico.
Weaver

Married to furnituremaker Maximo L. Luna, Crisostoma produced traditional handwoven, natural-dyed Rio Grande-style blankets at the Taos Vocational School in the 1930s. The patterns for Luna's blankets—simple geometric forms inserted between horizontal stripes—were based on weaving bulletins published by the New Mexico State Department of Vocational Education.

## LUNA, MAXIMO L.
Born 1896, Taos, New Mexico; died 1964, Taos.
Furnituremaker, teacher

Luna was best known for his Spanish Colonial-style cabinets and other furniture, which featured his own hand-forged iron fittings and tinwork. From 1925 until 1960, he taught woodworking in the Taos Vocational School.

## MACE, SHADRACK
Mars Hill, North Carolina; no dates available.
Furnituremaker

Using pioneer methods, Mace made chairs that exhibited the traditions of his pre–Civil War forefathers. His wife made the twisted corn-shuck seats.

## MANUELITO, GLADYS (MRS. SAM)
fl. 1920s–30s

## MANUELITO, IRENE (MRS. JIM)
fl. 1920s–30s
Weavers

Irene and Gladys were trained as weavers by their uncle Hosteen Klah, a respected Navajo medicine man and one of the first weavers to do sandpainting textiles. The women married two brothers, Jim and Sam Manuelito, and were often called "Mrs. Jim" or "Mrs. Sam." They made seventy ceremonial rugs with their uncle. When he died, his last piece was still on the loom. They finished it.

*See also Hosteen Klah:* ARTISTS' BIOGRAPHIES

## MARGOLIS, NATHAN
Born Russia; no dates available.
Furnituremaker

A Russian immigrant, Margolis settled in Hartford, Connecticut, and with his brothers Harold and Jacob, he opened a shop and began making colonial reproduction furniture. Wallace Nutting called Nathan's pieces the "best work in America."

## MARSHALL, BEULAH WATKINS
Born 1899; died 1975.
Quiltmaker

In 1923, Beulah Watkins married the Rev. T. O. Marshall. Using patterns from the *Farm Home Journal* and the local newspaper, from exchanges with her neighbors as well as a family heirloom, Beulah produced quilts in such traditional patterns as Bear Paw, Trip Around the World, and Princess Feather. The last pattern, which she used in a quilt in the early 1930s, was renamed in honor of George Washington, whose two hundredth birthday was widely celebrated in 1932. *Washington's Plume Quilt* was a precise reproduction of a nineteenth-century appliqué pattern, created with traditional color combinations and the straight edges typical of early Tennessee quilts.

## MARTINEZ, JULIAN
Born 1885, New Mexico; died 1943, New Mexico.
Ceramist

Martinez was among the workers hired by Edgar Lee Hewett in 1908 to help excavate prehistoric sites on the Pajarito Plateau. Married to Maria Martinez, "the Potter of San Ildefonso," Julian began by painting her pots with geometric and symbolic designs. In 1919, he developed a method of producing matte black on polished black pottery. By teaching this technique to other San Ildefonso potters in 1921, Martinez provided a livelihood for the other pueblo artisans.

*See also Edgar Lee Hewett:* SCHOLARS AND ADVOCATES' BIOGRAPHIES

## MARTINEZ, MARIA POVERA
Born 1887, San Ildefonso Pueblo, New Mexico; died July 20, 1980, San Ildefonso Pueblo.
Ceramist

Internationally known as "the Potter of San Ildefonso," Martinez was a self-taught potter who helped stimulate interest in Native American ceramics. In 1919, her husband, Julian, improved on the plain black pottery, which she had been making for seven years, by developing a technique for combining matte black and polished black surfaces in her pieces. By teaching their skills to other

San Ildefonso potters, they created a thriving business for the pueblo. Martinez won international renown for her work, which she demonstrated at the 1934 Chicago Century of Progress Exposition and the 1939 San Francisco Golden Gate International Exposition. At the time of her death, her pottery was among the most coveted Indian artwork, bringing between fifteen hundred and fifteen thousand dollars per piece.

*See also Popovi Da:* ARTISTS' BIOGRAPHIES

*Golden Gate International Exposition—Federal Building Indian Exhibition:* EXHIBITIONS

## MEEM, JOHN GAW
Born November 17, 1894, Pelotas, Brazil; no death date available.
Architect

In the 1920s, Meem began his career by designing homes for wealthy members of Santa Fe's art colony. Originally coming to the area as a patient at Dr. Frank Mera's Sunmount Sanatorium, he became interested in Spanish pueblo architecture, and soon was a leading proponent of the Santa Fe style and the preservation of mission churches. In Albuquerque, his works include the main buildings at the University of New Mexico and the Little Theater. In Colorado, he designed the Colorado Springs Fine Arts Center.

*See also Works Progress Administration—Albuquerque Little Theater:* GOVERNMENT AND PRIVATE AGENCIES AND INSTITUTIONS

## MOULTON, JULIA A. TILTON
Born 1860; died August 15, 1938.
Weaver

In 1925, Julia Moulton helped Mary Coolidge set up the first exhibition of old and new hooked rugs. The success of this one-hundred piece exhibition prompted Mary and her husband, Joseph Randolph Coolidge, to establish the Sandwich Home Industries, in Center Sandwich, New Hampshire, the following year. Mary particularly encouraged the production of hooked and braided rugs and the revival of spinning, weaving, and knitting. Julia Moulton produced a rectangular hooked throw rug in neutral colors, with a black border, showing the Burleigh House—Center Sandwich's oldest standing home. Her rug was one of the first sold by the Sandwich Home Industries.

## NAMPEYO
Born c. 1860, First Mesa Village, Hano, Arizona; died 1942.
Ceramist

As a child, Nampeyo became a skilled potter, using traditional Hopi shapes and designs. Following Jesse Walter Fewkes's 1895 excavation of Sityatki, she began re-creating prehistoric pieces and quickly found a market. Other Hopi artists followed, and pottery became a major source of income for the First Mesa. After she went blind, Nampeyo continued to shape pots, and her husband, Lesou, decorated them. She passed on her skills to her daughters Annie, Fannie, and Nellie, who achieved similar success with their work.

## NUSBAUM, JESSE
Born September 3, 1887, Greeley, Colorado; no death date available.
Furnituremaker, photographer

In 1909, Nusbaum became staff photographer for the Museum of New Mexico, in Santa Fe. Interested in Sylvanus Morley's delineation of the Santa Fe style, he documented houses in the town's unimproved Spanish sections. In 1917, he designed and built furniture for the Women's Board Room in the Santa Fe Fine Arts Museum. Nusbaum continued to make furniture for private clients as well as the National Park Service. A member of the 1906 archaeological expedition to Mesa Verde, in Colorado, he later returned there to serve as superintendent of the national park, from 1921 to 1930.

*See also Sylvanus Griswold Morley:* SCHOLARS AND ADVOCATES' BIOGRAPHIES

## NUTTING, MARIET GRISWOLD
Born 1854; died August 31, 1944, Framingham Center, Massachusetts.
Textile designer

Born into a wealthy family and educated in private schools, Mariet Griswold married Wallace Nutting and helped inspire his interest in photographing colonial scenes by posing in period costumes for his tableaux. She also made large hooked rugs for her husband's company. After his death, she managed the business.

*See also Wallace Nutting:* SCHOLARS AND ADVOCATES' BIOGRAPHIES

## OSOLNIK, DAPHNE
No dates available.
Weaver

In 1938, Daphne married Berea College teacher Rude Osolnik. At Berea, she made a bold wool blanket similar to those produced by the college's students. She and her husband were instrumental in the development of the Southern Highland Handicraft Guild.

*See also Southern Mountain Handicraft Guild:* GUILDS AND SOCIETIES

## OSOLNIK, RUDE
Born March 4, 1915, Dawson, New Hampshire.
Woodworker, teacher

Osolnik graduated from Bradley University in 1937. After working briefly for the Caterpillar Tractor Company, he became an industrial-arts teacher at Berea College. In 1941, he assumed the chairmanship of the department and also directed the woodcutting industry. He started Osolnik Originals, in Berea, in 1956. His own products include lathe-turned candlesticks and free-form wooden containers made of twigs. A consultant to numerous craft organizations, Osolnik served as president of the Southern Highland Handicraft Guild from 1960 to 1962.

*See also Berea College:* SCHOOLS

## PARKER, MARY SALTONSTALL TUCKERMAN
Born July 12, 1856, Salem, Massachusetts; died June 26, 1923, Salem.
Embroiderer

Born into a prominent family on Boston's North Shore, Mary Tuckerman began doing needlework as a child, and, throughout her life, she produced household linens and cross-stitched samplers for her own pleasure and enjoyment. From 1900 on, she created a series of samplers—approximately one a year—in which she adapted the Colonial revival style to her own purposes. In addition to the typical motifs of baskets with fruit, flowers, birds, and urns, her samplers featured religious themes, events of local history, portrayals of modern life, and autobiographical incidents. She also filled her samplers with short, rhymed verse, many of which she wrote herself. Her marriage, in 1887, produced two sons. Two of her most unusual samplers, featuring planes, ships, artillery guns, and the names of her sons, were made while the young men were in the service during World War I.

## PERKINS, LAWRENCE BRADFORD
Born February 12, 1907, Evanston, Illinois.
Architect, designer

Although his career was just beginning, Perkins, in partnership with the more experienced Eliel Saarinen, won the contract for designing the Crow Island School, in Winnetka, Illinois, the first effort of the city's public school system to construct a building that would reflect its educational philosophy. Perkins visited Winnetka schools, studied the program's theories, and talked with teachers before helping to create a school that featured flexible classroom space and

movable furniture. Working for the WPA Illinois Craft Project in 1940, Perkins and Eero Saarinen (Eliel's son) designed molded chairs for the school. The school established Perkins's reputation and brought him assignments for other public schools and university buildings.

*See also Federal Art Project (FAP)— Illinois Craft Project:* GOVERNMENT AND PRIVATE AGENCIES AND INSTITUTIONS *Crow Island School:* SCHOOLS

## PICKETT, MAGGIE
fl. 1940s.
Seamstress

A Crow and Yellowtail Indian, Pickett created beaded moccasins and leggings with a semitraditional design.

## PLESS, SUSAN
Born during the Civil War or early postbellum period, probably in Tennessee; died 1944, Okfuskee County, Oklahoma.
Quiltmaker

Pless was a prolific quiltmaker. When her family migrated to Okfuskee County, near Okemah, Oklahoma, and moved into a two-room farmhouse, she quilted on a frame that hung from the ceiling but swung out of the way when the room was needed for other purposes. Pless raised fourteen children. The quilting tradition was carried on by her daughter Mary Jane Johnston (born 1890, Curvin, Tennessee) and her granddaughter Gracell Tate (born 1920).

## POPOVI DA
Born 1921, San Ildefonso Pueblo, New Mexico; died 1971, San Ildefonso Pueblo.
Ceramist, painter

In 1948, Antonio Martinez, the son of Maria and Julian Martinez, legally changed his name to Popovi Da, which means "red fox." In the early 1930s, he attended the Santa Fe Indian School Studio, where he was taught by Dorothy Dunn. After serving in World War II, he returned to the San Ildefonso Pueblo and opened the Popovi Da Studio of Indian Art, with his wife, Anita, to display and sell his mother's pottery. In 1950, he began painting her pots, and in 1956, he became her full partner; the signature "Maria/Popovi" began to appear at that time. In 1961, using a new firing technique, Popovi Da produced a sienna color; later, he developed a gunmetal finish. In 1965, he began making his own pots, which he signed "Popovi."

*See also Maria Martinez:* ARTISTS' BIOGRAPHIES

## POWESHIEK, SUSIE
Born 1898; died 1984.
Seamstress

A Mesquakie Indian, Poweshiek created a ribbon appliqué skirt with Great Lakes patterns in the silk borders and frontal area. A very important Mesquakie art form, ribbonwork dated to the Tama Settlement, Iowa, of the mid-nineteenth century, and subsequently became a traditional element in the dress of the women.

## QUINTANA, PEDRO
Born 1910.
Tinsmith

Trained by his father as a filigree jewelry-maker, Quintana switched to tinwork at the request of Brice Sewell, of the New Mexico State Department of Vocational Education. He wrote the department's instructional bulletin on tinwork. From 1934 to 1938, he demonstrated tin-smithing at Santa Fe's Native Market.

*See also New Mexico State Department of Vocational Education:* GOVERNMENT AND PRIVATE AGENCIES AND INSTITUTIONS

## REINHARDT FAMILY
fl. 1875–1946, Catawba Valley, North Carolina.
Ceramists

About 1875, Ambrose Reinhardt moved to Catawba Valley, North Carolina, and set up a pottery. There, he trained his sons Jim (1856–1929) and Pinkney (1864–1932) as potters. Pinkney's sons Enoch (1903–1978) and Harvey (1912–1960) carried on the family tradition. In 1928, Harvey worked at Jim Lynn's pottery, where he was known for his prodigious output. In 1932, Enoch and Harvey started Reinhardt Brothers, in Vale, North Carolina. Four years later, when Harvey began H. F. Reinhardt Pottery, Enoch started marking his work "E. W. Reinhardt Pottery." In 1942, when Harvey was drafted, he moved his family to Wilmington. He sold his business to Burlon B. Craig in 1946. Enoch left the pottery business that same year.

*See also Reinhardt Brothers:* CRAFT SHOPS AND PRODUCTION CENTERS—CERAMICS

## REISS, WINOLD
Born 1886, Karlsruhe, Germany; died August 29, 1953, New York, New York.
Illustrator, painter

Reiss believed it was possible to document distinctive racial types. A 1989 National Portrait Gallery exhibition of his work included portraits of Europeans, African Americans, Asian Americans, European Americans, and Native Americans, among others. During the 1920s, he illustrated *Survey Graphic* articles on sea island basketmakers and the Harlem Renaissance. The latter work, which also appeared in *The New Negro*, Alain LeRoy Locke's 1925 anthology of the Harlem Renaissance, reveals his attention to the variety of complexions and facial features among Harlem residents. He also illustrated *School Acres* (1930), Rossa B. Cooley's book on Penn Normal, Industrial, and Agricultural School, on St. Helena Island, South Carolina. Reiss traveled extensively to tribes in the United States and Canada to paint Native Americans, his favorite subject.

*See also Cooley, Rossa B.,* School Acres: An Adventure in Rural Education: BOOKS AND PERIODICALS

## REVIS, MARGARET MELINDA CARSON ("BIG MAMA")
Born 1886, Big Ivy, North Carolina; died 1971, Beech Community, North Carolina.
Dollmaker

Revis and her husband, Jim, raised ten children while living in a one-room house and farming leased land. One winter night, she dreamed that she was a little girl and came upon a cow eating her lost doll. The cow, taking pity on the child, taught her how to use corn shucks to make a doll. Soon after the dream, Revis began creating corn-shuck dolls, working to perfect the design and technique. She sold the dolls through the Allanstand Cottage Industries, in Asheville, and, in 1919, patented her "Husk Family," which included mother and father dolls, twelve-year-old brother and sister twin dolls, a six-year-old girl doll, and a "tiny tot" doll. Revis later designed aunt, uncle, and grandparent dolls. When Jim Revis died, seven children were still living at home, and the corn-shuck dolls became the family business. In the summer, they raised corn, and in the fall and winter, they assembled the dolls. Revis became known as Big Mama, not for her girth but for the size of her real and corn-shuck families.

*See also Allanstand Cottage Industries:* CRAFT SHOPS AND PRODUCTION CENTERS—TEXTILES

## RITCHIE, CORDELIA EVERIDGE ("AUNT CORD")
No dates available.
Basketmaker

Aunt Cord Ritchie was a self-taught basketmaker who took apart baskets to study how they were made. When asked where she got her patterns, she replied that "they're all in my head somewhere!" Ritchie's baskets were made of willow, oak, hickory, and honeysuckle vines. Her first husband, Soloman Everidge, was involved in the founding of Hindman Settlement School. Aunt Cord, who taught her basketmaking craft to others, was well-known and beloved at the school.

*See also Hindman Settlement School:* SCHOOLS

## ROOSEVELT, EDITH KERMIT CAROW
Born August 16, 1861, Norwich, Connecticut; died September 30, 1948.
Seamstress

In 1886, Edith Carow became the second wife of Theodore Roosevelt. A refined and socially conservative woman, she concentrated on the family's domestic life. After the death of her husband, she became active in a needlework guild, producing samplers and embroidered genre pictures, many depicting scenes from her husband's career or family events. These included a sampler portraying one of her husband's hunting expeditions and a petit point sampler, sewn, in 1933, in honor of the recognition of the U.S.S.R. by the United States.

## SACK, ISRAEL
Born September 15, 1883, Kaunas, Lithuania; died May 4, 1959, Brookline, Massachusetts.
Furnituremaker, antiques dealer

After apprenticing as a cabinetmaker in England, Sack moved to Boston in 1903, where, two years later, he opened a shop. There, he made cabinets and repaired furniture for antiques dealers and collectors. In time, he became an expert on seventeenth- and eighteenth-century American antiques, opening antiques shops in Marblehead, Massachusetts; New London, Connecticut; and New York City. Sack helped private individuals and museums build their collections. Among his clients were Henry Ford, who used his assistance in furnishing the Wayside Inn, at Greenfield Village, and John D. Rockefeller, Jr., who hired him to procure American and English antiques for Colonial Williamsburg.

*See also Colonial Williamsburg; Greenfield Village:* GOVERNMENT AND PRIVATE AGENCIES AND INSTITUTIONS

## SALAZAR, DAVID
Born 1901, Los Cerrilos, New Mexico; no death date available.
Weaver

Self-taught, Salazar began weaving in 1932. He also taught himself the arts of spinning and vegetable dyeing. In the 1930s, he demonstrated weaving at Santa Fe's Native Market and taught spinning, dyeing, and weaving for the New Mexico State Department of Vocational Education. Salazar made mohair draperies using a four-harness loom, and wove neckties and scarves that were sold at Lord & Taylor. He was also an accomplished leatherworker.

*See also New Mexico State Department of Vocational Education:* GOVERNMENT AND PRIVATE AGENCIES AND INSTITUTIONS

*Native Market:* CRAFT SHOPS AND PRODUCTION CENTERS—GENERAL

## SAMPSON, ANNA PENNINGTON
Born 1897; died 1981, Fulton, Arkansas.
Quiltmaker

Sampson was an active quilter in the Fulton area.

## SEGURA, GEORGE
No dates available.
Woodworker

In the early 1930s, Segura taught furnituremaking at the Spanish-American Normal School, in El Rito, New Mexico. He also supervised the National Youth Administration students who made furniture for the Albuquerque Little Theater.

*See also Works Progress Administration— Albuquerque Little Theater:* GOVERNMENT AND PRIVATE AGENCIES AND INSTITUTIONS

## SHELTON, JOSSIE
Born 1917, near Haynesville, Louisiana.
Quiltmaker

At eight, Jossie learned to quilt by watching her mother, which led to a lifelong interest. A few years after her marriage, in 1938, to Mitchell Shelton, she used whatever scraps she had available to make her *Mosaic/String Strip Quilt.* Piecing quilts by day and by night until her eyes began to fail, she then turned to local gospel singing performances with her guitarist husband.

## SIMMONS, PETER
Born 1855, St. Stephens, South Carolina; died 1954, Charleston, South Carolina.
Blacksmith, wheelwright

Born into slavery, Simmons learned blacksmithing from his father. His work consisted primarily of toolmaking and repair work, skills he passed on to Philip Simmons (no relation).

## SIMMONS, PHILIP
Born 1912, Wando, Daniel Island, South Carolina.
Blacksmith

Apprenticed in 1925 at the age of thirteen, Simmons acquired skills reflecting a tradition that can be traced back to 1825 and the work of Guy Simmons, the father of his mentor Peter Simmons (no relation). With the decline in the market for wrought-iron tools, Simmons began making decorative ironwork. Today, he is still producing gates and other distinctive pieces in Charleston, South Carolina. A small garden-museum is being established in Charleston for his work.

## SIMS, LUCY
Born c. 1874; died 1941.
Quiltmaker

An active quiltmaker in Mount Zion and Galveston, Texas, her only surviving piece, *Wild Goose Chase Quilt,* completed around 1925, demonstrates the endurance of a nineteenth-century pattern.

## STAHL, THOMAS
Born 1863, Carl's Hill, Upper Milford Township, Lehigh County, Pennsylvania; died December 10, 1942, Powder Valley, Pennsylvania.

## STAHL, ISAAC S.
Born September 15, 1872, Carl's Hill, Upper Milford Township, Lehigh County, Pennsylvania; died August 17, 1949, Bally, Pennsylvania.
Ceramists

Pennsylvania German folk potters Thomas and Isaac Stahl continued a family tradition. The Stahl interest in pottery began when their father, Charles Ludwig Stahl (1828–1896), entered an apprenticeship in 1843 in the pottery of John Krauss, in Kraussdale, Lower Milford Township, Lehigh County. In 1847, at nineteen, Charles bought land and started the Powder Valley Pottery, operating it until his death. Three of his sons—James, Thomas, and Isaac—followed the craft. At their father's death, Isaac, who had started working in the pottery when he was twelve and had been made foreman at twenty-two, took over and, for two years, managed the business under his own name. From 1898 to 1902, he managed it in partnership with his brother James, but competition put them out of business. For thirty years, the brothers pursued other professions. The death of folk potter Jacob Medinger, in 1932, prompted Isaac and Thomas to reestablish their pottery, continuing the folk-art tradition.

## STARK, TILLIE GABALDON
Born 1919, Santa Fe, New Mexico.
Embroiderer

Before learning to do *colcha* embroidery, Gabaldon made natural-dyed yarn for weavers. She studied embroidery with Dolores Perrault Montoya, of Taos, New Mexico, and became an expert in the craft. In the 1930s, Gabaldon was employed by Santa Fe's Native Market to demonstrate dyeing and colcha embroidery.

*See also Native Market:* CRAFT SHOPS AND PRODUCTION CENTERS—GENERAL

## STEPHENS, WALTER BENJAMIN
Born October 3, 1876, Clinton, Iowa; died 1961, Asheville, North Carolina.
Ceramist

As a boy on the family farm in Tennessee, Stephens first worked with his mother, a ceramist and teacher. In 1913, he moved to Asheville, North Carolina, and in the 1920s, he established the Pisgah Forest Pottery, in Arden, North Carolina. There, he developed American Cameo pottery, a technique of raised porcelain scenes of Americana on plain pottery bodies, similar to the work of Wedgwood. Stephens's designs, which included covered wagons, deer hunting motifs, and eventful moments in the life of Daniel Boone, were an outgrowth of his interest in American history and his own childhood experiences traveling to Nebraska in a covered wagon.

*See also Pisgah Forest Pottery:* CRAFT SHOPS AND PRODUCTION CENTERS— CERAMICS

## STONE, ARTHUR JOHN
Born September 26, 1847, Sheffield, England; died February 2, 1938, Gardner, Massachusetts.
Metalsmith

After serving an apprenticeship in Sheffield, England, Stone emigrated to the United States in 1884 and became a designer and head of the hollowware department at W. B. Durgin, in Concord, New Hampshire. In 1887, he left that position to establish the hollowware department at F. W. Smith and Company, in Gardner, Massachusetts, a position he retained until he opened his own shop, in 1901. Stone advocated handwrought silver during the Arts and Crafts period, developing a style of smooth surfaces and spare ornamentation. His artistry and craftsmanship rivaled the most acclaimed American silverwork, gaining Stone a reputation as the successor to Paul Revere.

*See also Arthur J. Stone Associates:* CRAFT SHOPS AND PRODUCTION CENTERS— METALS

## TAFOYA, MARGARET
Born August 17, 1904, Santa Clara Pueblo, New Mexico; no death date available.
Ceramist

Margaret learned the art of potterymaking from her mother, Sara Fina, who was known for her carved pottery, and her grandmother, aunt, and older sister. She attended the Santa Clara Pueblo School and, at eleven, was sent to the Santa Fe Indian School Studio, returning home in 1918 when a flu epidemic killed many Santa Clara residents. She was soon making pottery with her mother, but left the pueblo to work as a cook at the Jicarilla Apache Indian Reservation, in Dulce, New Mexico, for three years. In 1924, she came back to marry Alcario Tafoya. While raising their twelve children, ten of whom lived beyond infancy, Margaret returned to her craft. Creating both large and small pieces of evenly fired and highly polished blackware that her husband often painted and carved, she was soon trading her pots for clothing or selling them to pueblo visitors and through dealers in Santa Fe and Taos. Her large ceramic vessels often required months to dry and hours to polish, and the beauty and detail of these majestic and sizable ollas garnered her great public attention. In 1984, Tafoya was chosen Folk Artist of the Year by the National Endowment for the Arts; in 1985, she was given the Governor of New Mexico Award for Outstanding Achievement.

## TAFOYA, TEOFILO
Born 1915, Santa Clara Pueblo, New Mexico.
Painter

Tafoya studied at the Santa Fe Indian School Studio and, later, taught art there and at the Albuquerque Indian School. After World War II, he received his B.A. in art education from the University of New Mexico. His painting style was essentially conservative.

*See also Santa Fe Indian School Studio:* SCHOOLS

## TANTAQUIDGEON, JOHN W. (CHIEF MATAHGA)
Born February 3, 1865; died April 1, 1949, Norwich, Connecticut.

## TANTAQUIDGEON, HAROLD
Born June 18, 1904; died April 1989.
Woodcarvers

Descendants of the famed Mohegan chief Uncas, John Tantaquidgeon and his son Harold kept southern New England Indian culture alive during the interwar period. John Tantaquidgeon's daughter Gladys was the first specialist appointed by John Collier to serve as a field representative for the Indian Arts and Crafts Board. Today, in her midnineties, she manages the family museum on Mohegan Hill, in Uncasville, Connecticut. The museum features the basketry, stonework, and elegant woodcarving of the woodland Mohegan Indians.

## TELLER, MYRON S.
No dates available.
Architect

Teller specialized in the restoration and revival of Dutch colonial houses in Kingston, New York. He employed blacksmiths of Dutch colonial heritage to ensure the stylistic accuracy of hardware used. Two blacksmiths who worked for Teller were brothers George and Abram Van Kleeck. Their grandfather had operated a smith shop in Samsonville, New York, in which the smithing skills and tools of the trade had been passed down for three generations.

## TOMAH, SABATTIS
No dates available.
Basketmaker

Sabattis Tomah was the son of Tomah Joseph, a brilliant Passamaquoddy leader whose talents as a birchbark engraver were unsurpassed. His son carried on the tradition, producing both carved and birchbark work.

## TOREBIO, ISABEL
fl. 1920s, Santo Domingo Pueblo, New Mexico.
Ceramist

Torebio was a potter whose intricate and stylized jars demonstrated the artistic conservatism that prevailed in the area.

## TUCKER, JUANITA
fl. 1940s.
Dollmaker

Tucker, an Assiniboin dollmaker, defied the Plains dollmaking tradition of not making portraits when she fashioned a pair of dolls that specifically represented the deceased son and daughter-in-law of the last Montana Blackfeet chief. Her dolls of Two Guns White Calf and his wife were not designed to be playthings or souvenirs—rather, they were created as an intentional memorial of the couple.

## VAUGHAN, LESTER HOWARD
No dates available.
Metalsmith

Trained as a silversmith, Vaughan began to work with pewter about 1915. He helped popularize it, making many objects by hand, others by casting or spinning. Among his many awards were medals from the Boston Society of Arts and Crafts and the Art Institute of Chicago.

## WEND, MILTON
No dates available.
Blacksmith, writer

In the 1920s, while operating Half Moon Forge, Wend issued a catalogue: *A Guide to Some Old Fashioned Hand-Forged Wrought Iron.* He also demonstrated his skills at early craft fairs for the New Hampshire Arts and Crafts League. In 1944, he wrote *How To Live in the Country without Farming,* which offered advice and observations on country living.

*See also New Hampshire Arts and Crafts League:* GUILDS AND SOCIETIES

## WOODMAN, ROBERT
Born 1908; died 1983.
Tinsmith

Trained as an engineer, Woodman made durable tinwork pieces, including mirrors, wall sconces, and chandeliers. He worked with Spanish Colonial revival architects on both public buildings and private residences. His collaborations with John Gaw Meem include the Laboratory of Anthropology and the Zimmerman Library at the University of New Mexico, in Albuquerque.

*See also John Gaw Meem:* ARTISTS' BIOGRAPHIES

## YAZZ, BEATIEN (JIMMY TODDY)
Born 1928, near Wide Ruins Trading Post, Arizona.
Painter

Yazz's father worked for Sallie and William Lippincott at their Wide Ruins Trading Post. The couple recognized Yazz's talent and encouraged him to use art as a means of personal expression. In 1945, Alberta Hannum published a fictional biography of Yazz, *Spin a Silver Dollar: The Story of a Desert Trading Post,* and the young Indian artist illustrated it. After the Lippincotts introduced him to Chicano artist James Swann, Yazz began producing socially relevant paintings as well as landscapes, neither of which showed an Indian influence.

*See also Wide Ruins Trading Post:* CRAFT SHOPS AND PRODUCTION CENTERS— TEXTILES

## YELLIN, SAMUEL
Born March 2, 1885, Mogilev-Podolski, Russia; died October 3, 1940, New York, New York.
Metalsmith

Yellin lived and worked in Philadelphia. His Arch Street Metalworkers Studio included a showroom, library, museum, drafting room, and forge space for two hundred workers. Instrumental in the revival of wrought iron in America, Yellin was considered its foremost master craftsman.

## AMSDEN, CHARLES AVERY
Born August 18, 1899, Forest City, Iowa;
died March 3, 1941, Los Angeles,
California.
Curator

A 1922 graduate of Harvard, Amsden
served as United States vice-consul in
various cities in France, Switzerland, and
Mexico. In 1927, he became curator of
the Southwest Museum, in Los Angeles,
and from 1928 to 1941 was secretary-
treasurer. During his career, Amsden
participated in archaeological excavations in the Southwest, including the one
at Pecos Pueblo. Among his publications, based on his fieldwork, are *Navaho
Weaving: Its Technic and History* (1934)
and *The Ancient Basketmakers* (1939).

*See also Amsden, Charles Avery,* The
Ancient Basketmakers *and* Navaho
Weaving: Its Technic and History:
BOOKS AND PERIODICALS

## APPLEGATE, FRANK G.
Born 1882, Atlanta, Illinois; died
February 13, 1931, Santa Fe, New
Mexico.
Painter, collector

From 1908 to 1920, Applegate taught at
the Trenton Industrial Art School, in
New Jersey. In 1921, he moved to Santa
Fe to devote himself to painting. Recognizing the craftsmanship of native artists,
he became interested in Spanish colonial
culture and began collecting examples of
*bultos, santos,* and furniture. With Mary
Austin, he established the Spanish Colonial Arts Society, in 1929, to promote
and preserve these crafts. His book *Indian Stories from the Pueblos* (1929) details
his study of Indian culture.

*See also Society for the Revival of Spanish-
Colonial Arts:* GUILDS AND SOCIETIES

## AUSTIN, MARY HUNTER
Born September 9, 1868, Carlinville,
Illinois; died August 13, 1934, Santa Fe,
New Mexico.
Author, collector

As part of the staff of the 1918 Carnegie
Foundation study on Americanization,
Austin became interested in the Spanish
colonial arts. She coined the term *Spanish colonial* to refer to the descendants of
the Spanish colonists. She and Frank
Applegate became the prime movers
behind the formation of the Spanish
Colonial Arts Society, in 1929. Many of
her thirty-two books and more than two
hundred articles deal with the region and
its culture.

## BASCOM, WILLIAM RUSSELL
Born May 23, 1912, Princeton, Illinois;
death date not available.
Anthropologist

An expert on African culture, Bascom
was interested in finding evidence of its
traditions in the United States. Along
with Melville Herskovits and Guy Johnson, he advised the Savannah Unit of the
WPA's Georgia Writer's Project, which
searched for examples of African culture
among coastal black Georgians in the
late 1930s. Bascom taught at Northwestern University from 1939 to 1957 and,
later, at the University of California,
Berkeley. His books include *Continuity
and Change in African Cultures* (1959),
*African Arts* (1967), and *African Art in
Cultural Perspective* (1973).

## BREW, JOHN OTIS
Born March 28, 1906, Malden,
Massachusetts.
Anthropologist

From 1930 to 1967, Brew was associated
with the Peabody Museum at Harvard
University, his alma mater. He directed
the museum and the division of North
American archaeology from 1948 to
1967. For twenty-five years, he was the
Peabody Professor of American Archaeology and Ethnology at Harvard, becoming an emeritus faculty member in 1972.
His fieldwork includes the excavation, in
Arizona, of prehistoric pueblo murals of
the Awatovi.

## CAHILL, E. HOLGER
Born January 13, 1887, Snaefellsnessysla,
Iceland; died July 8, 1960, Stockbridge,
Massachusetts.
Curator, writer

Cahill began his career as a freelance
writer and journalist. In 1922, he joined
the staff of the Newark Museum and, in
time, became an expert on American
folk art. From 1932 to 1933, he served as
exhibitions director at the Museum of
Modern Art, in New York City. He then
worked with Mrs. John D. Rockefeller,
Jr., in developing what is now the Abby
Aldrich Rockefeller Folk Art Collection,
in Colonial Williamsburg. In 1935,
Cahill was appointed director of the
Works Progress Administration's Federal
Art Project, a post he held until 1943.
Following that, he became a novelist.

*See also Federal Art Project (FAP):* GOV-
ERNMENT AND PRIVATE AGENCIES AND
INSTITUTIONS

## CAMPBELL, JOHN CHARLES
Born September 14, 1867, La Porte,
Indiana; died May 2, 1919, New York,
New York.
Educator, writer

A graduate of Williams College and
Andover Theological Seminary, Campbell served as principal of a mountain
academy in Alabama, under the auspices
of the Congregational American Missionary Association, from 1895 to 1898.
He next spent a year teaching in a public
school in Stevens Point, Wisconsin,
before returning to Appalachia to serve
as principal of another mountain academy, in Tennessee, in 1899. Two years
later, he became affiliated with Piedmont
College, in Demorest, Georgia, eventually taking over as president. After
approaching the Russell Sage Foundation about conducting a field study in
Appalachia, he was hired to study its
problems and conditions. Beginning in
1908, and for the next year and a half, he
toured the area on horseback and by
wagon. In 1912, the foundation created
the Southern Highlands Division, with
Campbell as its director. He advocated
an educational curriculum based on
Danish folk schools as appropriate for
the region. In 1921, two years after his
death, *The Southern Highlander and His
Homeland* was published.

*See also Russell Sage Foundation:* GOV-
ERNMENT AND PRIVATE AGENCIES AND
INSTITUTIONS

## CAMPBELL, OLIVE DAME
Born 1882, Medford, Massachusetts; no
death date available.
Educator, school founder

After graduating from Tufts College, she
taught school, before becoming John C.
Campbell's second wife, in 1907. As her
husband toured the Southern Highlands
for the Russell Sage Foundation, she collected the words and music of the ballads she heard, while studying the
baskets and quilts of their informants.
With English folk-song scholar Cecil
Sharp (1859–1924), she continued studying the folk ballads and, in 1917, published *English Folk Songs of the Southern
Appalachians.* Campbell became interested in Danish folk schools as an appropriate way to enhance mountain life and
culture; in 1919, she received a fellowship from the American Scandinavian
Foundation to study their efforts first-
hand. In 1925, she opened the John C.
Campbell Folk School, in Brasstown,
North Carolina.

*See also John C. Campbell Folk School:* SCHOOLS

## COLLIER, JOHN
Born May 4, 1884, Atlanta, Georgia; died May 8, 1968, Talpa, New Mexico. Government administrator, teacher

From 1907 to 1919, Collier worked as the secretary of the People's Institute, in New York City, advocating city planning for recreational activities for children and adults. His experience with various immigrant groups convinced him that the process of Americanization did not necessitate the rejection of one's native culture. Applying this understanding to the Pueblo Indians, he became an advocate for preserving and promoting their rights and culture under the auspices of the Indian Welfare Committee of the General Federation of Women's Clubs and the American Indian Defense Association. From 1933 to 1945, Collier served as United States Commissioner of Indian Affairs, winning compensation for lost tribal lands, restoring surplus lands to tribes, promoting tribal corporations and self-government, and establishing the Indian Arts and Crafts Board to improve and protect Indian-made products. When government concerns for Indian affairs declined during World War II, Collier resigned and accepted teaching positions at City College of New York and Knox College.

*See also Indian Arts and Crafts Board:* GOVERNMENT AND PRIVATE AGENCIES AND INSTITUTIONS

## COOK, NANCY
Born August 26, 1884, Massena, New York; died August 16, 1962, Trumbull, Connecticut. Entrepreneur, teacher, woodworker

In 1922, while serving as executive secretary of the women's division of the New York State Democratic Committee, Cook met Eleanor Roosevelt. A 1912 graduate of Syracuse University, Cook was a skilled craftsperson who had taught arts and handcrafts in the Fulton, New York, public school system. During World War I, she worked for the Red Cross in England, where she used her woodworking skills to make artificial limbs. After learning of the Roosevelts' interest in providing employment for farmers unable to fully support themselves by farming, Cook suggested setting up a small industry to produce quality, early American reproduction furniture. This was the genesis of Val-Kill Industries, which lasted from 1927 to 1938. Cook supervised the Val-Kill Furniture Shop.

*See also Val-Kill Industries:* CRAFT SHOPS AND PRODUCTION CENTERS—GENERAL

## COOLEY, ROSSA BELLE
Born 1873, Albany, New York; died September 24, 1949, Greenport, New York. Educator

Cooley graduated from Vassar College in 1893, and devoted her life to improving the conditions of blacks. After teaching at Hampton Institute, in Virginia, for seven years, she was appointed principal of Penn Normal, Industrial, and Agricultural School, on St. Helena Island, South Carolina, in 1905, and served in that position until 1944. She wrote about her experiences in *Homes of the Freed* (1926) and *School Acres: An Adventure in Rural Education* (1930).

*See also Cooley, Rossa B.,* School Acres: An Adventure in Rural Education: BOOKS AND PERIODICALS

## DEFENBACHER, DANIEL S.
Born May 22, 1906, Dover, Ohio. Arts administrator

As state director for the North Carolina WPA Federal Art Project, Defenbacher established three community art centers, with galleries and instructional programs. His innovations were picked up by the national office, and he served as assistant to the director from 1936 to 1939. That year, Defenbacher became director of the Walker Art Center, in Minneapolis, Minnesota. Twelve years later, he assumed a similar position at the Fort Worth Arts Center, where he stayed until 1954. He moved to the private sector in 1959, becoming director of design and communications for the Raychem Corporation, until 1973.

## D'HARNONCOURT, RENÉ
Born May 17, 1901, Vienna, Austria; died August 13, 1968, New Suffolk, Long Island, New York. Curator, museum director

Originally a student of philosophy and chemistry, d'Harnoncourt moved to Mexico in 1926 and supported himself painting postcards for tourists and decorating shop windows. Working on an exhibition of pre-Columbian art at the Frederick Davis Gallery, he met the Mexican Minister of Education, who, in turn, introduced him to the United States Ambassador. D'Harnoncourt was chosen to coordinate an exhibition of Mexican art to circulate in the United States. In 1933, he became director of a nationwide broadcast on art for NBC radio. In 1935, he taught art history at Sarah Lawrence College. The following year, he became the general manager of the Indian Arts and Crafts Board, a position he held for eight years. D'Harnoncourt was the originator and coordinator of the Museum of Modern Art's "Indian Art of the United States" exhibition, in 1941. In 1944, he became vice president in charge of foreign activities and director of the Department of Manual Industries at the museum. From 1949 to 1968, he served as the museum's director.

*See also Museum of Modern Art—Indian Art of the United States:* EXHIBITIONS

## DICKERMAN, MARION
Born April 11, 1890, Westfield, New York; died May 16, 1983, Kennett Square, Pennsylvania. Educator

Dickerman was a longtime companion of Nancy Cook, a close friend of Eleanor Roosevelt. She and Cook began living together in 1909, during their graduate-school years at Syracuse University. After teaching high school in Canisteo and Fulton, New York, Dickerman served as dean of the New Jersey State Normal School, in Trenton, from 1920 to 1921. The following year, she started teaching at Todhunter, a girls school, in New York City. In 1926, Dickerman, Cook, and Roosevelt bought the school, and Dickerman served as principal from 1927 to 1939. She was a co-owner of Val-Kill Industries; because of her school responsibilities, though, she was not as closely associated with its activities.

*See also Val-Kill Industries:* CRAFT SHOPS AND PRODUCTION CENTERS—GENERAL

## DOUGLAS, FREDERICK HUNTINGTON
Born October 29, 1897, Evergreen, Colorado; died April 23, 1956, Denver, Colorado. Curator

Douglas received an A.B. degree from the University of Colorado in 1921 and studied at the Pennsylvania Academy of the Fine Arts, in Philadelphia, from 1922 to 1926. He worked as a painter and woodcarver for four years before beginning his association, in 1929, with the Denver Art Museum. Serving as curator of Indian arts and, later, Native arts, Douglas helped the museum build its Indian art collection and promote the aesthetic value of Indian art. With René d'Harnoncourt, he organized important Indian art exhibitions at the Golden Gate International Exposition, in San Francisco, and the Museum of Modern Art, in New York City. In 1946, he began serving as a commissioner on the Indian Arts and Crafts Board.

## EATON, ALLEN HENDERSHOTT
Born October 1878, Crestwood, New York; died December 7, 1962, Union, Oregon. Writer, arts administrator

Raised on a farm in Union, Oregon, Eaton trained as a sociologist at the University of Oregon, where he later became a lecturer on art appreciation. His involvement with craft exhibitions began in 1915 when his proposal for a crafts installation in the Oregon Building at the Panama-Pacific Exposition was accepted. In 1919, he was appointed field secretary of the American Federation of Arts; the following year, he joined the Surveys and Exhibits Division of the Russell Sage Foundation, mounting craft exhibitions and teaching others how to organize craft shows. After a chance meeting in 1926 with Olive Dame Campbell, widow of the director of the Southern Highlands Division of the foundation, Eaton traveled to Appalachia to address the Conference of Southern Mountain Workers. His lecture inspired the founding, in 1928, of the Southern Mountain Handicraft Guild. Over the next decade, Eaton promoted and documented Highlands crafts and craftspersons in such books as *Handicrafts of the Southern Highlands* (1937) and *Rural Handicrafts in the United States* (1937). In 1941, he was appointed director of the foundation's Department of Arts and Social Work. He expanded his craft interests by working with the Boston Society of Arts and Crafts. He later wrote *Handicrafts of New England* (1949).

EWERS, JOHN CANFIELD
Born July 21, 1909, Cleveland, Ohio.
Curator, museum director

A graduate of Dartmouth and Yale, Ewers worked as curator for the National Park Service between 1935 and 1940, serving in Morristown, New Jersey; Berkeley, California; and Macon, Georgia. From 1941 to 1944, he was curator at the Museum of the Plains Indian, in Montana. Beginning in 1945, he held several positions at the Smithsonian Institution, including associate curator of ethnology (1945–56) and assistant director (1959–64) and director (1964–65) of the Museum of History and Technology. His books include *Plains Indian Painting* (1940), *Artists of the Old West* (1965), and *Indian Life on the Upper Missouri* (1968).

FEWKES, JESSE WALTER
Born November 14, 1850, Newton, Massachusetts; died May 31, 1930, Forest Glen, Maryland.
Ethnologist

After earning a Ph.D. from Harvard in 1877, Fewkes studied zoology at the University of Leipzig, in Germany. He returned to his alma mater to work at the Museum of Comparative Zoology from 1890 to 1899. In 1895, he became associated with the Bureau of American Ethnology, a connection he maintained until his retirement, in 1928. During his career, Fewkes participated in excavations of prehistoric ruins in Arizona, New Mexico, Colorado, and Utah, as well as in Puerto Rico, eastern Mexico, Tennessee, and Georgia. He served as field director for the Hemenway Archaeological Expedition from 1891 to 1895. His contributions were numerous and important: an application of zoological methods to archaeology, including a comparison of ancient zoomorphic designs to modern Hopi culture; the discovery of a new type of pottery in Mimbres Valley, New Mexico; and his work tracing the migrations of the separate tribes that became the Hopi.

FROST, WILLIAM. G.
Born July 2, 1854, Le Roy, New York; died September 12, 1938, Berea, Kentucky.
Educator

Frost received his bachelor's and master's degrees from Oberlin College, in 1876 and 1879, respectively, and his Ph.D. from the University of Wooster in 1891. The following year, he became president of Berea College, in Kentucky, serving in that position until 1920. At Berea, Frost adapted the curriculum to meet the region's needs. In 1907, he helped found the Lincoln Institute of Kentucky, when the state legislature outlawed integrated schools.

*See also Berea College:* SCHOOLS

GLASSGOLD, C. ADOLPH
Born February 8, 1899, New York, New York; no death date available.
Arts administrator, editor, painter

Glassgold taught painting at a New York City high school from 1922 to 1925. After painting in Europe for two years, he taught at City College of New York, from 1927 to 1929. He edited *The Arts* (1928–30) and *Creative Art* (1930–32), and succeeded Ruth Reeves as national coordinator of the Index of American Design, from 1937 to 1940. Beginning in 1941, Glassgold pursued his interest in public housing and international relief work.

*See also Federal Art Project (FAP)— Index of American Design:* GOVERNMENT AND PRIVATE AGENCIES AND INSTITUTIONS

GORDON, ROBERT WINSLOW
Born September 2, 1888, Bangor, Maine; died March 29, 1961, Washington, D.C.
Folklife archivist

An early leader in documenting American folk songs, Gordon taught at the University of California at Berkeley from 1917 to 1924, a location that allowed him to collect sea songs at the San Francisco and Oakland waterfronts. In 1925, he became a freelance folk historian, writing in popular magazines and continuing to collect songs and piece together their histories. For the next four years, he recorded African American songs along the Georgia coast, near Darien. In 1928, Gordon became the first director of the Library of Congress's Archive of American Folk Song, a position that was eliminated in 1933. During his career, he collected more than nine hundred cylinder and disc recordings and ten thousand song manuscripts.

HERSKOVITS, MELVILLE J.
Born September 10, 1895, Bellefontaine, Ohio; died February 25, 1963.
Anthropologist

Herskovits received his Ph.D. from Columbia University in 1923, and lectured there on anthropology from 1924 to 1927. That same year, he began his association with Northwestern University, where he was to remain for the rest of his career, becoming a professor in 1935 and directing the Program of African Studies in 1951. Herskovits conducted field research in Dutch Guiana, Haiti, West Africa, Brazil, and Trinidad. He believed that elements of African culture were present in black folk dialect, music, dance, and folklore in the United States, although less so than in the Caribbean.

*See also Works Progress Administration —Georgia Writers' Project, Savannah Unit:* GOVERNMENT AND PRIVATE AGENCIES AND INSTITUTIONS

HEWETT, EDGAR LEE
Born November 23, 1865, Warren County, Illinois; died December 31, 1946, Albuquerque, New Mexico.
Anthropologist, educator, museum director

As an anthropologist, Hewett directed numerous excavations of ancient cliff dwellings and pueblos in Colorado, Utah, Arizona, and New Mexico. In addition, he held various administrative positions, serving as superintendent of Fairfax, Missouri, and Florence, Colorado, schools, from 1889 to 1892, and president of New Mexico Normal School, from 1898 to 1903. He encouraged the New Mexico territorial legislature to establish the Museum of New Mexico, and he served as the museum's director from its inception, in 1909, until 1917. From 1927 to 1940, he was professor of archaeology and anthropology at the State University of New Mexico.

*See also School of American Archaeology:* SCHOOLS

## HEYE, GEORGE GUSTAV

Born September 16, 1874, New York, New York; died January 20, 1957, New York.

Businessman, collector, museum director

Trained as an electrical engineer at Columbia University, Heye worked briefly in this field before forming the banking firm of Battles, Heye, and Harrison, where he was employed from 1901 to 1909. While working as an engineer in Arizona, he purchased a Navajo buckskin shirt; thus began what ultimately was to become one of the largest collections of American Indian artifacts. Beginning in 1904 and continuing throughout his lifetime, Heye participated in excavations and funded others through the Heye Foundation. In 1909, he housed his collection in the private Heye Museum, in New York City. With the death of his mother, in 1915, he inherited the family fortune and built the Museum of the American Indian, Heye Foundation, to which he donated his vast collection. Heye served as the director of the museum from 1916 to 1956.

## HODGE, FREDERICK WEBB

Born October 28, 1864, Plymouth, England; died September 28, 1956, Santa Fe, New Mexico.
Ethnologist

After working as a clerk in a law and publishing firm in Washington, D.C., Hodge accepted an appointment as a secretary for the United States Geological Survey. In 1886, he became secretary to the Hemenway Archaeological Expedition, which excavated Indian ruins in Arizona and New Mexico. Three years later, he began to work for the Bureau of American Ethnology at the Smithsonian Institution, serving as ethnologist-in-charge from 1910 to 1918. His next assignment took him to New York City, where he was an ethnologist for the Museum of the American Indian, Heye Foundation, until 1931. His final position was as director of the Southwest Museum, in Los Angeles. He retired in 1955, after building the museum's ethnology and archaeology collections on Indians of the Southwest.

## HRDLICKA, ALES

Born March 29, 1869, Humpolec, Bohemia; died September 5, 1943, Washington, D.C.
Anthropologist

As a young man, Hrdlicka worked in a cigar factory to support his family, who had emigrated to the United States in 1882. While ill with typhoid fever, he met a physician who encouraged him to pursue a medical degree. Hrdlicka grad

uated from the New York Homeopathic Medical College in 1894 and began to work for the State Homeopathic Hospital for the Insane. After performing numerous autopsies, he started to develop his own methods for using physical differences and skeletal measurements to distinguish races. In 1903, he helped organize the Smithsonian Institution's new Division of Physical Anthropology, serving as curator from 1910 to 1942. Based on his studies of skeletal remains, Hrdlicka believed that Native Americans were fairly recent descendants of Asians who had come to the Americas via the Bering Straits and Alaska.

## HUNTER, RUSSELL VERNON

Born 1900, Hallsville, Illinois; died March 20, 1955, Roswell, New Mexico.
Teacher, museum director, painter

After teaching art in the Los Cerrillos, New Mexico, schools, Hunter became director of the Puerto de Luna vocational school, in 1934. A year later, he was appointed WPA art director of New Mexico, a position he held until 1942. For five years, he worked as regional director of the USO. From 1948 to 1952, Hunter served as director of the Dallas Museum of Fine Arts; in 1952, he assumed a similar position at the Roswell Museum and Art Center, in New Mexico.

*See also Roswell Community Art Center:* GOVERNMENT AND PRIVATE AGENCIES AND INSTITUTIONS

## KIDDER, ALFRED VINCENT

Born October 29, 1895, Marquette, Michigan; died June 11, 1963, Cambridge, Massachusetts.
Archaeologist

After receiving his Ph.D. from Harvard University in 1914, Kidder participated in archaeological excavations in the American Southwest under the sponsorship of the Archaeological Institute of America (1907), University of Utah (1908), Harvard (1908), and the New Mexico Territorial Museum (1910–11). In 1910 and from 1912 to 1914, he taught at Harvard as an Austin teaching fellow. He directed excavations at Pecos, New Mexico, for the Phillips Academy from 1915 to 1929. Beginning in 1927, Kidder was associated with the Carnegie Institute of Washington, heading its division of historical research from 1930 to 1950. With S. J. Guernsey, Kidder wrote several books on his fieldwork, including *Archaeological Exploration in Northeastern Arizona* (1919) and *Basket-maker Caves of Northeastern Arizona* (1921). On his own, he wrote *The Artifacts of Pecos* (1932) and *The Pottery of Pecos* (1931 and 1936).

*See also Guernsey, Samuel James, and Alfred Vincent Kidder,* Basket-maker Caves of Northeastern Arizona *Kidder, Alfred Vincent,* The Artifacts of Pecos *and* The Pottery of Pecos: BOOKS AND PERIODICALS

## KROEBER, ALFRED LOUIS

Born June 11, 1876, Hoboken, New Jersey; died October 5, 1960, Berkeley, California.
Anthropologist, collector

A student of Franz Boas at Columbia University, Kroeber received his Ph.D. in 1901. His doctoral dissertation on "Decorative Symbolism of the Arapaho" reflected his interest in culture and languages. He became the first faculty member in the University of California at Berkeley's newly formed Department of Anthropology, and he stayed at the university until his retirement, in 1946. Kroeber collected Native American baskets and was interested in Native American art. His publications numbered more than seven hundred, including *Anthropology* (1923), which was the discipline's standard text for many years, *Handbook of the Indians of California* (1925), and *Cultural and Natural Areas of Native North America* (1939).

*See also Kroeber, Alfred Louis,* Handbook of the Indians of California: BOOKS AND PERIODICALS

## LA FARGE, OLIVER

Born December 19, 1901, New York, New York; died August 2, 1963.
Anthropologist, writer

La Farge pursued his childhood interest in Native Americans, participating in archaeological excavations, championing the rights of Indians, and writing both children's and adult novels and nonfiction works that drew upon Indian culture. His novel *Laughing Boy* won the Pulitzer Prize in 1929. From 1926 to 1928, La Farge taught ethnology at Tulane University. From 1931 to 1933, he was an anthropology fellow at Columbia University, and taught writing there from 1936 to 1941. He worked for the government as a field representative for the United States Indian Service (1936), a committee member to the Government on Indian Affairs (1949), and a member of the United States Department of the Interior's Committee on Indian Arts and Crafts. During the 1930s, he also directed the Eastern Association in Indian Affairs (1930–32), the National Association on Indian Affairs (1933–37), and the American Association of Indian Affairs (1937–42). In the 1960s, Secretary of the Interior Stewart L. Udall claimed La Farge knew "more about the American Indian than any non-Indian."

See also *American Association of Indian Affairs:* GUILDS AND SOCIETIES

## LOCKE, ALAIN LeROY

Born September 13, 1886, Philadelphia, Pennsylvania; died June 9, 1954, New York, New York.
Educator, writer

Locke was the first black Rhodes scholar at Oxford University, in England. A 1907 Harvard graduate, he became a professor of philosophy and education at Howard University in 1912, and served as head of the Department of Philosophy from 1917 to 1953. When *The New Negro* was published, in 1925, Locke became known as "the voice of the Harlem Renaissance." In that anthology, he described the Harlem Renaissance as an "artistic awakening of racial self-consciousness and a collective renewal for black people," for, during the 1920s, urban blacks had made Harlem the center of cultural activities in the literary and visual arts. Locke believed that a better understanding of African Americans' past and present contributions to American culture would help alleviate racism.

See also *Locke, Alain LeRoy,* The New Negro: BOOKS AND PERIODICALS

## LUHAN, MABEL DODGE

Born February 26, 1879, Buffalo, New York; died August 13, 1962, Taos, New Mexico.
Writer

Luhan is known for her informative memoirs and for her promotion of Indian cultures. Born into a socially prominent family, she moved to Florence, Italy, where she established an artistic and literary salon with her second husband, Edwin Dodge. Divorcing Dodge in 1913, she returned to New York City and established another literary salon, in Greenwich Village, attracting Emma Goldman, Margaret Sanger, and Lincoln Steffens, among others. In 1916, she married artist Maurice Sterne; when she joined him in Santa Fe, she became fascinated with the Pueblo Indians. She settled there, divorced Sterne, and, in 1923, married painter Tony Luhan, a full-blooded Taos Pueblo Indian. She wrote about her experiences with the artists, writers, and political radicals of the day in such books as *Lorenzo in Taos* (1932), *Winter in Taos* (1935), and *Edge of Taos Desert, An Escape to Reality* (1937).

## MINER, LEIGH RICHMOND

Born August 5, 1864, Cornwall, Connecticut; died June 9, 1935, Hampton, Virginia.
Teacher, photographer

Originally hired to teach drawing at the Hampton Institute, Miner became director of applied art from 1898 to 1904 and 1907 to 1935. From 1904 to 1907, he pursued his interest in photography, setting up a studio in New York City. In the early 1900s and again in 1923, Miner visited former Hampton students who were teaching at Penn Normal, Industrial, and Agricultural School, on St. Helena Island, South Carolina. Intrigued by the surroundings, he photographed the island people and school activities. His photographs appear in Edith Dabbs's *Face of an Island: Leigh Richmond Miner's Photographs of Saint Helena Island* (1970).

See also *Penn School:* SCHOOLS

## MORLEY, SYLVANUS GRISWOLD

Born June 7, 1883, Chester, Pennsylvania; died September 2, 1948, Mexico.
Archaeologist, writer

An expert on Mayan civilization, Morley also was interested in Spanish pueblo revival architecture. From 1909 to 1913, he conducted fieldwork in Central America and Mexico under the auspices of the School of American Archaeology. He served on the Santa Fe Planning Board, advocating a return to the Santa Fe style, which he differentiated from the California mission style. He applied his knowledge of historic preservation in New England to activities in Santa Fe, and was a member of the group working to remodel the Governors Palace for the Museum of New Mexico.

See also *School of American Archaeology:* SCHOOLS

*Museum of New Mexico:* GOVERNMENT AND PRIVATE AGENCIES AND INSTITUTIONS

## NEWCOMB, FRANC JOHNSON

Born March 30, 1887, Greenfield, Wisconsin; no death date available.
Researcher, writer

After attending teacher-training school in Wisconsin, Franc Johnson moved to the Navajo reservation to teach at Fort Defiance, Arizona, from 1913 to 1915. In 1914, she married Indian trader Arthur Newcomb, who owned the Blue Mesa Trading Post on the reservation. For more than twenty years, she studied Navajo culture and became friends with Hosteen Klah, a respected medicine man and weaver. With Mary Cabot Wheelwright, Newcomb encouraged Klah to translate his sandpaintings into weavings, convincing him that it was not sacrilegious to display rugs in a museum rather than use them as floor coverings. After being invited to ceremonies where drawing materials were forbidden, she sketched more than five hundred sandpaintings from memory. Newcomb is the author of *Hosteen Klah, Navajo Medicine Man and Sand-Painter* (1964) and *Navajo Bird Tales Told by Hosteen Klah Chee* (1970), in addition to articles on Navajo life for a variety of periodicals.

See also *Hosteen Klah:* ARTISTS' BIOGRAPHIES

## NORTHEND, MARY HARROD

Born May 10, 1850, Salem, Massachusetts; died 1925.
Writer

Northend began writing for *Good Housekeeping* magazine in 1904. She contributed articles on colonial architecture, home decorating, and gardens to *Century, Country Life in America, The Ladies' Home Journal, McCall's Magazine,* and *House and Garden,* and wrote several books on the same subjects. She collected more than thirty thousand photographs of American homes.

## NUTTING, WALLACE

Born November 17, 1861, Marlboro, Massachusetts; died July 19, 1941, Framingham Center, Massachusetts.
Clergyman, photographer, antiquarian, manufacturer, writer

Ordained as a Congregational minister in 1888, Nutting had pastorates in Newark, New Jersey; St. Paul, Minnesota; Seattle, Washington; and Providence, Rhode Island, before leaving the ministry in 1905 because of ill health. In 1897, he began taking and selling photographs of tramps, Vermont, and Palestine, among other subjects; in 1907, he opened Wallace Nutting, Inc., in Southbury, Connecticut, hiring girls to hand-tint his collection of more than fifty thousand photographs. In 1912, he moved the business to Framingham, Massachusetts, and, in 1922, he sold it. Having become interested in antique furniture and colonial interior decoration, he had started Wallace Nutting Furniture, in 1917, to produce quality reproductions. Nutting wrote and illustrated several definitive studies of early American furniture, including *Furniture of the Pilgrim Century* (1921–1923; rev. 1924) and *Furniture Treasury* (1928–1933).

See also *Mariet Nutting:* ARTISTS' BIOGRAPHIES

*Nutting, Wallace,* Furniture of the Pilgrim Century (of American Origin): 1620–1720: BOOKS AND PERIODICALS

## SANCHEZ, GEORGE ISIDORE
Born October 4, 1906, Barela, New Mexico; died April 5, 1972, Austin, Texas.
Sociologist, educator

Beginning as a teacher, in 1923, in a one-room schoolhouse in New Mexico, Sanchez pursued a career that included both educational administration and research. From 1930 to 1935, he headed the Division of Information and Statistics for the New Mexico State Department of Education. His research included studies of rural schools in Mexico and the southwestern United States, for the Julius Rosenwald Fund, and of the Taos, New Mexico, schools. Sanchez was a professor of Latin American education at the University of Texas, in Austin, from 1940 to 1972. His classic study, *The Forgotten People: A Study of New Mexicans* (1940), criticized both government treatment and public romanticization of New Mexicans and championed bilingual-bicultural education for Mexican Americans.

*See also Sanchez, George Isidore,* The Forgotten People: A Study of New Mexicans: BOOKS AND PERIODICALS

## SEWELL, BRICE
No dates available.
Educator, sculptor

Sewell taught in the art department of the University of New Mexico before becoming the state's director of vocational education and training in 1932. As a result of his and Leonora Curtin's campaign to revive Spanish New Mexican crafts, the state became the first to receive federal funding for crafts education under the Smith-Hughes Act (1917). Through his efforts, the statewide teaching of traditional skills in vocational schools fostered the 1930s craft revival in New Mexico.

*See also New Mexico State Department of Vocational Education:* GOVERNMENT AND PRIVATE AGENCIES AND INSTITUTIONS

## WELLS, JAMES LESESNE
Born November 2, 1902, Atlanta, Georgia; died January 20, 1993, Washington, D.C.
Teacher, painter, printmaker

For thirty-nine years, Wells taught art at Howard University, in Washington, D.C., before retiring in 1968. A painter and printmaker, his work reflects an ultramodern, African style. He directed the Harlem Art Workshop, in New York City, during the summers of 1933, 1934, and 1935.

*See also Harlem Art Workshop:* SCHOOLS

## WHEELWRIGHT, MARY CABOT
Born October 2, 1878, Boston, Massachusetts; died July 19, 1958, Sutton's Island, Maine.
Philanthropist, writer

Wheelwright bought a ranch near Alcalde, New Mexico, in 1923, and, at the same time, because of her love of the Maine coast, a shipmaster's cottage on Sutton's Island. From then on, she divided her time between her two homes. While stranded on the Navajo reservation during a snowstorm, she met medicine man Hosteen Klah and became fascinated with Navajo religious ceremonies. In 1936, she opened the Museum of Navajo Ceremonial Art, in Santa Fe, to display her collection of religious artifacts, which included Klah's sandpainting weavings, ceremonial objects, and recordings of chants. She studied primitive religions from around the world in order to compare their symbolism with that of the Navajo. Wheelwright wrote *Navajo Creation Chants* (1942) and *Water and Hail Chants* (1946). In 1976, the Santa Fe museum was renamed for her.

*See also Hosteen Klah:* ARTISTS' BIOGRAPHIES

*Museum of Navajo Ceremonial Art:* GOVERNMENT AND PRIVATE AGENCIES AND INSTITUTIONS

# GOVERNMENT AND PRIVATE AGENCIES AND INSTITUTIONS

## BUREAU OF INDIAN AFFAIRS
1834–present

Following the French and Indian Wars, each colony established its own superintendency of Indian affairs. In 1786, Congress, declaring that the general management of these activities was to be among the duties of the Secretary of War, established the Indian Department. The department's primary duties were negotiating tribal treaties and purchasing tribal lands. In 1824, the department received its own director, to relieve the Secretary of War of these responsibilities. The department's name was changed to the Bureau of Indian Affairs (BIA) in 1834, and it continued to be part of the war department until 1849, when it was transferred to the newly created Department of the Interior. The bureau's primary responsibilities have been to help Indians attain their full economic, social, political, and cultural status in American society. This has been done through public schools, adult education, and vocational training, as the BIA, beginning in the

1850s, established schools on and off the reservation. As a result of the 1887 General Allotment Act, the BIA became manager of Indian lands and was charged with the breakup of tribal political and social systems and the elimination of Indian culture to allow for complete acculturation. The Indian Reorganization Act of 1934 reversed this policy.

*Indian Reorganization Act of 1934*
Also known as the Wheeler-Howard Act, the Indian Reorganization Act was the initial step in the new federal policy toward Native Americans. The bill was one of the first to be discussed in tribal meetings prior to its passage. As passed, the act helped strengthen tribes as political and economic units, provided for Indian civil service, stopped land allotment, and emphasized the value of Indian culture. The government's goal no longer was to assimilate Indians individually but to incorporate Indian communities into mainstream culture. Tribal management was supported, Indian arts and crafts were encouraged, and the ban

on Indian costumes and ceremonies was lifted.

## CIVILIAN CONSERVATION CORPS (CCC)
1933–42

In 1933, Congress established the Civilian Conservation Corps to perform conservation activities and aid unemployed men between the ages of seventeen and twenty-four whose families were on relief. During its nine-year existence, the CCC employed two and a half million men in such activities as repairing national historic sites, building national park buildings, and fighting forest fires. Stressing educational activities, CCC staff taught thirty-five thousand men to read, while WPA Federal Art Project instructors offered courses in arts and crafts.

## COLONIAL WILLIAMSBURG
1926–present
Williamsburg, Virginia
Founder: John D. Rockefeller, Jr.

Started in 1926 with funds from John D. Rockefeller, Jr., Colonial Williamsburg is the largest restoration project in the United States. Through careful research, scholars and craftspeople have renovated and reconstructed more than one hundred and fifty major buildings on the one hundred and seventy acre site that served as the capital of Virginia from 1699 to 1780. Furnishings and landscaping re-create the colonial period, and costumed craftspeople and interpreters stage historical reenactments and demonstrate crafts using appropriate techniques and equipment.

## FEDERAL ART PROJECT (FAP)
1935–42

Under E. Holger Cahill's direction, the FAP helped unemployed artists preserve and develop their skills. More than one hundred and eight thousand paintings, twenty-five hundred murals, and eighteen thousand pieces of sculpture were created. Other activities included art education and exhibitions at community art centers, theater productions, and archaeological research. From 1935 to 1939, the FAP received federal funding under the Works Progress Administration (WPA) for projects in music, drama, literature, and art. In 1939, when the WPA became the Work Projects Administration, the FAP's theater program was eliminated, and other projects, in order to continue, had to receive 25 percent of their funding from state and local governments.

*Design Laboratory*
1935–37
New York, New York

Sponsored by the Federal Art Project, the Design Laboratory provided free adult courses in industrial and graphic arts. Volunteer professionals emphasized industrial design and techniques in the Bauhaus tradition. Industrial designer Gilbert Rohde began as director in 1936, serving for a further year after the laboratory lost its federal funding in 1937. The Design Laboratory continued privately for several years.

*Illinois Craft Project*
1935–43

Under the auspices of the Federal Art Project, Illinois promoted arts and crafts production throughout the state, including the coordination of nine craft shops. Each shop employed local artists and had its own specialty; for instance, the Decatur shop made toys while the Chicago shop focused on woodwork and weaving. In 1940, the Winnetka shop, which specialized in furniture, made molded and laminated chairs for the town's Crow Island School.

*Index of American Design*
1935–41

Sponsored by the Federal Art Project, the Index hired more than five hundred unemployed artists to document American decorative arts from the colonial period through the nineteenth century. The artists created more than twenty-two thousand plates, using rendering techniques developed by Egyptologists to document ancient tomb decorations. The plates (the originals are housed in the National Gallery of Art, in Washington, D.C.) provide a comprehensive survey of American design and craftsmanship. Ruth Reeves (1892–1966), a painter and textile designer, served as the first national coordinator for the Index. C. Adolph Glassgold replaced her, serving in the position from 1937 to 1940.

## GREENFIELD VILLAGE
1926–present
Dearborn, Michigan
Founder: Henry Ford

Henry Ford, an industrialist who collected Americana, purchased the Wayside Inn, in South Sudbury, Massachusetts, in 1923. Three years later, he began constructing Greenfield Village, his re-creation of an early American village, and the Henry Ford Museum, which traces the country's industrial development from the earliest colonial days. Together, the museum and village constitute the Thomas A. Edison Institute. Instead of concentrating on wars, treaties, and politics, Ford's enterprises focused on how ordinary people of the past had lived. The primary emphasis of the museum is agriculture, leisure, industry, domestic life, transportation, and communication; it also houses Ford's collections of automobiles, furniture, clocks, and domestic appliances. Central to the village is a reconstruction of the Menlo Park, New Jersey, research facility of Edison, who was much admired by Ford. It includes Noah Webster's New Haven, Connecticut, home; the log cabin in which William Holmes McGuffey was born; the Illinois courthouse where Abraham Lincoln first practiced law; and other reconstructed structures representative of village life during the course of America's history.

## INDIAN ARTS AND CRAFTS BOARD
1935–present

The 1935 Indian Arts and Crafts bill created this U.S. Department of the Interior commission "to promote the economic welfare of the Indian tribes and the Indian Wards of the government through the development of Indian arts and crafts and the expansion of the market for the products of Indian art and craftsmanship." Activities in the 1930s included reservation craft guilds, art classes, exhibitions, and the provision of government trademarks to authenticate Indian products.

## LABORATORY OF ANTHROPOLOGY
1931–47
Santa Fe, New Mexico

With funds from John D. Rockefeller, Jr., this private organization received a new Spanish Pueblo building to house the Pueblo Pottery Fund in addition to its own collection of Indian artworks. When the laboratory experienced financial difficulties in the 1940s, its holdings were divided between the School of American Research and the Museum of New Mexico.

*See also School of American Archaeology:* SCHOOLS

*Museum of New Mexico:* GOVERNMENT AND PRIVATE AGENCIES AND INSTITUTIONS

## MERIAM REPORT
1928

Written by Lewis Meriam, of the Brookings Institute, this report listed the recommendations of the Committee of One Hundred, appointed by Secretary of the Interior Herbert Work to study government relations with the Indians. It provided a new basis for government policy toward Native Americans under Presidents Hoover and Roosevelt. It cited integration into the white mainstream as the desired goal of federal relations with the Indians and stressed the necessity of education and the preservation of Indian resources as requisite steps toward this end.

## MUSEUM OF NAVAJO CEREMONIAL ART; WHEELWRIGHT MUSEUM OF THE AMERICAN INDIAN
1936–present
Santa Fe, New Mexico
Founder: Mary Cabot Wheelwright

In 1937, Wheelwright established the Museum of Navajo Ceremonial Art to display her collection of religious artifacts, including ceremonial objects and recordings of chants. Prominent among the collections were weavings of sacred sandpaintings by Navajo medicine man Hosteen Klah. The museum was renamed for Wheelwright after her death, in 1976.

*See also Mary Cabot Wheelwright:* SCHOLARS AND ADVOCATES' BIOGRAPHIES

## MUSEUM OF NEW MEXICO
1909–present
Santa Fe, New Mexico
Founder: Territorial Legislature of New Mexico

In 1909, Edgar Lee Hewett, among others, encouraged the territorial legislature of New Mexico to establish a museum in the old Governors Palace, in Santa Fe. The museum now encompasses four separate institutions: the Museum of Fine Arts, the Museum of Indian Arts and Culture, the Museum of International Folk Art, and the Governors Palace, which examines New Mexico's history and culture. *El Palacio* is the official journal of the museum.

*See also Edgar Lee Hewett:* SCHOLARS AND ADVOCATES' BIOGRAPHIES

## NATIONAL PARK SERVICE
1916–present

Created in 1916, the National Park Service promotes and protects more than three hundred national parks, preserves, monuments, memorials, and historic sites.

*Yosemite Park Indian Field Days*
1916–30

The National Park Service sponsored Indian Field Days in Yosemite Valley. The event featured a parade, horse races, Indian baby contests, and prizes for the best costume and war dance. Although not authentic, the field days attracted both Indians and tourists. Basket contests influenced traditional Miwok-Paiute basketmaking, as participants recognized that "the prettiest basket" awards were given to those that employed new colors and designs.

## NATIONAL YOUTH ADMINISTRATION (NYA)
1935–43

The goal of this federal program was to provide employment and education for young people without the regimentation considered an anathema to a democracy. Originally directed only at young men, the National Youth Administration eventually expanded its services to women, ultimately providing part-time jobs to more than four million young people. Among its projects were road and building construction and resident training centers to teach industrial skills to rural youth.

## NEW MEXICO STATE DEPARTMENT OF VOCATIONAL EDUCATION (SDVE)
State of New Mexico

During the 1930s, the department focused on teaching and reviving traditional Spanish crafts by establishing vocational schools that offered courses in weaving, tanning, leatherwork, furniture-making, and ornamental ironwork. Funded by state and federal money, the activities helped to preserve the traditional culture and alleviate economic distress in the Hispanic communities. Under the direction of Brice Sewell, the department prepared carefully researched craft bulletins detailing authentic New Mexican pieces in order to ensure the preservation of traditional designs and techniques. Dolores Perrault Montoya and Carmen Espinoza, weavers and textile instructors, prepared the bulletins on *colcha* embroidery. Montoya also wrote about vegetable dyeing, while Espinoza was responsible for the issues on tinwork and painted chests. Both artists, as well as David Salazar, a self-taught weaver, were textile instructors in the state vocational schools.

*See also Brice Sewell:* SCHOLARS AND ADVOCATES' BIOGRAPHIES

## PUBLIC WORKS OF ART PROJECT (PWAP)
1933–34

The Public Works of Art Project was the predecessor of the Federal Art Project. Under the sponsorship of the U.S. Treasury Department, the PWAP hired unemployed painters, sculptors, designers, and craftspeople to provide works of art for nonfederal public buildings and parks. Thirty-seven hundred artists created more than fifteen thousand pieces, at a cost of $1,312,177.

## ROSWELL COMMUNITY ART CENTER; ROSWELL MUSEUM AND ART CENTER
1937–present
Roswell, New Mexico

The Roswell Museum and Art Center is an example of an institution that outlasted its founding as a community art center under the Works Progress Administration. During the 1930s, as part of the New Mexico Federal Art Project, woodworker Domingo Tejeda supervised the construction of Spanish Colonial revival furniture for the Roswell Community Art Center, while carvings were executed for the wall niches of the museum by carver and painter Juan Sanchez. Today, the museum focuses on twentieth-century southwestern paintings and sculpture and features archaeological collections of Native American art.

## RUSSELL SAGE FOUNDATION SOUTHERN HIGHLANDS DIVISION
1912–19
Asheville, North Carolina

With sixty-five million dollars she inherited in 1906, Margaret Olivia Sage established the Russell Sage Foundation in 1907. Interested in the development of social work, the foundation staff responded positively to John C. Campbell's suggestion to conduct a social survey of the population, natural resources, and conditions in the southern mountains area. In 1912, the foundation formally established the Southern Highlands Division, with Campbell as director; a year later, the division opened its headquarters in Asheville, North Carolina. The division's province was the mountainous areas of Maryland, Virginia, West Virginia, Kentucky, North Carolina, South Carolina, and Alabama—a rural region covering one hundred and twelve thousand square miles and home to five million people. Its activities included gathering information about conditions, establishing connections between government agencies and churches, and improving the inhabitants' lives. The division closed in 1919, soon after Campbell's death.

*See also John C. Campbell:* SCHOLARS AND ADVOCATES' BIOGRAPHIES

## SANTA FE FINE ARTS MUSEUM; MUSEUM OF FINE ARTS
1917–present
Santa Fe, New Mexico

The Museum of Fine Arts is one of the four museums that constitute the Museum of New Mexico, in Santa Fe. The building's architectural elements are reminiscent of the traditional New Mexico style found in Pueblo Indian homes and Spanish mission churches. Its collections, which focus on fine arts of the Southwest, include paintings and sculpture by southwestern and American Indian artists.

## SCHOMBURG CENTER FOR RESEARCH IN BLACK CULTURE
1925–present
New York, New York

Originally called the Division of Negro Literature, History, and Prints, the Schomburg Center is located at the 135th Street branch of the New York Public Library. In 1926, the library purchased Arthur A. Schomburg's private collection of African, Caribbean, and African American materials. Schomburg worked as the center's curator from 1932 to 1938, when it was renamed for him. The center, which functions as both a history museum and reference library, houses books, prints, drawings, and sculpture by African Americans, as well as an extensive collection of reference materials about African American history and culture.

## SUBSISTENCE HOMESTEAD PROJECT
### 1933–35

As part of the National Industrial Recovery Act of 1933, twenty-five million dollars was provided to relocate twenty-five thousand urban families to rural areas. The government designed pilot programs featuring small handcraft industries to supplement the income of new rural residents. By 1935, fifty projects were launched—Arthurdale, West Virginia, being the best known. That same year, the project was taken over by the Resettlement Administration.

## ARTHURDALE, WEST VIRGINIA
### 1933–42

In October 1932, the Division of Subsistence Homesteads purchased one thousand acres of the Arthur estate, in Reedsville, West Virginia, for a planned community of two hundred families. One hundred and fifty families settled there, and the Religious Society of Friends (Quakers) helped establish the Mountaineer Craftsmen's Cooperative Association. Eleanor Roosevelt, an early advocate, hoped the community would allow for subsistence farming, to enable families to purchase whatever they could not produce themselves. The community homes proved too cold for the winter months, and it was too expensive to design homes that the families could afford. The experiment was judged a failure by Secretary of the Interior Harold Ickes. Liquidation began in 1942, at a loss to the government of two million dollars.

## WORKS PROGRESS ADMINISTRATION; WORK PROJECTS ADMINISTRATION
### 1935–43

Following the passage of the Emergency Relief Appropriation Act in 1935, President Franklin D. Roosevelt created the Works Progress Administration (WPA) to distinguish unemployment relief from other types of social aid. During its eight years, the WPA hired eight and a half million people in a wide variety of jobs, at a cost of $11.4 billion dollars. WPA workers built or improved two thousand five hundred hospitals, five thousand nine hundred school buildings, one thousand airport facilities, public parks, and thousands of miles of roads and sidewalks. Under the Federal Art Project, WPA workers participated in art, theater, and music projects. In 1939, the WPA came under the direction of the Federal Works Agency and was renamed the Work Projects Administration. WPA programs continued under this new affiliation, although construction was emphasized and the theater program was eliminated. Beginning in 1941, WPA activities focused on national defense; by 1943, private employment opportunities eliminated the need for the agency.

### *Albuquerque Little Theater*
Opened 1936
Albuquerque, New Mexico

In 1930, the Albuquerque Little Theater began operations, rehearsing in whatever space it could locate and hosting productions in the Kimo Theater. Recognizing the need for permanent space, the founders approached the Works Progress Administration and received funding to build their own theater. John Gaw Meem designed the building, which featured such handwork as tinsmith Eddie Delgado's wall sconces; woodcarver Patrocinio Barela's sculpture; weaver Stella Garcia's embroidered stage curtains; ironworker Pete Garcia's stairway railings; furniture by students at the Spanish-American Normal School, in El Rito; and straw appliqué on furniture by Ernesto Roybal.

### *Georgia Writers' Project, Savannah Unit*
1937–40

William Russell Bascom, Melville J. Herskovits, and Guy Johnson advised the Savannah Unit of the Georgia Writers' Project. Bascom, an expert on African culture, sought evidence of these traditions in the United States; for three years, writers interviewed and observed African Americans along the Georgia coast, near Savannah, looking for examples. Isaac Basden, a blind basketmaker who made fanners and large, round baskets, was interviewed in 1940, in Harris Neck, Georgia. The findings of the Savannah Unit appear in *Drums and Shadows: Survival Studies among the Georgia Coastal Negroes* (1940), a book that demonstrates the continuity between the Georgians' customs and their African heritage.

### *Indian Arts and Crafts Project*
c. 1935–41

As part of the Works Progress Administration handcrafts program, American Indians, in Kansas, Oklahoma, Washington, Montana, and other areas where there were sizable Indian populations, received training in tribal crafts in order to preserve their heritage. Kansas artisans produced objects used in museum displays on the American Indian. In New York State, one hundred Seneca Indians received training in traditional methods of making clothing, baskets, and jewelry, and also painted watercolors and oils of Indian life.

# EXHIBITIONS

## CHICAGO WORLD'S FAIR THE DESIGN FOR LIVING HOUSE
### 1933–34
Chicago, Illinois

The Design for Living House was one of several exhibitions at the fair purporting to show how houses would soon be built and decorated. Architect John B. Moore designed the house, which was decorated by Gilbert Rohde. It featured contemporary, factory-produced furniture that emphasized straight lines and polished metal hardware. Although the furniture was contemporary, the room settings were traditional. Rohde contrasted color and texture in the rooms, many of which featured electric clocks he had designed.

## GOLDEN GATE INTERNATIONAL EXPOSITION
February 1939–September 1940
San Francisco, California

With $3.8 million from the Works Progress Administration, the city built a four-hundred acre man-made island in San Francisco Bay. Organizers chose Pacific Unity as the official theme, and proclaimed peace and brotherhood as the exposition's purpose. The 1940 Art in Action program, held in the Palace of Fine Arts, featured craft demonstrations by such artists as the ceramists Maria Martinez and Glen Lukens. Miguel Covarrubias also painted murals for the exposition.

### *Golden Gate International Exposition Federal Building Indian Exhibition*
February 1939–September 1940
San Francisco, California

Utilizing funds from the Rockefeller and Carnegie foundations, the Indian Arts and Crafts Board organized an exhibition of Indian art for the exposition. René d'Harnoncourt, with the assistance of Frederick H. Douglas, directed the exhibition, which focused on the value and accomplishments of past and contemporary Indian works. It opened with the Hall of Indian History, which used charts and maps to outline the development of Indian culture. Visitors next toured galleries, encountering displays that highlighted the aesthetic value of the articles. The exhibition ended with a salesroom that featured demonstrations of contemporary Indian crafts and model settings showing how Indian art complemented modern interior design. Its success stimulated art and anthropology museums to cooperate on similar exhibitions.

*See also René d'Harnoncourt; Frederick H. Douglas:* SCHOLARS AND ADVOCATES' BIOGRAPHIES

## THE METROPOLITAN MUSEUM OF ART AMERICAN WING
1924–present
New York, New York

Funded by Robert W. and Emily Johnston de Forest, the American Wing is a permanent exhibition of American architecture, furniture, ceramics, glass, textiles, metalwork, and silver from colonial New England through the early Republic period. Room settings depict the homes of clergy, tradespeople, mariners, and merchants. Through the efforts of Richard T. Haines Halsey (1865–1942), an authority on and collector of early Americana and the first curator of the American Wing, the collection of American antiques was legitimized, prompting the use of antiques and reproductions in home decoration.

## THE MUSEUM OF MODERN ART INDIAN ART OF THE UNITED STATES
1941
New York, New York

In 1941, the museum devoted the entire building to an exhibition of Indian art under the direction of René d'Harnoncourt and Frederick H. Douglas. It began on the third floor, with simple displays focusing on the painting, sculpture, and ceramics of prehistoric North American civilization. The second floor, labeled "Living Traditions," presented the art of historic native America and employed dramatic lighting to demonstrate its supernatural aspects. "Indian Art for Modern Living" was on the first

floor. Additional galleries showcased contemporary painting and sculpture, Indian art as a subject worthy of study, and the art's compatibility with modern furnishings, jewelry, and clothing.

*See also René d'Harnoncourt; Frederick H. Douglas:* SCHOLARS AND ADVOCATES' BIOGRAPHIES

## NEW YORK WORLD'S FAIR CONTEMPORARY ART BUILDING AMERICAN ART TODAY
1940
New York, New York

The exhibition "American Art Today" was housed in the redwood Contemporary Art Building designed by Frederick L. Ackerman, Joshua D. Lowenfish, and John V. Van Pelt. Twenty-three galleries featured contemporary American paintings, sculpture, and prints; art historian Mildred Constantine served on the committee that organized the exhibition. In 1940, a WPA Federal Art Project community art center was re-created. It showcased more than eight hundred works of art by WPA artists and featured handcraft demonstrations.

## NEW YORK WORLD'S FAIR COMMUNITY INTERESTS EXHIBIT
1939–40
New York, New York

Designer Gilbert Rohde explored how technical changes had affected the social and cultural aspects of community life. He characterized the 1789 period as "Man AND Community," while 1939 represented "Man IN the Community." In the first period, people were self-sufficient, with little time for leisure. In the second period, science and technology had altered one's relationship to the community, so that modern man worked shorter hours, enjoyed better health, and received more schooling. Rohde envisioned a future with increased adult education, a richer cultural life, and more recreational activities. To illustrate his thesis, he arranged exhibits showing a colonial village green, inventions that changed the world, "Mrs. Modern" ordering dinner over the telephone, and modern man informed about the world.

## NEWARK MUSEUM OLD AND NEW PATHS IN AMERICAN DESIGN, 1720–1936
1936
Newark, New Jersey

In November 1936, the Newark Museum placed on display works of the Federal Art Project of the Works Progress Administration, with the primary focus

on renderings from the Index of American Design. At the opening of the exhibition, Holger Cahill delivered an address on American design that highlighted the strengths and features of American art.

*See also Federal Art Project (FAP)—Index of American Design:* GOVERNMENT AND PRIVATE AGENCIES AND INSTITUTIONS

## PHILADELPHIA SESQUICENTENNIAL EXHIBITION
June 1–November 30, 1926
Philadelphia, Pennsylvania

Nicknamed "the Rainbow City," in contrast to the World Columbian Exposition's "White City," in Chicago, in 1893, the Philadelphia Sesquicentennial featured monumental buildings in an array of colors. The event commemorated the one hundred and fiftieth anniversary of the signing of the Declaration of Independence. Among its patriotic displays was the re-creation of High Street—Philadelphia's main street in 1776—which included the Paul Revere Forge, a dame school, a Friends meetinghouse, and the Franklin Print Shop. Six million visitors attended the fair.

## SANTA FE FIESTA
Revived 1911–present
Santa Fe, New Mexico

The fiesta tradition reaches back to 1712 and the first celebration of Don Diego de Vargas's reconquest of New Mexico, following the successful Pueblo Rebellion of 1680. Held intermittently for almost two hundred years, the fiesta, which was revived in 1911, features reenactments of de Vargas's victory, as well as other dramatic performances based upon New Mexican history. Music, dancing, and art exhibits are all a part of the event.

## WORCESTER ART MUSEUM EXHIBITION OF CONTEMPORARY NEW ENGLAND HANDICRAFTS
October 10–December 12, 1943
Worcester, Massachusetts

This exhibition focused on artwork produced by New England craftspeople between 1938 and 1943. "Handicrafts," defined in the catalogue as "those things which people make with their hands, either for their own use or for others," embraced products made with tools and machinery as long as the handmade aesthetic was maintained. The exhibition included rugs, quilts, fine fabrics woven for commercial distribution, pottery, wood products, baskets, model ships, and pewter..

# GUILDS AND SOCIETIES

## AMERICAN ASSOCIATION OF INDIAN AFFAIRS; ASSOCIATION ON AMERICAN INDIAN AFFAIRS
1923–present
New York, New York

The American Association of Indian Affairs was created by the merger of the National Association of Indian Affairs and the American Indian Defense Association. In 1923, John Collier had been instrumental in founding the American Indian Defense Association, whose original goal was to oppose the Dawes Act and push for the preservation of Indian culture and political and economic rights. In 1946, it merged with the National Association of Indian Affairs to become the American Association of Indian Affairs. With a current membership of forty thousand, the Association on American Indian Affairs, as it is now called, provides legal and technical aid to tribes throughout the United States, focusing on such areas as health, education, and economic development.

## INDIAN POTTERY FUND
1922–present
Santa Fe, New Mexico
Founders: Kenneth Chapman, Harry P. Mera

The purpose of the Indian Pottery Fund was to collect and preserve examples of the development of southwestern pueblo pottery. Incorporated in 1925, the fund deeded its collection to the School of American Research, in Santa Fe, in 1966. Now part of the school, the collection formed the basis of the Indian Arts Research Center, which was built in 1978.

*See also School of American Archaeology:* SCHOOLS

## NEW HAMPSHIRE ARTS AND CRAFTS LEAGUE
1931–
Concord, New Hampshire
Founder: New Hampshire Commission of Arts and Crafts

Inspired by the success of the Sandwich Home Industries in producing and selling handcrafts, the New Hampshire Commission of Arts and Crafts established the league. There, instruction was provided in weaving, needlework, and carving; fairs were held periodically where artists were able to exhibit work; and shops were established for craftspersons to sell their ware.

## SOUTHERN MOUNTAIN HANDICRAFT GUILD; SOUTHERN HIGHLAND HANDICRAFT GUILD
1928–present
Penland, North Carolina

The guild began informally in 1928 when Allen H. Eaton, local craftspeople, and representatives from Berea College and community centers met at the Weaving Cabin, at Penland, in North Carolina, to explore ways in which they could cooperate. The guild formally began in 1930 in Knoxville, Tennessee, taking the name Southern Mountain Handicraft Guild. Three types of groups were represented: craftspeople, production centers, and persons interested in promoting the guild's purposes, which included preserving the local culture and marketing crafts. In 1931, the guild moved to Asheville, North Carolina, and, by 1933, it changed its name to the Southern

Highland Handicraft Guild. In 1982, the guild's headquarters relocated to the Southern Highland Folk Art Center on the Blue Ridge Parkway.

*See also Allen Hendershott Eaton:* SCHOLARS AND ADVOCATES' BIOGRAPHIES

## SOCIETY FOR THE REVIVAL OF SPANISH-COLONIAL ARTS; SPANISH COLONIAL ARTS SOCIETY
1925–present
Santa Fe, New Mexico

In 1925, Frank Applegate, Mary Austin, and Leonora Curtin, among others, established the Society for the Revival of Spanish-Colonial Arts to collect and preserve Spanish colonial handcrafts. The group was incorporated in 1929 as the Spanish Colonial Arts Society. Its activities included lectures, training, publications, and exhibits. The following year, it sponsored the Spanish Arts Shop, to provide a year-round market for artisans who produced traditional crafts. Industrialist Cyrus McCormick, Jr., who was interested in promoting Spanish colonial arts and advocated a return to earlier prototypes rather than the creation of new styles, helped fund the shop. During the 1930s and 1940s, when New Deal projects were sponsored that reflected the society's mission to preserve colonial craftsmanship, the society became inactive. In 1952, members revived the society's efforts.

*See also Mary Austin:* SCHOLARS AND ADVOCATES' BIOGRAPHIES
*Spanish Arts Shop:* CRAFT SHOPS AND PRODUCTION CENTERS—GENERAL

# BOOKS AND PERIODICALS

## ALEXANDER, HARTLEY BURR
*Pueblo Indian Painting*
Nice, France: C. Szwedzicki, Editions d'Art, 1932.

Five hundred copies of this oversize (15¼ x 20″) portfolio were printed. In addition to an English-French introduction, it featured fifty reproductions of watercolors by San Ildefonso and Zia Pueblo artists: Julian Martinez, Encarnacion Pena, Abel Sanchez, Romando Vigil, Louis Roybal, Richard Martinez, Alfonso Roybal, Awa Tsireh, Miguel Martinez, and Velino Herrera. Alexander summarizes the culture and condi-

tions of the pueblos, noting that, despite differences, the "tyranny" of little rainfall is evident in the artists' work: Many of the plates depict various dances related to the need for rain, as well as cloud and rain emblems.

## AMSDEN, CHARLES AVERY
*The Ancient Basketmakers*
Los Angeles, Calif.: Southwest Museum, 1939.

This brief, thirty-five page pamphlet provides an overview of the basketmaker culture. According to Amsden, these people lived in the four-corners region of

Utah, Colorado, New Mexico, and Arizona prior to the cliff dwellers. Hunters and gatherers who engaged in simple farming, they often are called Anasazi, which, in Navajo, means "the ancient people." The basketmakers lived in caves and wore little, although excavations uncovered beaded jewelry.

*See also Charles Avery Amsden:* SCHOLARS AND ADVOCATES' BIOGRAPHIES

## AMSDEN, CHARLES AVERY
*Navaho Weaving: Its Technic and History*
Santa Ana, Calif.: Fine Arts Press, 1934.

Amsden based his study on research conducted between 1929 and 1934. He discovered that Navajo weavers learned their trade from Pueblo women captured during raids on their homes in the mid-1700s. The Navajos' skills surpassed that of their teachers. Amsden describes various looms, dyes, and textiles, as well as blankets, ponchos, and dresses.

*See also Charles Avery Amsden:* SCHOLARS AND ADVOCATES' BIOGRAPHIES

## BENEDICT, RUTH
*Patterns of Culture*
Boston, Mass.: Houghton Mifflin Company, 1934.

*Patterns of Culture* was translated into fourteen languages and became one of the most widely read books in the field of anthropology. Benedict introduced the concept of culture and focused on human diversity, which she believed reflected the range of human personalities. She concentrated on New Mexico pueblos, the Dobu, and the northwestern coast of America in her discussion of customs, cultural diversity, and patterns of culture.

## BUNZEL, RUTH
*The Pueblo Potter: A Study of Creative Imagination in Primitive Art*
New York: Columbia University Press, 1929.

Bunzel reported on her research in New Mexico pueblos during the summers of 1924 and 1925. Her focus was the Zuni, Acoma, Hopi, and San Ildefonso Pueblos. She describes technique and form, design principles, personal elements, and symbolism, and includes an appendix of various designs. Bunzel concludes that there is great variation even in traditional designs, with change often the result of white influence.

## COOLEY, ROSSA BELLE
*Homes of the Freed*
New York: New Republic, 1926.

As noted by J. H. Dillard in the introduction, this book is a guide to promoting "more wholesome and seemly ways of living among the people who dwell in the background." Cooley, principal of Penn Normal, Industrial, and Agricultural School, on St. Helena Island, South Carolina, is interested in showing how an understanding of previous generations influences the way that field hands can learn through formal education. She relates how three generations of black women have changed since the time of slavery, enumerating the variety of roles women now play, including singers, teachers, midwives, farmers, and homemakers.

*See also Rossa Belle Cooley:* SCHOLARS AND ADVOCATES' BIOGRAPHIES

*Penn School:* SCHOOLS

## COOLEY, ROSSA BELLE
*School Acres: An Adventure in Rural Education*
New Haven, Conn.: Yale University Press, 1930.

In recounting her twenty-five years as principal of Penn Normal, Industrial, and Agricultural School, on St. Helena Island, South Carolina, Cooley gives information on its history and classes. In his introduction, Paul U. Kellogg claims that the book can benefit educators everywhere, as it shows how the classic New England curriculum is not appropriate for the rural conditions of the South. Cooley's story is complemented by Winold Reiss's crayon drawings.

*See also Rossa Belle Cooley:* SCHOLARS AND ADVOCATES' BIOGRAPHIES

*Penn School:* SCHOOLS

## EATON, ALLEN H.
*Handicrafts of the Southern Highlands*
New York: Russell Sage Foundation, 1937.

Eaton employs both an academic and popular approach in his study of the culture and crafts of the Southern Highlands. The result is a book that provides anecdotal information and research documenting not only the crafts but the people, schools, companies, and guilds involved in their production and marketing. Eaton was the craftsman's champion; he creates sensitive portraits of these highlanders, while the work that they produced is documented photographically by Doris Ulmann. Chapters focus on individual crafts, such as pottery, baskets, furniture, and instruments.

*See also Allen Hendershott Eaton:* SCHOLARS AND ADVOCATES' BIOGRAPHIES

## EATON, ALLEN H.
*Immigrant Gifts to American Life: Some Experiments in Appreciation of the Contributions of Our Foreign-born Citizens to American Culture*
New York: Russell Sage Foundation, 1932.

Eaton, then director of surveys and exhibits for the Russell Sage Foundation, discusses the contributions of various immigrant groups to American craftsmanship, focusing on how to organize exhibitions of foreign artists similar to those sponsored by the foundation. A resource section identifies foreign-born

sculptors, painters, graphic artists, and handcraft workers.

*See also Allen Hendershott Eaton:* SCHOLARS AND ADVOCATES' BIOGRAPHIES

## EL PALACIO
1913–present
Santa Fe, New Mexico

As its masthead reads, the focus of *El Palacio* is "the Arts and Sciences of Man in the Southwest." The official journal of the Museum of New Mexico, it is jointly sponsored by the School of American Research, the Archaeological Society of New Mexico, and the Santa Fe Society of the Archaeological Institute. Richly illustrated, the journal reports on the art, folklore, and architecture of New Mexico.

*See also Museum of New Mexico:* GOVERNMENT AND PRIVATE AGENCIES AND INSTITUTIONS

## FINLEY, RUTH E.
*Old Patchwork Quilts and the Women Who Made Them*
Philadelphia, Pa.: J. B. Lippincott Company, 1929.

Finley's purpose is to document a folk art and interpret its relationship to the period in which the book is produced. She believes that quilts provide insight into women's lives, as they were traditionally made in the home and conveyed symbolic meaning. Finley provides a history of patchwork quilts, including discussion of their production, patterns, appliqués, designs, and colors.

## GUERNSEY, SAMUEL JAMES, AND ALFRED VINCENT KIDDER
*Basket-maker Caves in Northeastern Arizona*
Cambridge, Mass.: Peabody Museum, 1921.

Excavating eleven caves in 1916 and 1917, the researchers found evidence of food, dress, and personal ornaments, cradles, baskets, skin pouches, mummies, and wood, stone, and clay objects. They conclude that basketmakers, who antedated the cliff dwellers, lived in perishable structures, with the caves used primarily for crop storage and burial. The book includes photographs, maps, and diagrams of the area and objects recovered during their excavations.

*See also Alfred Vincent Kidder:* SCHOLARS AND ADVOCATES' BIOGRAPHIES

## INDIANS AT WORK
1933–45
Washington, D.C.: Bureau of Indian Affairs.

"An Emergency Conservation News Sheet for Ourselves," this periodical initially reported on emergency conservation work conducted by employees of the Indian service and Indian-related legislation. It described activities on reservations throughout the United States and included field managers' reports. *Indians at Work* quickly expanded its focus to include articles on Indian schools, artists and their crafts, and book reviews. By January 15, 1934, the legend had changed to "A News Sheet for Indians and the Indian Service." While reports of the conservation activities of the Indian Service (and, after 1937, the Indian division of the Civilian Conservation Corps) remained a mainstay, *Indians at Work* became more feature-oriented, covering archaeological findings and health reports. With the advent of World War II, the periodical featured Indians in the armed services. According to the September 1941 issue, the bureau sent *Indians at Work* to major newspapers, as well as to thirteen thousand subscribers in all the states and seventeen foreign countries. Publication frequency varied from monthly to bimonthly.

*See also Bureau of Indian Affairs:* GOVERNMENT AND PRIVATE AGENCIES AND INSTITUTIONS

## KIDDER, ALFRED VINCENT
*The Artifacts of Pecos*
New Haven, Conn.: Phillips Academy/Yale University Press, 1932.

Kidder covers specimens other than pottery found at the Indian pueblo ruins in San Miguel County, New Mexico, between 1915 and 1925. These pueblos were inhabited from approximately 1250 to 1838, making them an especially valuable source for information during a period when most prehistoric pueblos were only briefly inhabited. Among the items recovered were objects made of stone, including implements, knives, and grinders; of clay—human effigies, animals, and bells; and of shells—beads and pendants.

*See also Alfred Vincent Kidder:* SCHOLARS AND ADVOCATES' BIOGRAPHIES

## KIDDER, ALFRED VINCENT
*The Pottery of Pecos*
New Haven, Conn.: Phillips Academy/Yale University Press, 1931 and 1936.

The first volume of Kidder's book, published in 1931, covers the dull-paint pottery, including black-on-white, biscuit, and modern painted ware, found at the Pecos Pueblo ruins, in San Miguel County, New Mexico. The section on black-on-white pottery was written by Charles Avery Amsden. Pottery, the primary interest of the excavators, helped establish that the site was inhabited from approximately 1250 to 1838. The first volume is primarily descriptive, as the researchers did not have the appropriate equipment to make detailed studies of the glazes. Kidder concludes that pottery played little part in the pueblo's development. Published in 1936, the second volume focuses on the glaze-paint, culinary, and other ware. Anna O. Shepard contributed a section on the technology of Pecos pottery, which includes discussion of binocular microscope examination. Kidder concludes that glazes were popular between 1375 and 1700, the same period that the pueblo attained its largest population, vigor, and prosperity.

*See also Alfred Vincent Kidder:* SCHOLARS AND ADVOCATES' BIOGRAPHIES

## KROEBER, ALFRED LOUIS
*Handbook of the Indians of California*
Washington, D.C.: U.S. Government Printing Office, 1925.

Based on seventeen years of research, Kroeber focuses on Indian civilization and its changes. He provides descriptions of fifty Indian nations, with comparisons of the "arts of life," including dress, fishing, food, textiles, pottery, society, and religion. The book, which contains ethnological and archaeological discussions of the various tribes, is *Bulletin* 78 of the Smithsonian Institution Bureau of American Ethnology.

*See also Alfred Louis Kroeber:* SCHOLARS AND ADVOCATES' BIOGRAPHIES

## LOCKE, ALAIN LEROY
*The New Negro*
New York: A. and C. Boni, 1925.

In 1925, Locke edited the March issue of *Survey Graphic,* which focused on Harlem. *The New Negro*, published later that year, served both to document the Harlem Renaissance of the 1920s and to assail the negative images of blacks in popular culture. His purpose, as stated in the book's foreword, was "to document the New Negro culturally and socially, to register the transformation of the inner and outer life of the Negro in America that have so significantly taken place in the last few years." The book's three sections provide insights on contemporary African American art, literature, and music; contemplative, sociological essays on blacks in the United States; and a bibliography of works by and about African Americans. Both black and white, male and female writers contributed to the book.

*See also Alain LeRoy Locke:* SCHOLARS AND ADVOCATES' BIOGRAPHIES

## NUTTING, WALLACE
*Furniture of the Pilgrim Century (of American Origin): 1620–1720*
1921 and 1923. Rev. ed. New York: Dover Publications, 1965.

Published in two volumes, in 1921 and 1923, the book was revised and enlarged in 1924. Nutting describes chests, desks, chairs, cupboards, and tables, among numerous other pieces, detailing various types, providing photographs and dimensions, and identifying owners.

*See also Wallace Nutting:* SCHOLARS AND ADVOCATES' BIOGRAPHIES

## POST, EMILY PRICE
*The Personality of a House: The Blue Book of Home Design and Decoration*
New York: Funk & Wagnalls Company, 1930.

The personality of a home, according to Post, lies not in the qualities that appeal to critical faculties but to personal emotions. She identified four essential foci for each home: outer appearance, formal hospitality, intimate rooms for occupants, and modern requirements of comfort. Post believed that home decoration should be suitable to both the situation and purpose and allow the home owners to express their own personalities. The book covers architectural styles, period furniture, remodeling, apartments, principles of color harmony, and arrangements of various types of rooms. It also includes diagrams and illustrations of room arrangements and furniture styles.

## SANCHEZ, GEORGE ISIDORE
*The Forgotten People: A Study of New Mexicans*
Albuquerque: University of New Mexico Press, 1940.

Sanchez provides an interpretive study of social and economic conditions of New Mexicans of Spanish descent who settled in the region between the sixteenth and eighteenth centuries and comprise more than half of the state's population. Although the book includes some statistics, Sanchez characterizes it primarily as a portrait of cultural defeatism. He is critical of both government treatment and public romanticization of New Mexicans, blaming limited educational opportunities for the New Mexicans' isolation and obsolete beliefs. In the 1967 edition (Albuquerque: Calvin Horn), Sanchez contends that the situation has not changed and the New Mexicans are still "a forgotten people."

*See also George Isidore Sanchez:* SCHOLARS AND ADVOCATES' BIOGRAPHIES

**SAVANNAH UNIT, GEORGIA WRITERS' PROJECT, WORK PROJECTS ADMINISTRATION**
*Drums and Shadows: Survival Studies among the Georgia Coastal Negroes*
1940. Reprint. Athens: University of Georgia Press, 1986.

*Drums and Shadows* is the 1940 report of the Savannah Unit of the Georgia Writers' Project of the WPA. Over the course of three years, field-workers interviewed one hundred thirty-four African Americans in twenty locations along the Georgia coast. Under the supervision of anthropologists Melville J. Herskovits, Guy Johnson, and William Russell Bascom, the interviewers sought proof of the continuation of African traditions rather than evidence of acculturation. The text contains a literary version of the informants' dialect and is accompanied by photographs taken by Muriel and Malcolm Bell, Jr. An appendix identifies seventy Georgia customs, such as festivals and funeral observances, that appear to have direct links to African culture.

*See also Works Progress Administration—Georgia Writers' Project, Savannah Unit:* GOVERNMENT AND PRIVATE AGENCIES AND INSTITUTIONS

*SURVEY GRAPHIC*
1921–52
New York, New York

In 1897, the Charity Organization Society of New York City began publishing *Charities: A Monthly Review of Local and General Philanthropy* to report on nationwide reform efforts in such areas as housing, child labor, temperance, and unemployment. *Charities* became *Charities and the Commons* in 1905 when it combined with *The Commons*, a Chicago journal on the settlement movement. In 1909, the publication changed its name to *The Survey* to reflect its new focus on urban social surveys. The first issue of each month appeared in magazine format while the subsequent weeklies were issued as news bulletins. In 1921, the news bulletins were combined into a monthly bulletin, and the heavily illustrated magazine issue became known as the graphic number. The March 1925 graphic issue, which focused on Harlem, served as a precursor to Alain Locke's *The New Negro*. From January 1933 to December 1948, the graphic number was issued as a separate publication entitled *Survey Graphic*. *The Survey*, meanwhile, continued as *Midmonthly Survey, Journal of Social Work* for four years, and then as *Survey Midmonthly*, until 1948. The following year, *Survey Midmonthly* and *Survey Graphic* were united in one publication as *The Survey*, and existed in that form until 1952.

*See also Alain LeRoy Locke:* SCHOLARS AND ADVOCATES' BIOGRAPHIES

**WORST, EDWARD F.**
*Foot-Power Loom Weaving*
Milwaukee, Wis.: Bruce Publishing Company, 1918.

First published in 1918, the book went through several revisions (the 6th edition, published in 1924, was reprinted in 1974 by Dover). Worst provided detailed information, with diagrams, explaining the weaving process, looms, and equipment; describing Danish, Norwegian, Swedish, and other styles of weaving; and providing weaving patterns and information on dyes.

*See also Penland School of Handicrafts, Inc.:* SCHOOLS

*Fireside Industries of the Appalachian School:* CRAFT SHOPS AND PRODUCTION CENTERS—GENERAL

# CRAFT SHOPS AND PRODUCTION CENTERS

## Ceramics

**COWAN POTTERY; ALSO CLEVELAND POTTERY AND TILE COMPANY**
1912–31
Cleveland, Ohio
Founder: R. Guy Cowan

Beginning as a commercial enterprise in New York City, Cowan Pottery also established a noncommercial laboratory in Cleveland. There, R. Guy Cowan taught pottery and utilized the talents of area ceramists, and, under the Public Works of Art Project, his pottery produced sculpture. The Cleveland School of Art supplied the pottery with a kiln and facilities, and the Cleveland Museum of Art displayed its work in special exhibitions.

**HILTON POTTERY**
c. 1917–34
Propst Crossroads, Catawba County, North Carolina
Founders: Ernest Auburn Hilton (1878–1948), Shuford Daniel Hilton (1875–1947), Claude Watson Hilton (1880–1946)

The Hilton brothers, who followed in the family pottery tradition, opened Hilton Pottery. While other Hilton-owned potteries specialized in utilitarian pottery, this company began to produce more art ware, including flower pots and vases. Hilton Pottery became known for its colorful glazes, including cobalt blue.

*See also Ernest Auburn Hilton:* ARTISTS' BIOGRAPHIES

**JUGTOWN POTTERY**
1922–50
Moore County, North Carolina
Founders: Jacques Busbee [James Littlejohn] (1870–1947), Julianna (Roycroft) Busbee

While painting North Carolina coastal scenes for the Jamestown Exposition, in 1907, Jacques Busbee became intrigued with native artisans who were descendants of English Staffordshire potters. He soon abandoned his career as a painter to teach pottery and organize a crafts center. In 1922, he and his wife opened Jugtown Pottery, to promote traditional craft. The Busbees employed a number of local potters, including Benjamin Wade Owen (1904–1983) and Charlie Teague (1901–1938), their first turner. Responsive to the market, the Busbees encouraged their potters to look for new forms and glazes.

**LOG CABIN POTTERY**
c. 1926–33
Guilford, North Carolina

Log Cabin Pottery was one of a handful of successful southern potteries offering traditional handmade ware.

**OLD PLANK ROAD POTTERY**
1959–72; 1982–present
Westmoore, Moore County, North Carolina
Founder: Benjamin Wade Owen (1904–1983)

Owen first made traditional pottery with his father, Benjamin Franklin Owen (1848–1917), and then worked for Jugtown Pottery for over a quarter of a century. In 1959, he opened Old Plank Road Pottery, where his work featured salt glazes. Owen retired in 1972; ten years later, his son Wade (born 1937) and grandson Ben (born 1968) reopened Old Plank Road Pottery.

## OMAR KHAYYAM POTTERY
1914–35
Buncombe County, North Carolina
Founder: Oscar Louis Bachelder

Bachelder became interested in pottery after visiting the Philadelphia Centennial International Exposition in 1876. He chose the name Omar Khayyam to indicate the pottery's emphasis on art ware. Bachelder worked forty years, in twenty-eight states and territories, but became known for his North Carolina shop, which produced both traditional and original forms that were notable for their rich, dark glazes. He was one of the first North Carolina folk potters to achieve a national reputation.

*See also Oscar Louis Bachelder:* ARTISTS' BIOGRAPHIES

## PISGAH FOREST POTTERY
c. 1920s–present
Arden, North Carolina
Founder: Walter B. Stephens
(1876–1961)

When the Pisgah Forest Pottery began in the 1920s, only the work of its owner was featured. Stephens favored pottery that displayed beautiful crystalline glazes, including an unusual turquoise blue. He also made cameo pottery similar to Wedgwood. Since 1932, the Pisgah Forest Pottery has been a Center Member of the Southern Highland Handicraft Guild. After Stephens's death, the pottery continued to operate under the supervision of his grandson John Thomas Case, who learned his craft from his grandfather.

*See also Walter Benjamin Stephens:* ARTISTS' BIOGRAPHIES

## REINHARDT BROTHERS; ALSO H. F. REINHARDT POTTERY; AND E. W. REINHARDT POTTERY
1932–46
Vale, North Carolina
Founders: Enoch W. Reinhardt (1903–1978), Harvey F. Reinhardt (1912–1960)

Growing up, Enoch and his brother Harvey helped their father in his pottery shop. In 1932, they started Reinhardt Brothers, in Vale, North Carolina. There, they produced utilitarian and fancy pottery, mastering swirl ware that they sold to gift and craft shops. In 1936, when Harvey began H. F. Reinhardt Pottery, Enoch began marking his work "E. W. Reinhardt Pottery." Harvey was drafted in 1942 and moved his family to Wilmington. Four years later, both brothers left the pottery.

*See also Reinhardt Family:* ARTISTS' BIOGRAPHIES

## ROYAL CROWN POTTERY
1939–42
Merry Oaks, Chatham County, North Carolina
Founder: Victor Obler

Obler, a New York businessman, reportedly named the company on a whim after spotting a Royal Crown Cola sign. He placed Jack Kiser in charge of the pottery and handled the marketing himself, which included managing a showroom on New York City's Fifth Avenue. Royal Crown was a large-scale operation; by 1940, it was using an electric pottery wheel. The company experimented with new forms and colors, including Spanish moss and colonial cream; its main product was a black florist's vase. In 1942, the wartime shortage of fuel and metallic oxides forced Obler to close.

## H. WILSON AND COMPANY
c. 1870–84
Guadalupe County, Texas
Founder: Hirum Wilson

Between 1857 and 1869, John Wilson, his son, and son-in-law ran a pottery in Guadalupe County, Texas, staffed with slaves. In 1870, one slave, Hirum Wilson, opened his own pottery; soon after Emancipation, he had attended Bishop College, in Marshall, Texas, and become a Baptist minister. Wilson made storage jars with a salt and local slip glaze. Two other black potters also opened their own potteries, using the Wilson name after Emancipation.

## Glass

## CLEVENGER BROTHERS
1930–present
Clayton, New Jersey
Founders: Henry Thomas Clevenger, Lorenzo Clevenger, William Elbert Clevenger

The intent of the Clevenger brothers was to carry on the South Jersey traditions of glassmaking by producing affordable reproductions of an American style in which applied decoration was added to the glass. Clevenger glass in the 1930s was principally free-blown. Lilypad decoration pitchers, bowls, double-handled vases, creamers, and sugar bowls were produced. Plain blown jumbo jugs, vases, flips, rose jars, footed tumblers, mugs, and camphor jugs were some of the many reproductions available. In 1939, the Ritter-Carlton Company, in New York City, sold Clevenger products, describing the work as a "rare collection of authentic hand blown replicas of Early American glass." The company was noted as "a haven for old men who

have had experience in a glass factory." In 1966, when James Travis, of Millville, New Jersey, bought and took over the glasshouse, the youngest employee was fifty-five years old.

## WPA GLASS FACTORY
fl. 1940s
Vineland, New Jersey

Under the government's Work Projects Administration, a New Jersey glass factory made idle by the Depression was reopened to preserve the hand-glass-blower's craft and to stimulate industry competition. Supervised by the former owner of the factory, the glassblowers—many of whom were descendants of New Jersey colonial glassblower Caspar Wistar—produced drinking cups, jugs, and vases with amber, amethyst, blue, green, ruby, milk, and yellow glass. The glass blown for the WPA was sent on a national exhibition tour and eventually was given to a number of public institutions, among them, the Newark Museum, in New Jersey.

## Metals

## GORHAM MANUFACTURING COMPANY
1831–present
Providence, Rhode Island
Founder: Jabez Gorham

Still an important presence in American silver, Gorham manufactures complete lines of silver tableware, as well as bowls, serving platters, and crystal. During the 1930s, when interest in the colonial era was fashionable, Gorham emphasized the ideal of the independent craftsperson through advertisements featuring an elderly silversmith. Gorham is now a part of Dansk International Designs Ltd.

## KEL-RIE-METALCRAFT
fl. 1930s
Williamsburg, Virginia
Founder: Max Rieg

A Bauhaus-trained craftsman, Rieg made pewter reproductions through his company, Kel-Rie-Metalcraft, for Colonial Williamsburg. He also trained apprentices and demonstrated his skills to visitors.

## ARTHUR J. STONE ASSOCIATES
1901–37
Gardner, Massachusetts
Founder: Arthur John Stone

Stone, a silversmith trained in Sheffield, England, emigrated to the United States. He opened a shop for the production of handwrought silver that catered to a renewed concern with both the craft process and the colonial style. Stone hired a number of gifted artisans, including Edward Billings, Herman Glendenning, Herbert Taylor, and Earle Underwood.

*See also Herman Glendenning; Arthur John Stone:* ARTISTS' BIOGRAPHIES

## Textiles

### ALLANSTAND COTTAGE INDUSTRIES
1897–
Asheville, North Carolina
Founder: Frances Louisa Goodrich
(1856–1944)

In 1890, Goodrich, an artist trained at the Yale School of Fine Arts, became involved in Appalachian missionary work, teaching school in Riceville, North Carolina, and, later, at Cove School. In 1895, she was given a Double Bowknot coverlet, which inspired her to begin a cottage weaving industry to revive the lost craft. Two years later, Allanstand Cottage Industries opened in the mountains north of Asheville. Goodrich added a salesroom in Asheville, in 1908, and incorporated her company in 1917. In 1932, she gave the Southern Highland Handicraft Guild full title to Allanstand Industries. Goodrich told the story of the coverlet in *Mountain Homespun* (1931).

### BLUE RIDGE WEAVERS
1922–
Tryon, North Carolina
Founders: Mr. and Mrs. George Cathey

Raised in the mountains, Mrs. Cathey became interested in handcrafts while working at Hull-House, in Chicago. In 1922, she and her husband opened Blue Ridge Weavers, after organizing a group of mountain women to do quality weavings, baskets, quilts, and rugs in their homes. Blue Ridge Weavers collected the products from workers' homes and displayed them in its Tryon salesroom.

### CHURCHILL WEAVERS
1923–
Berea, Kentucky
Founder: D. Carroll Churchill
(1873–1969)

Trained as a physicist and mechanical engineer, Churchill worked briefly for Westinghouse Electric Company before moving to Ahmadnagar, India, to head an industrial school, run by the Congregational Church, and begin the American Deccan Institute. While there, he designed a fly-shuttle loom with the capacities of a power loom. Churchill returned to the United States; in 1921,

Berea College hired him to teach physics and organize its mechanical-engineering department. He left this position and, in 1923, began Churchill Weavers. His goal was to create a financially successful company that would produce fine, hand-woven fabrics using his continuously improved fly-shuttle and finger-shuttle looms. Churchill Weavers trained local boys and girls in the craft. Depending on the season, it employed between five and one hundred and fifty weavers.

### FIRESIDE INDUSTRIES
1892–present
Berea, Kentucky
Founder: Berea College

Shortly after William G. Frost became president, Berea College began Fireside Industries, to encourage women to make and sell such crafts as weavings and quilts to help finance their children's education. By 1900, Fireside Industries had its own shop on campus, and the college served as the marketing agent. In 1911, Swedish weaving instructor Anna Ernberg was hired to take over. She used Swedish-style looms and designed a small hand loom that could be used easily in the classroom as well as at home. Her students wove both traditional and new patterns. Fireside Industries refers literally to the crafts carried on in the mountain home. The name was also used by the Appalachian School and Hindman Settlement School's production and marketing group.

*See also Berea College:* SCHOOLS

### KNOX WEAVERS
1933–
Santa Fe, New Mexico
Founder: E. M. Knox

After working twenty-one years as an investment banker and fifteen years as division manager for Metropolitan Life Insurance, in Kansas City, Missouri, Knox retired to Santa Fe. In 1933, he opened Knox Weavers, which employed young men who had learned weaving from their fathers and grandfathers. By 1938, Knox Weavers had twenty-two looms and employed forty Hispanic Americans.

### THE KRAFT SHOP
1931–
Santa Fe, New Mexico
Founders: Preston McCrossen, Helen McCrossen

In 1930, the Spanish Colonial Arts Society hired the McCrossens to run the Spanish Arts Shop, in Santa Fe. A year later, the couple left to open the Kraft Shop, where they exhibited and sold their own weaving. Between 1935 and 1938, the McCrossens annually sold

more than seventy-five thousand ties worldwide. Their staff in 1938 included seventy-two weavers, most of whom were Hispanic.

### MATHENY WEAVERS
1922–
Berea, Kentucky
Founders: Mr. and Mrs. F. E. Matheny

A member of the Berea College faculty, Matheny and his wife began a community hand-loom project, independent of the college. Thirty families worked for Matheny Weavers, with some able to completely support themselves through their work. Matheny Weavers emphasized special patterns and color schemes.

### MOUNTAIN CABIN QUILTERS
1931–
Wooten, Kentucky
Founder: Minnie Klar

Mountain Cabin Quilters was established to make quilts based on old mountain and colonial patterns. By 1933, the company employed sixty women to card the wool, make padding, and produce quilts in their homes. Two years later, the business office moved to Cashiers, North Carolina, although the company continued to employ women who lived in the Wooten area.

### PINE BURR STUDIO
c. 1920s
Apison, Tennessee
Founder: Mrs. F. D. Huckabee

An example of a self-supporting craft studio that was part of the Appalachian craft revival, it taught mountain women to make hooked rugs.

### SANTA FE WEAVERS
1930–
Santa Fe, New Mexico
Founder: Celima Padilla

In 1930, Padilla left government work to open Santa Fe Weavers. Descended from a long line of weavers, many of her family were also sheep owners. Her shop featured hand-carded spun wool and vegetable-dyed products.

### SHUTTLE-CRAFT GUILD
1922–56
Seattle, Washington; Cambridge, Massachusetts; Basin, Montana
Founder: Mary Meigs Atwater
(1878–1956)

Atwater, who taught weaving, founded Shuttle-Craft Guild and served as its president until her death, operating the guild from wherever she was living. She is the author of *Shuttle-Craft Course of Instruction* (1923) and *Shuttle-Craft Book of American Hand-Weaving* (1928).

## SHUTTLE-CRAFTERS
1923–c. 1930s
Russellville, Tennessee
Founders: The Dougherty sisters

Founded by the Dougherty sisters and run by sister Sarah, Shuttle-Crafters promoted traditional weaving. It emphasized standardized designs and colors and used a 1799 log cabin as a display center and workroom. In 1933, four women worked at the center while four worked at home.

## SPINNING WHEEL
1924–1930s; 1946–48
Asheville, North Carolina
Founder: Clementine Douglas
(1893–1967)

After teaching school in Wellesley, Massachusetts, Douglas, who had studied design at New York's Pratt Institute, became a teacher at Pine Mountain Settlement School, in North Carolina. In 1924, she established the Spinning Wheel, to make woolens, linens, hooked rugs, blankets, shawls, and other pieces. Spinning Wheel workers used old and new patterns and colored the wool with dyes made from hickory bark, walnut hulls, sumac berries, and other natural materials. Douglas encouraged creativity in her employees, allowing families to design their own special patterns and colors for rug weaving. In 1935, she became director of Southern Highlanders, Inc., a new marketing craft program funded by the Tennessee Valley Authority. Under Douglas's direction, the Spinning Wheel reopened again in 1946, but she sold the shop in 1948.

## WIDE RUINS TRADING POST
Eastern Arizona, between Chambers and Ganado
Owners: Sallie Lippincott, William Lippincott

After working as rangers at Canyon de Chelly, the Lippincotts bought the trading post at Wide Ruins, on the Navajo Reservation, in 1938. The post, which had several prior owners, had been built on the site of a major Anasazi ruin called Pueblo Grande. Culturally sophisticated, the Lippincotts encouraged local weavers and insisted on quality products. The rugs that they purchased are characterized by fine, even weaving with tightly spun yarns and little or no synthetic dyes. Sallie Lippincott helped to develop vegetal-dyed rugs with borderless patterns. Together, the Lippincotts attracted artists, writers, scholars, and sightseers as they traded with the Navajo, pumped gas, and offered hospitality to their visitors

## Wood

## DANERSK
c. 1920s–
North Carolina; Stamford, Connecticut
Founder: Ralph Erskine

Danersk furniture was originally made in the North Carolina mountains by "old-time chair makers." When the company later expanded, it moved to a factory in Stamford, Connecticut, and established a showroom in New York City. The company's advertisements during the post–World War I period suggested the prevailing nationalistic temper. They emphasized the positive attributes of decorating a home in the tradition of the Founding Fathers, promoting highboys and desks that combined Colonial revivalism, Arts and Crafts movement sensibility, and modern technology. Danersk furniture resembled colonial pieces, but they were made primarily by modern machinery, with some handcrafted details.

## KITTINGER COMPANY
1866–present
Buffalo, New York

In the 1930s, Kittinger made reproductions of Williamsburg furniture. Now part of the Maytag Company, it makes wood and upholstered office furniture.

## ONEIDACRAFT
fl. 1920s–30s
Oneida, New York

During the 1920s, Oneidacraft was a company known for its "authentic" early American furniture made by craftsmen intimately familiar with the original sources. In 1925, the company's president, Richard T. Haines Halsey, the original curator of the American Wing of the Metropolitan Museum of Art, chose the pieces of furniture for reproduction. During his years as president, Oneidacraft sold its replicas exclusively through W. and J. Sloane, of New York City.

## TRYON TOYMAKERS
c. 1930s
Tryon, North Carolina
Founders: Eleanor P. Vance, Charlotte L. Yale

Vance and Yale organized Tryon Toymakers to teach woodcarving and toymaking to young people. The students made toys designed by Vance.

## VIRGINIA CRAFTSMEN, INC.
c. 1930s–
Harrisonburg, Virginia

According to *Colonial Charm for Homes of Today*, a sales catalogue issued by Virginia Craftsmen in the 1930s, the company duplicated the standards and techniques of colonial furnituremakers. By purchasing its quality reproductions, home owners were guaranteed both "taste and liveableness." The catalogue described a wide variety of Windsor, ladder-back, and upholstered chairs; tables, drawers, and chests; and beds. Customers could purchase these in maple, walnut, or brown or red mahogany. The company claimed that the owners of the original pieces attested to the accuracy of the reproductions.

## WOODCRAFTERS AND CARVERS SHOP
c. 1920s–
Gatlinburg, Tennessee
Founders: O. J. Mattil, Pi Beta Phi Settlement School

Mattil established the Woodcrafters and Carvers Shop at the Pi Beta Phi Settlement School. There, men and boys were able to study the art of cabinetmaking, make quality furniture, and learn how to price their work. Mattil searched remote areas for old designs and also created original pieces. In addition, the shop made miniature furniture.

*See also Pi Beta Phi Settlement School:* SCHOOLS

## WOODY CHAIRS
No dates available.
Spruce Pine, North Carolina
Founders: Arval Woody, Frank Woody, Paul Woody, Walter Woody

The brothers' great-grandfather pioneered a style of spruce pine chairmaking. Following that style, and using tools they made themselves, the four brothers carried on the family craft

## General

## ARROW CRAFT SHOP
1926–
Gatlinburg, Tennessee
Founder: Pi Beta Phi Settlement School

The Pi Beta Phi Settlement School opened the Arrow Craft Shop as a marketing organization on the school grounds, in Gatlinburg. Staff workers coordinated area women who made woven goods and handcrafts to sell to alumnae and tourists visiting the Great Smoky Mountains National Park, which opened in 1934. According to a Women's Bureau study that year, sixty-five women made baskets and fans, woven goods, and chairs in their homes for sale at the shop.

*See also Pi Beta Phi Settlement School:* SCHOOLS

## BILTMORE ESTATE INDUSTRIES; BILTMORE INDUSTRIES
1901–
Asheville, North Carolina
Founder: Mrs. George Vanderbilt

The Biltmore Estate Industries began on the one hundred and thirty thousand acre estate built by George Vanderbilt in the 1890s. Mrs. Vanderbilt sent woodworkers Eleanor P. Vance and Charlotte L. Yale to England for training; on their return, the two women took a cottage on the estate and began offering woodcarving classes to young boys. Classes soon expanded to metalwork, weaving, and sheepraising. In 1917, Mrs. Vanderbilt sold the company to Fred L. Seely, and he shortened the name to Biltmore Industries. According to a 1934–35 Women's Bureau study, Biltmore Industries was a commercial craft center that specialized in handwoven suiting and employed forty-seven weavers.

## FIRESIDE INDUSTRIES OF THE APPALACHIAN SCHOOL; PENLAND WEAVERS AND POTTERS
1923–68
Penland, North Carolina
Founder: Lucy Morgan

Lucy Morgan learned weaving from Anna Ernberg at Berea College. In 1923, she began teaching women of the Penland community to weave on the counterbalance looms she had brought from Berea. Beginning in 1925, funding was received through the Smith-Hughes Act. The following year, the Weaving Cabin was constructed on school property, and the weavers became known as the Fireside Industries of the Appalachian School. In 1928, the name was changed to Penland Weavers and Potters, to reflect the addition of pottery to its repertoire. By 1933, thirty-four women were weaving, potting, and working in pewter in their homes. Edward Worst first visited the Penland Weavers and Potters in 1928; when he returned the following year, paying students from outside the community were also allowed to attend his classes. A weaving institute grew, and, soon, students were coming from twenty-two states to attend a two-week summer program. The Penland School of Handicrafts was incorporated in 1938, and Penland Weavers and Potters operated as a production arm of the school until 1968. The items produced were sold on consignment to various women's auxiliaries and gift shops throughout the United States.

*See also Appalachian Industrial School; Penland School of Handicrafts, Inc.:* SCHOOLS

## HUBBELL TRADING POST
1876–present
Ganado, Arizona
Founder: John Lorenzo Hubbell

After working in a trading post in the Utah territory, Hubbell opened his own on the Navajo Indian Reservation, near Ganado, Arizona. The post has been in continuous operation since 1876 and is now a national historic site. Hubbell bought and sold Indian crafts, traded goods, and operated as a pawnbroker. The Fred Harvey Company was one of his chief buyers in the 1930s, purchasing Ganado blankets and *yei* paintings to sell at its outlets.

## KIMO THEATER
Built 1937
Albuquerque, New Mexico

Italian immigrant Oreste Bacheli conceived this theater, constructed in the pueblo deco style, as a homage to his adopted homeland, and he hired architects Carl Boller and Carl Von Hassler to implement his vision. The theater was built of reinforced brick, heavily stuccoed to resemble adobe construction. Its interior featured murals, including trompe l'oeil scenes of Taos Pueblo. Other Indian motifs were a checkerboard design, *kachina* masks, and wrought-iron birds on the stairs.

## MOUNTAINEER CRAFTSMEN'S COOPERATIVE ASSOCIATION
1932–
Morgantown, West Virginia

The American Friends Service Committee of the Religious Society of Friends organized the Mountaineer Craftsmen's Cooperative Association in the bituminous coal regions of West Virginia. Five communities of destitute miners and their families learned a variety of crafts, some of which represented the types and techniques of pioneer handcrafts typically found in the state. Utilizing their newly acquired skills, the families made early American reproduction furniture; pewter-, iron-, and other metalwork; quilts, baskets, weavings, and plain and decorative needlework. This training allowed them to produce clothing and home furnishings for themselves, as well as objects to sell in the association's retail shops. The association also made furniture and furnishings for several of the homes in the Arthurdale federal project known as the Reedsville Experimental Community, in Preston County, West Virginia.

*See also Subsistence Homestead Project— Arthurdale, West Virginia:* GOVERNMENT AND PRIVATE AGENCIES AND INSTITUTIONS

## NATIVE MARKET
1934–39
Santa Fe, New Mexico
Founder: Leonora Curtin

Curtin, with the help of Dolores Perrault Montoya, who was on loan from the New Mexico State Department of Vocational Education, established and funded the Native Market. It replaced the Spanish Colonial Arts Society's Spanish Arts Shop as a promotion center and outlet for Hispanic crafts. Re-creating the atmosphere of traditional craft markets, Curtin hired such artisans as embroiderer Deolinda Baca to demonstrate *colcha* embroidery, weavers Margaret Baca and David Salazar to illustrate weaving, Tillie Gabaldon Stark to show dyeing techniques, and others to exhibit woodcarving. These demonstrations were intended to promote the market's sales. Furnituremaker Abad E. Lucero and tinsmith Francisco Sandoval (1860–1944) were two of the area artisans who sold their work through the shop. Although the market thrived while Curtin provided financial support, it closed within six months when management was turned over to an artisans' committee.

*See also Spanish Arts Shop:* CRAFT SHOPS AND PRODUCTION CENTERS—GENERAL

## SHENANDOAH COMMUNITY WORKERS
1927–c. 1930s
Bird Haven, Virginia
Founder: William Bernard Clark

A Virginia-based example of the independent industries established during the Appalachian craft revival, this group produced wood crafts, pottery, paintings, toys, and hooked rugs.

## SOUTHWESTERN MASTER CRAFTSMEN
c. 1930s
Santa Fe, New Mexico

Southwestern Master Craftsmen offered a complete line of interior furnishings made by Hispanic artists, including draperies, rugs, furniture, tinwork, and ironwork.

## SPANISH ARTS SHOP
1930–34
Santa Fe, New Mexico
Founder: Spanish Colonial Arts Society

In 1930, the Spanish Colonial Arts Society hired Helen and Preston McCrossen to run its Spanish Arts Shop, which they did for a year. The shop served as a year-round outlet for artisans, focusing exclusively on the Spanish New Mexican crafts the society wished to preserve and promote. One of the artisans, Francisco Sandoval, had learned tinsmithing in the

1870s from his father. He owned a plumbing shop in Santa Fe, and sold his tinwork through the Spanish Arts Shop and the Native Market.

*See also Native Market:* CRAFT SHOPS AND PRODUCTION CENTERS—GENERAL

## THE SPANISH CHEST
1929–
Santa Fe, New Mexico
Founders: Bruce Cooper (1905–1987), Benjamin Sweringen

Cooper and Sweringen opened the Spanish Chest to sell antiques, furniture, and lighting fixtures made in the traditional Santa Fe style. Both men were tinsmiths who created their own Hispanic craft pieces. Cooper's work in the 1940s and 1950s included colorfully painted glass and tinwork. He also collected and sold nineteenth-century tinwork.

## TUCSON NATIVE MARKET
c. 1930s
Tucson, Arizona

After serving as manager of the Native Market in Santa Fe, Eleanor Bedell assumed responsibility for the Tucson Native Market. It sold New Mexican crafts, which included locally made furniture from the Spanish Indian Trading Company.

## VAL-KILL COTTAGE
1925–
Hyde Park, New York

In 1925, Franklin Delano Roosevelt gave a lifetime lease to his wife, Eleanor, Nancy Cook, and Marion Dickerman to build a cottage on the Roosevelt family property at Hyde Park, New York. The land, a favorite picnic spot along a stream of the same name, was located several miles from the main Hyde Park residence. According to the lease, the property was to revert to his estate at the death of the last surviving leaseholder. In 1925, Henry Toombs, of McKim, Mead and White, designed the stone cottage, with the assistance of the Roosevelts, Cook, and Dickerman. Val-Kill Industries began in the cottage, but the three women soon saw the need to build a separate factory. Cook and Dickerman continued to live in the original Val-Kill

Cottage, which became known as the "stone cottage" after Eleanor Roosevelt converted the factory into a home for herself in 1936 and began calling that the Val-Kill Cottage.

*Val-Kill Forge*
1934–38
Hyde Park, New York

In 1934, Roosevelt, Cook, and Dickerman set up Val-Kill Forge as part of a greater plan to expand Val-Kill Industries after the furnituremaking component proved successful. Arnold Berg ran the forge with the assistance of Clifford Smith, a local Hyde Park resident, and Frank Swift, a metalcrafter from Poughkeepsie. The partners studied metalwork in Europe, and the forge made copies of American or European objects, as well as pieces designed by Cook. Pewter became the primary material, and, by 1938, the forge produced more than fifty items, including salt and pepper shakers, inkstands, plates, candlesticks, and utensils.

*Val-Kill Furniture Shop*
1927–36
Hyde Park, New York

Val-Kill Furniture Shop was the first and primary endeavor of Val-Kill Industries. Cofounder Nancy Cook, a skilled woodworker, suggested setting up a small industry to produce quality, early American reproduction furniture. Although initially intended as a means of employing local workers, most were Italian and Norwegian craftspersons from New York City. Originally housed in the stone cottage at Val-Kill, a separate factory was soon built on the grounds. In 1936, when the factory closed, Eleanor Roosevelt converted the building into a home for herself, and she lived and worked there until 1962.

## VAL-KILL INDUSTRIES
1927–38
Hyde Park, New York

Val-Kill Industries was the brainchild of Eleanor Roosevelt, Nancy Cook, and Marion Dickerman, as well as Carolyn O'Day, who took a supportive rather than active role as a company vice-president. Its purpose was to provide remunerative work for farmers in the area

who were unable to fully support themselves and their families through farming. Because Cook's expertise was in furnituremaking, the enterprise began with the Val-Kill Furniture Shop, which specialized in making quality reproduction, early American furniture; pewter and woven goods were added later. In 1927, it received its first commission, from Franklin Delano Roosevelt, to build furniture for his new cottage at Warm Springs, Georgia. Val-Kill's first exhibit, held at the Roosevelt home on Sixty-fifth Street, in New York City, included pieces that ranged from a forty-dollar trestle table to a maple chest of drawers costing one hundred and seventy-five dollars. According to Dickerman, Val-Kill Industries closed when Cook's responsibilities with the Democratic State Committee interfered with her work. Scholars suggest that Eleanor Roosevelt's commitments as First Lady, and her reluctance to continue to subsidize operations, hastened liquidation.

*Val-Kill Looms; Val-Kill Weavers*
1929–37; 1934–49
Hyde Park, New York

Val-Kill Looms was established to help local women earn money. It offered weaving classes for women who, in their spare time, used small table looms in their homes to make scarves, luncheon sets, baby blankets, and bath sheets, among other items. The group ranged from fifteen to twenty local women. More of an educational experience than a lucrative business venture, this program was not an overwhelming success.

Val-Kill Weavers was a more businesslike enterprise. It was undertaken with Nelly Johannesen, a former Val-Kill housekeeper. At the suggestion of Eleanor Roosevelt, who recognized her former employee's aptitude for weaving, Johannesen set up a loom and added homespun weaving to the responsibilities of her tearoom. Between 1934 and 1949, at the Val-Kill Tearoom and Weaving Cottage, she seasonally wove fabric for dresses, coats, and suits, and made clothing for President and Mrs. Roosevelt. Although the weaving cottage was planned as part of Val-Kill Industries, Johannesen actually ran the business on her own after the first year.

APPALACHIAN INDUSTRIAL
SCHOOL; APPALACHIAN SCHOOL
1914–64
Penland, North Carolina
Founder: Missionary District of the
Episcopal Diocese of North Carolina

After studying at General Theological
Seminary and Columbia University,
Rufus Morgan returned to his home state
of North Carolina and served as the first
director of the Appalachian Industrial
School, until 1917. Under the auspices of
the Episcopal Church, the school provided educational training for mountain
children. In 1920, after teaching in the
Midwest and working for the Chicago
Children's Bureau, Lucy Morgan followed her brother at the school, teaching
first through third grade until 1923. That
year, Amy Burt came to Penland to serve
as the permanent director of the school,
shifting the focus to younger children.
The name changed in the early 1920s;
although there were many transforma-
tions, the school continued to operate
until 1964.

*See also Penland School of Handicrafts,
Inc.:* SCHOOLS

*Fireside Industries of the Appalachian
School:* CRAFT SHOPS AND PRODUCTION
CENTERS—GENERAL

BEREA COLLEGE
1855–present
Berea, Kentucky
Founders: John G. Fee, John R. Rogers

In 1855, abolitionists Fee and Rogers
founded Berea College, admitting blacks
on an equal basis with whites. Students
earned part of their tuition by working in
the college's farms, gardens, and shops.
In 1893, with the encouragement of its
president, William G. Frost, Berea
became a focal point for the crafts
revival. A private liberal arts college, it
continues to advance the interests of the
Southern Appalachians, and 80 percent
of the student body is drawn from the
area. The college operates more than one
hundred labor departments, and students must still work at least ten hours a
week in one of them.

*See also William G. Frost:* SCHOLARS
AND ADVOCATES' BIOGRAPHIES

*Fireside Industries:* CRAFT SHOPS AND
PRODUCTION CENTERS—TEXTILES

BERRY SCHOOLS
1902–
Rome, Georgia
Founder: Martha Berry

Established as a mission school in Rome,
Georgia, Berry Schools were active in the
crafts revival in Appalachia. The school
emphasized weaving and the production
of linens and rugs made from flax grown
on its farm. Students performed all manual labor at the school and built the Sun-
shine Cottage, where courses in arts and
crafts were provided.

JOHN C. CAMPBELL FOLK
SCHOOL
1925–present
Brasstown, North Carolina
Founder: Olive Dame Campbell

Modeled after folk schools that Olive
Dame Campbell visited in Denmark, the
John C. Campbell Folk School (named
for her deceased husband) strove to preserve and encourage rural culture and
life. Instructors emphasized a variety of
crafts, although carving took center
place. Today, the school continues to
emphasize the preservation and marketing of arts and crafts. Adults visit from
around the country for intensive week-
end and one- or two-week training sessions in weaving, basketry,
blacksmithing, dollmaking, and music
and dance.

*See also Olive Dame Campbell:* SCHOL-
ARS AND ADVOCATES' BIOGRAPHIES

CLEVELAND SCHOOL OF ART;
CLEVELAND INSTITUTE OF ART
1882–present
Cleveland, Ohio

Through instruction and exhibitions, the
school offers an important and well-
known preparatory program in ceramics.
In 1949, it changed its name to the
Cleveland Institute of Art. Today, the
institute awards baccalaureate degrees.

CROSSNORE
c. 1910–40
Crossnore, Avery County, North
Carolina

Founded as a mission school, Crossnore
became associated with the Appalachian
crafts revival. In 1917, in response to the
Smith-Hughes Act promoting vocational
education, the school added a weaving

department. A 1934–35 Women's
Bureau study reported that Crossnore
offered adult craft classes and employed
twenty women to make weavings and
hook rugs.

CROW ISLAND SCHOOL
1940–
Winnetka, Illinois
Founder: Winnetka Public School
System

In 1919, the Winnetka public school system pioneered an innovative curriculum:
It recognized students' different learning
styles and allowed them to progress at
their own rate through a combination of
group projects and individual instruction. In 1940, the school system acquired
property near Crow Island, a Winnetka
city park, to construct a school whose
architecture and furnishings reflected its
educational philosophy. Architects
Lawrence Perkins and Eliel Saarinen
observed Winnetka classrooms and
talked with teachers before designing a
building with flexible classroom space
and movable furniture. Special features
included a basement pioneer room that
replicated a pioneer home, an art room
with many sinks, and a large manual
workshop. Under the auspices of the
Winnetka division of the FAP Illinois
Craft Project, Perkins and Eero Saarinen
(Eliel's son) designed molded-and-
laminated birch chairs for the school.
Crow Island established Perkins's reputation as a school architect, and its plan
was duplicated throughout the country.

*See also Lawrence Perkins:* ARTISTS'
BIOGRAPHIES

HAMPTON NORMAL AND
AGRICULTURAL INSTITUTE;
HAMPTON INSTITUTE
1868–present
Hampton, Virginia
Founder: Samuel Chapman Armstrong

With the aid of the American Missionary
Association, Armstrong founded Hampton Normal and Agricultural Institute to
train students to teach in a separate,
black educational system in the South.
He believed that African Americans
should accept their position as laborers
in the southern economy, in direct contrast to Negro educators who desired
equality and opportunity for their students. The two-year Hampton program,
which qualified students to receive a

common school teaching certificate, was designed to inculcate Christian morals and diligent work habits through required manual labor. By the 1920s, Hampton's goals changed and more closely mirrored those of other black institutions of higher education.

## HARLEM ART WORKSHOP
c. 1933–35
New York, New York

Located at the 135th Street branch of the New York Public Library, the Harlem Art Workshop provided adult and children's classes in drawing, sculpture, maskmaking, block printing, and linoleum cut-and-block work. James Lesesne Wells, a Howard University art professor, directed the workshop, with the assistance of painter Palmer Hayden. In 1935, twenty-five students over the age of fourteen were taking classes.

*See also Palmer Hayden:* ARTISTS' BIOGRAPHIES

*James Lesesne Wells:* SCHOLARS AND ADVOCATES' BIOGRAPHIES

## HINDMAN SETTLEMENT SCHOOL
1902–
Hindman, Knott County, Kentucky
Founders: Katherine Pettitt, May Stone

The guiding principles of this mission school were similar to the activities of urban settlement houses and industrial schools. Hindman's Fireside Industries (not to be confused with the Fireside Industries of Berea College or the Appalachian School) promoted weaving, basketmaking, and chairmaking. Pettitt and Stone managed the school's daily operations and supervised the day and boarding students. Soloman Everidge, a local man, was also instrumental in the founding of the school. His wife, Cordelia ("Aunt Cord"), made baskets now owned by the school.

*See also Cordelia Everidge ("Aunt Cord") Ritchie:* ARTISTS' BIOGRAPHIES

## HOWARD UNIVERSITY
1867–present
Washington, D.C.

Howard was originally intended as a training school for African American ministers and teachers, a purpose that reflected contemporary prejudices about the abilities of blacks in higher education. When the final charter was written by Congress, however, strong support had been built to create a coeducational liberal arts college and university. Howard University has become the largest black comprehensive university in the United States, with colleges of liberal arts, fine arts, pharmacy, and dentistry, and schools of engineering and architecture, medicine, law, religion, and social work.

## PENLAND SCHOOL OF HANDICRAFTS, INC.; PENLAND SCHOOL OF CRAFTS, INC.
1938–present
Penland, North Carolina
Founder: Lucy Morgan

The school emerged from classes taught by Chicago weaving expert Edward Worst. He first came to Penland, in 1928, at the request of Lucy Morgan, who had taken weaving classes with him, in Chicago, at the suggestion of Allen Eaton. Weaving courses became popular with Penland Weavers and Potters and people from outside the community, who began taking classes in 1929. A summer weaving institute developed; from it, the Penland School of Handicrafts was incorporated as a nonprofit institution in 1938. Morgan served as director for more than thirty years. She was a brilliant businesswoman, with a keen ability to identify emerging markets. Her activities at the school also reflected her beliefs in the value of all people and in the capacity of craftwork to provide spiritual sustenance. The school added mountain crafts, as well as courses in jewelrymaking, metalwork, lapidary, and shoemaking, and students came to Penland from around the world. After World War II, occupational crafts were stressed, and special sessions were set up for home demonstration agents working for the U.S. Department of Agriculture; the school also trained workers for the blind. Morgan's handpicked successor, Bill Brown, became the director at Penland in 1962, shifting the focus of the school to a retreat for university-trained craftspersons. The school's name was officially changed in 1984.

*See also Appalachian Industrial School:* SCHOOLS

*Fireside Industries of the Appalachian School:* CRAFT SHOPS AND PRODUCTION CENTERS—GENERAL

## PENN SCHOOL; PENN NORMAL, INDUSTRIAL, AND AGRICULTURAL SCHOOL
1862–present
St. Helena Island, South Carolina
Founders: Ellen Murray, Laura Towne

In 1862, Quaker abolitionists Murray and Towne, with support from the Philadelphia Commission, founded the Penn School, to demonstrate that slaves could become useful, productive citizens. The school's name was changed in 1904 when it adopted the industrial-education program championed by Hampton Institute. The teachers, many of whom had been trained at Hampton, sought to improve the island's agricultural practices and public schools. Rossa Belle Cooley was appointed principal in 1905, after teaching at Hampton for seven years, and served until 1944. In 1916, George Brown, a graduate of the school, became the head of the basket shop, and remained there until 1950. Brown invited island basketmakers to improve their products by working at the school's shop. Other courses offered were carpentry, cobbling, and blacksmithing.

*See also Rossa Belle Cooley:* SCHOLARS AND ADVOCATES' BIOGRAPHIES

## PI BETA PHI SETTLEMENT SCHOOL; ARROWMONT SCHOOL OF ARTS AND CRAFTS
1912–present
Gatlinburg, Tennessee

In 1912, Pi Beta Phi, the first national college sorority, established a rural settlement house in Gatlinburg, Tennessee, the site recommended by the U.S. Commissioner of Education. The Pi Beta Phi School, which fostered home industries, focused on weaving and reintroducing spinning to the region. In 1925, when Winogene Redding became director, she recruited thirty women to work from their homes, selling their ware from the Arrow Craft Shop on the school grounds. O. J. Mattil was one of the teachers. He had moved to Chattanooga, Tennessee, as a vocational agriculture teacher, and, in addition to classes in poultryraising and crop rotation, he taught furnituremaking and remodeling. When he came to Pi Beta Phi, he established the Woodcrafters and Carvers Shop. In 1945, the University of Tennessee and the Pi Beta Phi Settlement School began offering Summer Craft Workshops in Gatlinburg. In 1970, the workshops became known as the Arrowmont School of Arts and Crafts. Today, one thousand students attend workshops taught by some of the best craftspeople in the country.

*See also Arrow Craft Shop; Woodcrafters and Carvers Shop:* CRAFT SHOPS AND PRODUCTION CENTERS—GENERAL; WOOD

## PINE MOUNTAIN SETTLEMENT SCHOOL
1913–
Pine Mountain, Harlan County, Kentucky
Founders: Katherine Pettitt, May Stone

In 1913, the Harlan County community gave land to establish the Pine Mountain Settlement School to Katherine Pettitt and May Stone, cofounders of Hindman Settlement School. Pine Mountain emphasized quilting and became part of the craft revival. In 1933, twenty-three people were employed as weavers, with six working from their homes.

## SANTA FE INDIAN SCHOOL STUDIO
1932–37
Santa Fe, New Mexico

In 1932, Dorothy Dunn, a graduate of the Art Institute of Chicago, who had researched Indian art in the late 1920s and early 1930s, organized an art studio at the government's Santa Fe Indian School to explore the personal and professional benefits of art training for Indian students. As one of the first programs of its kind, Dunn's studio became a model for other Indian schools, especially after the Reorganization Act of 1934 encouraged such activities. As the school's only art teacher, Dunn influenced a generation of painters. Her techniques can be identified in nearly all Indian painters born between 1915 and 1940, as she taught a number of students at the Santa Fe school, and they, in turn, taught other Indians at government schools around the country. Typical paintings by Dunn-trained artists display certain characteristics: disciplined brush strokes; the use of opaque, water-mixed paints; a nonspecific background environment; and content that is asocial and idealized. They are often images of Native Americans at work or taking part in ceremonies. Dunn encouraged her students to paint *yei* and *kachina* figures.

## SCHOOL OF AMERICAN ARCHAEOLOGY; SCHOOL OF AMERICAN RESEARCH
1907–present
Santa Fe, New Mexico
Founder: Archaeological Institute of America

On December 30, 1907, the Archaeological Institute of America established the School of American Archaeology, to conduct research in North America and train students. Under the direction of Edgar Lee Hewett, the school sponsored field schools, excavated southwestern pueblos, and published its findings, thus becoming instrumental in the revived interest in Indian crafts. In 1909, the school moved into the Governors Palace, in Santa Fe, along with the Museum of New Mexico, and Hewett became director of the school and museum. In 1917, its name was changed to the School of American Research, to reflect its broader interests in art and ethnology. With the dissolution of the Laboratory of Anthropology in 1947, the school received its collections, which are now housed in the Indian Arts Research Center, built in 1978. The school and museum ended their relationship in 1959. Since 1967, the school has offered postdoctoral seminars in anthropology, although archaeology remains its primary focus.

*See also Edgar Lee Hewett:* SCHOLARS AND ADVOCATES' BIOGRAPHIES

## SNOW LOOMS SCHOOL OF WEAVING AND CRAFTS
1921–
New York, New York
Founder: Edith H. Snow

After teaching at Flambeau Weavers, in New York City, from 1918 to 1919, Snow opened her own weaving school. She served as its president until 1931.

## TUSKEGEE NORMAL AND INDUSTRIAL INSTITUTE; TUSKEGEE UNIVERSITY
1881–present
Tuskegee, Alabama
Founder: Booker T. Washington

Washington founded Tuskegee Normal and Industrial Institute as Alabama's first training school for black teachers. Known as Tuskegee Institute, the school derived its curriculum from Washington's belief that only through the development of vocational skills, and the resulting economic gains, would blacks achieve civil and political rights. The institute employed a self-help program that allowed students to earn all or part of their expenses while pursuing courses in carpentry, farming, mechanics, or teacher education. In 1985, the school became Tuskegee University. It now encompasses a college of arts and sciences and schools of agriculture and home economics, business, education, engineering and architecture, nursing and allied health, and veterinary medicine.

### KARDON
### *Within Our Shores*

1. "A Neglected History: 20th-Century American Craft," a two-day symposium held at the American Craft Museum, January 19 and 20, 1990. A transcript of the proceedings was published by the American Craft Museum in 1990.

2. This despite Walker Evans's harsh photographic depictions in the Evans–James Agee collaboration *Let Us Now Praise Famous Men*.

3. Lincoln Kirstein, *Exhibition of American Folk Painting in Connection with the Massachusetts Tercentenary Celebration* (pamphlet prepared for Harvard Society for Contemporary Art, Cambridge, 1930), unpaged. Readers are referred to Ian Quimby and Scott T. Swank, eds., *Perspectives on American Folk Art* (New York: Winterthur Museum/W. W. Norton, 1980).

4. E. Holger Cahill, *American Folk Art: The Art of the Common Man in America, 1750–1900* (New York: Museum of Modern Art, 1932).

5. Janet Catherine Berlo, ed., *The Early Years of Native American Art History: The Politics of Art History and Collecting* (Seattle: University of Washington Press, 1992).

6. Ivan Karp and Steven D. Lavine, eds., *Exhibiting Cultures: The Poetics and Politics of Museum Display* (Washington, D.C.: Smithsonian Institution Press, 1991), 5–6.

7. Svetlana Alpers, "A Way of Seeing," in Karp and Lavine, *Exhibiting Cultures*.

8. Assisting us in identifying certain specific objects were Dale Rosengarten and Winifred Owens-Hart.

9. For a discussion of René d'Harnoncourt's impact upon the display and understanding of Native American objects, readers are referred to W. Jackson Rushing, "Marketing the Affinity of the Primitive and the Modern," in Berlo, *Early Years of Native American Art History*, 191–236.

### GREEN
### *Culture and Crisis*

1. Caroline Bird, *The Invisible Scar* (New York: David McKay, 1986).

2. Anglo-Saxonism had been a highly visible part of American popular and academic culture since the early nineteenth century, but the cry of "racial purity" gained both adherents and volume after the Civil War. The alteration of immigration patterns from a preponderance of Anglo-Saxon, Anglo-Celtic, and northern European immigrants in the first three-quarters of the century to a far greater percentage from southern and eastern Europe helped fuel the fires of xenophobia that were burning throughout the United States by 1900. See John Higham, *Strangers in the Land: Patterns of American Nativism, 1860–1925* (New York: Atheneum, 1969); Harvey Green, "Popular Science and Political Thought Converge: Colonial Survival Becomes Colonial Revival, 1830–1910," *Journal of American Culture*, vol. 6, no. 4 (Winter 1983): 3–24.

3. Janet Catherine Berlo, "The Formative Years of Native American Art History," in Berlo, ed., *The Early Years of Native American Art History: The Politics of Art History and Collecting* (Seattle: University of Washington Press, 1992), 1–21.

4. Irene Sargent, "Indian Basketry: Its Structure and Design," *The Craftsman*, vol. 7, no. 3 (December 1904): 321–34; Natalie Curtis, "A Bit of American Folk Music: Two Pueblo Indian Grinding Songs," *The Craftsman*, vol. 7, no. 1 (October 1904): 35–41; Frederick Monsen, "Pueblos of the Painted Desert," *The Craftsman*, vol. 12, no. 1 (April 1907): 16–33; Natalie Curtis, "The Creation Myth of the Cochans (Yuma Indians)," *The Craftsman*, vol. 16, no. 5 (August 1909): 559–62.

5. It was ironic that at the very moment many white Americans, armed with reverence, reverie, and, perhaps, some guilt about white dealings with the Indians, were "discovering" the handcrafts of these Native Americans, industrial production of some of their goods was moving ahead at full speed. Between 1900 and 1930, there were five major industrial producers of woolen robes and blankets of Native American design—J. Capps and Sons, Oregon City Woolen Mills, Buell Manufacturing Company, Racine Woolen Mills, and Pendleton Woolen Mills. Only Pendleton continued production after the Depression. See Charles J. Lohrmann, "Language of the Robe," *NaTive Peoples*, vol. 6, no. 3 (Spring 1993): 22–28.

6. Henry Shapiro, *Appalachia on Our Mind: The Southern Mountains and Mountaineers in the American Consciousness, 1870–1920* (Chapel Hill: University of North Carolina Press, 1978); David E. Whisnant, *All That Is Native and Fine: The Politics of Culture in an American Region*, The Fred W. Morrison Series in Southern Studies (Chapel Hill: University of North Carolina Press, 1983).

7. On Powell's racism, see Whisnant, *All That Is Native and Fine*, 237–52.

8. Quoted in Stanley Coben, *A. Mitchell Palmer* (New York: Columbia University Press, 1963), 198.

9. Having begun as a white supremacist vigilante group after the defeat of the Confederacy, in 1865, the Klan had gradually lost much of its power base by 1900. But, within a decade, a renewed and reinvigorated Klan formed around the old hatred of African Americans as well as some new foci of intolerance: Jews, "new" immigrants, Catholics, antiprohibitionists, urban political machines, and other "moral" evils, such as prostitution and Darwinian evolutionary theory. See Kenneth Jackson, *The Ku Klux Klan in the City, 1915–1930* (New York: Oxford University Press, 1967).

10. Harold Stearns, ed., *Civilization in the United States: An Inquiry by Thirty Americans* (New York: Harcourt, Brace, and World, 1922).

11. Walter Lippmann, *Public Opinion* (New York: Harcourt, Brace, and World, 1922).

12. Lothrop Stoddard, *The Revolt against Civilization* (New York: Charles Scribner's Sons, 1922).

13. William Ogburn, *Social Change with Respect to Culture and Original Nature* (New York: Viking Press, 1922).

14. The American Country Life Association, *Proceedings* (Chicago: University of Chicago Press, 1929), 2.

15. Among the multitude of studies, Margaret Byington's *Homestead: The Households of a Mill Town* (1910; reprint, Pittsburgh, Pa.: University of Pittsburgh Press, 1974) is the most famous.

16. Roland Marchand, *Advertising and the American Dream: Making Way for Modernity, 1920–1940* (Berkeley: University of California Press, 1985).

17. Michael Williams, *Americans and Their Forests: A Historical Geography* (Cambridge, Mass.: Cambridge University Press, 1989).

18. See Richardson Wright, "Williamsburg: What It Means to Architecture, to Gardening, to Decoration," *House and Garden*, vol. 72, no. 11 (November 1937): 68–79; "New Williamsburg Inn," *House Beautiful*, vol. 79, no. 7 (July 1937): 24–25.

19. The literature on the Colonial revival is vast and still a big business. See Alan Axelrod, ed., *The Colonial Revival in America* (New York: W. W. Norton, 1985); Sarah L. Giffen and Kevin D. Murphy, eds., *"A Noble and Dignified Stream": The Piscataqua Region in the Colonial Revival, 1860–1930* (York, Maine: Old York Historical Society, 1992); Michael Kammen, *Mystic Chords of Memory: The Transformation of Tradition in American Culture* (New York: Alfred A. Knopf, 1991).

20. Cranbrook is one example of Modernist activity that will be treated in Volume III of this series, *Craft in the Machine Age: European Influence on American Modernism, 1920–1945*.

21. United States Bureau of the Census, *Historical Statistics of the United States, Colonial Times to 1957* (Washington, D.C.:

Government Printing Office, 1960), 636.

22. See Mirra Komarovsky, *The Unemployed Man and His Family* (New York: Dryden Press, 1935). In Studs Terkel, *Hard Times: An Oral History of the Great Depression* (New York: Pantheon, 1970), Terkel found that Americans tended to blame themselves and feel intense shame for their plight.

## RHOADS
### Colonial Revival

1. William B. Rhoads, *The Colonial Revival* (New York: Garland Publishing, 1977); Karal Ann Marling, *George Washington Slept Here: Colonial Revivals and American Culture, 1876–1986* (Cambridge: Harvard University Press, 1988).

2. George Leland Hunter, "Modern American Furniture," *Arts and Decoration,* vol. 20, no. 3 (January 1924): 55.

3. William B. Rhoads, "The Colonial Revival and the Americanization of Immigrants," in Alan Axelrod, ed., *The Colonial Revival in America* (New York: W. W. Norton, 1985), 341–61.

4. Wendy Kaplan, ed., *"The Art That Is Life": The Arts and Crafts Movement in America, 1875–1920* (Boston: Museum of Fine Arts/Little, Brown and Company, 1987), 173–81, 383; William B. Rhoads, "The Colonial Revival and the Arts and Crafts Movement," in Bert Denker, ed., *The Substance of Style: New Perspectives on the American Arts and Crafts Movement* (New York: W. W. Norton, forthcoming).

5. John Crosby Freeman, introduction, *Wallace Nutting Checklist of Early American Reproductions* (Watkins Glen, N.Y.: American Life Foundation, 1969), unpaged; Louis M. MacKeil, *Wallace Nutting* (Saugus, Mass.: Saugus Historical Society, 1984), 31–42; Michael Ivankovich, *The Guide to Wallace Nutting Furniture* (Doylestown, Pa.: Diamond Press, 1990).

6. *Wallace Nutting Checklist.*

7. Wallace Nutting, *Furniture of the Pilgrim Century (of American Origin): 1620–1720* (Framingham, Mass.: Old America, 1924), 8; *Wallace Nutting Checklist.* Ivankovich, *Nutting Furniture,* 77, suggests that Nutting turned to mahogany and the more elaborate eighteenth-century styles to meet public demand.

8. *Wallace Nutting Checklist.*

9. Wallace Nutting, *Wallace Nutting's Biography* (Framingham, Mass.: Old America, 1936), 246; Nutting to Nathan Margolis, October 27, 1922 (Winterthur Museum). H. I. Brock, "The Hunt for the Old Widens," *The New York Times Magazine* (September 20, 1925): 1, observed that most cabinetmakers were foreign-born.

10. *Wallace Nutting Checklist.* Nutting made office furniture advertised as adaptations, not reproductions. Wallace Nutting, *Supreme Edition General Catalog* (Framingham, Mass., 1930; reprint, West Chester, Pa.: Schiffer Publishing, 1984), 140–45.

11. Patricia E. Kane, *Three Hundred Years of American Seating Furniture* (Boston: New York Graphic Society, 1976), 265.

12. David L. Barquist, *American Tables and Looking Glasses* (New Haven: Yale University Art Gallery, 1992), 249, 347.

13. *Windsor Chairs, Being a Description and Price List of the Windsor Chairs Made by Hand in the Danersk Shops* (New York and Tryon, N.C.: Erskine-Danforth, n.d.), unpaged; *Danersk Decorative Furniture* (New York: Erskine-Danforth, 1917); Karen C. Donnelly, Stamford Historical Society, to author, March 1, 1993.

14. *Arts and Decoration,* vol. 7, no. 4 (August 1992): 241; Ralph Erskine, "Tradition in the Livable Home," *The International Studio,* vol. 77, no. 316 (September 1923): 469; *Arts and Decoration,* vol. 26, no. 5 (March 1927): 73.

15. *Arts and Decoration,* vol. 24, no. 5 (March 1926): 67; *Arts and Decoration,* vol. 25, no. 5 (September 1926): 63. Another maker of Colonial revival furniture, Berkey and Gay Furniture Company, warned that if parents provided inferior furnishings, their sons would feel "ashamed" and escape to speakeasies like Malucio's; *House and Garden,* vol. 48, no. 3 (September 1925): 58.

16. *The International Studio,* vol. 79, no. 328 (September 1924): ix.

17. *Arts and Decoration*, vol. 25, no. 10 (May 1926): 69; *The International Studio,* vol. 84, no. 348 (May 1926): 89; *Antiques,* vol. 19, no. 6 (June 1931): 469. Jacob Margolis to Francis Garvan, November 2, 1927, condemned Danersk's "commercialized . . . reproductions," lacking "exactness and true feeling"; Barquist, *American Tables,* 249.

18. *Antiques,* vol. 20, no. 6 (December 1931): 369; *Antiques,* vol. 20, no. 5 (November 1931): 301.

19. Lewis Mumford, "American Interiors," *The New Republic,* vol. 41, no. 526 (December 31, 1924): 139.

20. Erskine, "Tradition in the Livable Home," 471.

21. R. T. H. Halsey and Elizabeth Tower, *The Homes of Our Ancestors As Shown in the American Wing of the Metropolitan Museum of Art* (Garden City, N.Y.: Doubleday, 1937), xxii, 239, 288.

22. *Antiques,* vol. 8, no. 3 (September 1925): 129; *The New York Times* (September 12, 1926): 4:14–15 Like Halsey, William Sloane Coffin was an advocate of Americanization; as president of the City Mission Society, he sought "to bring about a practical realization of the American idea of democracy among the polyglot population of New York." *The New York Times* (December 18, 1933): 18. Jacob Margolis lumped Sloane's furniture with Danersk's and condemned both; see note 17.

23. A brochure, *Val-Kill Shop, Roosevelt Industries, Hyde Park, New York,* c. 1927, acknowledges the aid of Cornelius, antiques expert Morris Schwartz, and architect Henry Toombs. Furnituremaker Otto Berge remembered extracting designs from "Nutting's book, not the catalogs," although it is unclear which of Nutting's historical books Berge employed. Emily L. Wright, summary of Berge interview, July 31, 1978, in her "Eleanor Roosevelt and Val-Kill Industries, 1925–1938," October 1978 (typescript at National Park Service, Hyde Park, N.Y.).

24. Kenneth S. Davis, *Invincible Summer: An Intimate Portrait of the Roosevelts* (New York: Atheneum, 1974), 57, 64; Franklin D. Roosevelt, introduction, Rosalie Fellows Bailey, *Pre-Revolutionary Dutch Houses and Families in Northern New Jersey and Southern New York* (New York: William Morrow, 1936), unpaged.

25. William B. Rhoads, "Franklin D. Roosevelt and Dutch Colonial Architecture," *New York History,* vol. 59, no. 4 (October 1978): 436–39; Frieda Wyandt, "A Governor's Wife at Work," *Your Home* (September 1929): 68–69.

26. Otto Berge, interviewed by Thomas F. Soapes, September 19, 1977 (transcript in Franklin D. Roosevelt Library, Hyde Park, N.Y.). Berge remembered the Jefferson magazine rack and a Queen Anne lowboy as the only "correct" pieces.

27. Eleanor Roosevelt, "Columbia Syndicate," Eleanor Roosevelt papers, Box 3031, Franklin D. Roosevelt Library, cited by Wright, "Val-Kill," Appendix VII.

28. Nancy McClelland, *Furnishing the Colonial and Federal House* (Philadelphia: J. B. Lippincott Company, 1947), 33; Rexford G. Tugwell, *In Search of Roosevelt* (Cambridge: Harvard University Press, 1972), 46.

29. *Arthurdale Assn. Mountaineer Craftsmen's Unit. Arthurdale, W. Va.* (undated catalogue in Winterthur Library); Jeanne S. Rymer, "Arthurdale: A Social Experiment in the 1930s," in Axelrod, *Colonial Revival in America,* 320–40.

30. William F. McDonald, *Federal Relief Administration and the Arts* (Columbus: Ohio State University Press, 1969), 462; *An Exhibition of Contemporary New England Handicrafts* (Worcester, Mass.: Worcester Art Museum, 1943), 39; *The New York Times* (September 22, 1940).

31. Holger Cahill, introduction, Erwin O. Christensen, *The Index of American Design* (New York: Macmillan, 1950), xvii.

32. *The New York Times* (January 19, 1936): 9:13; Robin Dustin, director, Sandwich Historical Society, to author, November 25, 1992.

33. Wallace Nutting to Nathan Margolis, October 27, 1922 (Winterthur Museum).

34. Harold Margolis to Office of Price Administration, April 17, 1944 (Winterthur Museum). *Hartford Daily Times* (June 15, 1931); Aetna commissioned Pilgrim Century furniture by Nutting for the Pine Room, a corporate boardroom. William Hosley, *Wallace Nutting: A Search for New England's Past* (Hartford, Conn.: Charter Oak Temple Cultural Center, 1989), unpaged. For Temple Beth Israel, in West Hartford, Harold Margolis designed altar chairs whose Byzantine style related to that of the building; *Hartford Daily Courant* (September 16, 1936).

35. Elenita C. Chickering, *Arthur J. Stone: Handwrought Silver, 1901–1937* (Boston: Library of the Boston Athenaeum, 1981); Barbara McLean Ward and Gerald W. R. Ward, eds., *Silver in American Life* (New Haven: Yale University Art Gallery, 1979), 86; Elenita C. Chickering to author, April 15, 1993; Rilla Evelyn Jackman, *American Arts* (New York: Rand McNally, 1928), 34.

36. Margaretha Gebelein Leighton, *George Christian Gebelein: Boston Silversmith, 1878–1945* (Boston: M. Leighton, 1976); Edward S. Cooke, Jr., in *Collecting American Decorative Arts and Sculpture, 1971–1991* (Boston: Museum of Fine Arts, 1991), 75–76; Ward and Ward, *Silver in American Life*, 101.

37. *House and Garden*, vol. 49, no. 5 (May 1926): 159.

38. David L. Barquist, *American and English Pewter at the Yale University Art Gallery: A Supplementary Checklist* (New Haven: Yale University Art Gallery, 1985), 52–53; *Antiques*, vol. 15, no. 5 (May 1929): 412; Nutting, *General Catalog*, 31; Howard Herschel Cotterell et al., *National Types of Old Pewter* (New York: Weathervane, 1972), 33; *Colonial Williamsburg Approved Reproductions* (Williamsburg, Va.: Colonial Williamsburg, 1937), 24.

39. Myra Tolmach Davis, *Sketches in Iron: Samuel Yellin* (Washington, D.C.: George Washington University, 1971).

40. Ivankovich, *Nutting Furniture*, 55–59; William L. Dulaney, "Wallace Nutting Collector and Entrepreneur," *Winterthur Portfolio* 13 (1979): 56–57.

41. *Touchstone*, vol. 5, no. 3 (June 1919): 255–56; *House Beautiful*, vol. 52, no. 1 (July 1922): 85.

42. *Architecture* (June 1925): 235; "Types of Wrought Iron Hardware Applicable to Early American Architectural Treatment," *Antiques*, vol. 12, no. 4 (October 1927): 311.

43. David E. Tarn, "A Study in Local Adaptation," *Architectural Record*, vol. 34 (October 1913): 323; Helen Wilkinson Reynolds, *Dutch Houses in the Hudson Valley before 1776* (New York: Payson and Clarke, 1929), 230; "He Couldn't Buy It . . . So He Made It," *American Architect*, vol. 137 (February 1930): 48–51; Myron S. Teller to Harriet S. Gillespie, February 2, 1939 (copy in author's possession); Harriet Sisson Gillespie, "Early Dutch Architecture in the Hudson Valley," *Arts and Decoration*, vol. 35, no. 2 (June 1931): 28–29, 72. Myron S. Teller, "Early Colonial Hand Forged Iron Work," *Architectural Record*, vol. 57, no. 5 (May 1925): 395–96; Nutting, *General Catalog*, 147; E. L. Austin and Odell Hauser, *The Sesqui-centennial International Exposition* (Philadelphia: Current Publications, 1929), 167.

44. Herman Hjorth, "Reproducing Antique Furniture in the Schools," *Industrial Arts Magazine*, vol. 11 (April 1922): 137; Albert Sack, *Fine Points of Furniture: Early American* (New York: Crown, 1950), dedication page; *Antiques*, vol. 11, no. 6 (June 1927): 477, 493; I. Sack, *Reproductions of Antique Fittings* (Boston: I. Sack, n.d.); *Antiques*, vol. 16, no. 3 (September 1929): inside front cover.

45. *Exhibition of Contemporary New England Handicrafts*, 8, 23, 25, 38.

46. *Wallace Nutting Checklist*; *Arts and Decoration*, vol. 23, no. 2 (June 1925): 7; "Rosemont," Marion, Virginia, undated catalogue; *Daughters of the American Revolution Magazine*, vol. 62, no. 4 (April 1928): unpaged.

47. *Arts and Decoration*, vol. 21, no. 4 (August 1924): 55.

48. *Antiques*, vol. 29, no. 5 (May 1936): 214; *Antiques*, vol. 12, no. 1 (July 1927): 3; *Antiques*, vol. 5, no. 1 (January 1924): 6.

49. Federal Writers' Project, *Maine, A Guide "Down East"* (Boston: Houghton Mifflin, 1937), 109.

50. George Leland Hunter, *Decorative Textiles* (Philadelphia: J. B. Lippincott Company, 1918), 133; Ethel Stanwood Bolton and Eva Johnston Coe, *American Samplers* (Boston: Massachusetts Society of the Colonial Dames of America, 1921); Judith Reiter Weissman and Wendy Lavitt, *Labors of Love: America's Textiles and Needlework, 1650–1930* (New York: Alfred A. Knopf, 1987), xiii; "Rosemont," 34.

51. Mary Harrod Northend, "Renaissance of the Sampler," *The International Studio*, vol. 77, no. 316 (September 1923): 492.

52. Marguerite Fawdry and Deborah Brown, *The Book of Samplers* (New York: St. Martin's Press, 1980), 124–25.

The revival of interest in samplermaking was primarily inspired by ancestral piety, but Stephen F. Whitman and Son, practitioners of "candy craft" in Philadelphia, had another explanation: The revival was stimulated, in part, because the "Whitman's Sampler has gone into practically all the tasteful homes in the land, showing on the package a fine example of cross-stitch needlework"; *House and Garden*, vol. 46, no. 2 (August 1924): 81.

53. Northend, "Renaissance," 491; Ruth E. Finley, *Old Patchwork Quilts and the Women Who Made Them* (Philadelphia: J. B. Lippincott Company, 1929), 7–8.

54. Weissman and Lavitt, *Labors of Love*, 67; Eleanor Roosevelt papers, 150.4 Handicrafts, 1934–35 (Franklin D. Roosevelt Library).

55. *The Renaissance of South Jersey Blown Glass* (Providence, R.I.: Grant and Lyon, 1934), n.p.

56. Gay LeCleire Taylor, *Clevenger Brothers Glass Works: The Persistence of Tradition* (Millville, N.J.: Museum of American Glass, 1987), 3–4.

57. Gay LeCleire Taylor, of the Museum of American Glass, provided photocopies of "American Glass Design" publicity for the WPA project in Vineland; Morley Cassidy, "Artists at Bubble Blowing Revive an Ancient Craft," *Philadelphia Evening Bulletin* (c. 1940). See also *The New York Times* (September 22, 1940).

58. Cornelius Weygandt, *The Dutch Country: Folks and Treasures in the Red Hills of Pennsylvania* (New York: Appleton-Century, 1939), 27; Lester Breininger, "The Stahl Family Potters," *Antique Collecting* (February 1979): 22–27; Wallace Nutting, *Pennsylvania Beautiful* (Framingham, Mass.: Old America, 1924), 155; Guy F. Reinert, "Passing of Stahl Brothers," *Town and Country* (March 17, 1950); Ann Hark, *Blue Hills and Shoofly Pie in Pennsylvania Dutchland* (Philadelphia: J. B. Lippincott Company, 1952), 195; "Die Brüder Stahl, Pennsylvanien, USA," *Unsere Heimat* (Kaiserslautern, Germany: 1938), n.p.

59. Helen Painter, "Mrs. Keyser of Plymouth Meeting," *American Home*, vol. 29 (May 1943): 40, 42; *Ambler Gazette* (April 21, 1966); Mrs. C. Naaman Keyser, *Method of Making Pennsylvania German Pottery* (Plymouth Meeting, Pa.: the author, 1943).

60. Writers' Program of the Work Projects Administration in the State of Virginia, *Virginia* (New York: Oxford, 1940), 155; "Development of Products Division before 1945," typescript provided by Bland Blackford, Colonial Williamsburg Foundation, April 12, 1993; Rutherfoord Goodwin, *A Brief & True Report Concerning Williamsburg in Virginia* (Williamsburg, Va.: Colonial Williamsburg, 1941), 120; *House Beautiful*, vol. 80, no. 1 (January 1938): 36, 73; *Colonial Williamsburg Approved Reproductions*, 5, 7.

61. Goodwin, *Brief & True Report*, 121; John D. Rockefeller, Jr., "The Genesis of the Williamsburg Restoration," *National Geographic*, vol. 71, no. 4 (April 1937): 401.

62. Barquist, *American and English Pewter*, 48–49; *Colonial Williamsburg Approved Reproductions*, 24.

63. Lewis Mumford, "American Interiors," *The New Republic*, vol. 41, no. 526 (December 31, 1924): 139; *The International Studio* (June

1928): 78. Edward D. Andrews and Faith Andrews, *Shaker Furniture: The Craftsmanship of an American Communal Sect* (New Haven: Yale University Press, 1937), 63, called for renewed production of Shaker designs as an alternative to simple modern furnishings marred by "smartness."

64. Wallace Nutting, "Antique Humbugs," *The Saturday Evening Post*, vol. 202 (March 22, 1930): 150; *Colonial Charm for Homes of Today* (Harrisonburg, Va.: Virginia Craftsmen, n.d.), 4, 19. *Antiques*, edited by Alice Winchester, advocated reproductions and adaptations of American antiques as perpetuating "an honorable tradition that is . . . distinctly American," while condemning "ultra-modernistic furniture" as "esthetic monstrosities"; *Antiques*, vol. 37, no. 6 (June 1940): 281, and *Antiques*, vol. 38, no. 2 (August 1940): 59.

65. *House and Garden*, vol. 47, no. 1 (January 1925): 45.

66. Richardson Wright, "The Modernist Taste," *House and Garden*, vol. 48, no. 4 (October 1925): 77–78.

67. T. H. Robsjohn-Gibbings, *Goodbye Mr. Chippendale* (New York: Alfred A. Knopf, 1945), 54–55.

68. Mary Davis Gillies, "Mr. and Mrs. McCall Know What They Want," *Architectural Forum*, vol. 82, no. 4 (April 1945): 102; Emily Price Post, *The Personality of a House: The Blue Book of Home Design and Decoration* (New York: Funk and Wagnalls Company, 1939), 267, 495.

69. McClelland, *Furnishing the Colonial and Federal House*, 5, 7.

## YORK
### New Deal Craft Programs

1. Edward Bruce was the director of the PWAP, which came to an end in 1934. Initially, WPA stood for Works Progress Administration; later, it was changed to Work Projects Administration. Francis V. O'Connor, *Federal Support for the Visual Arts: The New Deal and Now*, 2d edition (Greenwich, Conn.: New York Graphic Society, 1971), remains an invaluable introduction to the nature and structure of the New Deal art programs and the research resources. Researchers should note that since O'Connor's publication, material in the National Archives in Record Group (RG) 69 has been recatalogued and boxes have been renumbered.

2. Richard D. McKinzie, *The New Deal for Artists* (Princeton: Princeton University Press, 1973), 28.

3. Allen H. Eaton, *Handicrafts of the Southern Highlands* (1937; reprint, New York: Dover, 1973), 292–99. See also Eaton, *Handicrafts of New England* (New York: Harper and Brothers, 1949); Eaton and Lucinda Crile,

"Rural Handicrafts in the United States" (Washington, D.C.: U.S. Department of Agriculture, Extension Services, 1937); Nathaniel Fairbanks, "Report for the Division of Self-Help Cooperatives," Federal Emergency Relief Administration (June 1, 1934).

4. Holger Cahill, personal papers, June 25, 1940, Archives of American Art, microfilm roll 1107.

5. *Old and New Paths in American Design, 1720–1936*, exhibition catalogue (Newark, N.J.: Newark Museum, 1936), 3.

6. Daniel S. Defenbacher, "Art in Action," in Francis V. O'Connor, ed., *Art for the Millions: Essays from the 1930s by Artists and Administrators of the WPA Federal Art Project* (Greenwich, Conn.: New York Graphic Society, 1973), 223–26.

7. These reports may be found in RG 69, WPA general correspondence, Archives of American Art, microfilm roll DC 51.

8. O'Connor, *Art for the Millions*, 208–27, 306–7.

9. Holger Cahill, personal papers, "Community Art Centers," Archives of American Art, microfilm roll 1107.

10. Francis V. O'Connor, "The Usable Future: The Role of Fantasy in the Promotion of a Consumer Society for Art," in Helen A. Harrison, ed., *Dawn of a New Day: The New York World's Fair, 1939–40*, exhibition catalogue (New York: Queens Museum, 1980), 63.

11. McKinzie, *New Deal for Artists*, 134; Sharon S. Darling, *Chicago Furniture: Art, Craft, and Industry, 1833–1983* (New York: W. W. Norton/Chicago Historical Society, 1984), 290–91.

12. The WPA required that many programs have state and/or local sponsorship and financial support.

13. Patrocinio Barela, interview by Sylvia Loomis, July 2, 1964, Archives of American Art, microfilm roll 3418; Wendell Anderson, Mildred Crews, and Judson Crews, *Patrocinio Barela: Taos Wood Carver*, 3d edition (Taos, N.M.: Taos Recordings and Publications, 1976); and Russell Vernon Hunter, "Concerning Patrocinio Barela," in O'Connor, *Art for the Millions*, 96–99.

14. Stephen Trimble, *Talking with the Clay: The Art of Pueblo Pottery* (Santa Fe, N.M.: School of American Research Press, 1987), 38–46.

15. Gerald E. Markowitz and Marlene Park, *New Deal for Art: The Government Art Projects of the 1930s with Examples from New York City and State*, exhibition catalogue (New York: Gallery Association of New York State, 1977), 75.

16. National Archives, RG 69, WPA Division of Information, Primary Files 1936–42, "Arts

and Crafts."

17. René d'Harnoncourt was manager of the Indian Arts and Crafts Board of the Department of the Interior, which was set up to develop a market for Native American crafts.

18. See Vertis Hays, "The Negro Artist Today," 210–12, Gwendolyn Bennett, "The Harlem Community Art Center," 213–15, and Harry H. Sutton, Jr., "High Noon in Art," 216–17, in O'Connor, *Art for the Millions*.

19. Bessie May Carlton, letter of May 14, 1941, National Archives, RG 69, WPA State Files, Alabama.

20. D. Michael Gormley and Karal Ann Marling, *Federal Art in Cleveland 1933–1943*, exhibition catalogue (Cleveland: Cleveland Public Library, 1974), 29–30, 58–59; Ross Anderson and Barbara Perry, *The Diversions of Keramos: American Clay Sculpture, 1925–1950*, exhibition catalogue (Syracuse, N.Y.: Everson Museum of Art, 1983), 64–72.

21. Edris Eckhardt reference file, American Craft Council Library; see also Ralph Woehrman, "Edris Eckhardt Interviewed," *Link*, vol. 12, no. 3 (Spring 1978): 4ff.

22. Hildreth York, *New Deal Art: New Jersey*, exhibition catalogue (Newark, N.J.: Robeson Center Gallery/Rutgers, The State University of New Jersey, 1980).

23. There were considerable differences from state to state in the organization of craft programs. Not all states had a separate category.

24. For instance, the tile panels in the Newark subway, by Domenick Mortellito, depicting the Morris Canal and the subway that replaced it; York, *New Deal Art*, 32.

25. Ibid., 48–49; Anderson and Perry, *Diversions of Keramos*, 2–24; O'Connor, *Art for the Millions*, 94–95.

26. *The Builders of Timberline Lodge*, with text by the Oregon Writers' Project (Portland, Oreg.: Works Progress Administration, 1937). The organization Friends of Timberline Lodge is responsible for the continuing restoration. Linny Adamson, curator of Timberline Lodge, provided information to the writer. See also Margery Hoffman Smith, personal papers, Archives of American Art, microfilm roll 2550.

27. For a review of Lukens's career, see Susan Peterson, "Glen Lukens, 1887–1967," *Craft Horizons*, vol. 28, no. 2 (March–April 1968): 22–25.

28. Beatrice Wood reference file, American Craft Council Library, in *American Craft* (August–September 1983): 24. Wood studied with Lukens at the University of Southern California in 1938.

29. See Whitney Atchley and Adrian Dornbush records, Archives of American Art, microfilm roll DC 51. Works of these artists will be included in the third exhibition of this series,

"Craft in the Machine Age: European Influence on American Modernism, 1920–1945."

30. Alberta Redenbaugh, "Crafts Programs," National Archives, RG 69, Records of the Work Projects Administration, Division of Service Projects, February 1942–June 1943; Final State Reports, Crafts Program. (Box 16, PC 37, Entry 30. Copies of this report exist in several locations within the archival records.) It is worth noting that Redenbaugh and administrators Dornbush and Atchley all comment frequently on the need for better design and better designers.

31. Donald R. Gillies and Emerson Ross, "Handicraft Activities on WPA Projects," WPA Final State Reports, Washington, D.C., February 1939.

32. Ruth Reeves, personal papers, Archives of American Art, microfilm roll 3093.

33. See C. Adolph Glassgold, transcript of an interview by Harlan B. Phillips, December 9, 1964, Archives of American Art; see also Erwin O. Christensen, *The Index of American Design* (New York: Macmillan, 1967).

34. "Olive Lyford Gavert: The WPA Federal Art Project and the New York World's Fair, 1939–40," in Francis V. O'Connor, ed., *The New Deal Art Projects: An Anthology of Memoirs* (Washington, D.C.: Smithsonian Institution Press, 1972), 263–67.


O'CONNOR
*WPA Federal Art Project*

1. I have derived most of the details from Rachael Griffin and Sarah Munro, eds., *Timberline Lodge* (Portland, Oreg.: Friends of Timberline, 1978), which contains a history of the lodge and its restoration, an inventory of its furnishings, and useful biographical sketches. For background, I have relied on Federal Writers' Project, "The Builders of Timberline Lodge," in Francis V. O'Connor, ed., *Art for the Millions: Essays from the 1930s by Artists and Administrators of the WPA Federal Art Project* (Greenwich, Conn.: New York Graphic Society, 1973), 182–89; Carl Gohs, "The House the Artists Built," *Northwest* (January 5, 1969): 6–11, which contains excerpts from FDR's dedication address; and Judith Rose et al., eds., *Timberline Lodge: A Love Story* (Portland, Oreg.: Friends of Timberline/Graphic Arts Center Publishing Company, 1986), which contains a good bibliography.


COE
*Native American Craft*

1. *The Memoirs of Ray Lyman Wilbur, 1875–1949*, eds. Edgar Eugene Robinson and Paul Carroll Edwards (Stanford, Calif.: Stanford University Press, 1960), 479–80.

2. Letter from John Collier to John Randolph Haynes, May 1992, quoted in Lawrence C. Kelly, *The Assault on Assimilation: John Collier and the Origins of Indian Policy Reform* (Albuquerque: University of New Mexico Press, 1983), 133. Among the numerous articles and books by and about John Collier, the most readily available, in addition to Kelly's, are Kenneth R. Philip, *John Collier's Crusade for Indian Reform, 1920–1954* (Tucson: University of Arizona Press, 1977), and Robert Fay Schrader, *The Indian Arts & Crafts Board: An Aspect of New Deal Indian Policy* (Albuquerque, N.M.: University of Albuquerque Press, 1983), each with extensive bibliographical references. Books by Collier himself include *Indians of the Americas* (New York: W. W. Norton, 1947) and *From Every Zenith: A Memoir and Some Essays on Life and Thought* (Denver, Colo.: Sage Books, 1963).

3. What has been described as "one of the most penetrating and fair-minded analyses of Collier" appears in a letter written by Harold L. Ickes, Secretary of the Department of the Interior during the Roosevelt administration, April 18, 1933, explaining his choice of Collier as Commissioner of Indian Affairs: "I think you know that I have had serious differences of opinion with John Collier. . . . I do believe, however, that no one exceeds him in knowledge of Indian matters or his sympathy with the point of view of the Indians themselves. I want some one in that office who is the advocate of the Indians. The whites can take care of themselves, but the Indians need someone to protect them from exploitation. I want a man who will respect their customs and have a sympathetic point of view with reference to their culture"; cited in Lawrence C. Kelly, "Choosing the New Deal Indian Commissioner: Ickes vs Collier," *New Mexico Historical Review*, vol. 49 (October 1974): 284.

4. Lewis Meriam and Associates, *The Problem of Indian Administration* (Baltimore: Institute for Government Research, The Johns Hopkins Press, 1928), generally referred to as the Meriam Report.

5. Schrader, *Indian Arts & Crafts Board*, 20.

6. Ibid., 19. For a detailed discussion of the ramifications of the report, ibid., 22–43.

7. Ibid., 299.

8. Collier and d'Harnoncourt met in Mexico in the summer of 1936 at a conference sponsored by the government. Because of his interest in learning about the status of the arts and crafts of the Mexican Indians, Collier was introduced to d'Harnoncourt, who had arrived in Mexico from Vienna in 1926, almost penniless and unable to speak either Spanish or English. Supporting himself as a commercial artist, he met artists and dealers, for whom he began to arrange exhibitions. After several conversations, Collier offered him the job. D'Harnoncourt, who later served as director of the Museum of Modern Art, in New York City, from 1949 to 1968, had a unique combination of knowledge, intelligence, diplomacy, humor, tact, taste, and infinite charm. For more on him, see Schrader, *Indian Arts & Crafts Board*, chs. 7–12; *René d'Harnoncourt: A Tribute, October 8, 1968*. Sculpture Garden, Museum of Modern Art, New York City; *René d'Harnoncourt Oral History* (New York: Columbia University Research Office, 1969); René D'Harnoncourt papers, National Archives of American Art, Washington, D.C.

9. Schrader, *Indian Arts & Crafts Board*, 129, quoting from Library of Congress, *Reports and Documents Concerning the Activities of the Arts and Crafts Board*, introduction, 7.

10. René d'Harnoncourt, "Activities of the Indian Arts and Crafts Board since Its Organization in 1936," *Indians at Work*, vol. 7 (April 1940): 33–35.

11. Ruth Bunzel, *The Pueblo Potter: A Study of Creative Imagination in Primitive Art* (New York: Columbia University Press, 1929), 5.

12. Ibid.

13. Lawrence P. Frank and Francis H. Harlow, *Historic Pottery of the Pueblo Indians, 1600–1880* (Boston: New York Graphic Society, 1974), 5.

14. Bunzel, *The Pueblo Potter*, 4.

15. Mary Histia's pottery was distributed to many government offices and United States embassies under the aegis of John Collier, Commissioner of Indian Affairs, who held her work in high esteem.

16. As an example of continuity, it should be pointed out that excellent specimens of this type of jar are still being made by Margaret Tafoya's descendants, often in redware as well as blackware.

17. Rick Dillingham, with Melinda Elliott, *Acoma and Laguna Pottery* (Santa Fe, N.M.: School of American Research, 1992), 143–44.

18. Unpublished manuscript by Sallie Lippincott Wagner, written at the request of the School of American Research; quotation courtesy Mrs. Wagner.

19. Ibid.

20. Tyrone Campbell and Joel and Kate Kopp, *Navajo Pictorial Weaving, 1880–1950: Folk Art Images of Native Americans* (New York: Dutton Studio Books, 1991), 4.

21. A number of the sandpainting tapestries woven by Klah and his family remain at the Wheelwright Museum. The collection also contained watercolor renderings of chants, as well as medicine material and medicine bundles. The latter have since been returned to the Navajo people in accordance with the principle of repatriation, although some members of Klah's family have objected to the dispersal of this material, as the objects had been of traditional preservation in the first place.

22. Collectors of these baskets are considered important enough to warrant an entire chapter in the authoritative book on the subject, Craig D. Bates and Martha J. Lee, *Tradition and Innovation: A Basket History of the Indians of the Yosemite-Mono Lake Area* (Yosemite National Park, Calif.: Yosemite Association, 1990), 109.

23. Ibid., 117. Both women were invited to demonstrate their craft at the 1939 Golden Gate International Exposition, in San Francisco.

24. During the period under consideration, there was a decisive development in the Southwest, especially in Santa Fe and Oklahoma, in the field of easel painting. Since this art form is outside the purview of a history of craft, no examples have been included.

25. Rosita Worl and Charles Smythe, "Jennie Thlunaut: Master Chilkat Blanket Artist," in *The Artist behind the Work: Life Histories of Nick Charles, Sr., Frances Dementiess, Lena Sours, and Jennie Thlunaut*, ed. Suzi Jones (Fairbanks: University of Alaska Museum, 1986), 127–45.

26. Katherine Kuh, "Alaska's Vanishing Art," *Saturday Review*, vol. 49 (October 22, 1966): 27.

27. Ibid., 28. "They deliberately set out to destroy the works," Kuh remembers, "declaring unsalvageable that which could have been saved, and which, properly handled, could have still provided Indians with jobs. The result remains a travesty to this day"; telephone conversation with the author, May 1993. In Viola E. Garfield and Linn A. Forrest, *The Wolf and the Raven: Totem Poles of Southeastern Alaska* (Seattle: University of Washington Press, 1961), a comparison of the original thunderbird and whale from Klinkwan (fig. 36) with the copy (fig. 37), or the original eagle carving from Howkan (fig. 38) with the copy (fig. 39), bears out the truth of Kuh's condemnation.

28. Frederic H. Douglas and René d'Harnoncourt, *Indian Art of the United States* (New York: Museum of Modern Art, 1941), 176. During the time of the exhibition, the three-story-high pole was set up outside the museum, after which it stood in the museum's garden for almost three decades. The museum's records indicate that the pole was returned to the Department of the Interior in 1968, but repeated efforts to locate it, or records of it, within that department have failed.

29. Ann T. Walton, John C. Ewers, and Royal B. Hassrick, *After the Buffalo Were Gone: The Louis Warren Hill, Sr., Collection of Indian Art* (St. Paul, Minn.: Northwest Area Foundation/University of Washington Press, 1985), 44, 174–75.

30. For more on Gladys Tantaquidgeon, see "'Last of the Mohicans' Works for Her People," *Indians at Work* (September 15, 1934): 24, and the entry under "Uncas" in *Biographical Dictionary of Indians of the Americas*, vol. 2 (Newport Beach, Calif.: American Indian Publishers, 1983), 517. For articles by Gladys Tantaquidgeon, see "New England Indian Council Fires Still Burn," *Indians at Work* (February 1, 1935): 20–24, and "Notes on Mohegan-Pequot Basketry Designs," *Indians at Work* (April 15, 1935): 43–46.

TREMBLAY
*Cultural Survival*

1. Editor's note: This terminology—like the use of conqueror, nonnative, captive, Native American, tribal, and indigenous—refers to European colonialism in the Americas. Whether native peoples were not themselves immigrants is still a question, as is the idea that these continents were originally unoccupied.

2. Susan Peterson, *The Living Tradition of Maria Martinez* (New York: Harper and Row, 1977), 98.

3. Alice Marriot, *Maria: The Potter of San Ildefonso* (Norman: University of Oklahoma Press, 1948), 158–81.

4. Nancy J. Parezo, *Navajo Sandpainting: From Religious Act to Commercial Art* (Tucson: University of Arizona Press, 1983), 25–26.

5. Will Roscoe, ed., *Living in the Spirit: A Gay American Indian Anthology* (New York: St. Martin's Press, 1988), 63.

6. Susan McGreevy, "Navajo Sandpainting Textiles at the Wheelwright Museum," *American Indian Art Magazine*, vol. 7, no. 1 (Winter 1981): 57, and Parezo, *Navajo Sandpainting*, 46.

7. McGreevy, *Navajo Sandpainting Textiles*, 55, and Parezo, *Navajo Sandpainting*, 46.

8. McGreevy, *Navajo Sandpainting Textiles*, 58.

9. Ibid., 58–59.

10. Elsie Allen, *Pomo Basketmaking: A Supreme Act for the Weaver*, rev. ed. (Healdsburg, Calif.: Natureal Press, 1972), 7–14.

11. J. M. Gogol, *American Indian Basketry Magazine*, vol. 1, no. 2, see plate 16.

WROTH
*The Hispanic Craft Revival*

1. Initial research for this article was made possible by a National Endowment for the Humanities grant, "Government Support of the Arts in New Mexico, 1933–1943," received in 1979 by this writer and Dr. Marta Weigle, of the University of New Mexico. I am also grateful to those participants in the events of the 1920s and 1930s who gave generously of their time for interviews, providing me with much valuable insight into the revival, and to the many other individuals who, over the years, have assisted me with this research.

This article is dedicated to the memory of Elidio Gonzales, master furnituremaker of Taos, one of the highly committed artists who kept the crafts alive from the 1930s through the 1980s.

2. *El Palacio*, vol. 7, no. 4 (August 1919): 89; see also *El Palacio*, vol. 4, no. 3 (July 1917): 93. Although this furniture was loosely based upon New Mexican prototypes—from Jesse Nusbaum's photographs of original pieces—the designers could not resist adding a few California mission touches. As Taylor and Bokides point out, the through-mortise-and-tenon joint, with tenon extending through to the outside, was not part of the New Mexican repertoire but, rather, a characteristic of California mission and Craftsman styles. See Lonn Taylor and Dessa Bokides, *New Mexican Furniture, 1600–1940: The Origins, Survival, and Revival of Furniture Making in the Hispanic Southwest* (Santa Fe: Museum of New Mexico Press, 1987), 216–17 and plates 214, 234, 258.

3. Mary Austin, "New Mexico Folk Poetry," *El Palacio*, vol. 7, nos. 7 and 8 (November 30, 1919): 149, 147. In this article, Austin appropriately gave credit to the earlier work of pioneering Hispanic folklorist Aurelio Espinosa.

4. For a detailed history of the early years of the society, see Marta Weigle, "The First Twenty-five Years of the Spanish Colonial Arts Society," in Weigle, Claudia Larcombe, and Samuel Larcombe, eds., *Hispanic Arts and Ethnohistory in the Southwest* (Santa Fe, N. M.: Ancient City Press, 1983), 181–203.

5. Mary Austin, "Frank Applegate," *New Mexico Quarterly*, vol. 2 (1932): 214.

6. See also Mary Austin, *Earth Horizon* (New York: Houghton Mifflin and Company, 1932), 358. Austin's overemphasis on things Spanish derives from the earlier romanticization of "Spanish" California begun in the 1880s by Anglo writers such as Bret Harte, Helen Hunt Jackson, and Gertrude Atherton. See John R. Chavez, *The Lost Land: The Chicano Image of the Southwest* (Albuquerque: University of New Mexico Press, 1984), 85–92. For a discussion of the blend of cultural influences upon Hispanic crafts in the colonial period, see William Wroth, "Crafts, Spanish Borderlands," in *Encyclopedia of the North American Colonies* (New York: Scribner's, 1993).

7. On José Dolores López and his descendants, see Charles L. Briggs, *The Woodcarvers of Córdova, New Mexico: Social Dimensions of an Artistic Revival* (Knoxville: University of Tennessee Press, 1980).

8. Quoted in Robert Coles, *The Old Ones of New Mexico* (1973; reprint, Albuquerque: University of New Mexico Press, 1989), 22. The woman was paraphrasing the words of Christ in Matt. 17:26, "For what is a man prof-

ited if he shall gain the whole world and lose his own soul?"

9. John Collier, "Mexico: A Challenge," *Progressive Education* (February 1942): 95–98, and his autobiography, *From Every Zenith: A Memoir and Some Essays on Life and Thought* (Denver: Sage Books, 1963). George I. Sanchez, *Mexico: A Revolution by Education* (Westport, Conn.: Greenwood Press, 1936). See also the discussion in Suzanne Forrest, *The Preservation of the Village* (Albuquerque: University of New Mexico Press, 1989), 63–78.

10. William Lumpkins, interview with the author, January 2, 1982, and Mela Sedillo Brewster (now Mrs. Robert Koeber), interview with the author, March 29, 1982. See also "The San José Training School," University of New Mexico *Bulletin*, Training School Series, vol. 1, no. 1 (1930), and vol. 1, no. 2 (1931), and L. S. Tireman, Mela Sedillo Brewster, and Lolita Pooler, "The San José Project," *New Mexico Quarterly*, vol. 3, no. 4 (November 1933): 207–16. L. S. Tireman, director of the San José Project, visited Mexico in 1931 to study the rural schools. See L. S. Tireman, "The Rural Schools of Mexico," University of New Mexico *Bulletin*, Training School Series, vol. 2, no. 1 (1931); his report is followed by Mary Austin, "Rural Education in New Mexico." Mary Austin and George I. Sanchez served on the board of the San José Project.

11. Brice Sewell, "The Problems of Vocational Education in New Mexico," manuscript in Governor Seligman papers, State of New Mexico Records Center (SNMRC), Santa Fe. Glassmaking and ceramics never became important parts of the SDVE program, probably because, in New Mexico, strong Hispanic traditions in these crafts did not exist.

12. Brice Sewell, SDVE *Trade Industrial News*, vol. 2, no. 2 (c. 1936).

13. William Wroth, "New Hope in Hard Times: Hispanic Crafts Are Revived during Troubled Years," *El Palacio*, vol. 89, no. 2 (Summer 1983): 22–31. Several of the SDVE mimeographed booklets have been reprinted in new editions, edited by this writer: *Furniture from the Hispanic Southwest* (Santa Fe, N.M.: Ancient City Press, 1984), and *Weaving & Colcha from the Hispanic Southwest* (Santa Fe, N.M.: Ancient City Press, 1985).

14. Crisostoma Luna, interview with the author, Taos, N.M., 1978.

15. On Pedro Quintana, see Sarah Nestor, *The Native Market of the Spanish New Mexican Craftsmen: Santa Fe, 1933–1940* (Santa Fe: Colonial New Mexico Historical Foundation, 1978), 29–30 passim, and Lane Coulter and Maurice Dixon, Jr., *New Mexican Tinwork: 1840–1940* (Albuquerque: University of New Mexico Press, 1990), 149–51. On Tillie Gabaldon Stark and David Salazar, see Nestor, *The Native Market*, 21, 25, 47, and 53, and William Wroth, ed., *Hispanic Crafts of the Southwest* (Colorado Springs, Colo.: Taylor

Museum of the Colorado Springs Fine Arts Center, 1977), 111–12.

16. Nestor, *The Native Market*, 31, 53–54.

17. Advertisement for the Knox Weavers, *New Mexico* (November 1938): 1.

18. Anna Nolan Clark, "The Art of the Loom," *New Mexico* (November 1938): 9–11, 35–36.

19. Advertisement for Southwestern Master Craftsmen, *New Mexico* (July 1938): 51.

20. Concerning Sandoval, Carmen Espinosa wrote in 1937: "Francisco Sandoval, another veteran tinworker of Santa Fe, relates that he has been engaged in tin craft since the age of thirteen. He is now approaching eighty. . . . He recalls the time when the stables of the American army were in the vicinity where the federal building now stands. Some of the army supplies, including oil for lamps and lanterns, were kept there. The lamp oil was brought from the Middle West in five-gallon tin containers. When the containers were empty, native tinworkers bought them for two cents each, and fashioned them into decorative articles." From *Tin Craft in New Mexico*, foreword by Carmen Espinosa (Santa Fe: New Mexico State Department of Vocational Education, 1937).

21. Coulter and Dixon, *New Mexican Tinwork*, 144–53. On Majel Claflin, see Ina Sizer Cassidy, "Art and Artists of New Mexico: Adventures in Tin," *New Mexico* (August 1937): 28, 56.

22. At the same time, and possibly serving as an inspiration for these American entrepreneurs, architect-craftsman William Spratling was reviving silverwork in Taxco, Mexico, where, beginning in 1932, dozens of young silversmiths worked under his tutelage and made silver of his design. With inspiration from Ambassador Dwight Morrow, who was a vigorous promoter of Mexican popular arts, Spratling was responsible for making Taxco the silverworking center of Mexico. He also employed tinworkers, ironworkers, and weavers in his shops. See his *File on Spratling: An Autobiography* (1932; reprint, Boston: Little, Brown, and Company, 1967), 60ff. Even earlier, in 1929, René d'Harnoncourt was also in Mexico, reviving village crafts, such as the famed lacquerwork of Olinalá, Guerrero. In 1930, he and Spratling organized an important exhibition of Mexican crafts that traveled all over the United States, including a showing in Albuquerque, where artist William Lumpkins, later a SDVE teacher, served as its local coordinator. See Robert Fay Schrader, *The Indian Arts & Crafts Board: An Aspect of New Deal Indian Policy* (Albuquerque N.M.: University of Albuquerque Press, 1983), 125–27.

23. Joy Yeck McWilliams (assistant to Russell Vernon Hunter on the WPA/FAP), interview with the author, December 28, 1981.

24. *Roswell Museum, Spring River Park, Roswell, New Mexico,* pamphlet (n.d., c. 1939).

25. For an overview of the WPA/FAP, see Richard D. McKinzie, *The New Deal for Artists* (Princeton: Princeton University Press, 1973), 75–177. On the Index of American Design, see Erwin O. Christensen, *The Index of American Design* (New York: Macmillan, 1950), and for the Hispanic Southwest, see *The Art of the Spanish Southwest: An Exhibition of Water-Color Renderings from the Index of American Design, National Gallery of Art, Washington, D.C.* (Washington, D.C.: United States-Mexico Commission for Border Development and Friendship, n.d., c. 1960s).


DE CURET AND KINGSLEY
*Lacemaking*

1. Aurelio Tio, *Biography of Diego Alvarez Chanca* (San Juan: Medical Association of Puerto Rico, ICPR, 1966), 53.

2. Ibid.

3. From an interview with a number of unidentified women in *Entretejidos: El Arte Del Tejido y El Encaje en Puerto Rico*, a videotape produced by Lucy Betancourt and the Borinquen Lacers for the Puerto Rican Endowment for the Humanities in 1984. *Entretejidos* is very difficult to translate; it means both the intertwined lace itself and the way the lives of the people making it are enmeshed in its weave.

4. The exhibition was held in the art gallery of the San Juan City Hall, March 1980.


VLACH
*"Keeping On Keeping On"*

Editor's note: In this series of Centenary publications, it is our policy to render dialectal speech as it was intended to be understood and not as it was presumably heard, but, at the request of the author, we have made an exception in this essay.

1. Allen H. Eaton, *Immigrant Gifts to American Life: Some Experiments in Appreciation of the Contributions of Our Foreign-born Citizens to American Culture* (New York: Russell Sage Foundation, 1932).

2. Marta Weigle, "The First Twenty-five Years of the Spanish Colonial Arts Society," in Weigle, Claudia Larcombe, and Samuel Larcombe, eds., *Hispanic Arts and Ethnohistory in the Southwest* (Santa Fe, N.M.: Ancient City Press, 1983), 181–203; Robert Fay Schrader, *The Indian Arts & Crafts Board: An Aspect of New Deal Indian Policy* (Albuquerque, N.M.: University of Albuquerque Press, 1983), 105–23; Garry G. Barker, *The Handcraft Revival in Southern Appalachia, 1930–1990* (Knoxville: University of Tennessee Press, 1991), 17–34.

3. A. Philip Randolph is quoted in Richard D. McKinzie, *The New Deal for Artists* (Princeton:

Princeton University Press, 1973), 145.

4. Harmon Foundation, *Negro Artists: An Illustrated Review of Their Achievements* (1935; reprint, Plainview, N.Y.: Books for Libraries Press, 1971), 24–26.

5. On black migration, see August Meier and Elliott Rudwick, *From Plantation to Ghetto*, rev. ed. (New York: Hill and Wang, 1970), 213–16.

6. Alain Locke, *The New Negro* (1925; reprint, New York: Atheneum, 1975), 7.

7. James D. Anderson, *The Education of Blacks in the South, 1860–1935* (Chapel Hill: University of North Carolina Press, 1988), 45.

8. Alain Locke, "The American Negro As Artist," *The American Magazine of Art* (Summer 1931), reprinted in *The Critical Temper of Alain Locke: A Selection of His Essays on Art and Culture*, ed. Jeffrey C. Stewart (New York: Garland, 1983), 171.

9. On Aaron Douglas, see David C. Driskell, *Two Centuries of Black American Art* (New York: Los Angeles County Museum of Art/Alfred A. Knopf, 1976), 62, 153.

10. Locke, *The New Negro*, 254.

11. James A. Porter, *Modern Negro Art* (New York: Dryden Press, 1943), 13–28.

12. There is much new research on the origins of southern folk pottery that discusses the significance of South Carolina's Edgefield District pottery. For a convenient summation, see Catherine Wilson Horne, ed., *Crossroads of Clay: The Southern Alkaline-Glazed Stoneware Tradition* (Columbia, S.C.: McKissick Museum, 1990), especially the essays by John Michael Vlach, "International Encounters at the Crossroads of Clay: European, Asian, and African Influences on Edgefield Pottery," 17–39, and Cinda K. Baldwin, "The Scene at the Crossroads: The Alkaline-Glazed Stoneware Tradition of South Carolina," 41–87.

13. M. V. Brewington, *Chesapeake Bay Log Canoes and Bugeyes* (Cambridge, Md.: Cornell Maritime Press, 1963), 31; see also Philip D. Morgan, "Black Life in Eighteenth-Century Charleston," in *Perspectives in American History*, new series, vol. 1 (1984): 196–200, and Peter H. Wood, *Black Majority: Negroes in Colonial South Carolina from 1670 through the Stono Rebellion* (New York: W. W. Norton, 1975), 200–205.

14. See John Michael Vlach, "'Us Quarters Fixed Fine': Finding Black Builders in Southern History," in Vlach, *By the Work of Their Hands: Studies in Afro-American Folklife* (Charlottesville: University Press of Virginia, 1991), 161–78; Catherine W. Bishir, "Black Builders in Antebellum North Carolina," *The North Carolina Historical Review*, vol. 61 (1984): 423–61.

15. See Vlach, "Black Craft Traditions in Texas:

An Interpretation of Nineteenth-Century Skills," in *By the Work of Their Hands*, 73–104, for an inventory of antebellum craft activity in one slaveholding state. For examples of the continuity of African crafts into the twentieth century, see Savannah Unit, Georgia Writers' Project, Work Projects Administration, *Drums and Shadows: Survival Studies among the Georgia Coastal Negroes* (1940; reprint, Athens: University of Georgia Press, 1986).

16. For a general account of the black coiled-basket tradition, see John Michael Vlach, *The Afro-American Tradition in Decorative Arts* (1978; reprint, Athens: University of Georgia Press, 1990), 7–19.

17. See Dale Rosengarten, *Row upon Row: Sea Grass Baskets of the South Carolina Lowcountry* (Columbia, S.C.: McKissick Museum, 1987), 40, and Doris Adelaide Derby, "Black Women Basket Makers: A Study of Domestic Economy in Charleston County, South Carolina" (Ph.D. diss., University of Illinois at Urbana-Champaign, 1980), 160–67.

18. Rosengarten, *Row upon Row*, 23–27.

19. For a forecast of the future of the Mt. Pleasant basketmaking community, see Dale Rosengarten, "'Bulrush Is Silver, Sweet Grass Is Gold': The Enduring Art of Sea Grass Basketry," in James Hardin and Alan Jabbour, eds., *Folklife Annual, 88–89* (Washington, D.C.: Library of Congress, 1989), 148–63, esp. 162–63.

20. See J. L. Dawson and H. W. De Saussure, eds., *Census of the City of Charleston for the Year 1848* (Charleston, S.C.: J. B. Nixon, 1849), 32–35.

21. W. E. B. Du Bois and Augustus Granville Dill, eds., *The Negro American Artisan* (Atlanta, Ga.: Atlanta University Press, 1913), 76.

22. The details of Philip Simmons's career can be found in John Michael Vlach, *Charleston Blacksmith: The Work of Philip Simmons*, rev. ed. (Columbia: University of South Carolina Press, 1992). See also "Philip Simmons: Afro-American Blacksmith," in Vlach, *By the Work of Their Hands*, 127–60.

23. On the history of the preservation movement in Charleston, see Charles B. Hosmer, Jr., *Preservation Comes of Age: From Williamsburg to the National Trust, 1926–1949*, vol. 1 (Charlottesville: University Press of Virginia, 1981), 232–74.

24. Philip Simmons, interview with the author, Charleston, S. C., May 31, 1978.

25. Ibid.

26. Vlach, *Charleston Blacksmith*, 105.

27. George P. Rawick, ed., *The American Slave: A Composite Autobiography*, vol. 13, part 4 (Westport, Conn.: Greenwood Press, 1972), 74; Norman R. Yetman, *Life under the "Peculiar Institution": Selections from the Slave*

*Narrative Collection* (New York: Holt, Rinehart, and Winston, 1970), 227.

28. Pecolia Warner, interview with the author, Memphis, Tenn., 1980.

29. For an illustration of the strip quilt made between 1939 and 1945 by Rosalie Lovette Martin, of Wilkes County, North Carolina, before she was ten years old, see Ruth Haislip Roberson, ed., *North Carolina Quilts* (Chapel Hill: University of North Carolina Press, 1988), 28.

30. Vlach, *Afro-American Tradition in Decorative Arts*, 55–75.

31. W. E. B. Du Bois, *The Souls of Black Folk* (1903; reprint, New York: Fawcett, 1961), 17.

32. Eli Leon, *Who'd a Thought It: Improvisation in African-American Quiltmaking* (San Francisco: San Francisco Craft and Folk Art Museum, 1987), 37.

33. For the WPA projects designed for African Americans, see Francis V. O'Connor, ed., *Art for the Millions: Essays from the 1930s by Artists and Administrators of the WPA Federal Art Project* (Greenwich, Conn.: New York Graphic Society, 1973), 210–17.

34. Anderson, *Education of Blacks in the South*, 35–36, 49.

ROSENGARTEN
## The Lowcountry Basket

Field notes, tapes, and transcripts of interviews cited in this essay are available at the McKissick Museum, University of South Carolina, Columbia.

1. Founded in 1862 by Quaker abolitionists, staffed by missionary schoolteachers, and supported by northern relief agencies, the school was part of an early Reconstruction venture known as the Port Royal Experiment. In 1904, the school was reorganized along the lines of Virginia's Hampton Institute and renamed the Penn Normal, Industrial, and Agricultural School.

2. For a detailed discussion of the relationship between the Arts and Crafts and manual-training movements, see Carlton Edward Bauer, "A Study of the Arts and Crafts Movement and of Art Nouveau in Relation to Industrial Arts Design" (Ph.D. diss., New York University, 1955). See also Oscar Lovell Triggs, *Chapters in the History of the Arts and Crafts Movement* (1902; reprint, New York: Benjamin Blom, 1971), 1, and Robert Judson Clark, ed., *The Arts and Crafts Movement in America, 1876–1916* (Princeton: Princeton University Press, 1972), 9.

3. *Annual Report of the Penn Normal, Industrial, and Agricultural School* (1924), 32, South Carolinian Library (SCL), University of South Carolina, Columbia.

4. Elizabeth Jacoway, *Yankee Missionaries in the South: The Penn School Experiment* (Baton Rouge: University of Louisiana Press, 1980), 88.

5. Leroy E. Browne, Sr., interview with the author, November 21, 1985, St. Helena Island, S.C. (At some point, the spelling of the name was changed from Brown to Browne.)

6. *Annual Report of the Penn Normal, Industrial, and Agricultural School* (1914), 14, SCL.

7. Henry Yaschik, interview with the author, May 21, 1992, Charleston, S.C. See also Henry Yaschik, *From Kaluszyn to Charleston: The Yaschik Family in Poland, Argentina, and South Carolina* (Charleston, S.C.: H. Yaschik, 1990), 42–43.

8. See Dale Rosengarten, *Row upon Row: Sea Grass Baskets of the South Carolina Lowcountry* (Columbia, S.C.: McKissick Museum, 1987), 30–31.

9. Charlotte Smith, "The Last of the Old-Time Basket Makers," *The Savannah News* (July 17, 1960).

10. *The Hammock Shop, Gifts and Novelties from the Carolina Lowcountry* (n.d., c. 1939), SCL.

11. Miss Cooley had initiated the project through her acquaintance with Paul U. Kellogg, the journal's editor. Her object was to promote Penn Normal and stimulate financial support from *Survey Graphic* readers. See Jeffrey C. Stewart, *To Color America: Portraits by Winold Reiss* (Washington, D.C.: Smithsonian Institution Press/National Portrait Gallery, 1989), 81.

12. Neil V. Rosenberg and Debora G. Kodish, eds., liner notes for sound recording, *"Folksongs of America": The Robert Winslow Gordon Collection, 1922–1932* (Washington, D.C.: Archive of American Folk Song, Library of Congress, 1978), 22–23.

13. Charles W. Joyner, *Down by the Riverside: A South Carolina Slave Community* (Urbana: University of Illinois Press, 1984), see photographs 126ff.

14. Collection of Brookgreen Gardens, Murrells Inlet, S.C.

15. Samuel Gaillard Stoney and Bayard Wootten, *Charleston: Azaleas and Old Bricks* (Boston: Houghton Mifflin, 1937). Wootten's photographs are housed in the North Carolina Collection, University of North Carolina Library, Chapel Hill.

16. Savannah Unit, Georgia Writers' Project, WPA, *Drums and Shadows: Survival Studies among the Georgia Coastal Negros* (1940; reprint, Athens: University of Georgia Press, 1986), 8, 121–22.

17. William Bascom, "Interview with Gullah (?) Negroes, U.S.A.," 41, 124, 118, 53, Carton 59; see also Bascom to "Dearest," June 10, 1939, Savannah, Georgia, and to Frazier Moore, July 2, 1939, Carton 25, William Bascom papers (WBP), Bancroft Library, University of California at Berkeley.

18. Clarence W. Legerton, Jr., interview with the author, July 2, 1985, Charleston, S.C. See also business record of Legerton & Co., collection of John E. Huguley, Charleston, S.C., and *"Seagrassco" Hand Made Baskets*, a two-page pamphlet in the collection of Clifford L. Legerton, North Charleston, S.C.

19. Jeanette Lee, interview with the author, January 20, 1992, and Harriett Bailem Brown, interview with the author, February 11, 1992, Mt. Pleasant, S.C.

20. Leola Wright, interview with the author, February 11, 1992, Mt. Pleasant, S.C.

21. For a description of transactions between Legerton and the Mt. Pleasant basketmakers, see Rosengarten, *Row upon Row*, 31–34. Other people besides Sam Coakley served as basket "agents"—James and Mae Bell Turner, for example, who lived in the community called Phillip—but, in scope and scale, none rivaled the Legerton-Coakley connection.

22. Quoted in Kate Porter Young [Kay Young Day], unpublished field notes, 1978.

23. Evelyina Foreman, interview with the author, October 23, 1985, Mt. Pleasant, S.C.

24. Jack Leland, "Basket Weaving African Art Survival?" *News and Courier* [Charleston, S.C.] (March 27, 1949).

25. Bascom, "Interview with Gullah (?) Negroes," 41, Carton 59, WBP.

26. For a discussion of making and selling baskets as an economic activity and a source of power for women, see Kay Young Day [Kate Porter Young], "My Family Is Me: Women's Kin Networks and Social Power in a Black Sea Island Community" (Ph.D. diss., Rutgers University, 1983), and Doris Adelaide Derby, "Black Women Basket Makers: A Study of Domestic Economy in Charleston County, South Carolina" (Ph.D. diss., University of Illinois at Urbana-Champaign, 1980).

27. Joyce V. Coakley, "Basketweavers," in *Folklife Annual, 88–89*, eds. James Hardin and Alan Jabbour (Washington, D.C.: Library of Congress, 1989), 164.

28. Marie Rouse, interview with the author, March 19, 1992, Mt. Pleasant, S.C.

OWENS-HART
*Ceramics*

1. As an African American ceramist, the lack of information on traditional African ceramics made it essential that I study clayworking in Africa, and I have spent years researching my African American antecedents.

2. In 1977, and, intermittently, until 1980, I was a field investigator in Ipetumodu, Nigeria. I became an apprentice to female master potters in a traditional village, studying their techniques and gathering information, over the course of three years, about the apprenticeship system. I learned that direct lines of knowledge transfer concerning the ceramics they produced went back one hundred twenty-five to two hundred years, meaning that they were producing pottery in that village during the years of the slave trade.

3. Leland Ferguson, *Uncommon Ground: Archaeology and Early African America, 1650–1800* (Washington, D.C.: Smithsonian Institution Press, 1992), 19.

4. Ibid., 3.

5. Antebellum face jars are generally attributed to African Americans. The original ancestors are thrown jugs that had been manipulated into a human face while the clay was still damp. Occasionally, contrasting pieces of kaolin were added as teeth in the form of slip decoration.

6. John Michael Vlach, *The Afro-American Tradition in Decorative Arts*, exhibition catalogue (Cleveland: Cleveland Museum of Art, 1978), 77.

7. Ibid., 79. Apparently, at the time Dave made this pot, he was in the service of a Mr. Miles.

8. Georgeanna H. Greer, "The Wilson Potteries," *Ceramic Monthly*, vol. 29, no. 6 (Summer 1981), 44–46.

9. Ibid.

10. Margaret W. Morley, *The Carolina Mountains* (Boston: Houghton Mifflin Company, 1913), 187–88.

11. Mrs. Helen Lyles, telephone interview with April Kingsley, October 5, 1993.

12. Mrs. Helen Lyles, interview with the author, in Washington, D.C., 1992.

13. Evangeline J. Montgomery, *Sargent Johnson: A Retrospective*, exhibition catalogue (San Francisco: Oakland Museum Art Division Special Gallery, 1971), 18.

14. This designation was attributed to African Americans at that time.

KINGSLEY
*Ruth Clement Bond*

I am indebted to Merikay Waldvogel for her original research into the TVA quilts and Ruth Clement Bond's life; see Waldvogel, *Soft Covers for Hard Times: Quiltmaking and the Great Depression* (Nashville, Tenn.: Rutledge Hill Press, 1990), 78–82.

1. Their daughter, Jane Bond Howard, is professor of European history at Lincoln University; their son George Clement Bond is professor of anthropology at Teachers College, Columbia University; and their son J. Max Bond, Jr., is dean of the School of Architecture, City College of New York. See Waldvogel, *Soft Covers*, 78.

2. Ruth Clement Bond, in an interview with the author, in May 1993, said that her husband had insisted that housing be built for the black workers just as it was for the white workers, but he did not anticipate it being erected in another area. The Bonds, who had been living in a house in a nearby town, decided they should live instead with the workers at the Wheeler Dam site.

3. Ruth Clement Bond, interview with the author, June 4, 1993. The remaining quotations that are not cited are from this interview.

4. This furniture was placed in storage in Knoxville, Tennessee, and, subsequently, lost, as the Bonds traveled to Haiti, East and West Africa, and even as far as Afghanistan over the ensuing years, to take a series of prestigious university positions.

5. The figural style Bond developed seems too close to that of Aaron Douglas for her not to have been influenced, though she doesn't believe she was. She does recall owning a copy of James Weldon Johnson's *God's Trombones*, however, which Douglas illustrated with similar figures. It was published in 1925, during the Harlem Renaissance, and her father surely would have known about the book. She probably had or saw a copy long before making the TVA designs, and later forgot, but she no longer has the book.

6. Her *Black Power Quilt* apparently was stolen from storage in the Knoxville home to which they moved after the Wheeler Dam project. Grace Reynolds Tyler's *Black Power Quilt*, an abbreviated Bond design featuring a fist holding a lightning bolt, was presented by Bond's husband to David Lilienthal, or another dignitary, at a meeting of TVA officials.

7. Waldvogel, *Soft Covers*, 81.

8. They made plain, monochrome corn-shuck rugs very well, but Bond made designs for them to use that had tonal variations going from dark to light.

9. Waldvogel, *Soft Covers*, 80.

KESSLER
*From Mission to Market*

1. Horace Kephart, *Our Southern Highlanders: A Narrative of Adventure in the Southern Appalachians and a Study of Life among the Mountaineers* (New York: Macmillan Company, 1922), 13.

2. Ibid., 18.

3. William H. Turner and Edward J. Cabbell, eds., *Blacks in Appalachia* (Lexington: University Press of Kentucky, 1985), 56.

4. Ibid.

5. David E. Whisnant, *All That Is Native and Fine: The Politics of Culture in an American Region*, The Fred W. Morrison Series in Southern Studies (Chapel Hill: University of North Carolina Press, 1983), 12.

6. Frances Louisa Goodrich, *Mountain Homespun* (1931; reprint, with an introduction by Jan Davidson, Knoxville: University of Tennessee Press, 1989), 9.

7. Frances Louisa Goodrich, "The Story of the Allanstand Cottage Industries," *The Tar Heel Woman* (September 1933): 3, 6.

8. Frances Louisa Goodrich, in Eileen Boris, *Art and Labor: Ruskin, Morris, and the Craftsman Ideal in America* (Philadelphia: Temple University Press, 1986), 126.

9. Allen H. Eaton, *Handicrafts of the Southern Highlands* (1937; reprint, with a preface by Ralph Rinzler, New York: Dover, 1973), 60.

10. Philis Alvic, *Weavers of the Southern Highland: The Early Years in Gatlinburg* (Murray, Ky.: P. Alvic, 1991), 1.

11. Ibid., 7.

12. This is the price given in the Appalachian Museum Collection, Berea, Kentucky.

13. Whisnant, *All That Is Native and Fine*, 155.

14. Boris, *Art and Labor*, 122.

15. Other craft industries included the Shenandoah Community Workers, organized by William Bernard Clark, in Bird Haven, Virginia; the Blue Ridge Weavers, established by Mr. and Mrs. George Cathey, in Tryon, North Carolina; the Shuttle-Crafters, established by Sarah Dougherty, in Russellville, Tennessee; the Mountain Cabin Quilters, established by Minnie Klar, in Wooten, Kentucky; the Matheny Weavers, established by F. E. Matheny, in Berea, Kentucky; the Pine Burr Studio, established by Mrs. F. D. Huckabee, in Pine Burr, Tennessee; and the Woodcrafters and Carvers, established by O. J. Mattil, in Gatlinburg, Tennessee.

16. Garry G. Barker, *The Handcraft Revival in Southern Appalachia, 1930–1990* (Knoxville: University of Tennessee Press, 1991), 16.

17. "Handicraft Guild Lauds Mrs. Patten," *The Chattanooga Times* (October 4, 1935), unpaged clipping, Archives, Southern Highland Handicraft Guild, Asheville, North Carolina.

18. Susan Morgan Leveille, interview with the author, March 1993.

19. Charles E. Martin, "Appalachia's Art of the Useful," *Natural History*, vol. 96, no. 7 (July 1987): 52.

20. The artist's daughter, Mable Westbrook, interview with the author, January 1993.

21. Mace's friend and collector, Robert Brunk, interview with the author, May 1993.

22. Edward Dupuy, *Artisans of the Appalachians* (Asheville, N.C.: Miller Printing Company, 1967), 110.

23. John Parris, *Mountain Bred* (Asheville, N.C.: Citizens-Times Publishing Company, 1967), 352.

24. Eaton, *Handicrafts of the Southern Highlands*, 171.

25. Parris, *Mountain Bred*, 250.

26. Ibid.

27. Leveille, interview with the author, March 1993.

28. Helen Bullard, *Crafts and Craftsmen of the Tennessee Mountains* (Falls Church, Va.: Summit Press, 1976), 137.

29. Daisy Wade Bridges, ed., "Potters of the Catawba Valley," *Journal of Studies, Ceramic Circle of Charlotte*, vol. 4 (Charlotte, N.C.: Mint Museum of Art, 1980), 13.

30. Charles G. Zug, III, *Turners and Burners: The Folk Potters of North Carolina*, The Fred W. Morrison Series in Southern Studies (Chapel Hill: University of North Carolina Press, 1986), 91.

31. Bridges, "Potters of the Catawba Valley," 43.

32. Ibid.

33. Ibid., 31.

34. Ibid.

35. Pat H. Johnston and Daisy Wade Bridges, "O. L. Bachelder and His Omar Khayyam Pottery," *Journal of Studies, Ceramic Circle of Charlotte*, vol. 5 (Charlotte, N.C.: Mint Museum of Art, 1984), 17.

36. Ibid.

37. "Walter Stephen, 85, Pisgah Forest Pottery Founder, Is Taken by Death," unidentified newspaper clipping, Archives, Southern Highland Handicraft Guild, Asheville, North Carolina.

38. Gay Mahaffy Hertzman, *Jugtown Pottery: The Busbee Vision* (Raleigh: North Carolina Museum of Art, 1984), 3.

39. Muriel Earley Sheppard, *Cabins in the Laurel* (Chapel Hill: University of North Carolina Press, 1935), 254.

# SELECTED BIBLIOGRAPHY

Only books and exhibitions are listed in this bibliography; readers may also refer to the following periodicals: *American Indian Art Magazine; Art and Archeology; Art Quarterly; Artspace: Southwestern Contemporary Arts Quarterly; Bulletin of the Women's Bureau; Ceramic Monthly; Craft Horizons; Crafts; El Palacio; Folklife Annual; Historic Preservation; The International Studio; Journal of Studies, Ceramic Circle of Charlotte; Natural History; New Mexico; New Mexico Quarterly; New Mexico Studies in the Fine Arts; The North Carolina Historical Review; Winterthur Portfolio.*

Adair, John. *The Navajo and Pueblo Silversmiths.* Norman: University of Oklahoma Press, 1944.

Allen, Elsie. *Pomo Basketmaking: A Supreme Act for the Weaver.* Rev. ed. Healdsburg, Calif.: Naturegraph, 1972.

Alvic, Philis. *Weavers of the Southern Highland: The Early Years in Gatlinburg.* Murray, Ky.: P. Alvic, 1991.

———. *Weavers of the Southern Highland: Penland.* Murray, Ky.: P. Alvic, 1992.

Anderson, James D. *The Education of Blacks in the South, 1860–1935.* Chapel Hill: University of North Carolina Press, 1988.

Anderson, Ross, and Barbara Perry. *The Diversions of Keramos: American Clay Sculpture, 1925–1950.* Syracuse, N.Y.: Everson Museum of Art, 1983.

Anderson, Wendell, Mildred Crews, and Judson Crews. *Patrocinio Barela: Taos Wood Carver.* 3d ed. Taos, N.M.: Taos Recordings and Publications, 1976.

Applegate, Frank Guy. *Indian Stories from the Pueblos.* 1929. Reprint. Glorieta, N.M.: Rio Grande Press, 1971.

*The Art of the Spanish Southwest: An Exhibition of Water-Color Renderings from the Index of American Design, National Gallery of Art, Washington, D.C.* Washington, D.C.: United States-Mexico Commission for Border Development and Friendship [1985].

Austin, Mary. *Earth Horizon.* New York: Houghton Mifflin Company, 1932.

Axelrod, Alan, ed. *The Colonial Revival in America.* New York: W. W. Norton, 1985.

Barker, Garry G. *The Handcraft Revival in Southern Appalachia, 1930–1990.* Knoxville: University of Tennessee Press, 1991.

Bates, Craig D., and Martha J. Lee. *Tradition and Innovation: A Basket History of the Indians of the Yosemite-Mono Lake Area.* Yosemite National Park, Calif.: Yosemite Association, 1990.

Batteau, Allen, ed. *Appalachia and America: Autonomy and Regional Dependence.* Lexington: University Press of Kentucky, 1983.

Bauer, Carlton Edward. "A Study of the Arts and Crafts Movement and of Art Nouveau in Relation to Industrial Arts Design." Ph.D. diss., New York University, 1955.

Becker, Jane, and Barbara Franco, eds. *Folk Roots, New Roots: Folklore in American Life.* Lexington, Mass.: Museum of Our National Heritage, 1988.

Benedict, Ruth. *Patterns of Culture.* 1934. 3d ed. Boston, Mass.: Houghton Mifflin Company, 1989.

Berlo, Janet Catherine, ed. *The Early Years of Native American Art History: The Politics of Art History and Collecting.* Seattle: University of Washington Press, 1992.

Bermingham, Peter. *The New Deal in the Southwest: Arizona and New Mexico.* Tucson: University of Arizona Museum of Art, 1980.

*A Bibliography of National Parks and Monuments West of the Mississippi River.* 2 vols. Washington, D.C.: U.S. Department of the Interior, National Park Service, 1941.

Blair, Mary Ellen, and Lawrence R. Blair. *Margaret Tafoya: A Tewa Potter's Heritage and Legacy.* West Chester, Pa.: Schiffer Publishing, 1986.

Bloxom, Marguerite D., comp. *Pickaxe and Pencil: References for the Study of WPA.* Washington, D.C.: Library of Congress, 1982.

Blythe, LeGette. *Gift from the Hills: Miss Lucy Morgan's Story of Her Unique Penland School.* Chapel Hill: University of North Carolina Press, 1958.

Boyd, E. *Popular Arts of Colonial New Mexico.* Santa Fe, N.M.: Museum of International Folk Art, 1959.

———. *Popular Arts of Spanish New Mexico.* Santa Fe, N.M.: Museum of New Mexico Press, 1974.

Breeze, Carla. *Pueblo Deco.* New York: Rizzoli, 1990.

Brewington, M. V. *Chesapeake Bay Log Canoes and Bugeyes.* Cambridge, Md.: Cornell Maritime Press, 1963.

Bridges, Daisy. *In Prayse of Potts.* Charlotte, N.C.: Mint Museum of Art, 1993.

Briggs, Charles L. *The Woodcarvers of Córdova, New Mexico: Social Dimensions of an Artistic "Revival."* Knoxville: University of Tennessee Press, 1980.

Brody, J. J. *Indian Painters and White Patrons.* Albuquerque: University of New Mexico Press, 1971.

Bronner, Simon J., ed. *American Material Culture and Folklife: A Prologue and Dialogue.* Ann Arbor, Mich.: UMI Research Press, 1985.

Brown, Charlotte Vestal. *Vernacular Pottery of North Carolina: 1982–1986, From the Collection of Leonidas J. Betts.* Raleigh: University Center Gallery, North Carolina State University, 1987.

Bullard, Helen. *Crafts and Craftsmen of the Tennessee Mountains.* Falls Church, Va.: Summit Press, 1976.

Bunzel, Ruth. *The Pueblo Potter: A Study of Creative Imagination in Primitive Art.* 1929. Reprint. New York: Dover Publications, 1972.

Cahill, E. Holger. *American Folk Art: The Art of the Common Man in America, 1750–1900.* New York: Museum of Modern Art, 1932.

———. *American Folk Sculpture.* Newark, N.J.: Newark Museum, 1931.

———. *American Primitives.* Newark, N.J.: Newark Museum, 1930.

Campbell, Doak S., Frederick H. Bair, and Oswald L. Marvel. *Educational Activities of the Works Progress Administration.* Washington, D.C.: U.S. Government Printing Office, 1939.

Campbell, John C. *The Southern Highlander and His Homeland.* New York: Russell Sage Foundation, 1921.

Campbell, Tyrone, and Joel and Kate Kopp. *Navajo Pictorial Weaving, 1880–1950: Folk Art Images of Native Americans.* New York: Dutton Studio Books, 1991.

Chase, Judith Wragg. *Afro-American Art and Craft.* New York: Van Nostrand Reinhold Company, 1971.

Chavez, John R. *The Lost Land: The Chicano Image of the Southwest.* Albuquerque: University of New Mexico Press, 1984.

Christensen, Erwin O. *The Index of American Design.* 1950. Reprint. New York: Macmillan, 1967.

Clark, Garth. *A Century of Ceramics in the United States, 1878–1978: A Study of Its Development.* New York: E. P. Dutton, 1979.

Coles, Robert. *The Old Ones of New Mexico.* 1973. Reprint. Albuquerque: University of New Mexico Press, 1989.

Collier, John. *From Every Zenith: A Memoir and Some Essays on Life and Thought.* Denver, Colo.: Sage Books, 1963.

———. *Indians of the Americas.* New York: W. W. Norton, 1947.

Conn, Richard. *Native American Art in the Denver Art Museum.* Seattle: University of Washington Press, 1979.

———. *A Persistent Vision: Art of the Reservation Days.* Denver, Colo.: Denver Art Museum, 1986.

Cooper, Patricia, and Norma Bradley Buferd. *The Quilters: Women and Domestic Art.* Garden City, N.Y.: Doubleday, 1977.

Coulter, Lane, and Maurice Dixon, Jr. *New Mexican Tinwork: 1840–1940.* Albuquerque: University of New Mexico Press, 1990.

Covarrubias, Miguel. *The Eagle, the Jaguar and the Serpent, Indian Art of the Americas. North America: Alaska, Canada, and the United States.* New York: Alfred A. Knopf, 1954.

Crawford, Jean. *Jugtown Pottery: History and Design.* Winston-Salem, N.C.: John F. Blair, 1964.

Crews, Mildred, and Judson Crews. *Patrocinio Barela: Taos Wood Carver.* Wharton, Tex.: Wharton College, 1970.

Dabbs, Edith M. *Face of an Island: Leigh Richmond Miner's Photographs of Saint Helena Island.* Columbia, S.C.: R. L. Bryan, 1970.

Davis, W. W. H. *El Gringo; or New Mexico and Her People.* New York: Harper and Brothers, 1857.

Derby, Doris Adelaide. "Black Women Basket Makers: A Study of Domestic Economy in Charleston County, South Carolina." Ph.D. diss., University of Illinois at Urbana-Champaign, 1980.

Dillingham, Rick, with Melinda Elliott. *Acoma and Laguna Pottery.* Santa Fe, N.M.: School of American Research, 1992.

Dockstader, Frederick J. *Indian Art in America: The Arts and Crafts of the North American Indian.* Greenwich, Conn.: New York Graphic Society, 1961.

Donhauser, Paul S. *History of American Ceramics: The Studio Potter.* Dubuque, Iowa: Kendall/Hunt Publishing Company, 1978.

Douglas, Frederick H., and René d'Harnoncourt. *Indian Art of the United States.* New York: Museum of Modern Art, 1941.

Driskell, David C. *Hidden Heritage: Afro-American Art, 1800–1950.* San Francisco, Calif.: Art Museum Association of America, 1985.

———. *Two Centuries of Black American Art.* New York: Los Angeles County Museum of Art/Alfred A. Knopf, 1976.

Duberman, Martin. *Black Mountain: An Exploration in Community.* New York: E. P. Dutton, 1972.

Du Bois, W. E. B. *The Souls of Black Folk.* 1903. Reprint. New York: Fawcett, 1961.

Du Bois, W. E. B., and Augustus Granville Dill, eds. *The Negro American Artisan.* Atlanta, Ga.: Atlanta University Press, 1913.

Dunn, Dorothy. *American Indian Painting of the Southwest and Plains Areas.* Albuquerque: University of New Mexico Press, 1968.

Eaton, Allen H. *Handicrafts of New England.* New York: Harper and Brothers, 1949.

———. *Handicrafts of the Southern Highlands.* 1937. Reprint. New York: Dover, 1973.

———. *Immigrant Gifts to American Life: Some Experiments in Appreciation of the Contributions of Our Foreign-born Citizens to American Culture.* New York: Russell Sage Foundation, 1932.

Eaton, Allen H., and Lucinda Crile. *Rural Handicrafts in the United States.* Washington, D.C.: U.S. Department of Agriculture, Extension Services, 1937.

Ewers, John C. *The Blackfeet: Raiders on the Northwestern Plains.* Norman: University of Oklahoma Press, 1958.

———. *Plains Indian Sculpture: A Traditional Art from America's Heartland.* Washington, D.C.: Smithsonian Institution Press, 1986.

Feder, Norman. *American Indian Art.* New York: Harry N. Abrams, 1971.

Ferguson, Leland. *Uncommon Ground: Archaeology and Early African America, 1650–1800.* Washington, D.C.: Smithsonian Institution Press, 1992.

Fewkes, Jesse Walter. *Hopi Katchinas Drawn by Native Artists.* Glorieta, N.M.: Rio Grande Press, 1969.

Finley, Ruth E. *Old Patchwork Quilts and the Women Who Made Them.* Philadelphia: J. B. Lippincott Company, 1929.

Gallegos, Matthew E. "The Arts and Crafts Movement in New Mexico, 1900–1945." Master's thesis, University of Virginia School of Architecture, 1987.

Garfield, Viola Edmundson, and Linn A. Forrest. *The Wolf and the Raven:*

*Totem Poles of Southeastern Alaska.* 1961. Rev. ed. Seattle: University of Washington Press, 1986.

George, Phyllis. *Kentucky Crafts: Handmade and Heartfelt.* New York: Crown, 1989.

Giffen, Sarah L., and Kevin D. Murphy. *"A Noble and Dignified Stream": The Piscataqua Region in the Colonial Revival, 1860–1930.* York, Maine: Old York Historical Society, 1992.

Goldstein, Rosalie, ed. *American Folk Art: The Herbert Waide Hemphill Jr. Collection.* Milwaukee, Wisc.: Milwaukee Art Museum, 1981.

Goodrich, Frances Louisa. *Mountain Homespun.* 1931. Reprint, with an introduction by Jan Davidson. Knoxville: University of Tennessee Press, 1989.

Gormley, D. Michael, and Karal Ann Marling. *Federal Art in Cleveland, 1933–1943.* Cleveland, Ohio: Cleveland Public Library, 1974.

Greer, Georgeanna H. *American Stonewares: The Art and Craft of Utilitarian Potters.* West Chester, Pa.: Schiffer Publishing, 1981.

———. *The Meyer Family: Master Potters of Texas.* San Antonio, Tex.: San Antonio Museum Association/Trinity University Press, 1971.

Griffin, Rachael, and Sarah Munro, eds. *Timberline Lodge.* Portland, Oreg.: Friends of Timberline, 1978.

Harlow, Francis Harvey. *Matte-paint Pottery of the Tewa, Keres, and Zuni Pueblos.* Santa Fe: Museum of New Mexico, 1973.

Harmon Foundation. *Negro Artists: An Illustrated Review of Their Achievements.* 1935. Reprint. Plainview, N.Y.: Books for Libraries Press, 1971.

Hartigan, Lynda Roscoe. *Made with Passion: The Hemphill Folk Art Collection in the National Museum of American Art.* Washington, D.C.: Smithsonian Institution Press, 1990.

Horne, Catherine Wilson, ed. *Crossroads of Clay: The Southern Alkaline-Glazed Stoneware Tradition.* Columbia, S.C.: McKissick Museum, 1990.

Horwitz, Elinor Lander. *Mountain People, Mountain Crafts.* New York: J. B. Lippincott Company, 1974.

Hosmer, Charles B., Jr. *Preservation Comes of Age: From Williamsburg to the National Trust, 1926–1949.* 2 vols. Charlottesville: University Press of Virginia, 1981.

Irwin, John Rice. *Baskets and Basket Makers in Southern Appalachia.* West Chester, Pa.: Schiffer Publishing, 1982.

———. *Musical Instruments of the Southern Appalachian Mountains: A History of the Author's Collection Housed in the Museum of Appalachia, Norris, Tennessee.* 2d ed. West Chester, Pa.: Schiffer Publishing, 1983.

Ivankovich, Michael. *The Guide to Wallace Nutting Furniture.* Doylestown, Pa.: Diamond Press, 1990.

Jacoway, Elizabeth. *Yankee Missionaries in the South: The Penn School Experiment.* Baton Rouge: University of Louisiana Press, 1980.

James, George Wharton. *Indian Basketry.* 1909. Reprint. New York: Dover, 1972.

Joyner, Charles W. *Down by the Riverside: A South Carolina Slave Community.* Urbana: University of Illinois Press, 1984.

Kent, Kate Peck. *Navajo Weaving: Three Centuries of Change.* Santa Fe, N.M.: School of American Research Press, 1985.

Kephart, Horace. *Our Southern Highlanders: A Narrative of Adventure in the Southern Appalachians and a Study of Life among the Mountaineers.* Enl. ed. New York: Macmillan, 1922.

Konrad, Lee-Ann, and Christine Nicholas. *Artists of the Dawn: Christine Nicholas and Senabeh.* Orono, Maine: Northeast Folklore Society, 1987.

Lauterer, Jock. *Runnin' on Rims: Appalachian Profiles.* Chapel Hill, N.C.: Algonquin Books of Chapel Hill, 1986.

Leftwich, Rodney, Tom Patterson, and John Perreault. *From Mountain Clay: The Folk Pottery Traditions of Buncombe County, Inc.* Cullowhee, N.C.: Belk Art Gallery, Western Carolina University, 1989.

Leon, Eli. *Who'd a Thought It: Improvisation in African-American Quiltmaking.* San Francisco: San Francisco Craft and Folk Art Museum, 1987.

Livingston, Jane, and John Beardsley. *Black Folk Art in America,*

*1930–1980*. Jackson: University of Mississippi Press and Center for the Study of Southern Culture/Corcoran Gallery of Art, Washington, D.C., 1980.

Locke, Alain. "The American Negro As Artist." 1931. *The American Magazine of Art*. Reprint in *The Critical Temper of Alain Locke: A Selection of His Essays on Art and Culture*, edited by Jeffrey C. Stewart, 170–80. New York: Garland, 1983.

———. *The New Negro*. 1925. Reprint. New York: Atheneum, 1975.

Lyford, Carrie A. *The Arts and Crafts of the Iroquois*. Washington, D.C.: U.S. Department of the Interior, Bureau of Indian Affairs, Division of Education, n.d.

———. *Ojibwa Crafts*. 1943. Reprint. *The Crafts of the Ojibwa (Chippewa)*. Stevens Point, Wis.: R. Schneider, 1982.

McDonald, William F. *Federal Relief Administration and the Arts*. Columbus: Ohio State University Press, 1969.

McKinzie, Richard D. *The New Deal for Artists*. Princeton, N.J.: Princeton University Press, 1973.

McMullen, Ann, and Russell G. Handsman, eds. *A Key into the Language of Woodsplint Baskets*. Washington, Conn.: American Indian Archeological Institute, 1987.

Mainzer, Janet C. "The Relation between the Crafts and the Fine Arts in the United States from 1876 to 1980." Ph.D. diss., New York University, 1988.

Malone, James M., Georgeanna H. Greer, and Helen Simons. *Kirbee Kiln, A Mid-19th Century Texas Stoneware Pottery*. Austin: Office of the State Archeologist, Texas Historical Commission, 1979.

Markowitz, Gerald E., and Marlene Park. *New Deal for Art: The Government Art Projects of the 1930s with Examples from New York City and State*. New York: Gallery Association of New York State, 1977.

Marling, Karal Ann. *George Washington Slept Here: Colonial Revivals and American Culture, 1876–1986*. Cambridge: Harvard University Press, 1988.

Marriot, Alice. *Maria: The Potter of San Ildefonso*. Norman: University of Oklahoma Press, 1948.

Mavigliano, George J., and Richard A. Lawson. *The Federal Art Project in Illinois, 1935–1943*. Carbondale: Southern Illinois University, 1990.

Meier, August, and Elliott Rudwick. *From Plantation to Ghetto*. Rev. ed. New York: Hill and Wang, 1970.

Morgan, Lucy, with LeGette Blythe. *Gift from the Hills: Miss Lucy Morgan's Story of Her Unique Penland School*. Chapel Hill: University of North Carolina Press, 1971.

Morley, Margaret W. *The Carolina Mountains*. Boston: Houghton Mifflin Company, 1913.

Nestor, Sarah. *The Native Market of the Spanish New Mexican Craftsmen: Santa Fe, 1933–1940*. Santa Fe: Colonial New Mexico Historical Foundation, 1978.

New Mexico State Department of Vocational Education. *Tin Craft in New Mexico*. 1937.

Niles, John Jacob. *The Appalachian Photographs of Doris Ulmann*. Penland, N.C.: Jargon Society, 1971.

North Carolina Museum of Art. *Jugtown Pottery: The Busbee Vision: From the Collection of the North Carolina Museum of Art*. Raleigh: North Carolina Museum of Art, 1984.

Nutting, Wallace. *Furniture of the Pilgrim Century (of American Origin): 1620–1720*. 1921 and 1923. Rev. ed. New York: Dover, 1965.

O'Connor, Francis V. *Federal Support for the Visual Arts: The New Deal and Now*. 2d ed. Greenwich, Conn.: New York Graphic Society, 1971.

———. "Olive Lyford Gavert: The WPA Federal Art Project and the New York World's Fair, 1939–40." In *The New Deal Art Projects: An Anthology of Memoirs*, edited by Francis V. O'Connor, 263–67. Washington, D.C.: Smithsonian Institution Press, 1972.

———. "The Usable Future: The Role of Fantasy in the Promotion of a Consumer Society for Art." In *Dawn of a New Day: The New York World's Fair, 1939–40*, edited by Helen A. Harrison. New York: Queens Museum, 1980.

O'Connor, Francis V., ed. *Art for the Millions: Essays from the 1930s by Artists and Administrators of the WPA Federal Art Project*. Greenwich, Conn.: New York Graphic Society, 1973.

*Old and New Paths in American Design, 1720–1936*. Newark, N.J.: Newark Museum, 1936.

Olson, James S. *Historical Dictionary of the New Deal*. Westport, Conn.: Greenwood Press, 1985.

*Ottawa Quillwork on Birchbark: An Historical Exhibition of Ottawa Quillwork on Birchbark Executed between 1830 and 1983*. Foreword by Stephen B. Graham. Harbor Springs, Mich.: Harbor Springs Historical Commission, 1983.

Parezo, Nancy J. *Navajo Sandpainting: From Religious Act to Commercial Art*. Tucson: University of Arizona Press, 1983.

Park, Marlene, and Gerald E. Markowitz. *Democratic Vistas: Post Offices and Public Art in the New Deal*. Philadelphia: Temple University Press, 1984.

Parris, John. *The Living Tradition of Maria*. Tokyo: Kodhansa International, 1979.

———. *Mountain Bred*. Asheville, N.C.: Citizens-Times Publishing Company, 1967.

Peterkin, Julia Mood. *Roll, Jordan, Roll*. Photographic studies by Doris Ulmann. New York: R. O. Ballou, 1933.

Porter, James A. *Modern Negro Art*. New York: Dryden Press, 1943.

Ramsey, Bets, and Merikay Waldvogel. *The Quilts of Tennessee: Images of Domestic Life Prior to 1930*. Nashville, Tenn.: Rutledge Hill Press, 1986.

Rawick, George P., ed. *The American Slave: A Composite Autobiography*. 19 vols. Westport, Conn.: Greenwood Press, 1972.

Reynolds, Gary A., and Beryl J. Wright. *Against the Odds: African-American Artists and the Harmon Foundation*. Newark, N.J.: Newark Museum, 1989.

Rhoads, William B. *The Colonial Revival*. New York: Garland Publishing, 1977.

Roberson, Ruth Haislip, ed. *North Carolina Quilts*. Chapel Hill: University of North Carolina Press, 1988.

Rodee, Marian. *Weaving of the Southwest*. West Chester, Pa.: Schiffer Publishing, 1987.

Rosenberg, Neil V., and Debora G. Kodish, eds. Liner notes for *"Folksongs of America": The Robert Winslow Gordon Collection, 1922–1932*. Sound Recording. Washington, D.C.: Archive of American Folk Song, Library of Congress, 1978.

Rosengarten, Dale. *Row upon Row: Sea Grass Baskets of the South Carolina Lowcountry*. Columbia, S.C.: McKissick Museum, 1987.

Rosenzweig, Roy, ed. *Government and the Arts in Thirties America*. Fairfax, Va.: George Mason University Library, 1986.

Rossano, Geoffrey, ed. *Creating a Dignified Past: Museums and the Colonial Revival*. Savage, Md.: Rowman & Littlefield Publishers, 1991.

Royce, Craig Evan. *Country Miles Are Longer Than City Miles: The Story of the Only Truly American Artcrafts*. Pasadena, Calif.: Ward Ritchie Press, 1976.

Sanchez, George Isidore. *The Forgotten People: A Study of New Mexicans*. Albuquerque: University of New Mexico Press, 1940.

Savannah Unit, Georgia Writers' Project, Work Projects Administration. *Drums and Shadows: Survival Studies among the Georgia Coastal Negroes*. 1940. Reprint. Athens: University of Georgia Press, 1986.

Scarborough, Quincy, and Robert Armfield. *Seagrove Pottery: The Walter and Dorothy Auman Legacy*. Fayetteville, N.C.: Quincy Scarborough Companies, 1992.

Schrader, Robert Fay. *The Indian Arts & Crafts Board: An Aspect of New Deal Indian Policy*. Albuquerque, N.M.: University of Albuquerque Press, 1983.

Seymour, Tryntje Van Ness. *When the Rainbow Touches Down: The Artists and Stories behind the Apache, Navajo, Rio Grande Pueblo and Hopi Paintings in the William and Leslie Van Ness Denman Collection.* Phoenix, Ariz.: Heard Museum, 1988.

Sheppard, Muriel Earley. *Cabins in the Laurel.* Chapel Hill: University of North Carolina Press, 1935.

Southern Highland Handicraft Guild. *The Bicentennial Collection of the Southern Highland Handicraft Guild.* Oteen, N.C.: Southern Highland Handicraft Guild, 1976.

————. *A Catalogue of Mountain Handicrafts by the Members of the Southern Highland Handicraft Guild.* Washington, D.C.: American Federation of Arts, 1933.

Spivey, Richard L. *Maria.* Rev. ed. Flagstaff, Ariz.: Northland Publishing Company, 1989.

Steele, Thomas J. *Santos and Saints: The Religious Folk Art of Hispanic New Mexico.* 2d ed. Santa Fe, N.M.: Ancient City Press, 1982.

Steinfeldt, Cecilia. *Texas Folk Art: One Hundred Fifty Years of the Southwestern Tradition.* Austin: Texas Monthly Press, 1981.

Stewart, Jeffrey C. *To Color America: Portraits by Winold Reiss.* Washington, D.C.: Smithsonian Institution Press/National Portrait Gallery, 1989.

Sweezy, Nancy. *Raised in Clay: The Southern Pottery Tradition.* Washington, D.C.: Smithsonian Institution Press, 1984.

Tanner, Clara Lee. *Southwest Indian Craft Arts.* Tucson: University of Arizona Press, 1968.

Taylor, Lonn, and Dessa Bokides. *New Mexican Furniture, 1600–1940: The Origins, Survival, and Revival of Furniture Making in the Hispanic Southwest.* Santa Fe: Museum of New Mexico Press, 1987.

Thompson, Robert Farris. *Flash of the Spirit: African and Afro-American Art and Philosophy.* New York: Random House, 1983.

Tinkham, Sandra Shaffer, ed. *The Consolidated Catalogue to the Index of American Design.* Cambridge, England: Chadwyck-Healey, 1980.

Torrence, Gaylord, and Robert Hobbs. *Art of the Red Earth People: The Mesquakie of Iowa.* Seattle: University of Washington Press, 1989.

Trimble, Stephen. *Talking with the Clay: The Art of Pueblo Pottery.* Santa Fe, N.M.: School of American Research Press, 1987.

U.S. Works Progress Administration. Oregon. *The Builders of Timberline Lodge.* Portland, Oreg.: Willamette Printing Company, 1937.

Vlach, John Michael. *The Afro-American Tradition in Decorative Arts.* 1978. Reprint. Athens: University of Georgia Press, 1990.

————. *By the Work of Their Hands: Studies in Afro-American Folklife.* Charlottesville: University Press of Virginia, 1991.

————. *Charleston Blacksmith: The Work of Philip Simmons.* Rev. ed. Columbia: University of South Carolina Press, 1992.

Wade, Edwin L., and Rennard Strickland. *Magic Images: Contemporary Native American Art.* Norman: University of Oklahoma Press/Philbrook Art Center, 1982.

Waldvogel, Merikay. *Soft Covers for Hard Times: Quiltmaking and the Great Depression.* Nashville, Tenn.: Rutledge Hill Press, 1990.

Walton, Ann T., John C. Ewers, Royal B. Hassrick. *After the Buffalo Were Gone: The Louis Warren Hill, Sr., Collection of Indian Art.* In cooperation with the Indian Arts and Craft Board of the United States Department of the Interior, Washington, D.C., and the Science Museum of Minnesota, St. Paul, Minnesota. St. Paul, Minn.: Northwest Area Foundation, 1985.

Washburn, Wilcomb E. *The Indian in America.* New York: Harper and Row, 1975.

Weaver, Emma. *Crafts in the Southern Highlands.* Asheville, N.C.: Southern Highland Handicraft Guild, 1958.

Weaver, Emma, and Edward L. Dupuy. *Artisans of the Appalachians.* Asheville, N.C.: Miller Printing Company, 1967.

Weigle, Marta. "The First Twenty-five Years of the Spanish Colonial Arts Society." In *Hispanic Arts and Ethnohistory in the Southwest,* edited by Marta Weigle, Claudia Larcombe, and Samuel Larcombe, 181–203. Santa Fe, N.M.: Ancient City Press, 1983.

Whisnant, David E. *All That Is Native and Fine: The Politics of Culture in an American Region.* The Fred W. Morrison Series in Southern Studies. Chapel Hill: University of North Carolina Press, 1983.

White, John Franklin, ed. *Art in Action: American Art Centers and the New Deal.* Metuchen, N.J.: Scarecrow Press, 1987.

Whiteford, Andrew Hunter, Stewart Peckham, Rick Dillingham, Nancy Fox, and Kate Peck Kent. *I Am Here: Two Thousand Years of Southwest Indian Arts and Culture.* Santa Fe: Museum of New Mexico Press, 1989.

Wood, Peter H. *Black Majority: Negroes in Colonial South Carolina from 1670 through the Stono Rebellion.* New York: W. W. Norton, 1975.

Worcester Art Museum. *An Exhibition of Contemporary New England Handicrafts.* Worcester, Mass.: Worcester Art Museum, 1943.

Wroth, William. *Christian Images in Spanish New Mexico: The Taylor Museum Collection of Santos.* Colorado Springs, Colo.: Colorado Springs Fine Arts Center, 1982.

————. "Crafts, Spanish Borderlands." In *Encyclopedia of the North American Colonies.* New York: Scribner's, 1993.

Wroth, William, ed. *Furniture from the Hispanic Southwest.* Santa Fe, N.M.: Ancient City Press, 1984.

————. *Hispanic Crafts of the Southwest.* Colorado Springs, Colo.: Taylor Museum of the Colorado Springs Fine Arts Center, 1977.

————. *Weaving & Colcha from the Hispanic Southwest.* Santa Fe, N.M.: Ancient City Press, 1985.

Wyman, Leland C., ed. *Beautyway: A Navajo Ceremonial.* New York: Pantheon, 1957.

Yetman, Norman R. *Life under the "Peculiar Institution": Selections from the Slave Narrative Collection.* New York: Holt, Rinehart, and Winston, 1970.

York, Hildreth. *New Deal Art: New Jersey.* Newark, N.J.: Robeson Center Gallery/Rutgers, The State University of New Jersey, 1980.

Zug, Charles G., III. *Turners and Burners: The Folk Potters of North Carolina.* The Fred W. Morrison Series in Southern Studies. Chapel Hill: University of North Carolina Press, 1986.

# CHECKLIST OF THE CATALOGUE

Note: Within each section, checklist entries are in alphabetical order. For all dimensions, height precedes width precedes depth.

## AFRICAN AMERICAN

Anonymous
*Covered Basket.* c. 1920s
Sweetgrass, palmetto cane,
2¾ x 5⅛ x 5⅛″
Collection The Charleston Museum, South Carolina

Anonymous
*Our Lady of the Horse Shrine.*
c. 1910–30
Pine, metal, glass beads, paper, paint, 16 x 11 x 6½″
Private collection

Anonymous
*Cradle-shaped Field Basket.* c. 1920s
Rush, palmetto butt, 7 x 25¼ x 16¼″
Collection Edisto Island Historic Preservation Society, South Carolina

Anonymous
*Cross-handled Basket.* c. 1930
Sweetgrass, pine needles, palmetto leaf, 10½ x 9 x 9″
Collection Harriet Clarkson Gaillard

Anonymous
*Gullah Cane.* c. 1939
Wood, length: 34″
Phoebe Hearst Museum of Anthropology, University of California, Berkeley. Bascom Collection

Anonymous
*Mt. Pleasant Sewing Basket with Lid.* c. 1920
Coiled sweetgrass, palmetto butt, cloth, Confederate bill,
3⅞ x 7½ x 7½″
Collection Edisto Island Historic Preservation Society, South Carolina

Anonymous
*Sea Island Basket.* c. 1930s
Rush, 4¾ x 17¾ x 17¾″
Phoebe Hearst Museum of Anthropology, University of California, Berkeley

William E. Artis
*Bowl.* c. 1945
Ceramic, 4¾ x 7 x 7″
Collection Howard University Gallery of Art, Washington, D.C.

William E. Artis
*Dish.* c. 1945
Ceramic, 11⅝ x 9⅛″
Collection Howard University Gallery of Art, Washington, D.C.

William E. Artis
*Dish.* c. 1945
Ceramic, 8 x 5¼″
Collection Howard University Gallery of Art, Washington, D.C.

Wini Austin
*Log Cabin Quilt Top.* c. 1920–30
Cotton, 76 x 85″
Collection Robert Cargo Folk Art Gallery

Welcome Beese
*Waccamaw River Rice Fanner Basket.* c. 1935
Rush, oak splints,
4⅝ x 20½ x 20½″
Collection Alberta Lachicotte Quattlebaum

Elmer W. Brown
*Rip Van Winkle and the Little Men.*
1935–38
Ceramic, height: 7⅝″
Collection Cleveland Public Library

George W. Brown
*St. Helena Island Sewing Basket with Lid.* 1940
Bulrush, palmetto, 4½ x 8 x 8″
Collection Leroy E. Browne, Sr.

Ned Cheadham
*Table.* c. 1910–30
Painted mixed hardwood,
29½ x 22 x 22″
Private collection

Anna Mae Grace
*Pig in the Pen/Spiderweb Strip Quilt.* c. 1943
Cloth, 91 x 74″
Collection Eli Leon

Amalia Lowery Holmes
*Strip Quilt.* c. 1927
Cotton, 76½ x 69″
Collection Lizzetta LeFalle-Collins and Willie E. Collins

Caesar Johnson
*Hilton Head Basket.* c. 1930
Rush, palmetto butt,
11 x 14 x 14″
Collection South Carolina State Museum, Columbia, South Carolina

Henry Letcher
*Blue Vase.* 1934
Ceramic, 8¼ x 4 x 4″
Collection Howard University Gallery of Art, Washington, D.C.

Henry Letcher
*Sgraffito Vase.* c. 1930s
Ceramic, 6¾ x 3½ x 3½″
Collection Howard University Gallery of Art, Washington, D.C.

Sorena Jefferson Linnen
*Covered Sewing Basket.* 1929
Sweetgrass, palmetto leaf, pine needles, 2½ x 3½ x 3½″
Collection M. Jeannette Lee

Rubie (Kesiah) Booker Lucas
*Green Luster Plate.* October 1921
Ceramic, 1$^{15}/_{16}$ x 8⅝ x 8⅝″
Collection Helen Bright Lyles

Rubie (Kesiah) Booker Lucas
*Poppy Vase.* c. 1920
Ceramic, 9⅞ x 3½ x 3½″
Collection Helen Bright Lyles

Maggie Mazyck
*Sewing Basket with Contents.*
c. 1930
Coiled sweetgrass, palmetto leaf,
6 x 10¼ x 10¼″
Collection Mrs. Jervey D. Royall

Peaches
*Spider Legs Variation Quilt.*
c. 1930–40
Cotton, 77 x 72″
Collection Robert Cargo Folk Art Gallery

Susan Pless
*Strip Quilt.* c. 1940s
Cloth, 86 x 81″
Collection Eli Leon

Anna Pennington Sampson
*Double Wedding Ring Quilt.*
c. 1940s
Cloth, 67½ x 82½″
Collection Eli Leon

Philip Simmons
*Window Grill.* c. 1940
Wrought iron, 39 x 27″
Collection Philip Simmons

Rose Phillips Thomas
*Tennessee Valley Authority Appliqué Quilt Design of a Black Fist.* 1934
Designed by Ruth Clement Bond
Cotton, 11¼ x 13″
Collection Rose Phillips Thomas

Rose Phillips Thomas
*Tennessee Valley Authority Appliqué Quilt Design of Man with Crane.*
1934
Designed by Ruth Clement Bond
Cotton, 13⅝ x 17¼″
Collection Rose Phillips Thomas

Rose Phillips Thomas
*Tennessee Valley Authority "Lazy Man" Appliqué Quilt.* 1934
Designed by Ruth Clement Bond
Cotton, 85¾ x 70″
Collection Ruth Clement Bond

Rich Williams
*Decorated Storage Jar.* c. 1930s
Stoneware, 13¼ x 33 x 33″
Collection Mr. and Mrs. Gary S. Thompson, Jr.

Rich Williams
*Storage Jar.* c. 1930s
Stoneware, 14⅝ x 36 x 36″
Collection Mr. and Mrs. Gary S. Thompson, Jr.

Ellis Wilson
*Dish.* c. 1940s
Pottery, diameter: 7⅛″
Collection Howard University Gallery of Art, Washington, D.C.

## APPALACHIAN

Anonymous
*Coverlet, Overshot Variation of Sunrise.* c. 1940
Wool and cotton, 106 x 77″
Collection Southern Highland Handicraft Guild. Folk Art Center, Asheville, North Carolina

Anonymous
*Egg Basket.* c. 1940–50
Oak splint, 14½ x 18 x 15½″
Collection Robert S. Brunk

Anonymous
*"Love Seat."* c. 1930s
Wood, woven corn shuck,
38 x 37½ x 17″
Collection Susan Morgan Leveille

Oscar L. Bachelder
*Pitcher.* c. 1928
Stoneware, Albany-slip glaze,
11¼ x 7¾ x 6⅓″
Collection Mint Museum of Art, Charlotte, North Carolina. Museum Purchase

Margaret Bergman
*"Constellation" Tablecloth.* c. 1937
Cotton, 35 x 37½″
Collection Nordic Heritage Museum, Seattle

Daniel Boone, VI
*Fireplace Set.* c. mid–1940s
Iron, screen: 28 x 32″; holder: 38 x 14″; shovel length: 30″; andirons: 20 x 13″ each
Collection Mrs. Francis Stroup

Rowena Bradley
*Cherokee Basket.* c. 1940–50
River cane, walnut dye, 11 x 11″
Collection Robert S. Brunk

Tom Brown
*Cow and Calf.* c. 1940
Carved walnut, 6 x 6 x 3¼″
Collection Southern Highland Handicraft Guild. Folk Art Center, Asheville, North Carolina

Cherokee
*Storage Basket.* c. 1920–40
River cane, walnut, bloodroot dyes,
11 x 21 x 21″
Collection Robert S. Brunk

Churchill Weavers
*Cloth 65, Kashan Stole.* 1931
Wool, 35 x 85″
Collection Churchill Weavers

Charles C. Cole
*Garden Urn.* c. 1940
Earthenware, 15¼ x 12⅜″
Collection Mint Museum of Art,
Charlotte, North Carolina. Gift of
Mint Museum Auxiliary and Daisy
Wade Bridges

Ruffin Cole
*Jug with Wooden Stopper.*
c. 1935–40
Salt-glazed stoneware, wood,
19¼ x 11″
Collection Mint Museum of Art,
Charlotte, North Carolina. Gift of
Mint Museum Auxiliary and Daisy
Wade Bridges

Kate Clayton ("Granny") Donaldson
*Cow Blanket.* c. 1930
Vegetable-dyed wool, cotton,
48 x 36″
Collection Southern Highland
Handicraft Guild. Folk Art Center,
Asheville, North Carolina

Kate Clayton ("Granny") Donaldson
*Mountain Cow Blanket.* c. 1930–35
Vegetable-dyed wool, cotton,
34 x 33″
Collection Berea College Appala-
chian Museum, Kentucky

Burlon B. Craig
*Voo Doo Jug.* c. 1935–40
Stoneware, alkaline glaze, porcelain
teeth, 19 x 12″
Collection Mint Museum of Art,
Charlotte, North Carolina. Gift of
Mint Museum Auxiliary and Daisy
Wade Bridges

Park Fisher
*Dulcimer.* 1933
Cherry wood, 36¼ x 2⅛″
Collection University of Kentucky
Libraries, John Jacob Niles
Collection

Ernest Auburn Hilton
*Vase.* c. 1935
Earthenware, glass glaze,
4 x 6 x 6″
Collection Mint Museum of Art,
Charlotte, North Carolina. Gift of
Daisy Wade Bridges

Shadrach Mace
Ladder-back Chair. c. 1940–50
Walnut, 45¼ x 17½ x 14¼″
Collection Robert S. Brunk

Beulah Watkins Marshall
Washington's Plume Quilt. 1931–35
Cotton, 72 x 74″
Collection Mable M. Westbrook

W. J. Martin
*Carved Turkey.* c. 1930

Wood, 5½ x 1½ x 4″
Collection John C. Campbell Folk
School, Brasstown, North Carolina

Ralph Siler Morgan II
*Shallow Bowl.* c. 1930
Pewter, 1½ x 12 x 12″
Collection Ralph Siler Morgan II

Rude Osolnik
*Turned Bowl.* c. 1940
Walnut, 2½ x 19 x 18″
Collection Rude Osolnik

Attributed to Benjamin Wade Owen
*Four-Handled Dragon Vase.* c. 1940s
Jugtown Pottery
Red stoneware, Chinese blue glaze,
14 x 5 x 5″
Collection Milton Bloch and Mary
Karen Vellines

Benjamin Wade Owen
*Pair of Candlesticks.* c. 1922
Jugtown Pottery
Stoneware, cobalt-blue decoration,
11¼ x 5⅓″
Collection Mint Museum of Art,
Charlotte, North Carolina. Gift of
Mint Museum Auxiliary and Daisy
Wade Bridges

Penland Weavers
*Table Runner.* c. 1930s
Wool, cotton, summer-winter
weave, Pine Tree pattern, 31 x 60″
Collection Berea College Appala-
chian Museum, Kentucky

Penland Weavers and Potters
*Pewter Plate with Etched Floral
Design.* c. 1935
Pewter, 1 x 9⅞ x 9⅞″
Collection Jan Brooks Loyd

Mary Prater
*Oak Splint Basket.* c. 1930–40
Oak splint, 8 x 9 x 8¼″
Collection Robert S. Brunk

Enoch William Alexander
Reinhardt
*Teapot and Cover.* c. 1935
Stoneware, 6½ x 3½ x 3½″
Collection Mint Museum of Art,
Charlotte, North Carolina. Gift of
Mint Museum Auxiliary and Daisy
Wade Bridges

Margaret Carson Revis
*Corn-shuck Dolls.* c. 1920
Corn shucks, corn silk, ink; female
figure: 10½ x 3 x 2″; male figure:
12 x 3 x 3″
Collection Southern Highland
Handicraft Guild. Folk Art Center,
Asheville, North Carolina

Cordelia Everidge ("Aunt Cord")
Ritchie
*Dream Basket.* c. 1920
Willow, 8 x 13″
Collection Southern Highland
Handicraft Guild. Folk Art Center,
Asheville, North Carolina

Walter Benjamin Stephen
*Cameo Vase.* 1944
Pisgah Forest Pottery
Stoneware, cobalt-blue glaze band,
13¼ x 5½ x 5½″
Collection Mint Museum of Art,
Charlotte, North Carolina. Gift of
Dr. and Mrs. Arthur Mourot

Walter Benjamin Stephen
*Vase.* c. 1930
Porcelain, crystalline glaze,
11¼ x 6″
Collection Southern Highland
Handicraft Guild. Folk Art Center,
Asheville, North Carolina

Tryon Toymakers
*Carved Gothic Bench.* c. 1936
Walnut, 17 x 20 x 9½″
Collection Robert S. Brunk

Arval Woody
*Dining Chair.* c. 1930
Walnut, 32 x 17 x 13½″
Collection Arval Woody


COLONIAL REVIVAL

Edward Billings
*Connecticut Tercentenary Bowl.* 1936
Arthur J. Stone Associates
Silver, 4¼ x 10½ x 10½″
Collection Mr. and Mrs. Thomas C.
Babbitt

Clevenger Brothers
*Lilypad Pitcher.* 1939
Glass, 9⅝ x 6 x 6″
Collection Museum of American
Glass, Wheaton Village, New Jersey

Danersk
*Joint Stool.* c. 1930
Oak, 19 x 19 x 13″
Collection Sterling Memorial
Library, Yale University, New
Haven

George C. Gebelein
*Coffee and Tea Service.* 1929
Silver, coffeepot: 8¼ x 9½″; teaket-
tle: 12¼ x 9″; teapot: 8¼ x 9½″
Courtesy Museum of Fine Arts,
Boston. Anonymous Gift

George C. Gebelein
*Inkstand.* c. 1930
Silver, 7⅛ x 10³⁄₁₆ x 10³⁄₁₆″
Collection Yale University Art
Gallery, New Haven. Gift of Mrs.
Edwina Mead Gagge

Herman Glendenning
*Sugar Bowl and Creamer.* 1927 and
1928
Arthur J. Stone Associates
Sterling silver, ivory, sugar bowl:
6⁵⁄₁₆ x 3¹⁄₁₆ x 4¼″; creamer:
4⅛ x 2⁷⁄₁₆ x 2⅞″
Collection Yale University Art
Gallery, New Haven. Bequest of
Peter J. Meyer

Samuel Isaac Godlove
*Godlove Chair.* c. 1937
Maple, hickory, 33 x 16 x 13″
Collection Jeanne S. Rymer

Mildred D. Keyser
*Wedding Plate.* 1938
Red clay, 2½ x 14 x 14″
Collection Mrs. Rosemary Keyser
Wood

Mountaineer Craftsmen's Coopera-
tive Association
*Sewing Rocking Chair.* c. 1937
Maple, hickory, rush,
38 x 18 x 34″
Collection Jeanne S. Rymer

Wallace Nutting
*Ballfoot Chest of Drawers.*
c. 1917–36
Walnut, pine, brass,
42 x 39¼ x 19¼″
Collection Gordon William Gray

Wallace Nutting
*Carver Armchair.* c. 1917–36
Maple, rush, 47 x 24¼ x 18″
Collection Gordon William Gray

Wallace Nutting
*Queen Anne Daybed.* c. 1917–36
Mahogany, rush,
39¼ x 25 x 75½″
Collection Gordon William Gray

Wallace Nutting and Edward Guy
*Chandelier.* c. 1920
Wrought iron, 46½ x 11½ x 1¼″
Collection Gordon William Gray

Oneidacraft
*Bombé Secretary with Bust of Lord
Howe.* c. 1926
W. and J. Sloane
Wood, 98 x 46 x 25″
Collection New York State Histori-
cal Association

Mary Saltonstall Parker
*Sampler.* 1920
Cotton embroidery on linen,
20 x 27″
Collection Peabody Essex Museum,
Salem, Massachusetts

Max Rieg
*Bowl.* c. 1937–50
Pewter, 2½ x 10½ x 10½″
Collection Yale University Art
Gallery, New Haven. Gift of Mr.
and Mrs. W. Scott Braznell

Edith K. Roosevelt
*Sampler.* 1925
Cloth, 20¼ x 16¼″
Sagamore Hill National Historic
Site, National Park Service

Isaac Stahl
*Plate.* September 9, 1940
Clay, 1⅜ x 8⅜ x 8⅛″
Collection Lester P. Breininger, Jr.

Arthur Stone
*Small Bowl*. c. 1920–30
Silver, 2¼ x 4 x 4"
Collection Berkeley College, Yale
University, New Haven

Herbert Taylor
*Tankard*. 1927
Silver, 7 x 8 x 8"
Collection Berkeley College, Yale
University, New Haven

Timberline
*Balcony Writing Table*. 1937
Wood, 40¾ x 35¾ x 29½"
Collection Friends of Timberline

Timberline
*Balcony Writing-Table Chair*. 1937
Wood, 29½ x 29¼ x 23⅛"
Collection Friends of Timberline

Timberline
*Lounge Chair*. 1937
Iron, rawhide, 30¼ x 25 x 32½"
Collection Friends of Timberline

Val-Kill Industries
*Porringer with Decorative Handle*.
c. 1930
Pewter, 1¼ x 4 x 4"
Collection Franklin D. Roosevelt
Library, Hyde Park, New York.
Gift of Mrs. Robert Abelow

Val-Kill Shop
*Ladder-back Chair*. c. 1930
Wood, 44¼ x 22 x 16½"
Collection National Park Service/
Roosevelt-Vanderbilt National
Historic Sites

Abram Van Kleeck
*Door Knocker*. c. 1928
Wrought iron, 5 x 4⅝ x 4"
Collection E. Ronald and Shirley
Rifenberg

Abram Van Kleeck
*Thumb Latch*. c. 1928
Wrought iron, 14⅛ x 3¼ x 4"
Collection E. Ronald and Shirley
Rifenberg

Lester Howard Vaughan
*Cream or Mayonnaise Set*. c. 1927
Pewter, bowl: 7⅛ x 4¹¹⁄₁₆";
ladle: 4⅝ x 5⅝"
Collection Yale University Art
Gallery, New Haven. Gift of Mr.
and Mrs. W. Scott Braznell

Lester Howard Vaughan
*Inkstand*. c. 1930
Pewter, ceramic, 4 x 3¼ x 3¼"
Collection National Park Service/
Roosevelt-Vanderbilt National
Historic Sites

Lester Howard Vaughan
*Pitcher*. c. 1930
Pewter, 6⁵⁄₁₆ x 7⅞ x 5⅜"
Collection Yale University Art
Gallery, New Haven. Marie
Antoinette Slade Fund

Virginia Craftsmen, Inc.
*Pennsylvania Windsor Chair*. c. 1930
Wood, 48 x 36 x 30"
Collection Yale University Art
Gallery, New Haven

WPA Glass Factory, Vineland, New
Jersey
*Amethyst Vase*. c. 1940–42
Glass, 16 x 4¼ x 4¼"
Collection Newark Museum, New
Jersey. Gift of the WPA Art Project,
1943

WPA Glass Factory, Vineland, New
Jersey
*Pitcher*. c. 1940–42
Glass, 7⅞ x 6 x 6"
Collection Newark Museum, New
Jersey. Gift of the WPA Art Project,
1943

Samuel Yellin
*Andirons*. c. 1920s
Wrought iron and brass; each:
29 x 17 x 20"
Collection Metropolitan Museum of
Art, New York. Friends of the
American Wing Fund, 1943

HISPANIC TRADITIONS

Anonymous
*Girl's Blouse*. c. 1920
Battenburg lace, length: 20"
Collection Teresa Rodón de Comas

Anonymous
*Bobbin Lace Bedspread*. 1934
Cotton (Japanese thread),
170 x 71"
Collection Rosalina Brau Echeandia

Anonymous
*Carson Colcha Embroidery*. c. 1930s
Wool, 82 x 52"
Gift of Historical Society of New
Mexico to Museum of New Mexico,
Museum of International Folk Art,
Santa Fe

Anonymous
*Lace Insert*. c. 1938–40
Cotton thread, 3 x 265"
Collection Rosalina Brau Echeandia

José Maria Apodaca
*Box*. c. 1930
Tin, glass, wallpaper, 6 x 9 x 6½"
Spanish Colonial Arts Society, Inc.,
Collection on loan to Museum of
New Mexico, Museum of Interna-
tional Folk Art, Santa Fe

Patrocinio Barela
*Anuncio del Nacimiento*. 1936–39
Juniper, 15 x 6 x 3"
Collection Colorado Springs Fine
Arts Center

Federal Art Project
*Straw Appliqué Wood Niche with
Santo*. c. 1930

Straw, wood, 10⅜ x 5½ x 4½"
Collection Museum of New Mexico,
Museum of International Folk Art,
Santa Fe

Celso Gallegos
*Holy Family Relief Carving*.
c. 1920–30
Wood, 13¾ x 6¼ x 2¼"
Ann and Alan Vedder Collection of
the Spanish Colonial Arts Society,
Inc., Museum of New Mexico,
Museum of International Folk Art,
Santa Fe

Celso Gallegos
*San Gorge Relief Carving*.
c. 1920–30
Pine, 9 x 11½ x ¾"
Spanish Colonial Arts Society, Inc.,
Collection on loan to Museum of
New Mexico, Museum of Interna-
tional Folk Art, Santa Fe

José Dolores López
*High Chair*. 1920s
Juniper and pine, 23 x 10 x 10¼"
Spanish Colonial Arts Society, Inc.,
Collection on loan to Museum of
New Mexico, Museum of Interna-
tional Folk Art, Santa Fe

José Dolores López
*Straw Appliqué Cross*. c. 1920s
Straw, wood, 11½ x 5¾ x 3"
Spanish Colonial Arts Society, Inc.,
Collection on loan to Museum of
New Mexico, Museum of Interna-
tional Folk Art, Santa Fe

Crisostoma Luna
*Jerga Shawl*. c. 1938
Wool, 39 x 57"
Collection Lane Coulter

Crisostoma Luna
*Rio Grande Revival Blanket*.
c. 1938–39
Wool, 70 x 42"
Collection Colorado Springs Fine
Arts Center

Sam Matta
*Crucifix*. c. 1930s
Carved stone, 13 x 9 x 8"
Caddy Wells Bequest to Museum of
New Mexico, Museum of Interna-
tional Folk Art, Santa Fe

Native Market
*Candlesticks*. c. 1930s
Iron, 11 x 4 x 4"
Collection Mrs. Y. A. Paloheimo

Native Market
*Chair*. c. 1930s
Pine, wool, 34 x 24 x 26"
Collection Mrs. Y. A. Paloheimo

Native Market
*Painted Chest with Stand*. c. 1930s
Pine chest: 14 x 29 x 13¾"; stand:
10½ x 35¼ x 17¼"
Collection Mrs. Y. A. Paloheimo

Native Market
*Storage Chest*. c. 1930s
Pine, 15¾ x 33⅞ x 15⅛"
Collection Mrs. Y. A. Paloheimo

Native Market
*Table*. c. 1930s
Pine, 28¼ x 35⅞ x 47⅝"
Collection Mrs. Y. A. Paloheimo

Pedro Quintana
*Tin Nicho*. c. 1935
Terneplate, reverse painted glass,
10½ x 12 x 4"
Collection Lane Coulter

Juan Sanchez
*Retablo, Santa Librado*. c. 1930s
Gesso and water-soluble paint on
wood, 9 x 7½"
Gift of Historical Society of New
Mexico to Museum of New Mexico,
Museum of International Folk Art,
Santa Fe

Francisco Sandoval
*Lantern*. c. 1930
Tin, glass, 17 x 5 x 4½"
Collection Museum of New Mexico,
Museum of International Folk Art,
Santa Fe

School of Notre Dame
*Baby's Receiving Blanket*. 1935
Irish linen, pulled thread edging,
42 x 42"
Collection Teresa Rodón de Comas

George Segura
*Chair*. c. 1936–40
Pine, 40 x 22 x 19"
Collection Albuquerque Little
Theater

Tillie Gabaldon Stark
*Colcha Pillow*. c. 1936–38
Cotton, wool, 14¼ x 18"
Collection Mrs. Y. A. Paloheimo

Domingo Tejeda
*Trastero*. c. 1937
Wood, straw, iron, 66½ x 42 x 15"
Collection Roswell Museum and Art
Center

Encarnacion Ubarri
*Wedding Bedspread*. 1922
Linen, cotton (Japanese thread),
84 x 83"
Collection Rosalina Brau Echeandia

NATIVE AMERICAN

Carrie Bethel
Mono Lake Paiute
*Basket*. c. 1930s
Sedge root, redbud, bracken fern
root, 21 x 32½ x 32½"
Collection Yosemite Museum,
National Park Service

Rose Cata
San Juan Pueblo

*Large Incised Jar.* c. 1930
Micaceous clay, 15¼ x 16½″
Collection School of American
Research, Santa Fe, New Mexico.
Amelia White Estate

Chimuhuevi
*Jar-shaped Basket.* c. 1920
Sedge, 5 x 6 x 6″
Collection School of American
Research, Santa Fe, New Mexico.
Indian Arts Fund

Crow
*Purse.* c. 1920–40
Leather, beads, 8 x 8″
Collection The Denver Art Museum

Mary Histia
Acoma Pueblo
*"National Recovery Act" Jar.* c. 1930
Ceramic, 10½ x 13 x 13″
Collection Franklin D. Roosevelt
Library, Hyde Park, New York

Hopi
*Cylindrical Vase.* c. 1910–20
Clay, paint, 10½ x 6 x 6″
Collection Museum of Indian Arts
and Culture/Laboratory of Anthro-
pology, Museum of New Mexico,
Santa Fe

Hopi
*Large Coiled Basket (kachina and
terrace designs).* c. 1920
Bunched grass, 16 x 18 x 18″
Collection School of American
Research, Santa Fe, New Mexico.
Given in memory of Margaret
Moses

Lucy Lewis
Acoma Pueblo
*Seed Jar.* c. 1910–25
Clay, paint, 6 x 11½ x 11½″
Collection School of American
Research, Santa Fe, New Mexico.
Gift of Carlos Vierra

Hosteen Klah and Irene Manuelito
Navajo
*Nightway Sandpainting Tapestry.*
c. 1925–30
Wool, dyes, 84 x 100″
Collection School of American
Research, Santa Fe, New Mexico.
Gift of Miss Mary Cabot Wheel-
wright, Alcalde, New Mexico

Maria and Julian Martinez
San Ildefonso Pueblo
*Portrait Plate.* c. 1920
Blackware, diameter: 12½″
Collection School of American
Research, Santa Fe, New Mexico

Matahga
*Wolf Head Club.* c. 1930s
Wood, 18 x 3 x 2½″
Collection Gladys Tantaquidgeon

Navajo
*Bracelet.* c. 1920
Silver, ¹⁵⁄₁₆ x 2½″
Collection Museum of Indian Arts
and Culture/Laboratory of Anthro-
pology, Museum of New Mexico,
Santa Fe

Navajo
*Concha Belt.* c. 1920s
Silver, turquoise, leather;
3¼ x 39¼″
Collection Museum of Indian Arts
and Culture/Laboratory of Anthro-
pology, Museum of New Mexico,
Santa Fe

Navajo (Four Corners)
*"Eye-dazzler" Rug.* 1945
Wool, dyes, 78 x 49″
Collection School of American
Research, Santa Fe, New Mexico

Navajo
*Girl's Dress and Blouse with Jewelry.*
c. 1930
Rayon, velveteen, silver, turquoise,
dress length: 14″; blouse length: 8″
Collection Michael Walsh

Navajo
*Revival-Style Bracelet.* c. 1930
Sheet silver, 1 x 2½″
Collection Museum of Indian Arts
and Culture/Laboratory of Anthro-
pology, Museum of New Mexico,
Santa Fe

Navajo
*Wide Ruins Rug.* c. 1939
Wool, vegetable dyes, 53½ x 30½″
Collection School of American
Research, Santa Fe, New Mexico.
Gift of Sallie Wagner

Ojibwa
*Bandolier Bag.* 1931
Beaded velveteen, 43 x 16″
Collection Sherman Holbert

Ojibwa
*Jingle Dress.* c. 1930s
Cotton, ribbon, metal jingles, skirt
length: 30¼″; blouse length: 22″
Collection A. M. Chisholm Muse-
um, Duluth, Minnesota

Ojibwa
*Minnesota Vest.* c. 1940
Glass beads, cotton thread,
22 x 23 x 6″
Collection James Economos

Penobscot
*"Shopper" Basket and Mold.* c. 1930s
Basket: ash splints, braided paper
cord, 8 x 13 x 7″; mold: wood,
9½ x 14 x 5″
Collection Children's Museum,
Boston

Susie Poweshiek
Mesquakie
*Skirt.* c. 1930
Wool, ribbon appliqué, silk, length:
36″
Collection Vivian Torrence

Santo Domingo Pueblo
*Jar* (Santa Melchor type). c. 1920–40
Clay, paint, 9¾ x 11¼ x 11¼″
Collection School of American
Research, Santa Fe, New Mexico.
Gift of Sheldon Parsons Memorial
Collection

Sioux
*Man's Necklace.* c. 1920
Otter fur, leather, quills, brass tacks,
ribbon, tin cones, feathers, mirrors,
48 x 22″
Collection The Denver Art Museum

Sioux
*Woman's Breastplate.* c. 1930
Rawhide, quills, glass and brass
beads, leather, tin cones, 39 x 11″
Collection The Denver Art Museum

Rose Spring
Iroquois
*Beaded Skirt* (detail). 1937
Wool, silk ribbon, glass beads,
34½ x 64″
Collection Rochester Museum &
Science Center, New York

Lottie Stamper
Cherokee
*Wastebasket.* 1930
River cane, 16 x 13 x 9½″
Collection Qualla Arts and Crafts

Arnold Sundown
Iroquois
*Circular Silver Brooch.* 1940
Silver, diameter: 2¼″
Collection Rochester Museum &
Science Center, New York

Margaret Tafoya
Santa Clara Pueblo
*Large Olla.* c. 1928
Blackware, 23 x 21″
Collection School of American
Research, Santa Fe, New Mexico

Harold Tantaquidgeon
*Crooked Knife.* c. 1930s
Wood, metal, length: 9″
Collection Gladys Tantaquidgeon

John and Harold Tantaquidgeon
*Bowl with Incised Carving.* c. 1930s
Maple, 16 x 9½ x 3½″
Collection Gladys Tantaquidgeon

Sabattis Tomah
Passamaquoddy
*Wastebasket.* c. 1920
Birchbark, sweetgrass, spruce root,
13½ x 12 x 12″
Collection Children's Museum,
Boston

Isabel Torebio
Zia Pueblo
*Large Storage Jar.* c. 1920–22
Clay, paint, 17 x 21 x 21″
Collection School of American
Research, Santa Fe, New Mexico.
Gift of H. P. Mera

Juanita Tucker
Assiniboin
*Commemorative Dolls (Blackfeet
style): "Two Guns White Calf and
His Wife."* c. 1941
Leather, beads, height: 12″ each
Collection The Science Museum of
Minnesota. On loan from North-
west Area Foundation

Western Apache
*Basket.* c. 1920
Fiber, 5¾ x 21¼ x 21¼″
Collection Museum of Indian Arts
and Culture, Santa Fe, New Mexico

References to illustrations are in *italics*. Footnote citations are indicated by the letter *n* directly following a page number.

Works Progress Administration, 30, 47, 96, 106, 110, 114, 116, 255, 272n1, 272n12, 272n23; Albuquerque Little Theater, Albuquerque, New Mexico, 91, 255; Arts and Crafts Program, 55–60; Community Arts Center, 56; Connecticut Craft Project, 47; Division of Statistics, 60; Division of Technical Services, 57; Farm Security Administration, 39–40; Federal Art Project. *See* Federal Art Project; Georgia Writer's Project, Savannah Unit, 111, 255, 260; Indian Arts and Crafts Project, 58, 75, 255; Michigan crafts project, 74–75; New Jersey Arts and Crafts Project, 47, 59; New Jersey Glass Project, 59; New Mex-ico Crafts Project, 57–58; Wisconsin Crafts Project, 57

World's Columbian Exposition (1893), Chicago, 81

Worst, Edward F., 264, 267; *Foot-Power Loom Weaving,* 127, 260

WPA. *See* Work Projects Administration; Works Progress Administration

WPA Glass Factory, Vineland, New Jersey, 261; *Amethyst Vase, 6, 187; Pitcher, 186*

Wright, Dean, 63

Wright, Richardson, 54

Wroth, William, 23, 27–28, 84–93

# Y

Yale, Charlotte L., 128, 263, 264

Yale University, New Haven, Connecticut: Art Gallery, 43; Sterling Memorial Library, 43

Yaschik, Nathan, 108

Yazz, Beatien (Jimmy Toddy), 246

Yellin, Samuel, 48–49, 246; *Andirons, 190*

Chief Yellow Tail, *66*

York, Hildreth J., 26, 55–61

Yosemite Park Indian Field Days. *See* National Park Service: Yosemite Park Indian Field Days

Young Doctor, 71

# Z

Zug, Charles, 131

Zuni tribe: *Silver Bracelet with 24 Turquoises, 71*

# Photograph Credits

Gavin Ashworth: 43, 44, 49; I. Wilson Baker: 143, 144, 218; Mrs. Russel Baker: 63; Tim Barnwell: 10, 130, 156, 164, 165, 166, 167, 174 left, 177 below, 178 above left; Berea College and the Doris Ulmann Foundation: 29, 123; Eric Boecherding: 206 below left and right; Eric Borg: 8, 182; Brookgreen Gardens, Murrells Inlet, South Carolina: 110; Tim Calloway, Little Traverse Historical Society: 74 left; The Charleston Museum, South Carolina: 98 below, 99, 115, 145 below; Blair Clark, Museum of Indian Arts and Culture/Laboratory of Anthropology, Museum of New Mexico, Santa Fe: 67, 222 below, 223, 226 below, 230; and Museum of International Folk Art, Museum of New Mexico: 15, 200, 203 above, 298, 209, 210 right, 211, 212, 213 ; Ralph T. Coe: 75; Colonial Williamsburg Foundation: 53; Colorado Springs Fine Arts Center: 205 below, 210 left; Lane Coulter: 89; Joe Dell: 189 above; Denver Art Museum: 65, 74 above, 216, 217, 219 above; Eleanor Roosevelt National Historic Site: 184 above right, 191 below right; David Fahrer, Rochester Museum and Science Center, New York: 218 below, 222 above; R. Farley: 12, 159; Albert Fenn, The Museum of Modern Art: 72 above; Francis Marion National Forest, McClellanville, South Carolina: 112 below; Franklin D. Roosevelt Library: 46, 47, 191 below left, 235; Charles Gay, McKissick Museum, University of South Carolina: 143 above; Rip Gerry: 228 above right; Jarvis Grant: 13, 146 above, 148, 149 left, 150, 151; Holly K. Green: 52; Abbott Gutshall, Sandwich Historical Society: 50; Robert Harris: 189 below; Greg Heins: 226 above; Henry Ford Museum and Greenfield Village: 48; Eva Heyd: 94, 134, 145 above, 173, 178 right, 190 above right and below left, 196, 221; High Museum of Art: 98 above; Jane Bond Howard: 120; Howard University: 114; Lawrence Hudetz, Timberline Lodge: 188; Joe Jordan: 149 right above and below; Carl Kauffman, Yale University Library: 185 below; Steve Keull, West Star Photography: 175, 176 below; Richard Khanlian: 88 middle, 198, 201 above left and right, 203 below, 204 above; Paul Kosovski: 154; Library of Congress: 31, 32, 34, 35, 36, 37, 38, 58, 103; Sallie Lippincot: 69; Harlee Little: 117 above, 140 above, 146 below, 147; Jesús Marrero: 206 above, 207; John May: 125; McKissick Museum, University of South Carolina, Clifford L. Legerton Collection: 112 above; Larry McNeil: 88 below, 202, 204 below; Metropolitan Museum of Art: 190 below right; Tom Mills: 174 right, 177 above; Michel Monteaux, Museum of International Folk Art, Museum of New Mexico, Santa Fe: 84, 85, 87, 90, 205 above; Gary Mortensen, Science Museum of Minnesota: 220; Museum of American Glass: 186 below; Museum of Fine Arts, Boston: 194 above; Museum of New Mexico: 27, 28 above, 80; National Archives: 55, 56, 57, 59, 86, 92, 93; National Gallery of Art, Washington, D.C.: 60, 61; National Museum of the American Indian, Smithsonian Institution: 72 below, 79; Newark Museum: 6, 186 above, 187; New York Public Library: 41, 54; New York State Historical Association: 45; North Carolina Division of Archives and History: 116; Oakland Museum: 117 below; Bruce Ojard: 215; Oregon Historical Society: 62; Penn School Collection, Penn Center, Inc., St. Helena Island, South Carolina: 108, 109; Phoebe A. Hearst Museum of Anthropology, University of California at Berkeley: 142 above left, 152 left; Philadelphia Museum of Art: 152 right; Terry S. Raby: 171; David Ramsey: 2, 126 above, 157, 158, 160, 161, 162, 163, 169, 176 above, 179; Mary Renzy: 126 below, 168, 172 below, 178 below; Richard Rhoads: 142 below right, 144 below; William B. Rhoads: 26; Roger Riley: 228 below, 229 middle and below; Sharon Risedorph: 104, 135, 137, 139; Jose Rivera, Roswell Museum: 9, 199; Tammie Roueche: 5, 155; Ron Ruehl: 228 above left; Jeanne Rymer and The Henry Francis Du Pont Winterthur Museum: 184 above left and below right; Saugus Historical Society: 42; Paige Sawyer: 142 below left; Schomburg Center, Art and Artifacts Division, New York Public Library: 97; School of American Research, Santa Fe: 1, 70, 224, 225, 226 middle, 229 above, 231, 232, 233; Mark Sexton, Peabody Essex Museum: 14, 197; Sheldon Jackson Museum, Sitka, Alaska: 72 below; Jackson Smith, North Carolina University Visual Arts Center: 153; South Carolina State Museum: 142 above right; Southern Historical Collection, University of North Carolina at Chapel Hill: 122, 127; Joseph Szasfai, Boston Athenaeum: 195 above; William Taylor: 180, 181, 183, 190 above left; J. E. Townley and Rainforest Studio: 88 above, 91; University of Iowa Museum of Art: 214; John Michael Vlach: 28 below, 102; Merikay Waldvogel: 140 below, 141; Wheelwright Museum of the American Indian, Santa Fe: 81, 82; Robert Woolard: 11, 227; Yale University Art Gallery: 185 above, 191 above, 192, 193, 194 below, 195 below.